PEARSON CUSTOM
Education

University of West Georgia
SPED 6706
Special Education in the Regular Classroom

PEARSON

Senior Vice President, Editorial: Patrick F. Boles
Senior Sponsoring Editor: Natalie Danner
Development Editor: Abbey Lewis
Operations Manager: Eric M. Kenney
Production Manager: Jennifer Berry
Art Director: Renée Sartell
Cover Designer: Kristen Kiley

Cover Art: "Textbooks and apple" used by permission of iStock; "Teacher and students" used by permission of iStock; "Classroom, globe on desk, US flag hanging from blackboard" Copyright © 1999–2008 Getty Images, Inc. All rights reserved. "Mulitcolored crayons"— Courtesy of iStockphoto. "Colorful crayons"— Courtesy of iStockphoto. "Toddler boy playing with alphabet puzzle"— Courtesy of Mimi Haddon/Getty Images. "School Hallway" courtesy of Matt symons/iStockphoto Lp. "Locker" courtesy of Jose Gil/iStockphoto Lp.

Printed in the United States of America.
V3NL
Please visit our website at *www.pearsonlearningsolutions.com*.

Attention bookstores: For permission to return any unsold stock, contact us at *pe-uscustomreturns@pearson.com*.

Pearson Learning Solutions, 501 Boylston Street, Suite 900, Boston, MA 02116
A Pearson Education Company
www.pearsoned.com

ISBN 10: 1-256-26011-8
ISBN 13: 978-1-256-26011-0

Contents

Special Education Procedures and Services

From Chapter 2 of *Including Students with Special Needs: A Practical Guide for Classroom Teachers,* 6/e. Marilyn Friend.
William D. Bursuck. Copyright © 2012 by Pearson Education. All rights reserved.

Special Education Procedures and Services

LEARNING Objectives

After you read this chapter, you will be able to

1. Explain the roles and responsibilities of the individuals who may participate in educating students with disabilities.
2. Describe the process through which a student may become eligible to receive special education services.
3. Name the components of individualized education programs (IEPs) and provide examples of them.
4. Describe the types of services that students with disabilities may receive and the settings in which they may receive them.
5. Discuss how parents participate in special education decision making and what occurs when parents and school district representatives disagree.
6. Outline the role of general education teachers in the procedures and services of special education, reflecting on their critical contributions to positive outcomes for students with disabilities.

Masterfile Royalty Free Division

MS. KUCHTA continues to worry about Christopher, one of her first-grade students, and she is preparing for a meeting with her school's Student Intervention Team (SIT) to discuss his slow learning progress. Christopher was identified as being at risk for school failure early in kindergarten. With intensive instruction and frequent monitoring of his progress, his learning accelerated. But now in first grade, problems are occurring again. Ms. Kuchta has been implementing what are referred to as Tier 1 interventions, research-based reading strategies, but Ms. Kuchta's data indicate they are insufficient. At today's meeting, Ms. Kuchta anticipates that the team—which includes the school psychologist, the assistant principal, the literacy coach, and another teacher—will decide to move Christopher to Tier 2. This means he will receive additional reading instruction three times each week for 40 minutes. If, after 10 weeks, that intervention is not increasing his learning rate, he will receive even more intensive interventions at Tier 3. The goal, if at all possible, is to address Christopher's academic deficits before they become so significant that special education might be needed. This process of data-driven and increasingly intensive interventions is referred to as *response to intervention*.

What actions do Ms. Kuchta and other teachers take when their students are struggling? How do educators decide whether Christopher's (and other students') learning challenges are so significant that they may constitute a disability and require special education services?

MS. LEE, a high school English teacher, has just pulled from her mailbox something titled "IEP at a Glance." As she reads through it, she realizes that it is a summary of the individualized education program (IEP) for Jennifer, one of her students. The summary includes a list of test accommodations Jennifer should receive, and it mentions steps being taken to help Jennifer prepare for a vocational program she will attend after high school. For example, Jennifer needs to complete unit tests in a small, structured environment. That means she will go to the special education classroom on test days instead of reporting to Ms. Lee's room. Ms. Lee notes that the speech/language therapist, the transition specialist, and the social worker are mentioned in the document, but the special education teacher is listed as the person to contact to answer questions.

What roles do general education teachers play in the writing and implementation of IEPs? How are they responsible for ensuring that IEP accommodations are available in the classroom? Who are the other service providers that teachers may work with as they educate students with disabilities?

MS. TURNER teaches science to seventh graders. Toward the end of the last school year, she was invited to become a member of her school's inclusive practices leadership team. At a summer professional development seminar, she learned that many of the students in her school still leave general education classes for a significant part of each day to receive special education services and that renewed effort is being made to ensure that these students have access to the same curriculum as other students by receiving more of their core academic instruction with their nondisabled peers. Ms. Turner and her colleagues are charged with planning professional development for all the professionals at their school on differentiation of instruction; designing ways to support students with disabilities in general education classes; and enlisting the assistance of administrators, parents, and teachers in refining the school's services.

What options exist for students with disabilities to receive the services to which they are entitled? To what extent does this occur in the general education setting? How are such decisions made? How do general education teachers and other school staff contribute to the education of students with disabilities?

PEARSON
myeducationlab

To check your comprehension on the content covered in chapter 2, go to the Book Resources in the MyEducationLab for your course, select your text, and complete the Study Plan. Here you will be able to take a chapter quiz, receive feedback on your answers, and then access review, practice, and enrichment activities to enhance your understanding of chapter content.

Regardless of the ages of the students you plan to teach, you will encounter students who struggle to learn. Some may appear to do everything they can *not* to learn. Others may try their best but still not be successful. Yet other students may have challenging behaviors, and you may find that the strategies effective with most students do not work with them. You may wonder whether some of these students should be receiving special education services and who will provide them.

This chapter introduces you to people who specialize in working with students with disabilities and procedures for deciding whether a student is eligible for special education services. You also will learn how students' individualized education programs (IEPs) are designed and monitored and which services students with disabilities use. You will discover that parents play a crucial role in special education procedures and that when they or students disagree with school professionals about special services, procedures exist to help them resolve these differences. Most important, you will learn about your role in working with other professionals and parents to determine student eligibility for special education, carrying out students' educational programs, and monitoring student learning.

Who Are the Professionals in Special Education?

Students with disabilities are entitled to a wide range of supports and services. Not surprisingly, many different individuals can be involved in the delivery of these services. You probably will interact with some of these professionals, such as special education teachers, almost every day. Others you might work with only occasionally. Some of these professionals serve students indirectly or work only with the few students who have the most challenging disabilities. Together, however, these educators create, implement, and evaluate the special education that students with disabilities receive.

General Education Teachers

As the *general education teacher,* you are the first professional discussed in this section because for many students with suspected or documented disabilities, you are the person who has the most detailed knowledge of their day-to-day needs in your classroom.

Your responsibilities span several areas. You are the person most likely to bring to the attention of other professionals a student whom you suspect may have a disability (Egyed & Short, 2006; McClanahan, 2009). That is, you may encounter a student who is reading significantly below grade level, a student whose behavior is so different from that of other students that you suspect an emotional disorder, or a student who has extraordinary difficulty focusing on learning. When you suspect a disability, you document the student's characteristics and behaviors that led to your concern by gathering samples of the student's work, compiling descriptions of his behavior, and keeping notes of how you have attempted to address the problem (Walker-Dalhouse et al., 2009). You work with special education colleagues and other professionals to systematically implement interventions in your classroom to clarify whether the student's problems need further exploration (Mercier-Smith, Fien, Basaraba, & Travers, 2009; Reutebuch, 2008). If the student is referred for assessment for special education, you contribute information about his academic and social functioning in your classroom and help identify the student's strengths, needs, and educational program components. For example, you might help others understand the curricular expectations in your classroom and the types of accommodations that may be necessary for the student to succeed there. If special education services are deemed necessary, you participate in deciding appropriate goals and, for some students, objectives. You also might assist special services staff members in updating parents on their

dimensions of DIVERSITY

Culturally and linguistically diverse students are more likely to succeed in school when their teachers create compassionate and flexible classroom environments, help students persist in spite of life challenges, and teach with "urgency." (Cartledge & Kourea, 2008).

child's quarterly and yearly progress. Most important, you are expected to work with special services staff to provide appropriate instruction within your classroom (Carter, Prater, Jackson, & Marchant, 2009; Munk, Gibb, & Caldarella, 2010). Several of the key responsibilities of a general education teacher are summarized in Figure 2.1.

When all your responsibilities are listed, your role in planning and providing special services to students may seem overwhelming. However, studies of general education teachers typically indicate that they are willing and able to contribute to the education of students with disabilities as long as some conditions are met. The most important conditions include having administrative leadership and staff preparation, sufficient time for teacher planning, and adequate funding and other resources for program support (Conderman, & Johnston-Rodriguez, 2009; Elhoweris & Alsheikh, 2006; Idol, 2006).

FIGURE 2.1 **General Education Teacher Responsibilities Related to Implementing IDEA**

Identify students with learning, behavior, or other needs serious enough to seek input from colleagues.
Jupiter Images – Food Pix – Creatas

Contribute to discussions of students as a member of an intervention assistance team.
iStockphoto.com

Implement strategies and gather data as part of a response to intervention (RtI) procedure.
Katelyn Metzger/Merrill

Provide evidence–based day–to–day instruction.
© Bob Daemmrich/Alamy

Collaborate with colleagues regarding students with disabilities.
Anthony Magnacca/Merrill

Communicate with parents regarding their child's strengths and needs.
Ellen B. Senisi/The Image Works

Participate in writing IEPs as a member of the multidisciplinary team.
Anthony Magnacca/Merrill

Special Education Teachers

Special education teachers are the professionals with whom you are most likely to have ongoing contact in teaching students with disabilities, and these professionals have increasingly complex roles (Fuchs, Fuchs, & Stecker, 2010). They are responsible for managing and coordinating the services a student receives, including writing and implementing the individualized education program (IEP). They typically also provide direct and indirect instruction to students who are assigned to them. In addition, they may consult with you regarding a student suspected of having a disability and work with you to determine whether a referral for assessment for possible special education is warranted, a process explained later in this chapter.

Depending on the state in which you teach and the disabilities of the students in your classroom, you may work with different types of special education teachers. Sometimes special education teachers are assigned to work with all of the students with disabilities in your class. For example, a special education teacher may support a student with learning disabilities and also a student with a moderate intellectual disability or a speech or language impairment. That professional may work indirectly with other special education professionals to ensure that each student's educational plan is being implemented and monitored. Sometimes, special education teachers work only with specific categories of students. For example, a teacher for students with visual impairments or hearing loss generally will be responsible only for students with those disabilities. In states that do not use categorical labels for students, some teachers work with students with high-incidence disabilities or low-incidence disabilities.

In other situations, special education teachers may be designated by the type of services they provide. For example, for some students with high-incidence disabilities in your class, you may work with a *consulting teacher* or perhaps an *inclusion facilitator* (Friend & Cook, 2010). This professional might meet with you regularly to monitor students' progress, problem solve with you about student concerns, and coordinate students' services, in some cases working directly with students but in other situations working indirectly by supporting teachers. You also might work with a *resource teacher* who divides time among directly instructing students, working with teachers regarding student needs, and co-teaching (Friend, Cook, Hurley-Chamberlain, & Shamberger, 2010). In some high schools, special education teachers now are assigned to work with a particular department, attending department meetings and providing supports for all students with disabilities enrolled in that department's courses.

For some groups of students, the special educator with whom you interact might be an *itinerant teacher*. Itinerant teachers often have roles like the professionals just described, but they travel between two or more school sites to provide services to students (For example, Dinnebeil, McInerney, & Hale, 2006). Teachers for students with vision or hearing disabilities often are itinerant. However, if you work in a school district where each school has only a few students with disabilities, even the special educator for students with high-incidence disabilities may deliver services this way.

One other type of special education teacher is a *transition specialist*. This professional typically works in a high school setting and helps prepare students to leave school for vocational training, employment, or postsecondary education (Brooke, Revell, & Wehman, 2009; Hartman, 2009). No matter what subject you teach in high school, you might work very closely with a transition specialist,

General educators, whether in core academic areas or related arts, are most likely to work with special educators to ensure that students with disabilities receive the specialized services to which they are entitled. Lori Whitley/Merrill

but this is especially likely in business education, consumer sciences, industrial and other vocational arts, and similar areas. This professional also spends time working directly with students to assess their skills and interests related to life after school. A transition specialist works with community businesses to arrange student job sites and resolve problems related to student workers. This professional also may serve as a *job coach,* accompanying a student to a job site and helping her master the skills needed to do the job successfully.

As the nature of special education services changes, so do the job responsibilities and titles of special educators. For example, you might find that the professionals in your school who used to be called *special education teachers* are now referred to as *intervention specialists (ISs).* This change in title represents an effort to delabel teachers and parallels the effort to deemphasize students' labels—that is, to focus on student strengths and needs rather than the language of disability. Regardless of the type of special education teachers with whom you work, you will find that they are important instructional partners who are no longer relegated to teaching just in the special education classroom. They support students by creating adapted materials, teaching with you in the general education classroom, working directly and separately with students who have disabilities, and often serving as coordinators for all the services any single student may receive.

Related Service Providers and Other Specialists

In addition to working with special education teachers, you will have contact with a variety of other service providers (National Dissemination Center for Children with Disabilities, n.d.). They, too, play important roles in educating students with disabilities. The following list includes the individuals with whom you are most likely to work.

School Psychologists   *School psychologists* offer at least two types of expertise related to educating students with disabilities. First, school psychologists often have a major responsibility for determining a student's intellectual, academic, social, emotional, and/or behavioral functioning. They typically contribute a detailed written analysis of the student's strengths and areas of need; in many school districts, this document is referred to as a "psych report" (that is, a psychological report). In a related role, school psychologists sometimes chair the multidisciplinary team that meets to decide whether a student has a disability and, if so, what types of services are needed (Arivett, Rust, Brissie, & Dansby, 2007).

A second major task for school psychologists is designing strategies to address students' academic and social or behavior problems, whether students have been identified as having a disability or not (Kaniuka, 2009). For example, these professionals typically are part of the team that designs and implements interventions prior to a decision about referral for possible special education services. Sometimes they serve as behavior consultants. Occasionally, they assist a teacher by working with an entire class group on social skills. They also might provide individual assistance to students with emotional or behavioral problems who are not eligible for special education.

Counselors   Although *counselors* most often advise high school students and assist students with disabilities as they transition from school to postschool options (Milsom & Hartley, 2005), they also work at other school levels and contribute to the education of students with disabilities (Mitcham, Portman, & Dean, 2009). For example, counselors in some school districts assess students' social and emotional functioning, including areas such as self-concept; motivation; attitude toward school, peers, and teachers; and social skills. Counselors also can provide services to both teachers and students. For teachers, they might suggest ways to draw out a student who is excessively shy, to incorporate activities designed to enhance students' self-concept into day-to-day classroom instruction, or to create an emotionally safe classroom environment. For students,

dimensions of
DIVERSITY

When middle school teachers were shown videos of students displaying "traditional walking" or stylized "strolling," they concluded the latter students had lower achievement, were more aggressive, and were more likely to need special education than the former students (Neal, McCray, Webb-Johnson, & Bridgest, 2003). The race or ethnicity of the student did not make a difference in the results.

counselors might provide individual assistance to a student struggling to understand a parent's death or unexplained departure from the family or other stressful events, arrange group sessions with several students who share specific needs, or work with an entire class on how to interact with a peer who has a disability.

Speech/Language Therapists   Many students with disabilities have communication needs. Some have mild problems in pronouncing words or speaking clearly. Others have an extremely limited vocabulary. Yet others rely on alternative means of communication, such as communication boards. The professionals who specialize in meeting students' communication needs are *speech/language therapists*, and they have a tremendously diverse range of school responsibilities (Harris, Prater, Dyches, & Heath, 2009). At the early elementary level, they might work with an entire class on language development or with an individual student on pronouncing sounds. At the intermediate elementary level, they might work on vocabulary with a group of students and might also help a student with a moderate cognitive disability pronounce some words more clearly or combine words into sentences. At the middle or high school level, they often focus on functional vocabulary and work mostly with students with low-incidence disabilities. For example, they might help a student with an intellectual disability learn to read common signs and complete tasks such as ordering in a restaurant or asking for assistance.

Social Workers   *Social workers'* expertise is similar to that of counselors in terms of being able to help teachers and students address social and emotional issues (Sabatino, 2009). Thus, social workers may serve as consultants to teachers and also may provide individual or group assistance to students. However, social workers have additional expertise. They often are liaisons between schools and families. For example, they can create a family history by interviewing parents and visiting a student's home; this information may be critical in determining whether a student needs special education services. Similarly, they may help other school professionals work with families on matters such as gaining access to community health services. The school social worker often follows up on teacher reports about the suspected abuse or neglect of students.

Administrators   The school principal, assistant principal, and sometimes a department chairperson or team leader are the *administrators* most likely to participate actively in the education of students with disabilities (Angelle & Bilton, 2009; Lasky & Karge, 2006). Their role is to offer knowledge about the entire school community and provide perspective on school district policies regarding special education and also to help address parents' concerns. Every team that determines whether a student is eligible for special education must have administrative representation. In one school, the mother of Marisha, a student with severe language delays, requested that her daughter receive speech/language therapy for 40 minutes daily. School professionals were in agreement that this amount of therapy was not appropriate. Dr. Wade, the principal, worked with the team and the parent to negotiate the amount of speech therapy needed to accomplish Marisha's goals.

In some locales, especially large urban and suburban districts where it is difficult to ensure that all required special education procedures are followed, a *special education coordinator* or *supervisor* is part of the district's administration. This professional specializes in understanding the sometimes complex procedures of special education. Coordinators help alleviate the pressure on principals and assistant principals to accurately interpret and follow guidelines. They also explain services and options to parents, problem solve with teachers when issues arise, and assist in monitoring to ensure that students with disabilities receive needed supports.

Paraprofessionals   Individuals who assist teachers and others in the provision of services to students with disabilities are *paraprofessionals* (Giangreco, Suter, & Doyle, 2010). These individuals usually have a certificate based on completing a community college or similar training program; some are even licensed teachers.

RESEARCH NOTE

Teachers who believe that their efforts truly make a difference in student learning (as opposed to those who believe that factors outside their control—such as conditions in the home—are more powerful) are more likely to be involved in their school teams for students struggling to learn and to be implementing RtI strategies (Nunn & Jantz, 2009).

P R O F E S S I O N A L **EDGE**

Working with Paraprofessionals

No matter what grade level you teach, you will likely find yourself at some point working closely with paraprofessionals, also called *paraeducators*. These individuals are employed by school districts to provide support to students with disabilities either by working with particular students one to one or by working in general or special education classrooms with several students.

Generally, paraprofessionals work under the direction of teachers or other professionals, and they do not have sole responsibility for any aspect of a student's educational program. If a paraprofessional is assigned to your classroom in order to support students with disabilities, these are some of the responsibilities that individual may carry out:

- Locate, arrange, or construct instructional materials.
- Assist students with eating, dressing, personal care, and bathroom use.
- Help prepare the classroom for students and keep work areas neat.
- Instruct students with disabilities individually, in small or large groups, and/or with typical peers, supervised by licensed educators and as specified in students' IEPs or by professionals on the service delivery team. Such instruction generally is review or reteaching rather than initial core instruction.
- Collect student data for professional team members regarding student progress toward goals.
- Score tests and certain papers using a key or rubric.
- Maintain files or records about students.
- Supervise playgrounds, halls, lunchrooms, buses, and loading zones.
- Address students' specific health needs (for example, suction tracheotomy tubes as assigned and trained by a school nurse).
- Assist and facilitate appropriate peer interactions.

- Assist students using adaptive equipment or devices (for example, a communication board).
- Support student behavior and social needs according to plans.
- Participate positively in evaluative or feedback sessions for improvement of their skills.
- Participate in training and coaching sessions to improve their skills associated with all duties and tasks assigned.
- Communicate with professionals about their work and students' progress on assigned tasks.
- Move or accompany students from one place to another, assisting students with mobility and transition.
- Contribute to the effectiveness of the special education team by using appropriate communication, problem solving, and conflict management strategies.

FROM THE RESEARCH

As the list suggests, paraprofessionals offer many valuable services to students and teachers in support of students. However, in a review of recent research, Giangreco and his colleagues found persistent issues in the roles and responsibilities of these school personnel, including practices for hiring and retaining them, their preparation for their jobs, specific job expectations, respect for the work paraprofessionals complete, problems related to supervision, and student perceptions of these support personnal.

Sources: "Managing Paraeducators in Your School: How to Hire, Train, and Supervise Non-Certified Staff," by N. K. French, 2003, Thousand Oaks, CA: Corwin; "Preparing and Managing Paraprofessionals," by M. L. Trautman, 2004, *Intervention in School and Clinic, 39*, pp. 131–138; "Paraprofessionals in Inclusive Schools: A Review of Recent Research," by M. Giangreco, J. Suter, & M. Doyle. (2010). *Journal of Educational & Psychological Consultation, 20*, pp. 41–57.

Regardless, these service providers generally complete their work under the direction of teachers and other professional staff members. Paraprofessionals also might be called *paraeducators, instructional assistants, teaching assistants, aides,* or other titles, depending on local practices.

School districts use paraprofessionals in many different ways (Carter, O'Rourke, Sisco, & Pelsue, 2009), but two roles are especially common. Some paraprofessionals are assigned to specific students who need ongoing individual assistance. For example, a student with no ability to move his arms may have a paraprofessional who takes notes for him and completes other tasks such as feeding. A few students have medical conditions requiring that a specially trained paraprofessional be present to monitor their status. Paraprofessionals in this role may be referred to as *personal assistants* or *one-to-one assistants.*

A second and more common role for paraprofessionals is to assist in the delivery of special services for many students. These paraprofessionals often work in both inclusive classrooms and special education classrooms as well as on the playground, at assemblies, and during bus duty. These paraprofessionals' primary responsibility is to work with students with disabilities, but they sometimes also help other students and the teacher as the need arises and time permits. The Professional Edge on the previous page contains more information about working with paraprofessionals.

Other Specialists   Depending on student needs and state and local practices, other professionals also may participate in the education of students with disabilities. Here is a list of these individuals and a brief description of their roles:

- *Physical therapist.* Assesses and intervenes related to gross motor skills, that is, large muscle activity.
- *Occupational therapist.* Assesses and intervenes related to fine motor skills, that is, small muscle activity.
- *Adaptive physical educator.* Designs physical education activities for students with physical, health, or other special needs that affect participation in traditional programs.
- *Nurse.* Key person for gathering needed medical information about students with disabilities and interpreting such information from physicians and other medical personnel.
- *Bilingual special educator.* Professional trained in both special education and bilingual education who specializes in serving students from diverse cultural and linguistic backgrounds.
- *Mobility specialist.* Helps students with visual impairments learn how to become familiar with their environments and how to travel from place to place safely.
- *Sign language interpreter.* Listens to classroom instruction and relays it to students who are deaf or hard of hearing using sign language.
- *Professional from outside agencies.* Provides services away from school (for example, private school, hospital, juvenile justice system) and serves as the liaison between such services and school personnel, especially during transitions from such services back to school.
- *Advocate.* Serves as an advisor and sometimes represents parents at meetings related to their children with disabilities, especially when parents believe they are not knowledgeable enough about the legal and educational requirements of special education.

Parents and Students

When decisions are being made concerning a student with a suspected or documented disability, the best interests of the student and her family must be represented. The parents—or a person serving in the role of a parent, such as a guardian or foster parent—have the right to participate in virtually all aspects of their child's educational program (Olivos, Gallagher, & Aguilar, 2010; Trainor, 2010), a topic addressed in more detail later in this chapter.

Often parents are strong allies for general education teachers. They can assist teachers by reviewing at home what is taught in school, rewarding their child for school accomplishments, and working with school professionals to resolve behavior and academic problems.

Whenever appropriate, students with disabilities also should be active participants in decision making about their own education. Increasingly, educators are involving students so they can directly state their needs and goals and learn to advocate for themselves, a concept referred to as **self-determination** (Branding, Bates, & Miner, 2009; Chambers, Wehmeyer, Saito, Lida, Lee, & Singh, 2007). The extent of student participation on the team depends on the age of the student, the type and impact of the

Some professionals, like sign-language interpreters, provide highly specialized services to specific groups of students. © Ilene MacDonald/Alamy

PROFESSIONAL **EDGE**

Self-Determination for Students with Disabilities

Think how you would react if other people constantly controlled your life, deciding what you should wear, where you should go, what career you should pursue, and what type of housing and roommates you should have. Beginning at a very young age, children typically begin to express their wishes, and they learn that they have a right to act on those wishes. (For example, have you ever tried to convince a 3-year-old that the two articles of clothing she selected to wear do not match?) But despite good intentions by professionals and parents, many students and adults with disabilities have been denied opportunities to make their own life decisions. Reversing this situation has become a goal for the field (for example, Martin, Van Dycke, Christensen, Greene, Gardner, & Lovett, 2006; Wehmeyer, 2007).

STUDENT-LED IEPS

When students lead their IEP meetings, they learn to think and advocate for themselves (Danneker & Bottge, 2009). They can learn to do this beginning at a very early age. For example, elementary students might have the role of introducing their parents to the team and describing to team members what they have been learning in school. Students in middle school might explain their disabilities and the impact of those disabilities, share their strengths, and discuss accommodations needed. In high school, students might lead the entire conference, working to ensure that the IEP and transition plan reflect their preferences and plans for the future.

General education teachers find that students who actively participate in their IEP meetings have better skills for interacting with adults, better understanding of their special needs, greater awareness of resources available to help them, and more willingness to accept responsibility for themselves (Test et al., 2004).

PERSON-CENTERED PLANNING

Another method of self-determination called *person-centered planning* was developed by professionals from both the United States and Canada and usually is related to IEP planning. It emphasizes these dimensions:

- *Community presence.* Identify the community settings that the student uses and the ones that would benefit him. The intent is to incorporate these settings into the educational planning process.
- *Choice.* Identify decisions made *by* the student and decisions made *for* the student. The goal of person-centered planning is to transfer as many choices to the student as possible.
- *Competence.* Identify the skills that will best assist the student to participate fully in the school and community and the strategies that will be most effective for teaching those skills.
- *Respect.* Clarify roles the student has in the school and local community. The goal is to strengthen and expand those roles and decrease or eliminate personal characteristics that might cause the student to be perceived by others in a stereotypical way.
- *Community participation.* Specify people with whom the student spends time at school and in other settings. The goal is to identify individuals who can advocate for the student and to foster friendships with age-appropriate peers.

A number of person-centered planning approaches have been developed, and you may find that one of these is used in your school district. They include Making Action Plans (MAPs), Planning Alternative Tomorrows with Hope (PATH), and Circle of Friends.

Sources: Adapted from "Benefits of and Barriers to Elementary Student-Led Individualized Education Programs," by J. Danneker and B. Bottge, 2009, *Remedial and Special Education, 30,* pp. 225–233; and *Person-Centered Practices: Building Personalized Supports That Respect the Dreams of People with Disabilities,* by REACH of Louisville, n.d., retrieved September 15, 2004, from http://www.reachoflouisville.com/person-centered/Default.htm. Reprinted with permission.

---

disability, and the professionals' and parents' commitment. In general, the older the student, the greater her ability to contribute, and the higher the value placed on her contribution, the greater the participation. Thus, first-grade students with disabilities usually are not expected to participate in making most decisions about their education. However, high school students with disabilities usually attend and participate in their team meetings, and their priorities and preferences are central to decision making (Arndt, Konrad, & Test, 2006). These students often have strong opinions about what they would like to do after high school, and they also take on more responsibility for monitoring their progress in reaching their goals (Hartman, 2009). You can learn more about student participation on teams in the Professional Edge.

How Can You Decide Whether a Student Need Might Be a Disability?

You will play a key role in deciding whether a student in your class should be evaluated for the presence of a disability. Although youngsters with obvious intellectual, sensory, and physical impairments usually are identified when they are infants or toddlers, learning, language, attentional, and behavioral disabilities—such as those displayed by Christopher, introduced at the beginning of the chapter—often are not diagnosed until children experience difficulty in school. Because you are the professional in daily contact with the student, you are the person most likely to notice an unmet need. It is your judgment that usually initiates the process of increasingly intensive interventions and, potentially, the special education decision-making process.

Analyze Unmet Needs

As you teach, you sometimes will discover that you have a nagging concern about a student. This concern might begin early in the school year, or it might take several months to emerge. For example, when you review a student's records of academic progress and consider your own impressions and evaluation of student work, you may decide that the student's achievement is not within the typical range, given the standards of your school district, community expectations, and state achievement standards. Should you ask other professionals to assess the student for interventions and eventually, if needed, for eligibility for special education? Perhaps. But first, you need to ask yourself some questions.

What Are Specific Examples of Unmet Needs? Having a vague worry about a student is far different from specifically stating a concern. For example, sensing that a student is unmotivated is not a clear concern. What does the student do that leads you to conclude that motivation is a problem? Is it that the student doesn't make eye contact when speaking to you or that the rewards and consequences that other students enjoy seem to have no effect, positive or negative, on this student? If you are thinking that the student is not making enough academic progress, what does that mean? Is it that classmates have mastered letters, sounds, and blends, but this student knows only about half the letters? Is it that other students easily use basic math procedures in solving multiple-step equations, but this student makes computational errors in eight out of ten problems? Vague concerns and hunches must be supported by specific information. Phrases such as "slow in learning," "poor attitude toward school," "doesn't pay attention," and "never gets work completed" might have very different meanings to different professionals. To prepare to share your concern with others, your first step is to ask yourself "When I say the student . . . , what examples, supported with data, clarify what I mean?"

Is There a Chronic Pattern Negatively Affecting Learning? Nearly all students go through periods when they struggle to learn, behave inappropriately, or otherwise cause you concern. Sometimes a situation outside school affects a student. For example, parents divorcing, the family being evicted from its apartment, elderly grandparents moving in with the family, or a family member being injured or arrested might negatively affect student learning or behavior. However, the impact of these traumatic events should not be permanent, and the student should gradually return to previous levels of functioning.

Students with disabilities also may be affected by specific situations and events, but their learning and behavior needs form a chronic pattern. In other words, they struggle over a long period of time regardless of the circumstances. For example, Betsy, who has a learning disability, has difficulty remembering sight words no matter what level they are or how creatively they are introduced. Jared, a high school student with an emotional disability, is withdrawn whether sitting in a large class or interacting in a small group. Julianna, an eighth grader who had a severe head injury last year, usually seems to grasp abstract concepts as they are taught, but she struggles to describe or apply them after instruction.

Are the Unmet Needs Becoming More Serious as Time Passes? Sometimes a student's needs appear to become greater over time. For example, Ben, who seemed to see well at the beginning of the school year, now holds books closer and closer to his face, squints when he tries to read, and complains about headaches. Karen, who began the school year reluctant but willing to complete assignments, refuses to do any work during class by November. Indications that a student's needs are increasing are a signal to ask for input from others.

Is the Student's Learning or Behavior Significantly Different from That of Classmates?   As you think about your concerns about a student, ask yourself how he compares to other students. For example, it has been demonstrated that students at risk for special education referral achieve at a significantly lower level than other students and are more likely to have serious behavior problems (Hosp & Reschly, 2003). However, if you have eight students who are all struggling, the reason might be that the information or skills are beyond the reach of the entire group or that your teaching approach is not accomplishing what you had planned. Even though self-reflection is sometimes difficult, when many students are experiencing problems, it is important to analyze how the curriculum or teaching might be contributing to the situation. In such instances, you should make changes in those two areas before seeking other assistance.

Keep in mind that many students have needs that *do* signal the presence of disabilities. Perhaps you are an elementary teacher who cannot seem to find enough books at the right level for one student in your fourth-grade class who is almost a nonreader. Perhaps you are an eighth-grade social studies teacher who is worried about two students' apparent inability to read the textbook or understand the themes of history integral to your curriculum. Maybe you are an algebra teacher who finds that one student seems to lack many prerequisite skills for succeeding in the course. Students with disabilities have needs that are significantly different from those of most other students.

Do You Discover That You Cannot Find a Pattern?   In some instances, the absence of a pattern in students' learning or behavior is as much an indicator that you should request assistance as is a distinct pattern. Perhaps Curtis has tremendous mood swings, and you arrive at school each day wondering whether he will have a good day or a bad day. However, you cannot find a way to predict which it will be. Or consider Becka, who learns science with ease but is failing English, according to a colleague on your seventh-grade team. You are not sure why her learning is so different in the two subjects. In a third example, in physical education, Tyrone seems to have average motor skills on some days but on other days frequently stumbles and cannot participate fully in the learning stations you have created.

Communicate Your Observations and Try Your Own Interventions

Your analysis of your students' unmet needs is the basis for further action. Although you eventually may decide to formally seek assistance for one of your students, part of your responsibility in attempting to help the student is gathering other information and trying to resolve the problem first.

Contact the Parents   One of your first strategies should be to contact the student's family (O'Connor, 2010). Parents or other family members often can inform you about changes in the student's life that could be affecting school performance. Family members also can help you understand how the student's activities outside school might influence schoolwork, including clubs, gang involvement, employment, and responsibilities at home. Further, by contacting the family, you might learn that what you perceive as a problem is mostly a reflection of a cultural difference. For example, a student whose family emigrated from Thailand is extremely quiet because silence signals respect in her native culture, not because she is unable to participate.

Parents also are your partners in working to resolve some student learning problems (for example, Benner & Mistry, 2007; Hughes & Kwok, 2007). They can assist you in monitoring whether homework is completed and returned to school, whether behavior problems are occurring on the walk home, or whether a physician is concerned about a child's medical condition. If you have students whose homes do not have a telephone or e-mail access and whose parents do not have transportation to come to school, your social worker or principal often can help you make needed contact.

www.resources

http://www.rtinetwork.org
The RTI Action Network, part of the National Center for Learning Disabilities, includes many resources to help you understand and implement RtI procedures. Included are separate sections with ideas and links for elementary, middle school, and high school teachers.

Contact Colleagues   Especially as a new teacher, you will want to informally discuss your concerns with other professionals to gain additional perspectives on the student's needs. In many schools, a special education teacher, assistant principal, department chairperson, literacy coach, or another professional can arrange to observe the student in your class and then discuss the observation. If your school psychologist is available, you might ask for consultation assistance. In schools where grade-level teams or other types of teams or departments meet, you can raise your concerns in that context. One hallmark of today's schools is an array of professionals with expertise in many areas. With a little exploration, you will likely find that your school has an in-house resource you can access to check your perceptions against a broader perspective.

Try Simple Interventions   Part of your responsibility as a teacher is to create a classroom where students can succeed. To cultivate such a setting, you can make simple changes as part of your efforts to address a student's unmet needs. Here are some examples:

- Have you tried moving the student's seat?
- Have you incorporated teaching strategies that help the student actively participate in lessons (for example, using choral responding, in which all students together repeat answers aloud)?
- Have you thought about ways to make your tests easier for the student to follow (for example, using more white space between items or sections)?
- Have you given the student only part of an assignment at one time to prevent him from becoming overwhelmed?
- Have you observed the student closely to determine whether helping her work one problem is enough to get her to work on the rest?

These are just a few instructional adjustments that many teachers make; many others are presented throughout this textbook. Sometimes these small accommodations are sufficient to help a student learn. In any case, you should try common interventions before deciding a student might need the far more intensive service of formal interventions or special education.

Document the Unmet Need   If you anticipate requesting assistance for a student, you need to demonstrate the seriousness of your concern and your systematic attempts to help meet the student's needs. If you have implemented a plan to improve student behavior, keep a record of how effective it has been. If you have contacted parents several times, keep a log of your conversations. If you have tried strategies to improve student learning, be prepared to describe those strategies and share the data you have gathered related to their impact. Documenting student needs serves two main purposes. First, it helps you do a reality check on whether the problem is as serious as you think it is. If you gather data from other students as a comparison, you can judge whether the unmet needs of one student are significantly different from those of typical students. Second, the information you collect will help you communicate with other professionals. Special service providers cannot possibly meet every need in every classroom. Their work is reserved in large part for extraordinary student needs, and your documentation will help in decision making about the amount and intensity of support a student may require.

How Do Students Obtain Special Services?

The majority of students who receive special education have high-incidence disabilities (such as learning disabilities) that you may be the first to recognize. If you teach at the elementary level, you probably will have students nearly every year who you refer for possible special services. If you teach in middle school, junior high, or high school, you will find that many students with disabilities already have been identified before they reach your classes. However, there are exceptions; students may be found eligible for special education at any time during their school years. As a teacher, you always have the option of asking a team of professionals to consider whether one of your students should be considered for special education services.

Having a serious and documented concern about a student is only the first step in considering whether a disability may be present. Your concern brings the student to the attention of other school professionals so that further information can be gathered and decisions made. The specific, formal procedures that must be followed to determine student eligibility for special education services are designed to ensure that only students who truly need these services receive them. These procedures are described in the following sections and summarized in Figure 2.2, which illustrates the flow of the procedures from beginning to end.

Initial Consideration of Student Problems

General education teachers, principals, special services personnel, parents, physicians, and social service agency personnel all may initiate the process of determining whether a student's needs constitute a disability. Most often, however, a general education teacher notices a pattern of academic underachievement, inconsistent learning, serious behavior problems, difficulties in social skills, or a persistent physical or sensory problem. When such problems occur, the teacher brings the student to the attention of others who help decide whether special education services are warranted.

Depending on the policies of your state and local district, there are two ways that the process of formally addressing student learning and behavior concerns can begin: (1) accessing an intervention assistance team or (2) using response-to-intervention procedures, an option available since implementation of the 2004 reauthorization of the Individuals with Disabilities Education Improvement Act (IDEA).

Intervention Assistance Team   One way to begin the process of helping a student suspected of having a disability is to bring the problem to the attention of a team (Friend & Cook, 2010). This team, often called an **intervention assistance team,** usually includes general education teachers, special services personnel, and an administrator. Teachers who want to "bring a student to the team" complete a referral form, on which they describe the student's strengths and problems and describe efforts they have made to assist the student. The teacher then meets with the team to discuss the written information, consider alternative strategies for assisting the student, and determine whether the student should have a detailed assessment for potential special education services (Lane et al., 2003). The unifying characteristic of this type of team is an emphasis on problem solving among all members.

Response to Intervention   A more clearly data-driven and structured procedure for analyzing students' learning problems is called **response to intervention (RtI).** Currently authorized in federal law just for students who may have learning disabilities but increasingly used to address a wide variety of student academic and behavior needs across all school levels, response to intervention calls for the systematic use of increasingly intensive, research-based interventions as a means for deciding whether a disability exists (Colvin, Flannery, Sugai, & Monegan, 2009; Lembke, McMaster, & Stecker, 2010). It is based on the assumption that approximately 75 to 80 percent of students will be able to learn if they receive high-quality instruction, that approximately 15 to 20 percent will benefit from moderately intensive instruction, and that the remaining 5 to 10 percent will need highly intensive instruction and possibly special education services. The Instructional Edge provides examples of interventions and how they vary by intensity.

Here is an example of an RtI procedure. Ms. Petersen is a first-grade teacher. She uses a district-adopted reading program in her class that has been demonstrated through research to be effective with students. This is called a *Tier 1 intervention.* The most recent screening assessment showed that one of Ms. Petersen's students, Jorgé, has not made much progress in reading; his skills are still at a kindergarten level. A team agreed that Jorgé's problems are significant and decided that he should

RESEARCH NOTE

Vannest, Temple-Harvey, & Mason (2009) identified 20 instructional strategies likely to improve academic outcomes for students with emotional disabilities. These included personalized instruction, including being allowed to retake tests, and increased opportunities to respond during instruction.

Although most RtI models have three tiers, after which students are considered for special education services, in some cases there are four tiers. In other models, Tier 3 consists of special education services rather than highly intensive interventions without special education eligibility.

FIGURE 2.2 The Decision–Making Process for Special Education

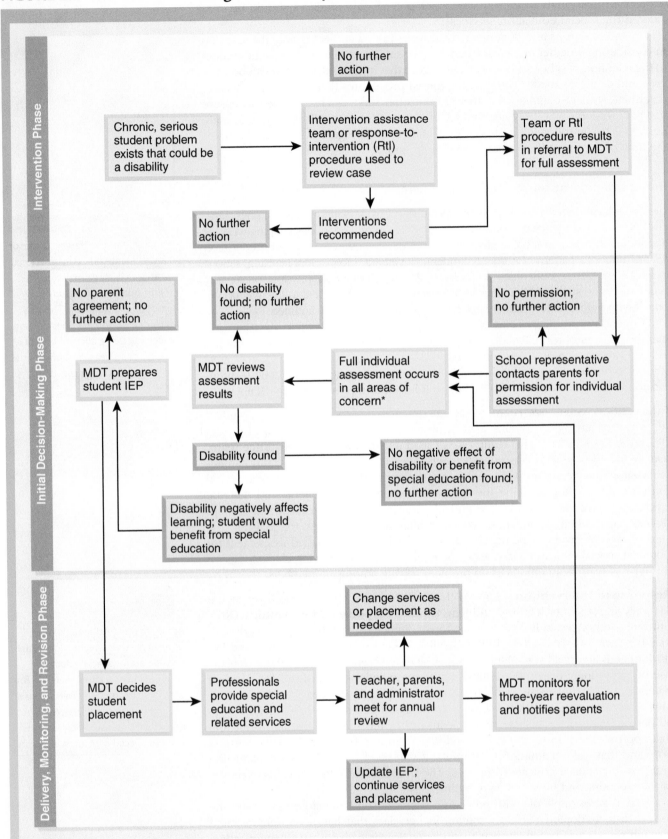

*Federal law permits the identification of students as having learning disabilities on the basis of Rtl procedures. When this option is used, the full assessment activities may be significantly reduced.

INSTRUCTIONAL **EDGE**

RtI and Intensity

Response to intervention is based on increasingly intensive interventions designed to avoid, if at all possible, the need for special education. Here are several dimensions that are used to determine intensity:

- *Frequency of intervention* In Tier 2 (sometimes called targeted intervention), an intervention may be offered three or four times each week. In Tier 3 (sometimes called intensive intervention), interventions typically occur five times per week.
- *Duration of intervention sessions* In Tier 2, the intervention might be implemented for 30 minutes per session. In Tier 3, the intervention might be implemented for 45 minutes per session.
- *Location of the intervention* In Tier 2, the intervention may be implemented in the general education setting. For example, three fourth-grade teachers skill group all their students and provide interventions in homogeneous groups to students in need while other students complete practice or enrichment activities. In Tier 3, intervention typically occurs in a setting away from the general education classroom.
- *Group size* Although specific group guidelines do not exist, Tier 2 interventions tend to be delivered in larger groups in middle or high school (for example, 6–10 students) and smaller groups in elementary school (for example, 3–4 students). Tier 3 interventions often require a small group size—usually fewer than four—and sometimes comprise one-to-one instruction.

- *Individual implementing the intervention* In Tier 2, the general education teacher often is responsible for implementing the intervention, and in some cases paraprofessionals may assist with this instruction. At Tier 3, a reading specialist, psychologist, special educator, or other specialist may be assigned to instruct the targeted students.
- *Type of intervention* Tier 2 includes research-based programs and strategies that supplement, enhance, and support Tier 1 instruction (Vaughn, 2003). Tier 2 instruction is systematic and explicit, and it provides students with multiple opportunities to practice skills essential for success in Tier 1. Two examples in reading at the elementary level are peer-mediated instruction (such as peer tutoring) and repeated readings (reading the same story or material several times to improve reading fluency and comprehension). In Tier 3, students receive highly concentrated interventions that are more tailored to their individual needs. Examples of these interventions include teaching specific strategies to improve vocabulary, comprehension, or pre-algebraic math skills.

As you might imagine, several of these dimensions can be changed at one time. Further, students may move up and down through the tiers, depending on what data indicate about their learning.

---

participate in a supplemental reading program in a small group led by the school's reading specialist. This service occurred four times each week for 30 minutes and was considered a Tier 2 intervention. After 12 weeks, the team reviewed the data gathered weekly about Jorgé's progress and noted that he still was not making adequate progress to catch up to his peers. The team enrolled Jorgé in an even more intensive skills-based reading program delivered five days a week for 50 minutes. If data indicate that the Tier 3 intervention does not work, the team may review the data, gather additional assessment information, and make a decision about Jorgé's eligibility for special education.

Although RtI is most likely to be implemented at the elementary level, it can occur whenever professionals determine a student is experiencing learning problems that are significant and interfering with achievement (National High School Center, National Center on Response to Intervention, and Center on Instruction, 2010). For example, Dana is a ninth-grade student whose assessed skills in written language are far below those of her peers. As a Tier 2 intervention she is enrolled in a composition class with 11 other students; in this one-semester class the teacher focuses on key elements of written language. The goal is for Dana to complete the course and improve her skills so that she can take a more traditional elective next semester. If her skills do not improve, she will probably be enrolled in a Tier 3 elective with a smaller group of students with a teacher as well as a literacy coach.

IDEA permits RtI but does not mandate it, and so although it is becoming common practice you should check locally to see whether an RtI procedure is in place. Further, the specific number of tiers of intervention, the length of time that interventions are implemented, and the exact nature of the interventions vary depending on state and local policies (Dexter, Hughes, & Farmer, 2008; Zirkel & Krohn,

fyi

The concept of response to intervention (RtI) arose from recognition that the traditional approach for identifying students with LD was a "wait-to-fail" model, in which students had to fall far enough behind in achievement to show a large discrepancy with their potential. RtI calls for intervention as soon as a problem is documented.

CASE IN PRACTICE

Response to Intervention: Looking at the Data

Mr. Thomas is a fourth-grade teacher attending a meeting to discuss Samuel, one of his students who is a struggling reader. Here is a brief segment of the conversation among Mr. Thomas, the school psychologist, and the reading specialist:

Mr. Thomas: With assistance from Ms. Jefferson (a paraprofessional), I completed the reading fluency measure for all my students last week. Overall, the students are just a little below average for this point in the school year, reading at 85 words per minute with fewer than five errors. But Sam is reading at only 50 words per minute, making an average of eight errors.

School psychologist: With these data and the other information you've provided, we should discuss whether Sam should start receiving more intensive instruction.

Reading specialist: Looking at his data, I can add that I already have a group that he could join, if we can work out the schedule. There are four other students with similar levels of skills, and I'm using the supplemental fluency materials from our reading program. But I would need you to do a quick curriculum-based check twice each week to see if his fluency is improving.

Mr. Thomas: We can work on the schedule. It's important to do something so we can see that Sam is making progress. And we just need to talk a little bit about the data collection.

School psychologist: I'd also like to suggest that Sam participate in the peer tutoring program with the sixth graders. I think he would benefit from repeated reading with one of the older students.

Mr. Thomas: That's a good idea. I do have some questions, though. For how long will we try these two interventions? What will happen if Sam's reading fluency does not improve? I'm a little concerned that we should refer him for an assessment for special education. I spoke with his mother on Monday, and she commented that Sam is talking about hating school and being embarrassed about his problems with reading. She is very worried about keeping his attitude positive.

School psychologist: The guideline is to intervene for 12 weeks, but if we don't see any change in six weeks, we can meet to decide if we should make a different decision. Will Sam's mother agree to assist by reading with him at home each evening? That would provide both her and us with an ongoing basis for communicating.

REFLECTIONS

Why are you, as an elementary, middle school, or high school teacher, responsible for implementing increasingly intensive interventions for your students who struggle to learn? Why do professionals consider data-based decision making so important in planning interventions for students? If you were Mr. Thomas, what additional questions would you have about the planned intervention?

RESEARCH NOTE

Response to intervention is being used to address behavior concerns as well as academic concerns. Fairbanks, Sugai, Guardino, and Lathrop (2007) found that an intervention more intensive than overall classroom management strategies (that is, Tier 2) was effective in addressing the behavior problems of half the students studied; the other half responded to an even more intensive intervention (that is, Tier 3).

2008). The Case in Practice illustrates what might occur at a team meeting when RtI is being implemented.

Regardless of variations among RtI models, one element of RtI is consistent: Even though it is included in federal special education law, it is largely the responsibility of general educators to carry it out (Mellard, McKnight, & Woods, 2009; Walker-Dalhouse et al., 2009). That is, as a general education teacher, you may be asked to work with a small group of students in your grade level during scheduled reading and language arts time, or you may be asked to assist in gathering data concerning student skill acquisition. Ultimately, the goal of RtI is to prevent some students from ever needing special education. At the same time, following RtI procedures will help ensure that students who need specialized instruction will receive it as soon as a problem is noticed.

Note that whether an intervention assistance team or RtI procedure is initiated, a parent is not legally required to be involved in the process. However, educators should notify parents of their concerns and enlist parental assistance in trying to solve the problem. In some schools, parents are routinely invited to team meetings. Parents should never be surprised when the possibility of providing special education is raised. They should be made aware of the existence of any serious problem as soon as it is noticed.

The Special Education Referral, Assessment, Eligibility, Planning, and Placement Process

If a student does not respond to increasingly intensive interventions or the intervention assistance team believes the student's needs are serious enough to consider special education as an option, the student's parents are formally contacted and the assessment process begins. At this point, a **multidisciplinary team (MDT)**—consisting of parents, educators, and others as appropriate—assumes responsibility for making educational decisions regarding the student. No student may receive special education unless the steps discussed in the upcoming sections are followed.

Parents' Rights   Before any discussion of how a student comes to receive special education services can proceed, it is essential that you understand how central parents are in all aspects of the referral, assessment, eligibility, planning, and placement process (Yell, Ryan, Rozalski, & Katsiyannis, 2009). As summarized in Figure 2.3, parents are key participants in all decision making related to their child's suspected or documented disability. They must be informed of their rights in their own language

www.resources

http://www.speakingofspeech.com/IEP_Goal_Bank.html
The Speaking of Speech website includes a bank of IEP goals appropriate for students with different types of needs. Do these examples meet the criteria for high quality goals as outlined in this chapter?

FIGURE 2.3 **Parents' Rights in Special Education**

IDEA stipulates procedural safeguards to ensure protection of parents' rights to be active participants in their child's education. The following are some of the major safeguards provided to parents:

1. Parents are entitled to be members of any group that makes decisions about the educational placement of their child.

2. Parents are to be given written notice before the school initiates, changes, or refuses to initiate or change the identification or educational placement of their child.

3. Parents can participate directly in the determination of their child's eligibility for special education and the development of the individualized education program (IEP) and its periodic review, generally at least annually (but in some cases, every three years).

4. The school must obtain written, informed parental consent before conducting an initial formal evaluation and assessment and before initially placing a student in a program providing special education and related services.

5. Parents can inspect and review any educational records maintained by the school district or other agency providing services under IDEA. Access to educational records will be granted to parents without unnecessary delay and before any meeting regarding an IEP or before any hearing relating to identification, evaluation, or placement of the child. In no case should access be delayed more than 45 days after the request has been made.

6. Parents may request and the school district must provide information on where an independent educational

evaluation may be obtained. In some instances, parents may have the right to an independent educational evaluation at public expense. The results of an independent evaluation obtained by the parents at private expense will be considered by the local school district in any decision about provision of a free appropriate public education to the child. Such results also may be presented as evidence at a due process hearing.

7. Parents have the right to request mediation as a means to resolving conflict with the school district concerning their child with a disability. Mediation must be available to parents prior to a due process hearing, but it may not delay a hearing. The district, not the parents, bears the cost of mediation.

8. Parents have the right to request a hearing before an impartial hearing officer in cases in which they disagree with school district decisions regarding their child's education. The hearing may relate to any aspect of special education. If the parents fail to win a due process hearing at the local level, they may appeal the results at the state department of education. After this step, if parents still are dissatisfied with the outcome of the hearing, they may initiate court action. Note, though, that if parents' legal actions are judged to be frivolous, the school district may seek to recover the funds spent in defending the district.

9. Parents must be fully informed of their rights and the procedural safeguards related to special education. These rights must be communicated in writing and in a form parents readily can understand.

Sources: Adapted from "Questions and Answers about IDEA," *NICHCY NewsDigest, 21* (2nd ed.), January 2000, Washington, DC: National Information Center for Handicapped Children and Youth, retrieved September 15, 2004, from http://nichcy.org/pubs/newsdig/nd21txt.htm; and "Parental Rights in Special Education," April 2004, Trenton: New Jersey Department of Education, retrieved September 15, 2004, from http://www.state.nj.us.njded/parights/prise.pdf.

Before a team can make a decision about a student's eligibility to receive special education, a comprehensive and individual assessment of strengths and needs must be completed. Syracuse Newspapers/The Image Works

and in a manner they can understand (Fitzgerald & Watkins, 2006). If you teach older students, you also should know that beginning at least one year before reaching 18 years of age, students also must be informed directly of their rights, and at age 18, most students assume the rights that parents have held for them (National Center on Secondary Education Transition, 2002).

The very first application of parents' rights comes before any assessment process begins. That is, parents must give written permission for their child to be individually assessed. Although it is not common for parents to deny permission, if they do, the process must stop unless the school district asks for a hearing to compel parents to comply. As you read about the rest of the procedures related to special education, you will notice many references to the rights parents have.

Components of Assessment Although the specific requirements regarding the types of data gathered vary somewhat by state and by the type of initial intervention processes used, assessment generally involves gathering information about a student's strengths and needs in all areas of concern. Typically, if the student has not had a vision and hearing screening and you have reason to suspect a sensory impairment, these tests precede other assessments. If sensory screening raises concerns, the parents are notified of the need for a more complete assessment by a physician or appropriate specialist.

Assessments completed by school professionals may address any aspect of a student's educational functioning (Yell, 2006). Often, for example, the student's intellectual ability is assessed. An individual intelligence test (often referred to as an *IQ test*) is administered and scored by a school psychologist or another qualified school professional. Academic achievement usually is assessed, too. The student completes an individual achievement test administered by a psychologist, special education teacher, educational diagnostician, or other professional. A third area often evaluated is social and behavior skills. This evaluation might involve a checklist that you and parents complete concerning a student's behavior, a test given by the school psychologist, or a series of questions asked of the student.

Another domain for assessment is the student's social and developmental history. A school social worker may meet with the parents to learn about the student's family life and major events in her development that could be affecting education. For example, parents might be asked about their child's friends and favorite out-of-school activities, their expectations for their child as an adult, and their child's strengths. Parents also might be asked whether their child has had any serious physical injuries, medical problems, or recurring social or behavior problems.

As another assessment component, a psychologist, counselor, or special education teacher often observes the student in the classroom and other settings to learn how he responds to teachers and peers in various school situations. For example, a psychologist may observe Scott, who usually plays with younger students during recess and gets confused when playground games are too complex. Scott also watches other students carefully and often seems to take cues for how to act from how they are acting. Similarly, a special educator may observe D. J., a sixth-grade student, in the cafeteria to try to understand what is triggering his many behavior incidents there. Such observations are helpful for understanding students' social strengths and needs.

If a potential need exists for speech, occupational, or physical therapy, another component is added to the assessment. The professionals in those areas complete assessments in their respective areas of expertise. A speech/language therapist might use a screening instrument that includes having the student use certain words, tell stories, and identify objects. The therapist also might check for atypical use of the muscles of the mouth, tongue, and throat that permit speech and for unusual speech

RESEARCH NOTE

According to IDEA, parents must receive a statement of their rights, written at a level they can easily understand (that is, seventh- or eighth-grade reading level). Fitzgerald and Watkins (2006) found that 92 percent or more of the parents' rights statements found on state department of education websites were written above this level.

habits such as breathiness in speaking or noticeable voice strain. Similarly, an occupational or physical therapist might assess a student's gait, strength and agility, range of motion, or ability to perform fine motor tasks such as buttoning and lacing.

Throughout the entire assessment process, IDEA specifically gives parents the right to provide information to be used as part of the evaluation. In addition, as the general education teacher, you typically provide details on the student's performance in class, patterns of behavior, and discrepancies between expectations and achievement. Your informal and formal observations play an important role in assessment.

Assessment Procedures   The exact procedures for assessing a student's needs vary according to the areas of concern that initiated the assessment process. The assessment must be completed by individuals trained to administer the tests and other assessment tools used; the instruments must be free of cultural bias; the student's performance must be evaluated in a way that takes into account the potential disability; and the assessment must provide data that are useful for designing an appropriate education for the student. School professionals are responsible for ensuring that these obligations are met.

RtI and Assessment   It should be noted that, at least for students being assessed to determine whether a learning disability exists, the data gathered as part of RtI procedures may be the basis for making that decision. Based on state and local policies, RtI data may be used in lieu of other assessments of ability and achievement, or, as is more common, these data may be used in addition to other assessment data.

Decision Making for Special Services

After a comprehensive assessment of the student has been completed, the multidisciplinary team (MDT) meets to discuss its results and make several decisions. The first decision the MDT must make is whether the student is eligible under the law to be categorized as having a disability. If team members decide that a disability exists, they then determine whether the disability is affecting the student's education and from that they decide whether the student is eligible to receive services through special education. In most school districts, these decisions are made at a single meeting, and parents must agree with the decisions being made or the student cannot receive special education services. Most school districts have specific guidelines to direct team decision making about the presence of a disability and the need for special education services. However, the decisions ultimately belong to the team. For example, most states specify that students identified as having a mild intellectual disability should have an IQ less than 70 as measured on an individual intelligence test and should have serious limitations in adaptive behaviors. However, if a student's score is slightly above 70 and her adaptive skills are particularly limited, a team can still decide that she has a mild intellectual disability. Likewise, if a student has a measured IQ lower than 70 but seems to have many adaptive skills, the team might decide that she does not have an intellectual disability.

If the MDT determines the student has a disability affecting her education and is eligible for services according to federal, state, and local guidelines, the stage is set for detailed planning of the student's education and related services. This planning is recorded in the student's **individualized education program,** or **IEP,** the document that outlines all the special education services the student is to receive. More details about IEPs and their preparation are provided later in this chapter.

The final decision made by the MDT concerns the student's placement. *Placement* refers to the location of the student's education. For most students (but not all), the placement is the general education classroom, often with some type of support offered, either there or part-time in a special education setting such as a resource room. According to IDEA, when a placement is a location other than general education, justification must be provided for that decision. Later in this chapter, special education services are discussed and placement options are outlined in more detail.

dimensions of
DIVERSITY

In IDEA 2004, the federal government for the first time required states (and thus local school districts) to take steps to correct the disproportionate representation of students from minority groups, a problem that is particularly serious in the areas of learning disabilities, intellectual disabilities, and emotional disabilities.

In your school district, the essentials of the procedures described in the preceding sections must be followed, but the specific steps, paperwork required, and names for the different parts of the process may vary. Nonetheless, all school district procedures are designed to ensure that students with disabilities are systematically assessed and that a deliberate and careful process is followed to provide for their education needs, and you are a critical participant throughout that process.

Monitoring Special Education Services

In addition to specifying the procedures that must be followed to identify a student as needing special education services, federal and state laws also establish guidelines for monitoring student progress. The monitoring process ensures that a student's educational program remains appropriate and that procedures exist for resolving disputes between school district personnel and parents.

Annual Reviews   The first strategy for monitoring special services is the **annual review.** At least once each year, a student's progress toward his annual goals must be reviewed and the IEP changed or updated as needed. Not all multidisciplinary team members who participated in the initial decisions about the student's disability and educational needs are required to play a part in the annual review. However, a teacher instructing the student and an administrator or other professional representing the school district must meet with the student's parents to discuss whether goals and objectives (as required) have been met and what the next steps in the student's education should be. In practical terms, if your school district completes all annual reviews during a given month, you will find that the special educators with whom you work are unavailable because of their other responsibilities, such as meeting with parents. Depending on local practices, you will likely be asked to attend annual reviews for some students. For many students, a general education teacher is most knowledgeable about their day-to-day functioning. This concept was highlighted with the mandate in IDEA that a general education teacher participate in the development of most students' IEPs, not necessarily by writing them but by contributing a classroom perspective.

The most recent reauthorization of IDEA included a new provision related to reviewing a student's educational program. In some cases, an IEP may be reviewed once every three years instead of every year. If a state has this option, the IEP must be reviewed at natural transition points for the student (for example, moving from middle school to high school), and parents have the right to request that an annual review be completed.

Three-Year Reevaluations   A second monitoring procedure required by law is the **three-year reevaluation.** At least every three years, and more often if deemed necessary by the MDT, students receiving special education services must be reassessed to determine whether their needs have changed. This safeguard is designed to prevent students with disabilities from remaining in services or programs that may no longer be appropriate for them, and parents are informed of this reevaluation but do not have to give permission for it to occur. In some cases, the reevaluation includes administering all the tests and other instruments that were used initially to identify the student as needing special education. However, in some cases IDEA permits existing information to be used for reevaluation instead of requiring new assessments. In fact, with parent and team agreement, the reevaluation may not involve any new assessment at all (Yell, 2006). On the basis of the three-year reevaluation, the MDT meets again to develop an appropriate IEP.

Additional Reviews   In addition to annual reviews and three-year reevaluations, IDEA stipulates that an IEP must be revised whenever a lack of expected progress toward achieving goals is noted, reevaluation information is gathered, or parents bring to the attention of the MDT information that affects the IEP. This suggests that an IEP may need to be revised more frequently than the once per year mandated by the basic requirements of the law. In some cases, necessary changes can be made with parent approval and without reconvening the team.

Parents have one more formal mechanism for obtaining information about their child's learning. IDEA specifies that the parents of students with disabilities have the right to receive progress reports about their children as often as do parents of typical learners. In many school districts, this means that formal communication about student learning progress now occurs every six or nine weeks during the school year, that is, at the end of each grading period.

Due Process   Yet another strategy for monitoring students receiving special education services is **due process,** the set of procedures outlined in the law for resolving disagreements between school district personnel and parents regarding students with disabilities (Bateman, 2009). Due process rights begin when a student is first brought to the attention of a team as potentially having a disability. Both the school district and parents are entitled to protection through due process, but parents typically exercise their due process rights when they fear the school district is not acting in the best interests of their child (Wright & Wright, 2006). For example, if parents have their child independently evaluated because they believe the assessment for special education did not accurately portray his needs and if the school district does not agree with the findings of the independent evaluator, the parents may request a due process hearing. Parents also may request a hearing if they disagree with the goals and objectives listed on the IEP and with the way services are being provided to meet those goals and objectives.

Due process hearings seldom address blatant errors on the part of the school or parents regarding special education; most often, they reflect the fact that many decisions made about students with disabilities are judgment calls in which a best course of action is not always clear. For example, Mr. and Mrs. Dotson filed a due process complaint in a dispute about the services their son Jeremiah would receive when he transitioned from middle school to high school. They wanted him to spend much of the day in general education classes with assistance from a paraprofessional and other supports. School district personnel maintained that Jeremiah's behavior outbursts when faced with frustrating tasks as well as his tendency to become overwhelmed in unfamiliar situations indicated the need for most of his education to occur in a separate setting. When discussion reached an impasse, a hearing officer was assigned by the State Department of Education to hear the case and issue a decision.

In practice, most school districts and parents want to avoid due process hearings, which tend to be adversarial and can damage the parent–school working relationship to the detriment of the student. To foster a positive working relationship, IDEA requires that all states have a system in place to offer **mediation** to parents at no cost as an initial means for resolving conflicts with schools (Wright & Wright, 2006). In mediation, a neutral professional skilled in conflict resolution meets with both parties to help them resolve their differences informally. Mediation, however, is not allowed to cause delay in the parents' right to a due process hearing. A hearing is preceded by mediation—a less formal dispute resolution strategy—unless parents decline this option.

Whether or not mediation occurs, IDEA also mandates a dispute resolution session, a sort of last chance for reaching agreement (Hazelkorn, Packard, & Douvanis, 2008; Mueller, 2009). If neither mediation nor a dispute resolution session is successful, a hearing is conducted by an independent and objective third party selected from a list provided by the state, but the school district bears the expense (D'Angelo, Lutz, & Zirkel, 2004). If either party disagrees with the outcome of a due process hearing, the decision can be appealed to a state-level review hearing officer. If disagreement still exists, either party can then take the matter to court.

If a due process hearing occurs concerning a student you teach, you may be called to testify. In such a case, you would be asked to describe the student's level of functioning in your classroom, the supports you provided, and your efforts with

Although nearly all students with disabilities participate in their school's music classes, a survey of 200 music educators indicated that they seldom participated in IEP meetings and believed they had inadequate preparation to work with these students (McCord & Watts, 2010).

fyi

When students who have IEPs transfer from district to district or even from state to state, IDEA requires the new school district to provide services similar to those provided by the previous school district until records can be reviewed and the previously received services adopted, amended, or dropped.

other special service providers to ensure the student was successful. An administrator and an attorney might help you prepare for the hearing, and they would answer any questions you might have about your role.

What Is an Individualized Education Program?

As mentioned earlier, the document that the multidisciplinary team uses to decide the best placement for a student with an identified disability and that serves as a blueprint for a student's education is called an *individualized education program* (IEP). The IEP addresses all areas of student need, including accommodations to be made in the general education setting and the services and supports to be provided there. The IEP also is the means through which student progress is documented (Etscheidt, 2006). General education teachers generally are involved as team participants in preparing an IEP if a student has any participation in the general education setting (Hackett, 2009; Turnbull, Huerta, & Stowe, 2006). Whether or not you are the teacher who serves in this role for particular students, if you have students with disabilities in your classroom, you will have opportunities to examine their IEPs or to meet with special educators to review highlights of these important plans, just as Ms. Lee, introduced at the beginning of the chapter, learned.

Accessing IEPs and learning about your state's requirements for them has been made more efficient with the increasing use of technology. The Technology Notes explains some of the electronic options related to IEPs and the procedures for developing them.

Required Components of an IEP

The essential components of the IEP were established by P.L. 94-142 in 1975, and they have been updated through the years. Although specific state requirements for IEPs vary somewhat, the federally required elements of IEPs are described in the following sections.

Present Level of Performance Information about a student's current level of academic achievement, social skills, behavior, communication skills, and other areas of concern must be included on an IEP. This information serves as a baseline and makes it possible to judge student progress from year to year. Often, highlights of the information collected from the individual assessment of the student or response to intervention data are recorded on the IEP to partially meet this requirement. Individual achievement test scores, teacher ratings, and summary assessments by specialists such as speech therapists and occupational therapists also can be used to report the present level of performance. Another component of this assessment is information about how the student's disabilities affect involvement in the general education curriculum.

Annual Goals and Short-Term Objectives *Annual goals* are the MDT's estimate of what a student should be able to accomplish within a year, related to meeting his measured needs resulting from the disability. For some students, annual goals may refer primarily to academic areas and may include growth in reading, math problem solving, and other curricular areas. Specifically, a student with a learning disability might have an annual goal to read and comprehend books at a particular grade level or demonstrate skills for finding and keeping a job. For other students, annual goals address desired changes in classroom behavior, social skills, or other adaptive skills. An annual goal for a student with a moderate intellectual disability, for example, may be to order a meal at a fast-food restaurant. A student with autism might have participating in conversation as a goal. Annual goals also may encompass speech therapy, occupational and physical therapy, and other areas in which a student has specialized needs. There is no right number of annual goals. Some students have as few as two or three, and others as many as eight or ten. However, IDEA specifies

Implementing Response to Intervention Using Technology

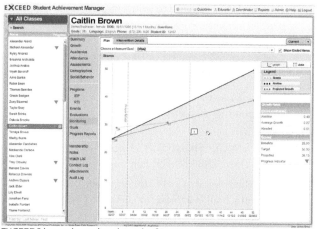

EXCEED® is a registered trademark of Spectrum K12 School Solutions, Inc.

Effectively implementing response to intervention requires familiarity with research-based interventions, frequent and valid monitoring to student learning progress, and analysis of the gathered data so that next steps can be identified. Fortunately, many websites are providing free materials to teachers so that they can implement RtI without having to develop interventions, assessments, and graphing tools on their own. Here are two of the most comprehensive sites to help you with RtI.

INTERVENTION CENTRAL (http://interventioncentral.org)

This website has so many ideas and options for RtI that you may need several visits to explore all the information available. Here are highlights:

- Under "Academic Resources" you will find research-based interventions for reading comprehension, reading fluency, math, writing, and other skill areas.
- Under "Behavior Resources" you will find many positive ideas for addressing behavior problems, including bullying

and unmotivated students. Strategies include the use of behavior contracts and "mystery motivators."

- In the "tools" section, you will find a variety of templates for graphing data. Other tools include random item generators so that you can easily create assessments on skills such as reading comprehension, writing, and math computation.
- The RtI blog includes issues and topics, including the importance of principal leadership in implementing RtI and the dilemma of sustaining RtI when budget cuts limit staff members available to assist in implementing intensive interventions.

RTI WIRE (http://www.jimwrightonline.com/php/rti/rti_wire.php)

This website boasts being the most complete, free set of RtI resources available to teachers. Examples of the materials and information you can find at the site include these:

- In "understand the model" you will find descriptions of various approaches to RtI as implemented across the United States.
- In "use teams to problem solve," you will find descriptions of the various team models being used across the states to make RtI a reality.
- In "select the right intervention" are links to many sites with academic interventions that span topics and skills areas as well as grade levels.
- In "monitor student progress" are links to sites with data templates using a variety of recording strategies, from simple tallies of behaviors to more complex approaches such as time sampling.
- In "graph data for visual analysis," the tools include several Excel® spreadsheets preformatted so that you can easily enter and graph your student data.

that annual goals must be measurable, and increased emphasis is placed on annual goals that enable a student to progress in the general education curriculum.

Short-term objectives are descriptions of the steps needed to achieve an annual goal, and they may or may not be required for all students, depending on state policies. Federal law requires that short-term objectives be written only for the IEPs of students with significant intellectual disabilities. For example, for a student with multiple disabilities whose annual goal is to feed herself, short-term objectives might include grasping a spoon, picking up food with the spoon, and using the spoon to transport food from plate to mouth. The number of short-term objectives for each annual goal relates to the type and severity of the disability, its impact on student learning, and the complexity of the goal. Examples of IEP goals and objectives are included in the Professional Edge on the next page.

Extent of Participation in General Education In keeping with the trend toward inclusive practices, the IEP must include a clear statement of justification for placing

dimensions of
DIVERSITY

Although most researchers express concern at the overrepresentation of boys in special education (particularly those who are African American), others are concerned that girls, who are underrepresented, are being denied services that they need in order to succeed later in life (Arms, Bickett, & Graf, 2008).

PROFESSIONAL **EDGE**

Sample IEP Goals and Objectives

The goals and objectives on IEPs are related to assessed student needs, and they are written in specific ways (Bateman & Linden, 2006). They must

- be aligned with the curriculum for the grade level of the student, regardless of the severity of the student's disability.
- be measurable and specify the conditions under which the student should be able to carry out an activity (such as the reading level of print material or the people with whom a student should communicate).
- indicate the level of mastery needed (such as a level of accuracy in an assignment).

Goals usually outline progress expected for approximately one school year. For all students with significant intellectual disabilities who take alternate assessments and, in some states, for all students with disabilities, goals are supplemented by short-term objectives or benchmarks that measure progress toward achieving the annual goal. The following are sample IEP goals and objectives:

STUDENTS WITH MILD/MODERATE DISABILITIES

- *Goal:* When assigned to write an essay of three paragraphs, Jerome will use complete sentences, capital letters, and punctuation with 80 percent accuracy.

Objective: When assigned to write one paragraph, Jerome will use periods, commas, question marks, and exclamation points with 90 percent accuracy.

- *Goal:* Susan will complete at least 80 percent of her homework assignments in English, algebra, and U.S. history.

Objective: Susan will write down homework assignments 90 percent of the time with 90 percent accuracy.

STUDENTS WITH SIGNIFICANT INTELLECTUAL DISABILITIES

- *Goal:* Maria will make eye contact when communicating with adults in school in at least five out of six trials.

Objective: Maria will make eye contact with the speech/language therapist during individual sessions in five out of six interactions initiated by the therapist.
Objective: Maria will make eye contact when the special education teacher calls her name and looks at her in at least five out of six interactions.
Objective: Maria will make eye contact when a classroom teacher calls her name and looks at her in at least five out of six interactions.

---

a student anywhere but in a general education classroom for all or part of the school day. Even for extracurricular and other nonacademic activities, if the team excludes the student from the setting for typical peers, a specific, evidence-based explanation of why that student cannot participate in such activities must be part of the IEP.

Services and Modifications Needed   The IEP contains a complete outline of the specialized services the student needs; that is, the document includes all the special education instruction to be provided and any other related services needed. Thus, a student receiving adaptive physical education has an IEP indicating that such a service is needed. A student's need for special transportation is noted on the IEP, too. A student who is entitled to transition or vocational assistance has an IEP that clarifies these services. Perhaps most important, the statement of services must include information about the supplementary aids and services, to be provided so that the student can access and progress in the general education curriculum.

One additional element of this IEP component concerns assessment. IDEA stipulates that if a student needs accommodations (for example, extended time) on district or state assessments, including high-stakes assessments, these should be specified on the IEP and implemented throughout the school year, not just for high-stakes tests. If a student is to be exempt from such assessments, the team must ensure the student will complete an alternate assessment that takes into account her functioning levels and needs. The Elementary and Secondary Education Act set specific limits on which students are exempt from high-stakes testing and eligible for alternate assessments, and these limits were confirmed and clarified in IDEA. Most of the students with disabilities you teach will be required to complete mandated assessments, and their scores must be considered for measuring adequate yearly progress (AYP).

Part of identifying services is indicating who is responsible for providing them. Any of the professionals introduced earlier in this chapter could be listed on the IEP to deliver special services. As a general education teacher, you may be included, too. For some students, you will be the teacher who completes most of the required instruction; for others, you will assist but not be primarily responsible. For example, a student with a mild intellectual or learning disability probably will be able to complete many class tasks with minor accommodations that you can make. However, if your student has significant intellectual and physical disabilities, other professionals undoubtedly will help develop the materials and activities you will use when the student is in your classroom.

Behavior Intervention Plan   Every student with significant behavior problems, not just those students labeled as having emotional disabilities, must have as part of the IEP an intervention plan based on a functional assessment of the student's behavior. This requirement reflects the increasing pressure for students to be supported in general education settings and the acknowledged difficulty of accomplishing that goal without fostering appropriate student behavior.

Date of Initiation and Frequency and Duration of Service and Anticipated Modifications   Each IEP must include specific dates when services begin, the frequency of the services, the types of accommodations and modifications that are part of the services, and the period of time during which services are offered. Because the law generally requires that student progress in special education be monitored at least once each year (or alternatively, three years), the most typical duration for a service is a maximum of one year. If during the year an MDT member sees a need to reconsider the student's educational plan, additional IEP meetings can be convened or amendments made by phone with parent approval.

Strategies for Evaluation   When a team develops an IEP, the members must clarify how to measure student progress toward achieving the annual goals and how to regularly inform parents about this progress (Etscheidt, 2006). For example, when short-term objectives are written, the team indicates the criteria and procedures to be used to judge whether each objective has been met. For the student learning to move around the school without assistance, the criteria might include specific point-to-point independent movement, and a checklist might be used to judge student progress toward reaching the goal.

Transition Plan   For each student who is 16 years of age or older, part of the IEP is an outcomes-oriented description of strategies and services for ensuring that the student will be prepared to leave school for adult life. This part of the IEP is called a **transition plan.** Students with disabilities who are college bound might have a transition plan that includes improvement of study skills, exploration of different universities and their services for students with disabilities, and completion of high school course requirements necessary to obtain admission to a university. For students who plan to work immediately after graduation, the transition plan might include developing skills such as reading employment ads and filling out job applications, as well as developing important job skills such as punctuality and respect toward people in authority and customers. This plan must be tailored to match the assessed strengths and needs of the particular student. It is updated annually, with participation by professionals from agencies outside the school typically increasing as the student nears graduation or school departure at age 21 or 22.

In addition to the basic components, IEPs have several other requirements. For example, they are signed by the individuals who participate in their development, including the student's parent or guardian. In addition, if a student has highly specialized needs, they must be addressed in the IEP. Examples of such needs are behavior, communication, braille (unless specifically excluded on the IEP), and assistive technology. In such cases, appropriate supports, services, and strategies must be specified (Yell, 2006).

RESEARCH NOTE

Although RtI can lead to improved academic outcomes for students from diverse backgrounds, research indicates that inadequate teacher preparation, a negative school culture, and misalignment of assessment and instruction can significantly limit its potential (Orosco & Klingner, 2010).

Working TOGETHER

Understanding the Intervention, Assessment, and Decision-Making Process

Even experienced teachers sometimes have questions about their roles and responsibilities related to intervention assistance teams, response to intervention procedures, the eligibility process, and the design of special education services. Here are a few common questions and their answers:

- I work in a high school, and most students already have been identified by the time they get to this level. Do high schools still need to have intervention assistance teams and procedures in place for response to intervention?

  Federal law requires that across all levels of schools, including high schools, a system must be in place to identify students who are not making expected academic progress. However, recent research indicates that RtI in high school must take into account significant context factors, including impact on graduation requirements, student choice in selecting interventions, involvement of parents, and staff members' perceptions of their roles (National High School Center et al., 2010).
- Do all the teachers on the middle school team need to attend the intervention assistance, response to intervention, and/or IEP team meetings for their students who have been referred or assessed?

In most cases, it is not reasonable to expect all the teachers on the middle school team to attend a meeting about a student with a suspected or identified disability. The composition of the prereferral team is a school's decision. In some cases, the middle school team might actually serve as the intervention assistance team. In others, a representative from the team might work with the team monitoring a student's response to intervention. When an initial IEP is written, in nearly all cases one general education teacher can provide a representative perspective for the team.

- Are general education teachers responsible for writing parts of the IEP?

Federal law requires participation of general education teachers in most IEP meetings because they bring an important viewpoint to them. However, those teachers generally do not write sections of the IEP. No matter what your role (for example, elementary, middle school, or high school teacher; related arts teacher; technology specialist), you are obligated to carry out any IEP provisions that pertain to you, including participating in services offered in the general education classroom and making adjustments to assignments and strategies as noted in the IEP.

The Value of IEPs

Although technical and potentially time consuming, IEPs guide the education of students with disabilities. An IEP helps you clarify your expectations for a student and provides a means for you to understand the student's educational needs. The document also informs you about the types of services the student receives and when the student's educational plan will next be reviewed.

Your job is to make a good-faith effort to accomplish the goals and/or short-term objectives on the IEP as they relate to your instruction. If you do that, you will have carried out your responsibility; if you do not do that, you could be held accountable. For example, suppose an IEP indicates that a student should learn the concept of freedom of speech. You can demonstrate that you are helping the student learn this by providing class discussion, role-play activities, and access to appropriate resources on the Internet, even if the student does not master this concept. If you state that the student is expected merely to read about the concept in the textbook chapter and you refuse to create opportunities for supported learning in this area, you may be violating the IEP.

Do you have questions about your role in the prereferral, referral, or IEP process? Additional considerations related to your role are presented in the Working Together.

Students with disabilities who are enrolled in faith-based private schools are entitled to some benefits from IDEA. Although these students must be identified by the public school district in that locale, they may receive only limited services that do not have to be available at the private school, only at the public school (Eigenbrood, 2004).

What Services Do Students with Disabilities Receive?

The services that a student with disabilities can receive are comprehensive, limited only by the stipulation that they must be necessary as part of that student's education. These services are provided in a variety of placements. Both the services and placements are determined by the multidisciplinary team.

Special Education and Related Services

The types of services students receive can be grouped into three categories: special education, related services, and supplementary aids and services. *Special education* refers to the specially designed instructional services students receive. These services may include a curriculum aligned with the standard curriculum but significantly simplified, access to a special education teacher qualified to teach students with a particular disability, and individualized instruction using specialized approaches. When a student's special education teacher comes to the classroom and teaches with the general education teacher, that is special education. When a student leaves a classroom for 30 minutes three times each week for intensive tutoring, that is special education. When a middle school or high school offers a life skills class for students with disabilities, that is special education, too.

Related services refer to all the supports students may need in order to benefit from special education. Examples of related services are speech therapy, transportation, physical and occupational therapy, adapted physical education, counseling, psychological services, and social work. A student's need to ride a special bus equipped with a wheelchair lift is a related service, as is a student's need for assistance with personal care such as toileting.

Supplementary aids and services are all means used to enable students to succeed in a general education setting. They include materials that are written at a different level or reformatted to make them easier for students to read, peer or paraprofessional support, assistive and other technology, and even special professional development for general education teachers so they know how to address students' instructional needs.

As you might guess, the range of possibilities for special education, related services, and supplementary aids and services is immense. Some students, particularly those with high-incidence disabilities, receive a limited number of special education services and perhaps no related services at all. For example, Lucas, a high school student with a learning disability in math, attends a geometry class in which a special education teacher teams with a math teacher. Lucas's assignments are sometimes shortened, and he is allowed extra time to complete tests. He already is looking into colleges that are recognized for their support of students with his special needs. Students with more complex or severe disabilities may have a more highly specialized special education as well as numerous related services. For example, Charmon, a student with physical and intellectual disabilities, receives the services of a physical and occupational therapist, and speech/language therapist, as well as a special education teacher.

Student Placement and Educational Environments

Where students receive their educational services is guided by the principle of least restrictive environment (LRE), that is, the setting in which they can succeed that is most like the setting for other students. In today's schools, the LRE for most students is general education for more than 80 percent of the school day. Nearly all school districts still have some separate special education classrooms, but the requirement that teachers delivering core academic instruction be highly qualified and the increasing recognition that students with disabilities can, with supports, succeed when educated with typical peers has caused educators to rethink such classrooms for all except students with extraordinary needs. As in Ms. Turner's school, which you read about at the beginning of the chapter, emphasis now is on designing systems of support in general education settings. Figure 2.4 shows the IDEA continuum of placements, now referred to as *educational environments,* that must exist for students with disabilities; it also provides recent data on the percentage of students with disabilities in each of those placements.

As discussed earlier, the decision about placement is made by the MDT and reviewed along with the IEP at least annually (or in some states and for some students, every three years). Placement can be changed as often as appropriate, with parental

FIGURE 2.4 IDEA Educational Environments for Students with Disabilities

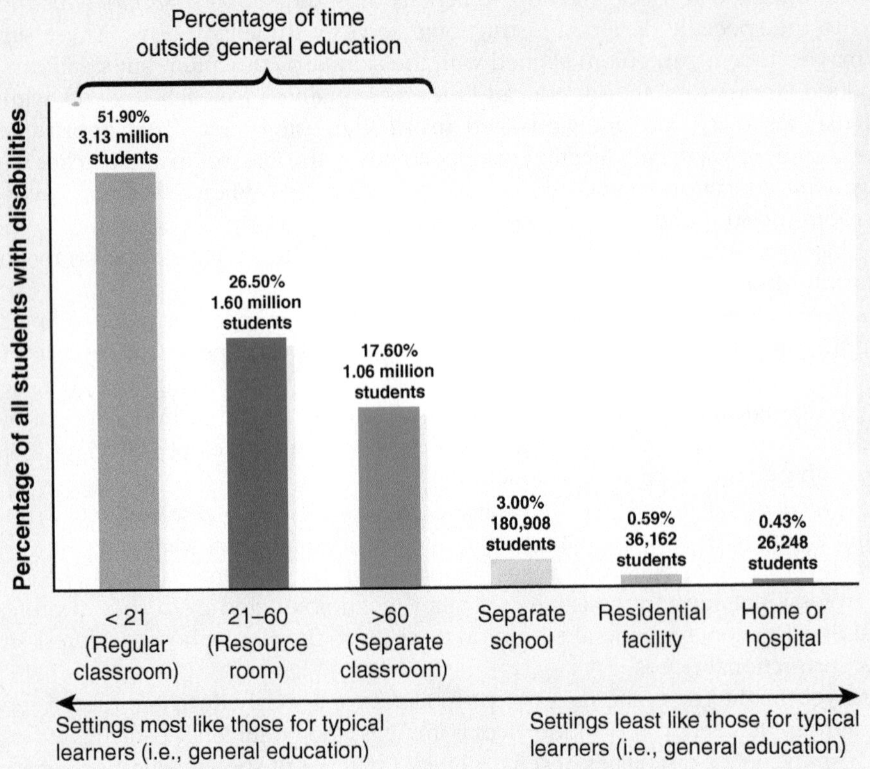

Source: U.S. Department of Education. (2009). *Twenty-eighth annual report to Congress on the implementation of the Individuals with Disabilities Education Act.* Washington, DC: Author.

permission. Generally, if the parents and school district representatives disagree about placement, the student remains in the current placement until the disagreement is resolved. Exceptions to this occur when discipline issues arise. Administrators may unilaterally change a student's placement (for example, through suspension) for up to 10 days in a school year, provided such methods are used with other students, too. If students with disabilities bring a weapon or drugs to school, they can be placed in an alternative educational setting for up to 45 school days while a decision is made concerning long-term placement (Yell, 2006).

Regular (General Education) Classes   More than half of students with disabilities spend more than 80 percent of the school day in a general education setting (U.S. Department of Education, 2009). A kindergartener with a communication disorder might be served by a speech/language therapist who comes to the classroom and teaches language lessons with the general education teacher. For a middle school student with intellectual and physical disabilities, an inclusion specialist might adjust a lesson on fractions by helping the student learn how to cut simple shapes into halves. For a high school student with a learning disability, a paraprofessional might provide assistance in biology class in carrying out lab directions and recording and completing assignments. This student also might have one special education class for instruction in study skills and learning strategies.

Resource Programs   Another group of students with disabilities attends school mostly in general education settings but also receives assistance in a special education classroom, often called a **resource room,** for 21 to 60 percent of the day (U.S. Department of Education, 2009). In elementary schools, resource programs sometimes are organized by the skills being taught. For instance, from 10:00 AM until 10:45 AM, basic math skills may be taught, and all the second- and third-grade students needing math assistance may come to the resource room at that time. Alternatively, some resource rooms are arranged by same-age groups. For example, all fifth graders with disabilities needing some separate service may go to the resource room together.

In middle schools and high schools, students are scheduled to have resource classes in the same way the rest of their classes are scheduled. For example, a student may attend a resource class that provides study strategies or reviews the curriculum being taught in general education classes. In some instances, core academic instruction is taught in the resource room by a special educator highly qualified in the academic area; this class might be called, for example, resource English or resource Algebra.

Separate Classes Some students with disabilities attend *separate classes* for more than 60 percent of the school day (U.S. Department of Education, 2009). In this placement, a special education teacher has the primary instructional responsibility for the students who receive grades from the highly qualified special educator for the subjects taught there. However, a separate class placement does not mean that students remain in a single classroom or that they do not interact with typical peers. They may receive instruction in different classrooms from several special educators, particularly in high school. They may attend a general education class for part of the day or a certain class period, and they also may participate with peers in related arts, assemblies, and other school activities.

Although Kurt is in a separate class most of the day at his high school, he takes a horticulture class with students without disabilities. A paraprofessional accompanies him because he has limited ability to understand directions and needs close guidance from an adult to participate appropriately. At Kyle's elementary school, 30 minutes each day is called *community time,* during which students read and write together, share important events from their lives, and learn about their neighborhood and community. For community time, Kyle goes to Mr. Ballinger's fifth-grade class. The students are about Kyle's age and assist him with the community activities and learning. Kyle's special education teacher helps Mr. Ballinger plan appropriate activities for him during that time.

Separate Schools A small number of students with disabilities attend public or private *separate schools* (U.S. Department of Education, 2009). Some separate schools exist for students with moderate or severe intellectual and physical disabilities, although such schools are, for the most part, becoming obsolete. Other separate schools serve students with multiple disabilities who need high levels of specialized services. For example, in a small community near Chicago, approximately 25 students are educated at a separate school. These students all need the services of a physical and occupational therapist; most have complex medical problems that must be closely monitored; and most cannot move unless someone assists them. These students have opportunities for contact with typical peers who are brought to the school through a special program to function as "learning buddies." Some students with serious emotional disabilities also attend separate schools. These students might harm themselves or others. They are not able to cope with the complexity and social stress of a typical school, and so the least restrictive environment for them is a school where their highly specialized needs, including therapeutic supports, can be addressed.

Residential Facilities A few students have needs that cannot be met at a school that is in session only during the day. If students in separate settings have even greater needs, they might attend school as well as live in a public or private *residential facility.* Few students with disabilities are educated in this manner (U.S. Department of Education, 2009). The students for whom this placement is the LRE often are those with severe emotional problems or severe and multiple intellectual,

www.resources

http://www.ed.gov/about/reports/
annual/osep/index.html
Many statistics about students with disabilities and how they receive education services come from the federally compiled annual reports to Congress on the implementation of IDEA. You can find copies of the reports from the past several years at this website.

sensory, and physical disabilities. In some states, students who are blind or deaf also might receive their instruction in a residential facility, an approach that is supported by some professionals and parents and opposed by others.

A somewhat different group of students also can be considered under the residential placement option. According to IDEA, children and young adults with disabilities who are incarcerated in the juvenile justice system must receive special education services. Further, children and young adults who are convicted of crimes and incarcerated as adults also may be entitled to special education services, unless the IEP team determines there is a compelling reason to discontinue services.

Home and Hospital Settings   A very small number of students with disabilities receive their education in a home or hospital setting (U.S. Department of Education, 2009). This placement often is used for students who are medically fragile, who are undergoing surgery or another medical treatment, or who have experienced an emotional crisis. For a few students with limited stamina, school comes to their homes because they do not have the strength to come to school. That is, a special education teacher comes to the home for a specified amount of time each week to deliver instruction. Home instruction also might be used for a student with serious behavior problems or for a student for whom there is disagreement about the appropriate school placement, pending resolution of the dispute.

One more point should be made about placement. For some students, the team may decide that their learning will suffer significantly if schooling stops during the summer. For these students, any of the services in any of the placements just described can be extended into school breaks and summer vacations through extended school year (ESY) programs.

Placements in separate classes and schools are far less preferred than those that support the education of students with disabilities in general education classrooms and schools. When placement includes a specialized setting, it often is appropriate for a specific skill or service and for a specific and limited period of time. The appropriate and required educational setting for most students with disabilities is the same classroom they would attend if they did not have a disability. This means that you, as a general education teacher, will play a central major role in the education of students with disabilities. Thus, it is important for you to understand the kinds of special services your students receive and your role in assisting to deliver them.

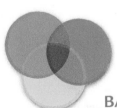

WRAPPING IT UP
BACK TO THE CASES

This section provides opportunities for you to apply the knowledge gained in this chapter to the cases described at the beginning of this chapter. The questions and activities that follow connect to the everyday activities of all teachers.

MS. KUCHTA will report information about the Tier 1 interventions she has used with Christopher at the meeting with the SIT. While some school districts have selected research-based Tier I interventions, other school districts may not have adopted specific strategies.

To help you understand RtI and the tiers of intervention, conduct a Google search using the key words "Response to intervention for reading disabilities" (or search for mathematics, writing, or another core academic area). Review at least three of the websites listed, noting the primary features of interventions described, and decide which you would consider for your own teaching. Share this information with two peers from your class and, as a group, determine which intervention you would recommend to the entire class.

MS. LEE is looking forward to working with the special educator and the speech/language therapist, but she is unsure of what to expect. Will this mean lots of meetings? Should she be keeping records of Jennifer's academic and language difficulties? Using information from the chapter, the Council for Exceptional Children (http://www.cec.sped.org/Content/NavigationMenu/SpecialEdCareers/Job_Profiles_Speci.htm), and the American Speech-Language-Hearing Association website (http://www.asha.org), outline how a special educator and speech/language therapist work with teachers and IEP teams. Then, explain what Ms. Lee should expect to happen in her classroom.

MS. TURNER, as you may remember, works with her school's inclusive practices leadership team. As time passes, she becomes concerned that students' right to an inclusive education may create unrealistic expectations for a general educator's ability to work with those who have exceptional learning needs. She has other concerns about the amount of paperwork and time required to meet the IDEA requirement that general education teachers participate in IEP meetings. How would you assure Ms. Turner that she is a necessary participant in the process and address her concerns? In your answer, specifically address both Ms. Turner's responsibilities and personal concerns. What resources might you access to supplement the information you found in this chapter?

SUMMARY

- The individuals who work to ensure that students with disabilities receive an appropriate education include general education teachers; special education teachers; related service providers such as school psychologists, counselors, speech/language therapists, social workers, administrators, paraprofessionals, and other specialists as well as parents and students.

- To determine whether special services are needed, general education teachers usually begin a process of deciding whether to request that a student be assessed for the presence of a disability by analyzing the nature and extent of the student's unmet needs; clarifying those needs by describing them through examples; determining that the needs are chronic and possibly worsening over time; comparing the student's needs to those of others in the class; possibly recognizing that no pattern seems to exist for the student's performance; and intervening to address the unmet needs and documenting those efforts.

- If concerns persist, the student's needs may be assessed by an intervention assistance team (IAT) or response to intervention (RtI) procedures.

- If increasingly intensive interventions do not resolve the concerns, a multidisciplinary team (MDT) follows federally established special education referral and assessment steps, including completing an individualized assessment with parental permission, making decisions about the need for special education, developing an individualized education program (IEP), and monitoring special education services.

- If parents and school district personnel disagree on any aspect of a student's special education program or services and if the disagreement cannot be resolved informally, due process procedures, including mediation and dispute resolution sessions, are used to ensure that the student receives an appropriate education.

- When an IEP is developed, it includes the student's present level of functioning, goals (and sometimes objectives), justification for any placement outside general education, needed services, the person(s) responsible for the services, beginning and ending dates for service delivery, and criteria for evaluation. The IEP also may include a behavior intervention plan and a transition plan and generally must be reviewed at least annually (in a few states, every three years).

- The services a student may receive, as outlined by the IEP, include special education, related services, supplementary aids and services, and a designation of placement: a general education classroom, resource program, or separate special education setting.

- General education teachers play an integral role in the education of students with disabilities, from the early identification of students who appear to have special needs, through assessment and identification, to IEP implementation.

APPLICATIONS IN TEACHING PRACTICE

A VISIT TO AN MDT MEETING

Ms. Richards teaches science to sixth graders. Beginning in the fall, she and her team members will be working with Natasha, a student newly identified as having a learning disability. Natasha enjoys many friends and extracurricular activities, but she has extraordinary difficulties with reading fluency, comprehension, and written expression. She also has significant problems organizing her work and remembering to complete and turn in assignments. To help set appropriate goals for the coming year, Ms. Richards is participating in an MDT meeting to create an IEP for Natasha. Although it would be ideal for all the sixth-grade team members to attend the meeting, that is not feasible, and so Ms. Richards is representing her colleagues as well.

General education (sixth-grade) science teacher: Ms. Richards
General education (fifth-grade) teacher: Mr. Tucker
Special education middle school teacher: Ms. Hill

(Continued)

APPLICATIONS IN TEACHING PRACTICE

A VISIT TO AN MDT MEETING (Continued)

Principal: Ms. Hubbert
Psychologist: Ms. Freund
Speech/language therapist: Mr. Colt
Parent: Ms. Wright

Ms. Hubbert: Our next task is to develop goals for Natasha. I'd like to suggest that we discuss academics first, then social areas, and wrap up with related services needed. Let's look at Natasha's strengths first—in all those areas.

Mr. Colt: Natasha has a very strong speaking vocabulary. She is considerably above average in that realm.

Ms. Freund: Along with that, according to the assessment data, Natasha's general knowledge is very good. She also is near grade level in basic math skills.

Mr. Tucker: It's not really academics, but one strength I see that Natasha has is her willingness to help classmates. She really wants to assist everyone in class to learn even when she herself is struggling. She also was very active in extracurricular activities this year. She participated in the service learning program, volunteered to read to the kindergarten class, and competed in the after-school sports program.

Ms. Hill: As we write academic goals, then, we need to remember that Natasha has strong vocabulary skills and general knowledge and that she does not need services in math. Perhaps we can use her social skills and other interests to help in the academic arena. Ms. Wright, what strengths do you see in Natasha?

Ms. Wright: Hmmm. She minds me, that's for sure. And she helps out around the house with chores. She likes to help me watch her baby brother.

Ms. Hill: Helping really seems to be Natasha's thing—let's keep that in mind.

Ms. Hubbert: Let's focus for a minute on academic areas of need.

Ms. Freund: Reading comprehension and written expression are by far the areas that need the most work. Natasha's comprehension is just at a beginning third-grade level, and her written expression is about a year below that.

Ms. Wright: She says she doesn't like reading because the other kids make fun of her when she can't read the words, and they tease her when Mr. Tucker gives her a "baby book."

Ms. Richards: In middle school, that could be even more of a problem. We need to be sure that she uses the same textbooks as the other students next year. I'm sure we can also arrange to get some supplemental materials for her to use at home. Before we finish today, let's be sure that we talk about that some more.

Ms. Freund: Ms. Richards and Ms. Hill, given what you know and have heard about Natasha, what might be priorities for next year?

Ms. Hill: I agree that comprehension is the key. Given the data and the other information we're discussing, I think a goal should be for her to improve her comprehension to a fourth-grade level on reading tasks that include stories, textbooks, and other materials such as children's magazines.

Ms. Hubbert: Ms. Wright, how does that sound to you? [*Ms. Wright nods.*]

The conversation continues.

Before the meeting ends, the MDT has generated the following additional goals in reading comprehension using materials at her instructional level:

- Natasha will identify with 90 percent accuracy the main characters and the problem and solution in literature that she reads at a third-grade level.
- Natasha will comprehend 80 percent of both narrative and expository material she reads aloud (third- to fourth-grade level) and 80 percent on material she reads to herself.

QUESTIONS

1. What are the responsibilities of the professionals represented at the MDT meeting? Which of the professionals are required to attend? How would your responses be different if this were an annual review?

2. What role does Ms. Richards take at the meeting? Why is her presence helpful in creating an educational program for Natasha? How else might she contribute during this meeting? Now apply what you said about Ms. Richards to your own teaching role. What contributions should you make when plans are being made for the educational services for a student with a disability?

3. What is the purpose of having both the fifth-grade teacher and a sixth-grade teacher attend the meeting? How might this improve the quality of the IEP? What problems might it cause?

4. What steps likely were completed prior to this meeting? How did the general education teacher prepare? What other team responsibilities were met?

5. What part of the IEP is the team addressing? What other parts have to be completed before the meeting ends? What must occur for the IEP to be valid?

6. How might this meeting be different if Natasha was a kindergartener going to first grade? A tenth-grader going to eleventh grade?

PEARSON
myeducationlab)

Go to Topic 6: Response to Intervention and Topic 7: IEP Process, in the My EducationLab (http://www.myeducationlab.com) for your course, where you can:

- Find learning outcomes for Reponse to Intervention and IEP Process along with the national standards that connect to these outcomes.
- Complete Assignments and Activities that can help you more deeply understand the chapter content.
- Apply and practice your understanding of the core teaching skills identified in the chapter with the Building Teaching Skills and Dispositions learning units.
- Examine challenging situations and cases presented in the IRIS Center Resources. (optional)
- Access video clips of CCSSO National Teachers of the Year award winners responding to the question, "Why Do I Teach?" in the Teacher Talk section. (optional)
- Check your comprehension on the content covered in the chapter by going to the Study Plan in the Book Resources for your text. Here you will be able to take a chapter quiz, receive feedback on your answers, and then access Review, Practice, and Enrichment activities to enhance your understanding of chapter content. (optional)

The Foundation for Educating Students with Special Needs

The Foundation for Educating Students with Special Needs

LEARNING Objectives

After you read this chapter, you will be able to

1. Explain key terms and concepts that describe special education.
2. Trace the historical events that have shaped contemporary special education services.
3. Outline the laws that govern current practices for educating students with disabilities.
4. Analyze your beliefs related to inclusive practices, taking into account contemporary knowledge and expectations about effective instruction and educational access, as well as parent perspectives.
5. Describe the categories of disabilities addressed in federal law.
6. Explain special needs other than disability that your students may have.

Pierre Tremblay/Masterfile Stock Image Library

THOMAS is one of those students who makes his presence known very quickly. He announced on the first day in his seventh-grade social studies class that the color of the walls was *xantho* (yellow). For several days later that fall, he came to school wearing only socks on his feet, because, as his mother explained, he had completely outgrown his old shoes but would not wear new, better-fitting ones because he said they "had knots in the toes." In all his classes, Thomas tends to keep to himself, and when group projects are assigned, he has difficulty knowing how to talk to his classmates about anything except the subjects he enjoys—French words commonly used in the English language and Alfred Hitchcock movies. When Thomas began elementary school, he was enrolled in a special education class for students with autism. However, most of his classmates had significant intellectual disabilities, and the teacher and Thomas's parents quickly realized that he needed to be challenged academically in a way that could not happen in that class. Since second grade, he has spent most of his time in general education classrooms. In some situations, a special education teacher worked in his classroom with the general education teacher, or a paraprofessional was present to assist the teacher and all the students. Now such support generally is not necessary. Thomas meets with his special education teacher, Ms. Meyer, once each day with several other students who have learning and behavior disabilities to learn strategies related to their schoolwork, and he receives social skills instruction from a counselor. If an issue arises in a general education class, Ms. Meyer problem solves with the teacher to address it. Thomas would like to be a linguist when he grows up.

What is autism? Why is it so important for Thomas to access the same curriculum as his peers? What provisions in current laws ensure that Thomas has the right to be educated in general education as much as possible?

PATRICIA is a fourth-grade student who was identified as having an intellectual disability (sometimes called mental retardation) when she was in the first grade. The cause of her disability cannot be pinpointed nor does it have a specific name, but there is a high likelihood that it was at least partly the result of her mother's drinking and drug use during pregnancy. Patricia already has lived in six foster homes because her mother was unable to take care of her and gave up custody. Happily, her current foster family has decided to adopt Patricia, a time-consuming process that should be completed before the end of this school year. In school, Patricia receives highly specialized instruction in language arts and math in a special education resource class, but she is a member of a general education class for science and social studies as well as for art, music, library/media, physical education, and technology skills classes. Spending time in both special education and general education settings was determined by a team to be the best option for Patricia, but Ms. Schwarz, her general education teacher, worries that the other students do not have enough interactions with Patricia to really get to know and value her and that Patricia's learning is actually made more difficult because she comes and goes from the classroom. Ms. Schwarz favors reducing the amount of time Patricia spends in the special education classroom. Ms. Ramos, the special educator, agrees; this topic will be addressed at a meeting to be held soon.

How likely are you to teach a student like Patricia? What is an intellectual disability? What factors have led teachers to advocate for educating students like Patricia in typical classrooms for all or much of the school day instead of in special education classrooms?

AARON has a learning disability that was identified when he was in second grade. He also takes medication for attention deficit–hyperactivity disorder (ADHD). Now in eleventh grade, Aaron is continuing to learn how to compensate for the academic difficulties he experiences. Although he is a bright and personable young man, he reads at about a seventh-grade level, and his writing is much like that of a student in second grade. He doesn't like to talk about his learning disabilities (LD); he doesn't want other students to make fun of him or treat him differently because he has LD. He is even more sensitive when asked to talk about why he takes medication. Even though his doctor has cautioned him to take the medication exactly as prescribed, he sometimes secretly skips taking it to see if he can get along without it. In his U.S. history class, Aaron is most successful on tests when he answers questions orally; he understands the concepts even if he sometimes cannot write down his thoughts. Because he doesn't like to be singled out, however, he sometimes refuses to take tests or get additional assistance during study period, so his grades are lower than they could be. Aaron is an excellent athlete, and on the basketball court, he feels equal to his friends. However, his parents are concerned that his interest in sports is distracting him from schoolwork.

How often will you meet students like Aaron? What is a learning disability? What types of supports and services do Aaron and other students with LD need to succeed in school?

Students like Thomas, Patricia, and Aaron are not unusual. They are among the 6.1 million school-age students in the United States who have disabilities that make them eligible for special education (U.S. Department of Education, 2009). But their disabilities do not tell you who they are: They are children or young adults and students first. Like all students, they have positive characteristics and negative ones, they have great days and not-so-great days, and they have likes and dislikes about school and learning. As a teacher, you probably will instruct students like Thomas, Patricia, and Aaron along with other students with disabilities or other special needs.

The purpose of this book is to help you understand these students and learn strategies for addressing their needs. Ultimately, you can be the teacher who makes a profound positive difference in a student's life. With the knowledge and skills you learn for teaching learners with exceptional needs, you will be prepared for both the challenges and the rewards of helping them achieve their potential.

What Key Concepts Guide Special Education?

As you begin your study of special education and think about your responsibility for teaching students like Thomas, Patricia, and Aaron, it is important that you understand that the field is guided by a number of critical concepts, some based directly on federal laws and the courts' interpretation of those laws and some based on a combination of research and recommended practices. What these key concepts illustrate clearly is the centrality of your role in the education of students with disabilities.

Special Education Services

When teachers refer to students with *disabilities*, they mean students who are eligible to receive special education services according to federal and state guidelines. **Special education** is the **specially designed instruction** provided by the school district or other local education agency that meets the unique needs of students identified as disabled according to federal and state eligibility criteria. Special education is a set of services that may include instruction in a general education or special education classroom, education in the community for students who need to learn life and work skills, and specialized assistance in areas such as physical education and vocational preparation.

Students with disabilities also may receive **related services,** that is, assistance required to enable students to benefit from special education. Examples of related services include speech/language therapy, transportation to and from school in a specialized van or school bus, and physical therapy. Additionally, students with disabilities are entitled to **supplementary aids and services.** This means they must receive, as needed, supports such as preferential seating, access to computer technology, and instructional adjustments (for example, more time to complete tests, simplified assignments) that enable them to be educated with their peers who do not have disabilities. All special education, related services, and supplementary aids and services are provided to students by public schools at no cost to parents.

You may encounter one additional set of terms relates to students' services. Students with disabilities are entitled to receive accommodations and modifications related to their instruction. **Accommodations** are changes in *how* the student learns key curriculum. For example, a student may be assigned fewer math problems because he takes longer than other students to complete each one. Another student may respond to an essay question on a history test by writing bullet points instead of paragraphs, because it reduces the writing task and the goal is to determine what she has learned about history. In each case, the curriculum has remained the same. **Modifications** refer to *what* the student learns and usually implies that some curriculum is removed. For example, a student with a significant intellectual disability may not learn all the vocabulary in a science unit, focusing instead on words that he is likely to encounter in day-to-day life. As you might surmise, many students with disabilities need accommodations, but only those with significant intellectual disabilities usually require modifications.

Least Restrictive Environment

As you read this textbook and complete the activities designed for your course, you will learn many important facts and skills related to working with students with disabilities. However, one of the most important concepts for you to understand as a general educator is **least restrictive environment (LRE),** a provision in the federal law that has governed special education for nearly four decades. The LRE provision guarantees a student's right to be educated in the setting most like that for peers without disabilities in which the student can be successful with appropriate supports provided (Palley, 2006). For most students, the least restrictive environment is full-time or nearly full-time participation in a general education classroom (Schwarz, 2007). In fact, in 2004–2005, approximately 51.9 percent of all school-age students with disabilities received 79 percent or more of their education in general education classrooms (U.S. Department of Education, 2009). This is true for Thomas, Patricia, and Aaron, who were introduced at the beginning of this chapter. Thomas and Patricia also receive instruction in a special education classroom each day. Aaron, who can succeed in social studies class when he gives test answers aloud, may leave his classroom for that purpose only. His LRE is a general education classroom; the test procedure is a supplementary service.

For some students—for example, some who have emotional or behavioral disabilities or autism—being in a general education classroom nearly all day may be academically and emotionally inappropriate. For these students, the LRE may be a general education classroom for part of the day and a special education classroom, sometimes called a *resource room*, for the remainder of the day. Yet other students' LRE may be a special education setting for most of the day, sometimes referred to as a *self-contained class*. Students with significant behavior problems and students who require intensive supports may be educated in this way. Finally, just a few students with disabilities attend separate or residential schools or learn in a home or hospital setting. These very restrictive options usually are necessary only for students with the most significant or complex disabilities.

Identifying an LRE other than a general education setting is a serious decision that usually is made by a team of professionals and a student's parents only after

In inclusive schools, all students are welcomed members of their learning communities.
Elizabeth Crews/The Image Works

intensive supports have been provided in the general education classroom without success. These supports can include alternative materials or curriculum, assistance from a paraprofessional (that is, a teaching assistant) or a special education teacher, adaptive equipment such as a computer, or consultative assistance from a psychologist or counselor. However, a few students' needs are so great that a setting outside general education is the only one considered. The points to remember are these: The LRE for most students with disabilities is general education, and you, as a professional educator, have a crucial role to play in these students' education.

Inclusive Practices

www.resources

http://www.disability.gov
Managed by the U.S. Department of Labor, this website is a comprehensive set of resources related to disabilities across the lifespan and includes links to resources available in each state.

Over the past two decades, the entire structure of special education services has undergone significant change (Fuchs, Fuchs, & Stecker, 2010). Although federal law continues to stipulate that a range of settings must be made available to meet the needs of students with disabilities, many professionals now seriously question the assumption that students who need more intensive services should routinely receive them in a restrictive setting such as a special education classroom. The concept of inclusive practices, while not directly addressed in federal special education law, implies that students are more alike than different and that all students are welcomed members of their learning communities (for example, Connor & Ferri, 2007; Downing & Eichinger, 2003; Fitch, 2003; Valle & Conner, 2011). In the past, many students with disabilities were only temporary guests in general education classrooms, and few efforts were made to provide assistance so they could be successfully educated with their nondisabled peers (for example, Artiles, Harris-Murri, & Rostenberg, 2006).

Many educators now find that all or most supports for students with disabilities can be provided effectively in general education classrooms when teachers are prepared to work with such students and related concerns are addressed (Dukes & Lamar-Dukes, 2009; McLeskey & Waldron, 2007a). They further maintain that if students cannot meet traditional academic expectations, the expectations should be changed, not the setting. These educators reject the assumption that the setting dictates the type and intensity of services, and they support instead inclusive practices (Roach & Salisbury, 2006).

The concept of **inclusive practices** is founded on the belief or philosophy that students with disabilities should be fully integrated into their school learning communities, usually in general education classrooms, and that their instruction should be based on their abilities, not their disabilities. Inclusive practices have three dimensions:

1. *Physical integration:* Placing students in the same classroom as nondisabled peers should be a strong priority, and removing them from that setting should be done only when absolutely necessary.
2. *Social integration:* Relationships should be nurtured between students with disabilities and their classmates and peers as well as adults.
3. *Instructional integration:* Most students should be taught in the same curriculum used for students without disabilities and helped to succeed by adjusting how teaching and learning are designed (that is, with accommodations) and measured. For some students with significant intellectual disabilities, instructional integration means anchoring instruction in the standard general curriculum but appropriately adjusting expectations (that is, making modifications).

Ultimately, the concept of inclusive practices as used in this book means that all learners are welcomed full members at their schools and in their classrooms and that they are seen as the responsibility of all educators (Frattura & Capper, 2006; Skilton-Sylvester & Slesaransky-Poe, 2009). It further implies that educators' strong preference is for these students to be educated with their peers without disabilities.

We also would like to note that we prefer the phrase *inclusive practices* to the term *inclusion* because the latter can imply that there is a single model or program that can serve all students' needs, while the former more accurately conveys that inclusiveness is made up of many strategies and options. Later in this chapter, we address in more detail how inclusive practices increasingly form the basis for contemporary education practices.

One more term should be mentioned in this discussion of how students with disabilities receive services. When the LRE concept became part of special education laws during the 1970s, the LRE for most students with disabilities was a part-time or full-time special education class. When such students were permitted to participate in general education, it was called mainstreaming. **Mainstreaming** involves placing students with disabilities in general education settings only when they can meet traditional academic expectations with minimal assistance or when those expectations are not relevant (for example, participation only in recess or school assemblies for access to social interactions with peers). In most locales, *mainstreaming* now is considered a dated term and has been replaced with the phrase *inclusion* or *inclusive practices*. However, as you participate in field experiences and speak to experienced educators, you may find that in some schools, the vocabulary of inclusion is used, but the practices implemented seem more like mainstreaming. That is, teachers may say that their school is inclusive but then explain that students like Aaron, featured in the beginning of the chapter, need to be in separate classes because of their below-grade reading levels. This practice is actually mainstreaming.

Finally, you also may find that teachers in your locale use words such as *LRE, mainstreaming,* and *inclusion* interchangeably, or they might have yet different terms to describe special education services. They may refer to *integrated classes* or *collaborative classes* when describing the general education classes in which students with disabilities participate. To assist you with the vocabulary of special education programs and instructional approaches, a glossary is provided at the back of this textbook. Keep in mind, though, that knowing the terms used in special education is not nearly as important as learning about your students, developing skills for addressing their needs, and celebrating your role in enabling them to achieve success.

How Did Today's Special Education Services Come to Exist?

Special education as it exists today has been influenced by a number of different factors. Although people with disabilities have been identified and treated for centuries, special education grew rapidly only in the twentieth century (Kode, 2002; Winzer, 1993). As special education has evolved, it has been shaped by federal law, the civil rights movement and related court cases, and changing social and political beliefs. Figure 1.1 illustrates some factors that have influenced the evolution of special education.

The Development of Education for Students with Disabilities

When compulsory public education began near the turn of the twentieth century, almost no school programs existed for students with disabilities (Kode, 2002; Scheerenberger, 1983). Students with disabilities that were relatively mild—that is, learning or behavior problems or minor physical impairments—were educated along with other students because their needs were not considered extraordinary. Many children with significant intellectual or physical disabilities did not attend school at all, and others were educated by private agencies or lived in institutions. In fact, for the first half of the twentieth century, many states explicitly legislated permission for school districts to prohibit some students with disabilities from attending (Yell, Rogers, & Rogers, 1998).

However, as compulsory education became widespread during the 1920s and 1930s, the number of special classes in public schools grew. Schools were expected

fyi

The Council for Exceptional Children (CEC), founded in 1922 by Elizabeth Farrell, is a professional organization for teachers, administrators, parents, and other advocates for the rights of students with disabilities (http://www.cec.sped.org).

www.resources

http://idea.ed.gov/explore/view/p/%2Croot%2Cdynamic%2CVideoClips%2C
At Building the Legacy: IDEA 2004 you can learn more detail about the requirements of federal special education law through a series of brief video clips.

FIGURE 1.1 Influences on Current Special Education Practices

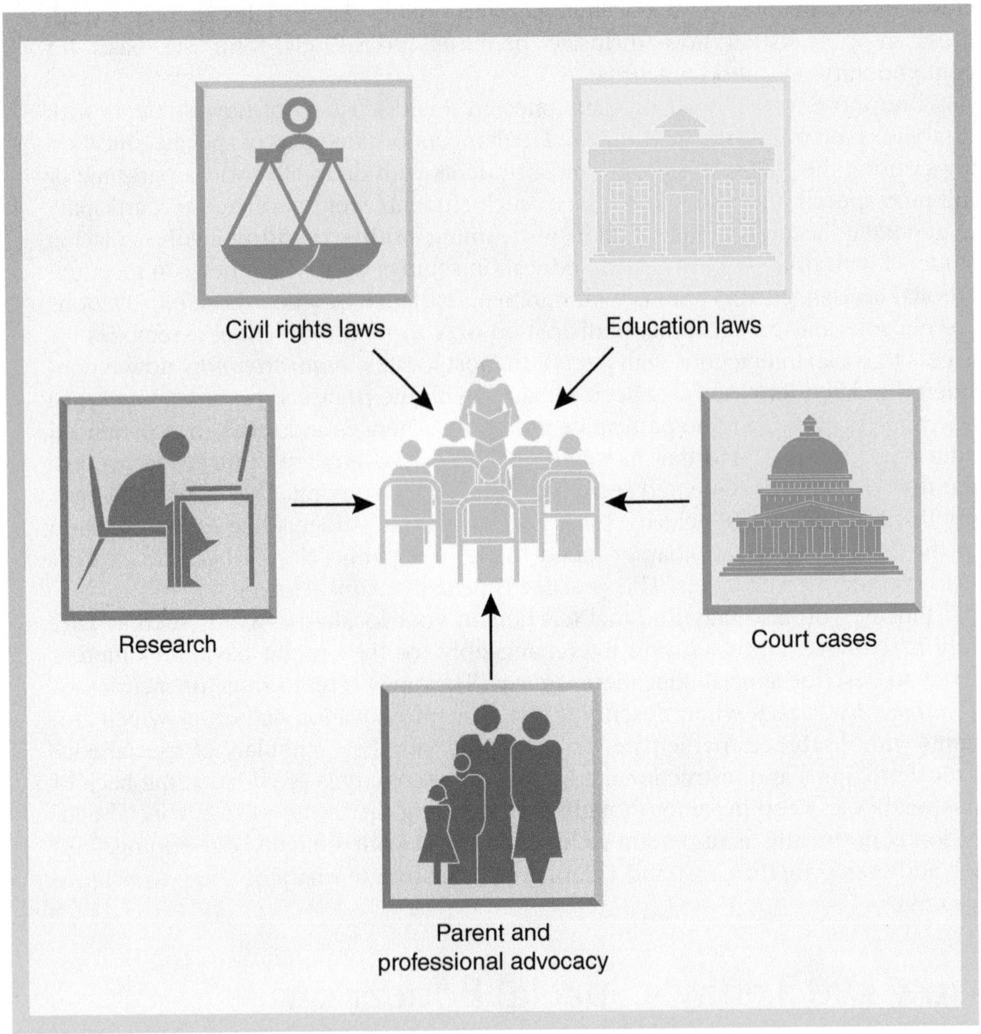

By the 1950s, special education programs were available in many school districts, but some undesirable outcomes were becoming apparent. For example, students in special classes often were considered incapable of learning academic skills. They spent their school time practicing what were called "manual skills" such as weaving and bead stringing. Researchers began questioning this practice and conducted studies to explore the efficacy of special education. When they compared students with disabilities who were in special education classes to similar students who had remained in general education, they found the latter group often had learned more than the former (Blatt, 1958; Goldstein, Moss, & Jordan, 1965). Parents at this time also became active advocates for better educational opportunities for their children (Blatt, 1987). By the late 1960s, many authorities in the field agreed

to be like efficient assembly lines, with each class of students moving from grade to grade and eventually graduating from high school as productive citizens prepared to enter the workforce (Patton, Payne, & Beirne-Smith, 1986; Scheerenberger, 1983). Special classes were developed as a place for students who could not keep up with their classmates. Because many students with disabilities still were not in school, most of the students sent to special classes probably had mild or moderate learning or intellectual disabilities. Educators at the time believed that such students would learn better in a protected setting and that the efficiency of the overall educational system would be preserved (Bennett, 1932; Pertsch, 1936).

dimensions of
DIVERSITY

As you prepare to be an educator, you will learn about the importance of developing *cultural competence.* Doing so involves valuing diversity, assessing your own views of diversity, being aware of the dynamics of intercultural interactions, developing cultural knowledge, and adjusting your teaching and other professional activities based on that knowledge (King, Sims, & Osher, 2007).

that segregated special classes were not the most appropriate educational setting for many students with disabilities (Blatt, 1958; Christopolos & Renz, 1969; Dunn, 1968; Hobbs, 1975; Lilly, 1971).

The Impact of the Civil Rights Movement on Special Education

During the 1950s and 1960s, another force began contributing to the development of new approaches for special education. The civil rights movement, although initially focused on the rights of African Americans, expanded and began to influence thinking about people with disabilities (Chaffin, 1975; Fleischer & Zames, 2001). In the **Brown v. Board of Education** decision in 1954, the U.S. Supreme Court ruled that it was unlawful under the Fourteenth Amendment to discriminate arbitrarily against any group of people. The Court then applied this concept to the education of children, ruling that the state-mandated separate education for African American students could not be an equal education. This court decision introduced the concept of *integration* into public education, the notion that the only way to protect students' constitutional right to equal opportunity was

The civil rights movements of the 1950s and 1960s strongly contributed to the recognition of the rights of individuals with disabilities. Don Cravens/Getty IMages/Time Life Pictures

to ensure that diverse student groups learned together. Soon people with disabilities were recognized as another group whose rights often had been violated because of arbitrary discrimination. For children, the discrimination occurred when they were denied access to schools because of their disabilities. Beginning in the late 1960s and continuing through today, parents and others have used the court system to ensure that the civil and educational rights of children with disabilities are preserved (Blanchett, Brantlinger, & Shealey, 2005; Rueda, Klingner, Sager, & Velasco, 2008). Figure 1.2 summarizes several influential court cases that have helped shape special education concepts and services.

Section 504   One of the outcomes of the civil rights movement was legislation designed to prevent discrimination against individuals with disabilities, whether children in schools or adults in the workforce. **Section 504** of the Vocational Rehabilitation Act of 1973 is a civil rights law that prevents discrimination against all individuals with disabilities in programs that receive federal funds, as do all public schools. For children of school age, Section 504 ensures equal opportunity for participation in the full range of school activities (Walker, 2006; Zirkel, 2009a). Through Section 504, some students not eligible for services through special education may be entitled to receive specific types of assistance to help them succeed in school.

For example, Sondra is a student with a severe attention problem. She cannot follow a lesson for more than a few minutes at a time; she is distracted by every noise in the hallway and every car that goes by her classroom window. Her teacher describes her as a student who "acts first and thinks later." Sondra does not have a disability as established in special education law, but she does need extra assistance and is considered disabled according to Section 504 because her significant attention problem negatively affects her ability to function in school. The professionals at her school are required to create and carry out a plan to help Sondra access education. Special education teachers may assist because they know techniques that will help Sondra, but Sondra does not receive special education services, and responsibility for the plan lies with the principal and teachers. Some of the other students who might receive assistance through Section 504 include those with health problems such as asthma and extreme allergies and those with physical disabilities who do not need special education (Zirkel, 2009b).

RESEARCH NOTE

In a qualitative study, Lindstrom, Doren, Metheny, Johnson, and Zane (2007) found that positive family relationships, involvement, advocacy, career aspirations, and career-related activities led to better employment for young adults with learning disabilities.

45

FIGURE 1.2 Court Cases Affecting Special Education

Since 1954, hundreds of legal decisions have clarified the rights of students with disabilities and the responsibilities of schools for educating them. The following cases have had a significant impact on special education.

Brown v. Board of Education (347 U.S. 483) (1954)

- U.S. Supreme Court case
- School segregation denies students equal educational opportunity
- Although referring primarily to racial segregation, this decision has since become the cornerstone for ensuring equal rights for students with disabilities

Pennsylvania Association for Retarded Children v. Commonwealth of Pennsylvania (343 F. Supp. 279) (1972)

- U.S. District Court of the Eastern District of Pennsylvania decision
- Schools may not refuse to educate students with mental retardation
- A free public education must be provided to *all* students

Larry P. v. Wilson Riles (793 F.2d 969) (1986)

- U.S. District Court for the Northern District of California decision
- Intelligence (IQ) tests cannot be used to determine whether African-American students have mental retardation because of the tests' racial and cultural bias
- In 1986, the ruling was expanded to include IQ testing of these students for any disability

Board of Education of Hendrick School District v. Rowley (632 F. 2d 945) (1982)

- U.S. Supreme Court decision
- Special education services must provide an appropriate education; the law does not require optimum services
- Parent request for an interpreter for their daughter with a hearing loss, who was achieving at an average level, was denied

Daniel R. R. v. State Board of Education (874 F.2d 1036) (1989)

- U.S. Court of Appeals for the Fifth Circuit decision
- Appropriate placement for students with disabilities depends on whether (1) a student can be satisfactorily educated in the general education setting with supplementary supports provided and (2) the student is mainstreamed to the maximum extent appropriate in cases in which the general education setting is not successful
- For Daniel, a student with Down syndrome, the school district did not violate his rights when he was moved from general education after an unsuccessful attempt to include him

Oberti v. Board of Education of Clementon School District (995 F.2d 204) (1993)

- U.S. Court of Appeals for the Third Circuit decision
- School districts must make available a full range of supports and services in the general education setting to accommodate students with disabilities, including the student with Down syndrome involved in the suit
- Just because a student learns differently from other students does not necessarily warrant that student's exclusion from general education

Doe v. Withers (20 IDELR 422, 426–427) (1993)

- West Virginia Circuit Court decision
- Michael Withers, a high school history teacher, refused to make oral testing accommodations needed by Douglas Doe, a student with learning disabilities, resulting in a failing grade and athletic ineligibility
- The family was awarded $5,000 in compensatory damages and $30,000 in punitive damages, illustrating general education teachers' very real responsibility to make a good faith effort to provide required accommodations for students with disabilities

Schaffer v. Weast (126 S. Ct. 528) (2005)

- U.S. Supreme Court decision
- The burden of proof in any disagreement about a student's individualized education plan lies with the party bringing suit—in this case, the Schaffer family
- Until this case, it typically had been assumed that a school district had to prove that its position in a suit was correct, even if the district had not filed the suit

Winkelman v. Parma City School District (2007 U.S. LEXIS 5902; 75 U.S.L.W. 4329) (2007)

- U.S. Supreme Court decision
- Parents of children with disabilities (in this case, the Winkelmans) have rights through IDEA and thus are entitled to represent themselves (and hence their children) in court
- Parents are not obligated to hire an attorney to represent them in court

Sources: Adapted from "Reflections on the 25th Anniversary of the Individuals with Disabilities Education Act," by A. Katisyannis, M. L. Yell, and R. Bradley, 2001, *Remedial and Special Education, 22,* pp. 324–334; "Medical Services: The Disrupted Related Service," by L. Bartlett, 2000, *Journal of Special Education, 33,* pp. 215–223; *Legal Issues in Special Educations,* by A. G. Osborne, 1996, Boston: Allyn & Bacon; "Adequate Access or Equal Treatment: Looking beyond the IDEA to Section 504 in a Post-Schaffer Public School," by C. J. Walker, 2006, *Stanford Law Review, 58,* pp. 1563–1622; and *Winkelman v. Parma City School District,* 2007, U.S. LEXIS 5902, 75 U.S.L.W. 4329.

Americans with Disabilities Act In July 1990, President George H. W. Bush signed into law the **Americans with Disabilities Act (ADA).** This civil rights law was based on the Rehabilitation Act of 1973, but it further extended the rights of individuals with disabilities. This law, amended and updated through the **Americans with Disabilities Act Amendments** (ADAA) in 2008, is the most significant disability legislation ever passed (National Council on Disability, 2006; Zirkel, 2009b). It protects all individuals with disabilities from discrimination, and it requires most employers to make reasonable accommodations for them. Although ADA does not deal directly with the education of students with disabilities, it does clarify the civil rights of all individuals with disabilities and thus has an impact on special education. This law also ensures that transportation, buildings, the workplace, and many places open to the public are accessible to people with disabilities. If you are a teacher with a disability, you might be influenced by ADA in the same way that it affects you in other situations. For example, if your school is not accessible to wheelchairs and undergoes renovation, then ramps, elevators, and wide entries with automatic doors probably will have to be installed. If you have a disability, this law also protects you from discrimination when you look for a teaching position.

The Legislative Basis for Contemporary Special Education

Influenced by researchers' growing doubts about the effectiveness of special education classes and by civil rights court cases, many states by the early 1970s had begun to address special education issues by passing laws to guarantee that students with disabilities would receive an appropriate education. Federal law soon mirrored this trend and continues to do so today (Valle & Conner, 2011). You can review the original core principles of and key subsequent additions to federal special education law in Figure 1.3.

The First Federal Special Education Legislation In 1975, Congress passed **Public Law (P.L.) 94-142,** the Education for All Handicapped Children Act (EHCA), thereby setting federal guidelines for special education and laying the foundation on which current special education practice rests. It took into account many of the early court decisions that established the civil rights of students with disabilities, and it mandated the concept of least restrictive environment (LRE). This law also specifically described categories of disabilities that make students eligible to receive special education and clarified the related services to which students might be entitled. In addition, it established procedures for identifying a student as needing special education and outlined the rights of parents who disapprove of the educational services offered to their children.

Revisions and Refinements to Special Education Legislation Since 1975, P.L. 94-142 has been reauthorized several times. As each reconsideration of the law has occurred, its core principles have been upheld. At the same time, the law has been extended and its provisions clarified. For example, in 1990 the name of the law was changed to the Individuals with Disabilities Education Act (IDEA) to reflect more contemporary person-first language. In addition, the term *handicapped* was removed from the law and the preferred term *disability* was substituted. This law also added significantly to the provisions for children from birth to age 5 with disabilities who had first been included in the law in 1986. It also bolstered provisions for supporting students with disabilities preparing to transition from school to work, postsecondary education, and other postschool options. One other important 1990 change in this law was the addition of two new categories of disability: autism and traumatic brain injury (TBI).

   IDEA was revised again in 1997. Perhaps most important for general education teachers, this law recognized that most students with disabilities spend all or

dimensions of
DIVERSITY

Guiberson (2009) found that Hispanic students are underrepresented in certain disability categories (e.g., intellectual and emotional/behavioral disabilities) and overrepresented in others (learning disability and speech-language impairment).

FIGURE 1.3 Provisions of the Individuals with Disabilities Education Improvement Act (IDEA)

Core Principles

- *Free appropriate public education (FAPE).* Students with disabilities are entitled to attend public schools and receive the educational services they need. This education is provided at no cost to parents.
- *Least restrictive environment (LRE).* Students with disabilities must be educated in the least restrictive environment in which they can succeed with appropriate supports provided. For most students, this environment is the general education classroom.
- *Individualized education.* The instructional services and other assistance for a student with disabilities must be tailored to meet his needs according to a prepared individualized education program (IEP) that is reviewed and updated annually.
- *Nondiscriminatory evaluation.* Students must be assessed using instruments that do not discriminate on the basis of race, culture, or disability. In considering eligibility for special education services, a student must be assessed by a multidisciplinary team in her native language using tests that are relevant to the area of concern. Eligibility cannot be decided on the basis of only one test.
- *Due process.* If a disagreement occurs concerning a student's eligibility for special education placement or services, whether raised by parents or the school district, no changes can be made until the issue has been resolved by an impartial hearing and, if necessary, the appropriate court, a procedure referred to as *due process*.
- *Zero reject–child find.* No student may be excluded from public education because of a disability. Further, each state must take action to locate children who may be entitled to special education services.

Additional Major Provisions

- *Transition services.* Transition services that prepare students for leaving school (for higher education, vocational training, or a job) must be addressed in IEPs for students beginning at age 16. Transition plans must include strategies to improve academic and functional achievement to foster student success and must be based on student strengths. These plans must be updated annually and be written to include measurable goals for the postsecondary years.
- *General education teacher roles and responsibilities.* At least one general education teacher must participate as a member of the team that writes a student's IEP, unless school professionals and parents agree for some reason that this would not be beneficial to the student. In addition, the IEP must directly address student participation in general education and justify any placement that is not in general education.
- *Highly qualified special education teachers.* Special education teachers who teach core academic subjects must obtain two types of credentials. First, they must have a special education teaching credential. In addition, in secondary schools, unless special education teachers work only with students with significant intellectual disabilities, they must be documented as being highly qualified in every core subject area in which they

teach. However, in most states, if they work in general education classrooms, ensuring that students with disabilities receive their needed supports there, they are not obligated to have the highly qualified status in those core academic areas. Elementary special educators usually are considered highly qualified to teach core subject areas at that level.

- *Parent participation.* Parents must be part of the decision-making team for determining eligibility for special education services as well as for determining the appropriate educational placement for their children. Furthermore, schools must report to parents on the progress of their children with disabilities at least as often as they report progress for students without disabilities.
- *Evaluation and eligibility.* School districts generally have 60 days from the time a parent agrees that the child can be evaluated until a decision must be reached about the child's eligibility for special education. Students are not eligible for special education simply because of poor math or reading instruction or because of language differences. For some students, the requirement that a complete reassessment be completed every three years can be modified. That is, for older students already existing information can be used in lieu of repeatedly administering standardized tests.
- *Disproportionate representation.* School districts must take specific steps to ensure that students from minority groups are not overidentified as being eligible for special education services. If disproportionate representation exists, districts must take steps to correct this problem.
- *Assessment of students.* States are required to measure the academic progress of students who have disabilities, either by including them in the standardized assessments other students take or, for students with significant intellectual disabilities, by using an alternate assessment process. Students are entitled to appropriate accommodations during assessment (for example, extended time, large-print materials).
- *Discipline.* As needed, strategies for addressing a student's behavior must be included as part of the IEP. If a student is suspended or placed in an alternative interim placement, a behavior plan must be developed. In some cases (for example, when students bring weapons or drugs to school), schools may place students with disabilities in alternative interim placements for up to 45 days, pending a meeting to determine the next steps. Students must continue to receive special education services during this time.
- *Paraprofessionals.* Paraprofessionals, teaching assistants, and other similar personnel must be trained for their jobs and appropriately supervised.
- *Procedural safeguards.* States must make mediation available to parents as an early and informal strategy for resolving disagreements about the identification of, placement of, or provision of services for students with disabilities. Parents are not obligated to mediate, and mediation may not delay a possible hearing. Unless waived with parent approval, the school district also must convene a dispute resolution session prior to a formal hearing regarding disagreements related to special education.

most of their school time in general education settings, and so it included a provision that the general education teacher usually should be a member of the team that writes the student's educational plan. Another important change occurred regarding assessment. Acknowledging that students with disabilities often were excluded from local and state assessments, the law added a requirement that students with disabilities be assessed like other students, using either the same assessment instrument employed with typical learners or some type of alternative instrument.

Current Special Education Legislation The most recent reauthorization of IDEA, signed into law in 2004 and sometimes called the **Individuals with Disabilities Education Improvement Act,** mandated yet further refinements in special education. For example, this legislation streamlined some procedures and paperwork, and it also specified that all students with disabilities must participate in all assessment conducted by local school districts with needed supports provided (Hyatt, 2007). The law also established that special education teachers must be **highly qualified** if they teach core academic content to students with disabilities. Yet another provision is this: IDEA now permits school districts to use some of the funds allotted to special education to design strategies for prevention. That is, by providing intensive teaching, behavior interventions, and other supports, it may be possible to prevent some students from needing special education at all.

The element of the current reauthorization of IDEA that may have the most direct impact on general education teachers is called response to intervention (RtI). RtI is a new and alternative way for students to be identified as having a learning disability. Rather than relying just on test scores, RtI permits states to decide to base that decision on whether or not increasingly intensive interventions implemented to address the student's academic problems have a positive impact on learning (Zirkel & Thomas, 2010). If they do, no disability exists. If little or no improvement occurs after research-based strategies and programs are carefully used more frequently and for longer periods of time, the student may be found to have a learning disability. Since its initial development, RtI also has been applied to student behavior problems. For now what is essential for you to remember is that RtI is implemented by general education teachers, reading specialists, and others; it is not a special education service. This means that it is likely you will have a role in an RtI process, and this is so whether you plan a career in elementary, middle, or high school.

Elementary and Secondary Education Act of 1965 (ESEA) Most recently reauthorized in 2002 and sometimes referred to as the **No Child Left Behind Act** (NCLB), it is the law that has the goal of ensuring that all students, including those who live in poverty, have equal access to a high quality education. Although the law directly addresses only schools whose students live in poverty, it generally mandates higher academic standards and increased accountability for all students, including those with disabilities. These are some of the law's key provisions:

- All students must be assessed to determine their academic progress. Nearly all students with disabilities take the same annual standardized assessments as their peers without disabilities; a few students, those with significant intellectual disabilities, take alternate tests designed to measure their learning.
- Each state must make adequate yearly progress (AYP) toward the goal of achievement at grade level for all students by 2014, and the scores of students with disabilities and other special needs (for example, those who live in poverty, those whose native language is not English) are part of this calculation.

www.resources

http://www.rti4success.org/
The National Center on Response to Intervention provides a straightforward explanation of RtI, training modules and other resources, and a free monthly newsletter.

INSTRUCTIONAL **EDGE**

Understanding Response to Intervention (RtI)

Response to intervention (RtI), part of IDEA, has rapidly become central to most schools' efforts to reach struggling learners. General education teachers, literacy and math specialists, administrators, and many other professionals have responsibility for implementing RtI, which is based on these core principles:

- An unwavering belief that all students can learn
- A focus on prevention in the academic, behavioral, and social domains
- Universal screening, that is, checking the academic, behavior, and social functioning of all students to determine which students are at-risk for failure so that interventions can be implemented
- A collaborative problem-solving approach to identifying and effectively addressing student learning, behavior, and social problems, one that includes professionals and parents/families

- Emphasis on implementing interventions with consistency (sometimes called fidelity of implementation)
- Decision making based on student data (rather than impressions or perceptions)
- Evidence-based practices, that is, academic, behavioral, and other supports implemented are only those demonstrated through research to be effective
- Continuous monitoring of student progress during interventions to determine in a timely manner whether those interventions are effective
- Multiple tiers of intervention; that is, increasingly intensive interventions matched to student needs implemented if evidence demonstrates those already in place are not reducing gaps
- If multiple tiers of intervention are not successful, referral for additional assessment and possibly special education services

At the school level, this means that if students with disabilities are not improving enough in terms of achievement, the school is identified as failing to make AYP, and sanctions may be applied.

- Assessments must include reporting individual student scores (not just aggregated scores) so that parents can be informed of their children's achievement.
- All students must be taught core academic subjects by teachers who are highly qualified in the content areas. This provision has helped to ensure that students with disabilities, especially those in middle school and high school, have more access to general education settings and teachers who generally have more extensive knowledge about the core academic subjects than do some special education teachers. This component of NCLB further strengthens the least restrictive environment provision of IDEA.
- Teaching practices and instructional programs, particularly those in reading and math, must be based on rigorous research. That is, they should have a strong basis in studies that demonstrate their positive impact on student learning. Consistent with this provision of the law, you will find as you read this textbook that the strategies presented for improving student achievement are grounded in such research.

Special education has evolved on the basis of many factors. When special education began, essentially no services were offered in public schools. Today comprehensive services in a wide variety of settings are supplied, and both very young children and young adults, as well as students in elementary and secondary schools, benefit from them. As the rights and needs of students with disabilities have been better understood and federal legislation has set higher standards for their education, general education teachers—in traditional core academic areas as well as in the essential related areas such as art, music, and physical education—have become increasingly involved in their education, a trend that surely will continue.

What Factors Influence Inclusive Practices in Today's Schools?

Now that you have learned about the key concepts that guide special education, the development of the field, and the litigation and legislation that have shaped special education services, it is important to return one more time to the topic of inclusion. The purpose of the following discussion is to draw your attention to the complexity of inclusive practices by briefly exploring several factors that have a significant influence on their implementation, including current and likely future legislation and policies; understanding of the concept of inclusive practices; the impact on stakeholders—students, parents, and educators; and resource limits that affect essential matters such as scheduling and staffing.

Legislation and Related Policies

Although the term *inclusion* does not appear in federal laws governing special education, provisions in those laws as well as other education and civil rights legislation you have read about in this chapter provide a strong foundation for inclusive practices (McLaughlin, 2010). This foundation is unlikely to be abandoned as new laws are enacted. For example, IDEA requires that students be educated in the least restrictive environment, and ESEA mandates access to the curriculum for all students. Together, these provisions have led state and local policymakers to stress inclusive practices. Similar comments could be made related to provisions such as the requirement for all students to participate in assessments and to make adequate yearly progress (AYP) and those related to teachers being highly qualified in core content areas. A useful activity is to scan back through all the information presented thus far to identify additional legislative provisions that probably have led to more inclusive practices in schools. This trend is not likely to vanish. Educational reformers maintain their commitment to holding all students, including those with disabilities, to high standards so that they leave school well-prepared for college or a vocation (U.S. Department of Education, 2010).

Not all the legislative influences are positive, however. For example, the requirements of ESEA have resulted in tremendous pressure for all students to reach achievement goals. In some schools, teachers fear that having students with disabilities in their classes may lower their average class scores. Others note that proposals to link teacher pay to the performance of their students may result in teachers resisting instructing students with disabilities out of concern they may miss out on bonuses and other financial incentives (Gratz, 2009). Concerns such as these should not be the basis for decisions about students' education, but they reflect the rather complicated situation that exists in schools today.

Understanding of Inclusive Practices

Although it is a bit surprising after so many years of discussion, a second influence on inclusive practices concerns its definition. Too often, research on inclusive practices and essays on their relative merits and drawbacks focus almost exclusively on where students are seated, that is, the amount of time they spend in general education classrooms (Friend & Shamberger, 2008; Idol, 2006). As a result, some professionals argue that students with disabilities sometimes need a small group, highly structured environment that is difficult to create in

General education teachers are accountable for the education of all the students in their classrooms, including those with disabilities.
Mac H. Brown/Merrill

PROFESSIONAL EDGE

Characteristics of Inclusive Schools

As you learn about your responsibilities as a teacher for students with disabilities, this list of characteristics can help you understand in a real-world way what an inclusive school is like.

- Every person who works in the school is committed to the goal of helping all students achieve their potential; inclusiveness is a school-level belief system.
- The principal is a strong and vocal advocate for all students, adamant that they access the general curriculum with a system of supports around them.
- Professionals and other staff routinely use respectful, person-first language.
- Emphasis is on abilities rather than disabilities.
- Special education and other services are seamless—their benefit to students is maximized and their cost to students is minimized.
- Special education and other services do not exist as separate entities (for example, "we have inclusion, resource, and self-contained programs; speech and ESL are pullout programs").
- Differentiation is considered the rule, not the exception.
- Assistive technology enhances access to the general curriculum.
- Parents are not just welcomed partners in the schools; their participation and collaboration are actively sought.
- A variety of support services are available to students, including instruction in a separate setting—but only when it is the last choice and only for as long as data indicate it is effective.
- Inclusiveness is communicated in many ways—materials displayed, books and other media available, adult interactions with students and each other, schedules, room assignments, and so on.
- The term *inclusion* is rarely needed because it is such an integral part of the school culture.

the general education classroom, and they conclude that inclusion—sometimes using the phrase *full inclusion*—is not sound educational practice.

Alternatively, in many school districts and among some authors (for example, Handler, 2003; McLeskey & Waldron, 2007), inclusive practices are conceptualized as a belief system that emphasizes welcoming all students in a school learning community (Frattura & Capper, 2006). Just as important, inclusiveness is not judged solely on the location of a student's education. In these schools, factors such as those listed in the Professional Edge are stressed. As you have learned, this broader view is the one taken in this textbook. In highly inclusive schools, professionals and parents realize that instruction sometimes must occur in a separate setting. However, their goal is to return the student to instruction with peers as soon as possible and for as much time as possible. Further, they judge the effectiveness of inclusive practices on a student-by-student basis, monitoring progress and making instructional decisions according to the student's individual needs and educational program (for example, Brigham, Morocco, Clay, & Zigmond, 2006).

Impact on Students, Parents, and Educators

Discussion about the best ways to educate students with disabilities should consider the key stakeholders. That is, consideration must be given to students and their parents and families. In addition, the perspectives of teachers and administrators should be taken into account.

Student Outcomes   Any discussion of inclusive practices must consider the effect on student achievement (Yell et al., 2006). That is, if students with disabilities in inclusive settings do not adequately progress in their learning, then inclusion is not in their best interests. At the same time, inclusive practices should not interfere with the achievement of other students. Generally, academic outcomes in inclusive schools have been found to be positive for students (Hang & Rabren, 2009; Idol, 2006). For example, in a statewide study, researchers found that students with disabilities who spent more time in general education passed the eighth-grade assessment at a higher rate than similar students with disabilities who were educated in special education settings. Students educated in general education settings also graduated at a higher rate from high school with a standard diploma (Luster & Durrett, 2003). Another

fyi

Although this textbook focuses on special education for students in kindergarten through twelfth grade, young children—those birth to age 5—also may be determined to be eligible for special education services.

statewide study found that school districts reporting the greatest achievement gains for students with disabilities focused on educating those students with nondisabled peers so that all had access to the same core curriculum (Silverman, Hazelwood, & Cronin, 2009).

Yet other researchers have found positive effects of inclusive practices on mathematics achievement (Kunsch, Jitendra, & Sood, 2007), language development (Rafferty, Piscitelli, & Boettcher, 2003), problem-solving skills (Agran, Blanchard, Wehmeyer, & Hughes, 2002; Ryndak, Ward, Alper, Storch, & Montgomery (2010), and discipline referrals (Cawley, Hayden, Cade, & Baker-Kroczynski, 2002). Although only a few studies have been reported on the impact of inclusive practices on typical students, they suggest that these students' achievement is not hindered (for example, McDonnell et al., 2003).

Few studies of students' perceptions of inclusive education have been reported, but those available generally indicate that students prefer to receive their education with their peers. For example, Connor (2006) reported on the experience of a student named Michael who was identified as being learning disabled and also lived in poverty. Michael discussed extensively the stigma of being labeled as disabled and receiving services in the special education classroom. He strongly preferred remaining in general education. Wilson and Michaels (2006) surveyed high school students with disabilities and their typical peers in a general education classroom with both a special education and a general education teacher. Both groups of students perceived the class as positive in terms of their access to multiple learning styles and assistance as needed.

Parent Perspectives Parents generally are positive about special education services, and they often prefer that their children be educated with peers in general education classrooms (Leach & Duffy, 2009; Purcell, Turnbull, & Jackson, 2006). They believe that inclusive practices are beneficial for academic achievement, and they also strongly believe that their children learn critical social skills when they spend most or all of the school day with their typical peers (Salend, 2006; Williams & Reisberg, 2003). One parent commented that when her fourth-grade son with autism was integrated into a general education classroom for most of the day, his behavior improved both at school and at home. She also noted that the other students in the class were clearly kind to her son, and she was grateful that they sought him out on the playground and chose him as a lunch partner.

When parents are uneasy about inclusive practices, their concerns usually relate to problems they have experienced or anticipate (for example, Hanline & Daley, 2002). For example, parents of children with physical disabilities have found that many teachers are poorly prepared to work with students with special needs and that these educators have not prepared students to have a classmate with a disability (Pivik, McComas, & Laflamme, 2002). Some parents find that their children seem more comfortable in a special education classroom that has fewer students and more structure (Johnson & Duffett, 2002). For all parents, perceptions of inclusive practices are more positive when they participate in collaborative decision making concerning their children's educational services (Matuszny, Banda, & Coleman, 2007).

Perspectives of Professionals The perceptions of teachers and administrators regarding inclusive practices can be represented along a continuum (for example, DeSimone & Parmar, 2006; Pavri & Monda-Amaya, 2001; Rea, McLaughlin, & Walther-Thomas, 2002). In some studies, general education teachers in elementary, middle, and high schools are found to believe strongly in inclusive practices based on high standards for students (King & Youngs, 2003; McLeskey et al., 2001). Teachers who support inclusive practices report making instructional accommodations to facilitate student learning and feeling positive about their work with students with disabilities (for example, Clayton, Burdge, Denham, Kleinert, & Kearns, 2006).

At the same time, some teachers' perceptions of inclusive practices are more ambivalent (for example, Kozik, Cooney, Vinciguerra, Gradel, & Black, 2009; Sze, 2009).

RESEARCH NOTE

Technology can improve outcomes for students with disabilities. Myles, Ferguson, and Hagiwara (2007) found that when they taught an adolescent with Asperger syndrome to use a personal digital assistant (PDA), he was motivated by the use of technology and significantly increased the number of times he independently recorded homework assignments.

They recognize the value of inclusive practices but are uncertain about implementation. In one study of mathematics teachers (DeSimone & Parmar, 2006), the educators indicated that they had not learned enough about students with disabilities in their professional preparation programs and were uncertain about students' needs and how to address them. As you think about teaching students with disabilities and other special needs, what knowledge and skills do you anticipate needing? Among the items frequently mentioned are a commitment to inclusive practices and knowledge of effective instructional strategies (Stanovich & Jordan, 2002).

In addition to the views of teachers, principals' support of inclusive practices is essential, because principals are responsible for keeping the vision focused, fostering among staff an understanding of inclusion, and nurturing the development of the skills and practices needed to implement these practices (Horrocks, White, & Roberts, 2008; Salisbury & McGregor, 2002). Generally, principals report positive attitudes toward inclusive practices (for example, Praisner, 2003). Like teachers, though, they express concern that general education teachers may not have the skills to effectively instruct students with disabilities in their classrooms (for example, Oluwole, 2009).

Limited Resources

The most immediate influences on inclusive practices and those often the most daunting challenges to them seldom relate directly to instruction. Instead they often relate to practical matters and other pressures that exist in schools (Sindelar, Shearer, Yendol-Hoppey, & Liebert, 2006). These are common concerns:

- *Adequate personnel:* Because inclusive schooling relies so heavily on the strong collaborative relationships among educators, staffing often is a critical issue. First, in many locales the overall size of classes has increased because of budget constraints. This leads to teachers having less time to spend with any individual student, including those with disabilities. Similarly, many special educators' caseloads have increased, and so their time has to be distributed among more students, and the same often can be said for other special service providers such as speech-language pathologists.
- *Scheduling:* The limited number of educators leads directly to problems in scheduling the inclusive programs and services needed by students with disabilities. For example, some students are best educated when their special education teacher joins the general education teacher in the general education and they co-teach. If one special educator is providing services to students in four, five, six, or even more classrooms, such partnerships are difficult to arrange. Similarly, in rural areas special education teachers and other service providers may may need to travel from school to school, limiting their availability for programs based on inclusive practices. In schools where teacher turnover is high, it is difficult to sustain efforts to support students with disabilities in general education classrooms.
- *Time for shared planning:* The success of inclusive practices ultimately relies on the extent to which general and special education teachers can collaborate to design instructional strategies and discuss student learning and behavior. Nearly every study of inclusive practices includes mention of planning time as a barrier to implementation (Horne & Timmons, 2009; Scruggs, Mastropieri, & McDuffie, 2007).

Putting the Pieces Together

In some ways, the various positive and negative influences on inclusive practices are like puzzle pieces. In today's schools some of the pieces may be missing and others difficult to fit into place; yet others may be readily addressed and fit easily into the larger picture. Even in your own course, classmates may have a wide range of opinions about inclusive practices and what is affecting them, and they may come across studies on inclusive practices that present contradictory results. In your field experiences, you are likely to discover that in some schools inclusive practices are the norm, while in others very traditional approaches are still in place. You may find yourself struggling to reconcile all these views.

One way that you can put the puzzle together is to learn to teach in a way that is responsive to a wide range of student needs (Sobel & Taylor, 2006; Zascavage & Winterman, 2009) and to use collaboration with colleagues and parents, as described in the Working Together, as a means for extending your expertise. As you will learn in the chapters that follow, much is known about effective ways to instruct students with disabilities, and many of those strategies will help other students learn as well (for example, Meo, 2008; McGuire, Scott, & Shaw, 2006; Pisha & Stahl, 2005). By welcoming all your students and making these strategies an integral part of your instruction, your pieces of the inclusive practices puzzle will fit right into place.

Finally, as you read about inclusive practices, keep in mind that the results researchers obtain and the viewpoints authors present are influenced by many variables in addition to those just discussed, including the abilities and disabilities, ages, and cultural backgrounds of students; the attitudes, knowledge, and skills of general and special education teachers; the commitment and participation of parents; school administration; policies and procedures; the type of outcomes measured; and even the predisposition of researchers and authors toward particular views of inclusive practices. As you develop your own understanding of inclusive practices, keep all these factors in mind to help you make sense of what you read. In this way, you will learn to be inclusive in your thinking but flexible in your approach to educating students with disabilities.

Working TOGETHER

The Importance of Collaboration for Meeting Student Needs

As you read this textbook and learn about your responsibilities for educating students with disabilities, you will find that *collaboration*—working together with others—is one of the keys to successful inclusive practices. Here are just a few examples of how you will collaborate on behalf of students:

- *Meeting with special education teachers:* You will meet frequently with special education teachers, both formally and informally. A special educator may contact you to see how a student is doing in your class, or you may contact a special educator to ask for new ideas for responding to a student's behavior. You and the special educator may share responsibility for meeting with parents during open houses or parent conferences.
- *Co-teaching:* Depending on local programs and services, you may co-teach with a special education teacher or related services professional such as a speech/language pathologist. In co-teaching, you share teaching responsibilities, with both educators working with all students.
- *Working with paraprofessionals:* If your class includes a student with a significant disability or several students who need support (but not co-teaching), you may collaborate with

a paraprofessional. You will guide the work of that individual in your class to ensure that student support is appropriately provided.

- *Meeting on teams:* Various school teams support inclusive practices. Your grade-level or middle or high school department team will likely spend part of its time discussing students with disabilities and problem solving to address their needs. You also may be part of a team that tries to address student learning and behavior problems prior to any consideration of the need for special education. If a student in your class is being assessed to determine whether special education is needed, you will be part of that team.
- *Interacting with parents:* Perhaps the most important part of collaborating on behalf of students with disabilities is working with parents. You may communicate with parents through notes sent home and through e-mail; meet with them occasionally as they express concerns about their children; confer with them at formal team meetings; and work with them as they volunteer at school, help with field trips, and participate in other school activities and initiatives.

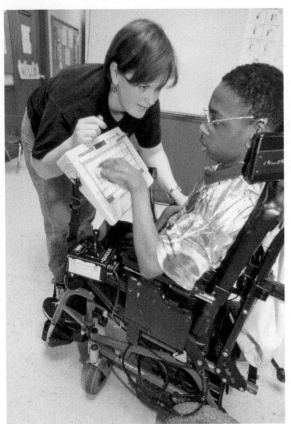

A disability label protects a student and gives access to resourses, but it does not provide information about a student's abilities and potential. © Jeff Greenberg/Alamy

Who Receives Special Education and Other Special Services?

Throughout this chapter, we have used the phrase *students with disabilities.* At this point, we will introduce you to the specific types of disabilities that may entitle students to receive special education services, as well as other special needs that may require specialized assistance. As you read the following definitions, remember that a disability label can only provide general guidelines about a student. Labels are a form of shorthand that professionals use, but no label can accurately describe a student. Your responsibility is to understand your students with disabilities in ways that extend beyond what any label communicates so you can help them reach their potential.

Categories of Disability in Federal Law

When we say that students have disabilities, we are referring to the specific categories of exceptionality prescribed by federal law. Each state has additional laws that clarify special education practices and procedures, and the terms used to refer to disabilities in state laws may differ from those found in federal law. For example, although federal law specifies the label *emotional disturbance* for some students, in some states, the term *behavior disorder* or *behavioral and emotional disability* is used. Similarly, although IDEA uses the term *mental retardation*, some states use the alternative *cognitive disability* or *intellectual disability.* Check with your instructor or your state department of education website for the terms used in your state.

According to IDEA, students with one or more of the following thirteen disabilities that negatively affect their educational performance are eligible for special education services. These disabilities also are summarized in Figure 1.4 on the next page.

Learning Disabilities   Students with *learning disabilities (LD)* have dysfunctions in processing information typically found in language-based activities. They have average or above-average intelligence, but they often encounter significant problems learning how to read, write, and compute. They may not see letters and words in the way others do; they may not be able to pick out important features in a picture they are looking at; and they may take longer to process a question or comment directed to them. They also may have difficulty following directions, attending to tasks, organizing assignments, and managing time. Sometimes these students appear to be unmotivated or lazy when in fact they are trying to the best of their ability. Aaron, described at the beginning of this chapter, has one type of learning disability, but many other types also exist, and no single description characterizes all students with LD. Learning disabilities are by far the most common special need: Slightly fewer than half of all students receiving special education services in public schools in 2004–2005 had a learning disability (U.S. Department of Education, 2009).

Speech or Language Impairments   When a student has extraordinary difficulties communicating with others for reasons other than maturation, a *speech or language impairment* is involved. Students with this disability may have trouble with *articulation,* or the production of speech sounds. They may omit words or mispronounce common words when they speak. They also may experience difficulty in *fluency,* such as a significant stuttering problem. Some students have far-reaching speech or language disorders, in which they have significant problems receiving and producing language. They may communicate through pictures or sign language.

FIGURE 1.4 IDEA Disability Categories

Federal Disability Term[1]	Brief Description[2]
Learning disability (LD)	A disorder related to processing information that leads to difficulties in reading, writing, and computing; the most common disability, accounting for almost half of all students receiving special education.
Speech or language impairment (SLI)	A disorder related to accurately producing the sounds of language or meaningfully using language to communicate.
Mental retardation (MR)	Significant limitations in intellectual ability and adaptive behavior; this disability occurs in a range of severity.
Emotional disturbance (ED)	Significant problems in the social-emotional area to a degree that learning is negatively affected.
Autism	A disorder characterized by extraordinary difficulty in social responsiveness; this disability occurs in many different forms and may be mild or significant.
Hearing impairment (HI)	A partial or complete loss of hearing.
Visual impairment (VI)	A partial or complete loss of vision.
Deaf-blindness	A simultaneous significant hearing loss and significant vision loss.
Orthopedic impairment (OI)	A significant physical limitation that impairs the ability to move or complete motor activities.
Traumatic brain injury (TBI)	A medical condition denoting a serious brain injury that occurs as a result of accident or injury; potentially affecting learning, behavior, social skills, and language.
Other health impairment (OHI)	A disease or health disorder so significant that it negatively affects learning; examples include cancer, sickle-cell anemia, and diabetes.
Multiple disabilities	The simultaneous presence of two or more disabilities such that none can be identified as primary; the most common is the combination of intellectual and physical disabilities.
Developmental delay (DD)	A nonspecific disability category that states may choose to use as an alternative to specific disability labels for students up to age 9.

[1]The terms used in your state may vary from those specified in federal special education law.

Some students' primary disability is a speech or language disorder, and they may receive services for this. For other students with disabilities, speech/language services supplement their other educational services. For example, a student with a learning disability also might receive speech/language services, as might a student with autism or traumatic brain injury. In these instances, speech/language services are often considered a related service, as defined earlier in this chapter.

Mental Retardation   Students with *mental retardation (MR)* have significant limitations in intellectual ability and adaptive behaviors. They learn at a slower pace than do other students, and they may reach a point at which their learning levels off. Although the federal description of disability categories does not distinguish between students with mild mental retardation and those with more significant intellectual disabilities, many state descriptions do. Most individuals with this disability can lead independent or semi-independent lives as adults and can hold appropriate jobs. Because the term *mental retardation* can be very stigmatizing, the alternative term *intellectual disability* is becoming more common. In this text, the two terms are used interchangeably. Patricia, one of the students you met in the introduction to this chapter, has an intellectual disability.

RESEARCH NOTE

Although many researchers have studied the effects of children with significant disabilities on their families, few have examined the effects of children with learning disabilities. Dyson (2010) found a surprising number of negative effects, including general stress, parent disagreements, and negative reactions from extended family members.

Emotional Disturbance When a student has significant difficulty in the social-emotional domain—serious enough to interfere with the student's learning—*emotional disturbance (ED)*, also sometimes called an *emotional and behavior disorder (EBD)*, exists. Students with this disability may have difficulty with interpersonal relationships and may respond inappropriately in emotional situations. That is, they may have extraordinary trouble making and keeping friends; they may get extremely angry when peers tease or play jokes on them; and they may repeatedly and significantly show little or inappropriate emotion when it is expected, such as when a family pet dies. Some students with ED are depressed; others are aggressive. Students with ED display these impairments over a long period of time, across different settings, and to a degree significantly different from their peers. Students with emotional disabilities are not just students whose behavior in a classroom is challenging to address; rather, they have chronic and extremely serious emotional or behavioral problems.

Autism Students with *autism*, sometimes referred to as *autism spectrum disorder* because of its many variations, usually lack appropriate social responsiveness from a very early age. They generally avoid physical contact (for example, cuddling and holding), and they may not make eye contact. Problems with social interactions persist as these children grow; they appear unaware of others' feelings and may not seek interactions with peers or adults. They may have unusual language patterns, speaking without inflection, repeating what others say, or repeating something heard on television over and over. To feel comfortable, they may need highly routinized behavior, such as a formalized procedure for putting on their clothes or eating their meals. Some students with autism have above-average intelligence; others have intellectual disabilities. The causes of autism are not well understood, and the best approaches for working with students with autism are still emerging.

Asperger syndrome, usually considered a type of autism, is receiving increased attention among professionals. Individuals with this disorder usually experience difficulty in social interactions and communication, and they often have a very narrow range of interests. However, with appropriate supports and teacher understanding, students with Asperger syndrome can be highly successful in school. Thomas, one of the students you met at the beginning of the chapter, is identified as having autism, and his characteristics are consistent with having Asperger syndrome. You can learn a little more about autism by reading the Case in Practice in which teachers meet to problem solve regarding another student with this disability.

Hearing Impairments Disabilities that concern inability or limited ability to receive auditory signals are called *hearing impairments (HI)*. When students are *hard of hearing*, they have a significant hearing loss but are able to capitalize on residual hearing by using hearing aids and other amplifying systems. Students who are *deaf* have little or no residual hearing and therefore do not benefit from traditional devices that aid hearing. Some students with hearing loss may be assisted through the use of advanced technology such as a cochlear implant, a small, complex electronic device implanted near the ear that can provide a sense of sound. Depending on the extent of the disability, students with hearing impairments may use sign language, speech reading, or other ways to help them communicate.

Visual Impairments Disabilities that concern the inability or limited ability to receive information visually are called *visual impairments (VI)*. Some students have *partial sight* and can learn successfully using magnification devices and other adaptive materials; students who are *blind* do not use vision as a means of learning and instead rely primarily on touch and hearing. Depending on need, students with visual impairments may use braille, specialized computers, and other aids to assist in learning. In addition, some students with vision loss need specialized training to help them learn to move around successfully in their environment.

CASE IN PRACTICE

Problem Solving in Inclusive Schools: The Classroom Teacher's Role

At Adams Middle School, staff members are meeting to discuss John, a seventh-grade student who has a formal diagnosis from a pediatric psychologist of pervasive developmental disorder (PDD) and who has many characteristics associated with autism. Ms. Diaz is David's English teacher, and Ms. Horton is the special educator who provides needed support. Mr. Powell, the school psychologist, also is present.

Ms. Diaz: John is a student with many dimensions. He usually does fairly well in class, and his behavior is much less disruptive than it was at the beginning of the school year, but whenever we transition from one activity to another, there is a fairly strong chance that John will refuse to change. If I insist, even using the strategies you've given me, Ms. Horton, John often starts rocking and singing in a loud voice and essentially shutting me out. I've had two calls from other parents who said their children reported that John takes up too much of my time in class. It was difficult to respond because I think that perception is fairly accurate. I hope we can come up with some ideas to improve the whole situation.

Ms. Horton: I know you also discussed John at your last team meeting. What did his other teachers have to say?

Ms. Diaz: Everyone except Mr. Bryant is experiencing the same problems. Mr. Bryant said that John really likes science and that his behavior problems might not be as pronounced there because John really wants to do the labs. He also said that sometimes he can tell by watching John's facial expression that John is trying very hard to transition between activities without a problem—and that it's very difficult for him.

Mr. Powell: You've mentioned the problem of transitioning between activities as one concern. Before we start addressing that, are there any other problems we should be aware of?

Ms. Diaz: No. Right now, it's the behavior during transitions—and I want to be clear that all of us on the team know John is quite capable of learning what we're teaching, and our data tell us he is making very strong gains academically. We are committed to finding more solutions before the problem becomes more serious.

Ms. Horton: One contribution I can make is to get into your classroom—and also into the classrooms of other teachers on

your team—to gather some additional information. It will help to gather data on the sequence of events in class that seem to prevent or lead to his behavior. For example, I'd like to observe how other students respond when he has a problem during a transition.

Ms. Diaz: That would be helpful, but I hope you can observe him within the next couple of days so we come up with new strategies. There is no time to waste. I've been cuing him as you suggested—it's not working now. I also tried to ignore him, but that made it worse.

Mr. Powell: Maybe we should focus for a minute or two on what is going well for John in your class.

Ms. Diaz: Let's see . . . He's usually fine and makes a good contribution when we're talking about assignments that are very concrete or literal. For example, he knows the nuances of parts of speech better than nearly any of the other students and always knows the answers and wants to share when an objective like that is the focus.

Mr. Powell: Our meeting time is nearly up—the bell is about to ring. Are we all clear on next steps? Ms. Horton, will you be able to observe in Ms. Diaz's class by the end of the week? I know you need answers right away, but I hope we can get a clearer sense of the pattern of John's behavior so we can find the right strategy for addressing it. If we can get in to observe this week, could we meet next Tuesday to try to generate some strategies?

Ms. Diaz: That would be great. Let's work out the details on observing.

REFLECTION

Why was this meeting a positive example of teachers addressing a student problem in an inclusive school? What did they do that has set them up for success? If you were trying to understand John better, what other questions would you ask about him? What would you like others to observe in the classroom in relation to him? In relation to you as the teacher? What do you think will happen at the next meeting? On the basis of this case, how would you describe the role of general education teachers in addressing the challenges of inclusion?

Deaf-Blindness Students who have both significant vision and hearing loss sometimes are eligible for services as *deaf-blind*. These students have extraordinarily unique learning needs, particularly in the domain of communication, and because of the highly specialized services they require. The degree of the vision and hearing loss may vary from moderate to severe and may be accompanied by other disabilities. Students in this category are likely to receive special education services beginning at birth or very soon thereafter.

Orthopedic Impairments Students with *orthopedic impairments (OI)* have physical conditions that seriously impair their ability to move about or complete motor activities. Students who have cerebral palsy are included in this group, as are those with other diseases that affect the skeleton or muscles. Students with physical limitations resulting from accidents also may be orthopedically impaired. Students with orthopedic impairments are difficult to describe as a group because their strengths and needs vary tremendously. For example, some students with this disability are unable to move about without a wheelchair and may need special transportation to get to school and a ramp to enter the school building. Others may lack the fine motor skills needed to write and may require extra time or adapted equipment to complete assignments.

Traumatic Brain Injury Students with *traumatic brain injury (TBI)* have a wide range of characteristics and special needs, including limited strength or alertness, developmental delays, short-term memory problems, hearing or vision losses that may be temporary or permanent, irritability, and sudden mood swings. Their characteristics depend on the specific injuries they experienced, and their needs often change over time. Because TBI is a medical condition that affects education, diagnosis by a physician is required along with assessment of learning and adaptive behavior. Students who experience serious head trauma from automobile accidents, falls, and sports injuries are among those who might be eligible for services as TBI.

Other Health Impairments Some students have a disease or disorder so significant that it affects their ability to learn in school. The category of disability addressing their needs is called *other health impairments (OHI)*. Students who have chronic heart conditions necessitating frequent and prolonged absences from school might be eligible for special education in this category, as might those with severe and chronic asthma. Students with diseases such as acquired immune deficiency syndrome (AIDS) and sickle cell anemia also may be categorized as having other health impairments, depending on the impact of their illnesses on learning. Some students—but not all—with attention deficit–hyperactivity disorder (ADHD) also receive special education services in this category.

Multiple Disabilities The category used when students have two or more disabilities is called *multiple disabilities*. Students in this group often have an intellectual disability as well as a physical disability, but this category also may be used to describe any student with two or more disability types (with the exception of deaf-blindness as noted above). However, this classification is used only when the student's disabilities are so serious and interrelated that none can be identified as a primary disability. Students with multiple disabilities often benefit from *assistive technology*, that is, simple or complex devices that facilitate their learning, as explained in the Technology Notes.

Developmental Delays The category *developmental delays (DD)* is somewhat different than the other disabilities recognized in IDEA. It is an option that states may use for children ages 3 through 9. This category includes youngsters who have significant delays in physical, cognitive, communication, social-emotional, or adaptive development, but it is applied instead of one of the more specific disability categories. This option has two advantages: First, it avoids the use of more stigmatizing labels for young children, and second, it acknowledges the difficulty of determining the nature of a specific disability when children are rapidly growing and changing.

A Cross-Categorical Approach to Special Education

Federal and state education agencies and local school districts use the categories of disability described in the previous section for counting the number of students receiving special education services and allocating money to educate them. When you prepare to teach a student, however, you probably will find that the specific category

---

fyi

A *primary disability* is one that most adversely affects a student's educational performance. A *secondary disability* is an additional disability that also affects a student's education but to a lesser degree. For example, a student identified with a learning disability as a primary disability could have an emotional disability as a secondary disability.

●—●—● TECHNOLOGY NOTES

The Opportunities of Assistive Technology

Whether the students you teach have mild or significant disabilities, they can use technology to help them to communicate, complete assignments, and fully participate in school and community. *Assistive technology*, which students with disabilities are entitled to access, refers to any device (that is, piece of equipment, product, or other item) used to increase, maintain, or improve the functional capabilities of an individual with a disability. Here are examples of the levels of assistive technology students might use.

NO TECHNOLOGY OR LOW TECHNOLOGY

No technology (no-tech) or *low technology (low-tech)* refers to items that do not include any type of electronics. Examples:

- A rubber pencil grip that enables a student with a disability to better grasp a pencil or pen
- A nonslip placemat on a student's desk that makes it easier for her to pick up items because it stops them from sliding
- A study carrel that helps a student pay closer attention to the schoolwork at hand

MID-TECHNOLOGY

Devices in the *mid-technology (mid-tech)* category use simple electronics. Examples:

- An audio recorder that a student uses to record lectures
- A calculator that assists a student in completing math computations
- A timer that lets a student know it is time to change from one activity to another

HIGH TECHNOLOGY

Items considered *high technology (high-tech)* incorporate more sophisticated, sometimes costly technology. Examples:

- Voice-recognition software that allows a student to use a microphone to dictate information that then appears in print on the computer
- Electronic communication boards on which a student can touch a picture and a prerecorded voice communicates for

Electronic communication boards are an example of high-tech assistive technology that benefits students with communication disorders.
Courtesy of AbleNet, Inc.

him. For example, a student touches a picture of himself and a voice says "Hello. My name is Danny. What is your name?"

Are you interested in assistive technology? These video clips demonstrate its use:

- http://teachertube.com/viewVideo.php?video_id=75646&title=Assistive_Technology_for_Writing_Low_High_Tech_Options
  This video demonstrates low-tech options for assisting students with writing tasks.

- http://teachertube.com/viewVideo.php?video_id=165020&title=Assistive_Technology
  This video shows both a younger and an older student using a communication device called a Dynovox.

- http://www.youtube.com/watch?v=fAdEOXD9Tvk
  In this video, Ellen, a college student with significant physical disabilities, demonstrates how she uses switches she touches with her head to control her wheelchair and communication device.

●—●—●

of disability does not guide you in discovering that student's strengths and devising appropriate teaching strategies. Further, students in different categories often benefit from the same instructional adjustments. Therefore, throughout this book, students generally are discussed in terms of only the following two groups:

1. *High-incidence disabilities* are those that are most common, including learning disabilities, speech or language impairments, mild intellectual disabilities, and emotional disturbance. Together these disabilities account for more than 80 percent of the disabilities reported in 2004–2005, the most recent year for which data are available (U.S. Department of Education, 2009).
2. *Low-incidence disabilities* are those that are less common and include all the other categories: moderate to severe intellectual disabilities, multiple disabilities, hearing impairments, orthopedic impairments, other health impairments, visual impairments, deaf-blindness, autism, traumatic brain injury, and developmental delays.

Most of the strategies presented throughout the text can be used effectively with most students, including students with disabilities. If you adopt a **cross-categorical approach** in your own thinking about teaching students with disabilities, you will see that many options are available for helping all students succeed.

Other Students with Special Needs

Not all students who have special learning and behavior needs are addressed in special education laws. The instructional strategies you learn in this book also can assist you in teaching many other students who may struggle in school, including those described in the following sections.

Students Who Are Gifted or Talented   Students who demonstrate ability far above average in one or several areas—including overall intellectual ability, leadership, specific academic subjects, creativity, athletics, and the visual or performing arts—are considered *gifted* or *talented*. Erin is included in this group; she seems to learn without effort, and she also is eager to learn about almost everything. Evan is considered talented; still in elementary school, he has participated in state and national piano recitals, and his parents have requested that he have access to the music room during recess so he can practice. Students who are gifted or talented are not addressed in federal special education law, but many states have separate laws that provide guidelines for identifying and educating students with special talents. Adequate funds are not always provided to implement these laws, however, and so the availability and scope of services for students with particular talents vary across the country and even within each state.

Students Protected by Section 504   Some students not eligible to receive special education services are entitled to protection through Section 504 and receive specialized assistance because of their functional disabilities, as described previously in this chapter. Among those likely to be included in this group are some students with attention deficit–hyperactivity disorder (ADHD). These students have a medical condition often characterized by an inability to attend to complex tasks for long periods of time, excessive motor activity, and/or impulsivity. The impact of this disorder on students' schoolwork can be significant. Students with ADHD may take medication, such as Ritalin or Strattera, that helps them focus their attention. Many students with learning disabilities or emotional disturbance also have ADHD, but these students receive assistance through IDEA, as do students with ADHD whose disorder is so significant that they are determined to be eligible for special education. Other students who may be protected by Section 504 include those with asthma, severe allergies, or epilepsy.

Students at Risk   Often, the general term *at risk* refers to students whose characteristics, environment, or experiences make them more likely than others to fail in school (and they also may have disabilities). Students whose primary language is not English—sometimes referred to as *English-language learners (ELLs)*—sometimes are considered at risk, and they may need assistance in school learning. They may attend bilingual education programs or classes for English as a second language (ESL) to have opportunities to learn English while also learning the standard curriculum, or they may receive assistance in their general education classrooms. Some ELLs also have disabilities; when this is the case, both English-language instruction and special education are provided. The checklist presented in the Professional Edge is a tool you can use to analyze your readiness to work with students and families from diverse backgrounds, including those who are English language learners.

dimensions of
DIVERSITY

Diversity has many faces. It includes ethnic, cultural, economic, linguistic, religious, ability, gender, and racial differences among the students you may teach.

PROFESSIONAL EDGE

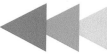

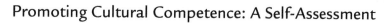

Promoting Cultural Competence: A Self-Assessment

Cultural competence refers to your understanding of and responses to diversity. Here is an excerpt from a tool designed to help professionals reflect on their awareness of a variety of factors that contribute to cultural competence. You can find the complete self-assessment checklist at http://nccc.georgetown.edu/documents/ChecklistCSHN.pdf.

DIRECTIONS: Please select A, B, or C for each item listed below

A = Things I do frequently, or statement applies to me to a great deal.

B = Things I do occasionally, or statement applies to me to a moderate degree

C = Things I do rarely or never, or statement applies to me to a minimal degree or not at all

- For children who speak languages or dialects other than English, I attempt to learn and use key words in their language so that I am better able to communicate with them during assessment, treatment, or other interventions.
- I use visual aids, gestures, and physical prompts in my interactions with children who have limited English proficiency.
- When interacting with parents who have limited English proficiency, I always keep in mind that:
  - Limitation in English proficiency is in no way a reflection of their level of intellectual functioning.
  - Their limited ability to speak the language of the dominant culture has no bearing on their ability to communicate effectively in their language of origin.
  - They may or may not be literate neither in their language of origin or English.
- I use alternative formats and varied approaches to communicate and share information with children and/or their family members who experience disability.
- I avoid imposing values that may conflict or be inconsistent with those of cultures or ethnic groups other than my own.
- I recognize and accept that individuals from culturally diverse backgrounds may desire varying degrees of acculturation into the dominant culture.

- I accept and respect that male-female roles in families may vary significantly among different cultures (e.g., who makes major decisions for the family, play and social interactions expected of male and female children).
- I recognize and understand that beliefs and concepts of emotional well-being vary significantly from culture to culture.
- I accept that religion and other beliefs may influence how families respond to illnesses, disease, disability and death.
- I recognize and accept that folk and religious beliefs may influence a family's reaction and approach to a child born with a disability or later diagnosed with a physical/emotional disability or special health care needs.
- I understand that traditional approaches to disciplining children are influenced by culture.
- I understand that families from different cultures will have different expectations of their children for acquiring toileting, dressing, feeding, and other self-help skills.
- I accept and respect that customs and beliefs about food, its value, preparation, and use are different from culture to culture.

NOTE: This checklist is intended to heighten the awareness and sensitivity of personnel to the importance of cultural diversity and cultural competence in human service settings. There is no answer key with correct responses. However, if you frequently responded "C," you may not necessarily demonstrate values and engage in practices that promote a culturally diverse and culturally competent service delivery system for children with disabilities or special health care needs and their families.

Checklist excerpts are included with express permission from the National Center for Cultural Competence.

Source: Goode, T. D. (2009). *Promoting cultural diversity and cultural competency: Self-assessment checklist for personnel providing services and supports to children with disabilities & special health needs and their families.* Washington, DC: Georgetown University Center for Child and Human Development. Retrieved October 23, 2010, from http://nccc.georgetown.edu/documents/ChecklistCSHN.pdf.

A second group of at-risk students includes *slow learners* whose educational progress is below average but who do not have a disability. These students are learning to the best of their ability, but they often cannot keep pace with the instruction in most general education classrooms without assistance. They are sometimes described as "falling between the cracks" of the educational system because while most professionals agree they need special assistance, they are not eligible for special education. They are likely to access and benefit from response to intervention (RtI) services described earlier in this chapter.

Other students who might be considered at risk include those who are homeless; those who live in poverty or move frequently; those who are born to mothers abusing drugs or alcohol or who abuse drugs or alcohol themselves; and those who are victims of physical or psychological abuse. Students in these groups are at risk for school failure because of the environment or circumstances in which they live.

fyi

Using *person-first language* is a way to ensure that you focus on students and not their labels. For example, say "students with disabilities" instead of "disabled students" and "my student who has autism" instead of "my autistic student."

You may find it challenging to find effective strategies to reach your students who have special needs but who do not have disabilities according to special education law. However, current trends in education can help you. First, you can access response to intervention procedures for research-based interventions for your struggling learners. In addition, as students with disabilities spend increasing amounts of time in general education classes, special education teachers and other special services providers often informally assist teachers in planning and adapting educational activities for them. Thus, other students with special needs often benefit from the trend toward inclusive education for students with disabilities.

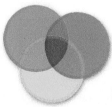

WRAPPING IT UP

BACK TO THE CASES

This section provides opportunities for you to apply the knowledge gained in this chapter to the cases described at the beginning of this chapter. The questions and activities that follow demonstrate how the concepts you have learned about connect to the everyday activities of all teachers.

THOMAS, as you may remember from the beginning of the chapter, is a student with autism. If you believe that being a member of a general education classroom has been successful for Thomas, explain what factors led you to that conclusion and how they may contribute to success for other students with disabilities. If you believe Thomas would be more successful learning in a special education setting, explain what factors led you to that conclusion and how they may prevent success for other students with disabilities.

PATRICIA, the elementary student with an intellectual disability, receives some of her education in general education and some in a special education setting. Why might this be a preferred option for some students? What could be the drawbacks to this approach for Patricia, her classmates, and her teachers? Which of the laws and court cases you learned about in this chapter led to the educational options Patricia has?

AARON, as you may recall, is troubled by his learning disability. Several of the assistive technologies mentioned in the Technology Notes on page 25 could provide support for Aaron's problems with attention and written tests. Select at least two technologies that you would recommend to Aaron. Remembering that Aaron does not want to stand out or be treated differently, what would you say to him to help him accept these assistive supports?

SUMMARY

- *Special education* refers to the specialized instruction received by the millions of students in the United States who have disabilities and is guided by the concept of the least restrictive environment (LRE).

- Current special education practices have evolved from a combination of historical factors, including the inception of compulsory public education early in the twentieth century, research questioning instructional practices for students with disabilities, the civil rights movement and related court cases, and a series of federal civil rights and education laws, including Section 504, P.L. 94-142, ADA, IDEA, and ESEA/NCLB.

- Inclusive practices today have been shaped by the historical, legislative, and litigative dimensions of special education. Although the primary goal of inclusion is to improve student outcomes by ensuring their rights, its implementation can be complicated by uncertainty about its meaning; professional understanding, attitude, and skill; and practical dilemmas related to funding and other resources.

- Federal law identifies 13 categories of disability that may entitle students to special education services: learning disabilities, speech or language impairments, mental retardation (increasingly called *intellectual disabilities*), emotional disturbance, autism, hearing impairments, visual impairments, deaf-blindness, orthopedic impairments, traumatic brain injury, other health impairments, multiple disabilities, and developmental delays.

- Many students have special needs not addressed through special education, including those who are gifted or talented; who have ADHD; who are at risk, including English-language learners and slow learners; and whose life situations comprise high risk for school failure. Students with disabilities also may have these special needs.

- Central to twenty-first-century education is the understanding that nearly all public school teachers are responsible for instructing students with disabilities and other special needs.

APPLICATIONS IN TEACHING PRACTICE
UNDERSTANDING CONTEMPORARY SPECIAL EDUCATION

It is a new school year—your first as a teacher in the Danville School District. You are excited about your new job but worried about following the district curriculum and making sure your students succeed on high-stakes tests. Then you learn that you will be responsible for the following students, and you find that you need all the skills for reaching diverse groups of students that you learned in your professional preparation program:

- Cassie is a bright student who has a visual impairment. To read, she uses a computer that greatly magnifies the materials. She also needs to work in bright light, and she gets fatigued from the effort required to use what little vision she has.
- Ramon is identified as having a learning disability. His reading ability is significantly below grade level. He also seems disorganized. He often forgets to bring materials and assignments to school, and he frequently asks for help immediately after directions for an assignment have been given.
- Tory lives in a foster home. He was removed from his mother's care because of several incidents of abuse. Tory is an angry child. He often refuses to work, he sometimes loses his temper and throws a book or crumples a paper, and he misses school frequently.

QUESTIONS

1. What are the possible strengths that Cassie, Ramon, and Tory might bring to your classroom? How can you emphasize their possible strengths instead of their difficulties? What is the rationale for assigning these students to a general education classroom like yours? How do the provisions of IDEA and ESEA affect these students' educational rights and responsibilities? What are appropriate goals you as a teacher should have as you begin to instruct them? Discuss with your classmates how Cassie, Ramon, and Tory's special needs might be demonstrated in an elementary school, middle school, or high school classroom.

2. What are some of the benefits and opportunities of educating these students in your classroom? What positive outcomes should you expect? How can you ensure these positive outcomes?

3. What are some of the risks and concerns related to educating these students in your classroom? What types of systemic supports could prevent or significantly reduce these risks and concerns? How might your own beliefs be either a benefit or a risk for these students?

4. If you spoke with the parents of Cassie, Ramon, and Tory, what might you expect them to say? What unique views might each student's parents have? How might their views be influenced by their family cultures and experiences? What could you do to encourage parent participation for your students?

5. What are your concerns and questions when you think about your responsibilities for educating students with disabilities and other special needs in your classroom—whether in the elementary grades, middle school, or high school? In what ways do you think you can make a contribution to your students' education? What types of support might you need? If you write your responses to these questions, keep them with your text.

myeducationlab

Go to Topic 1: Inclusive Practices and Topic 2: Law, in the MyEducationLab (http://www.myeducationlab.com) for your course, where you can:

- Find learning outcomes for Inclusive Practices and Law along with the national standards that connect to these outcomes.
- Complete Assignments and Activities that can help you more deeply understand the chapter content.
- Apply and practice your understanding of the core teaching skills identified in the chapter with the Building Teaching Skills and Dispositions learning units.
- Examine challenging situations and cases presented in the IRIS Center Resources. (optional)
- Access video clips of CCSSO National Teachers of the Year award winners responding to the question, "Why Do I Teach?" in the Teacher Talk section. (optional)
- Check your comprehension on the content covered in the chapter by going to the Study Plan in the Book Resources for your text. Here you will be able to take a chapter quiz, receive feedback on your answers, and then access Review, Practice, and Enrichment activities to enhance your understanding of chapter content. (optional.)

Assessing
Student Needs

Assessing
Student Needs

LEARNING Objectives

After you read this chapter, you will be able to

1. Explain how general education teachers can contribute significantly to the assessment process.

2. Describe the uses of high-stakes, standardized achievement, and psychological tests in making educational decisions for students with special needs.

3. Describe how alternate assessments for students with significant intellectual disabilities can be developed and scored.

4. Define curriculum-based assessment and explain how it can help general education teachers.

5. Construct and use probes of basic academic skills, prerequisite skills and knowledge in content areas, and independent learning skills.

6. Use curriculum-based assessment to make special education decisions.

Bob Daemmrich/PhotoEdit Inc.

MS. LYONS is concerned that Rob, a student in her second-grade class, is not keeping up with the rest of the class in math. She knows that he will be taking the state math test in third grade, and she is afraid that if he continues to fall behind, he won't meet state standards. Mr. Blair, the special education teacher, suggests that Ms. Lyons do some informal assessment herself before referring Rob for special education or other services.

What kinds of assessments can Ms. Lyons use to clarify Rob's problems in math? How might these assessments help her make changes in Rob's math instruction? Under what circumstances should she refer Rob for special education or other services?

MR. BLOUNT teaches a high school U.S. history class. He has learned that three students with disabilities will be in his class this fall. Mr. Blount was told that these students have some reading problems and may have trouble reading the textbook. He decides to make up a test to give at the beginning of the year to see how well all of his students are able to use the textbook. Using a section of a chapter from the text, he writes questions to test how well students can figure out the meanings of key vocabulary words, use

parts of the book (for example, the table of contents, glossary, and index), read maps, and read for information (for example, note main ideas and draw conclusions). When Mr. Blount gives the test, he finds that the three identified students have trouble reading the text, but many other students also have difficulty.

How might Mr. Blount use the information from this assessment to differentiate instruction for his students?

ROBERTO is a student with moderate to severe intellectual disabilities who is in Ms. Benis's sixth-grade social studies class. As a result of Roberto's cerebral palsy, he has significant cognitive, language, and motor deficits. Roberto can read his name, as well as some high-frequency sight words. He uses a wheelchair, and he has trouble with fine motor movements such as cutting and handwriting. Roberto speaks with the aid of a communication board.

How can Roberto meet state standards for sixth grade in social studies? What kinds of assessments can Ms. Benis use to determine whether Roberto is meeting standards in social studies?

As more and more students with disabilities are being served in general education classes, teachers need to make many important decisions that can greatly affect these students' success. This is particularly important in view of federal requirements in the Individuals with Disabilities Education Act (IDEA) that students with disabilities participate in district testing programs, have access to the general education curriculum, and make meaningful progress toward meeting general curriculum goals. For example, in the preceding vignettes, Ms. Lyons wanted to help Rob before he failed the state math test in grade 3. Mr. Blount wanted to find out whether his students could read the textbook for his history class to help him decide which students would benefit from adapting the book. Ms. Benis needed to include Roberto, who had significant disabilities, in her social studies class but had to figure out how he would meet state standards. To respond effectively in situations such as these, teachers need accurate, relevant information. Thus, they need to develop informal measures to help them make instructional decisions as well as participate in special education decision making. This chapter explores assessment strategies that help general education teachers contribute to the process of decision making for students with special needs. This process involves determining whether a student needs special education services; when a student is ready to learn in inclusive settings; when an alternative to state testing is required; and what classroom accommodations and modifications to try, continue to use, or change. The assessment strategies described are also helpful if your school is implementing RtI.

How Do Your Student Assessments Contribute to Special Education Decisions?

As a general education teacher, you make an important contribution to the process of identifying and meeting the needs of students with special needs. A major part of that contribution involves assessing student needs. **Assessment** has been defined as the process of gathering information to monitor progress and to make educational decisions when necessary (Overton, 2009). The most common ways of collecting information are through standardized, commercially produced tests, high-stakes state accountability tests, and informal tests devised by the teacher. Much of the information in this chapter is about ways in which these measures can be used to make decisions about students with special needs. General education teachers contribute assessment information in six important decision-making areas for students with special needs: screening, diagnosis, program placement, curriculum placement, instructional evaluation, and program evaluation.

Screening

Screening involves the decision about whether a student's performance differs enough from that of his or her peers to merit further, more in-depth assessments to determine the presence of a disability. For example, to clarify Rob's problems in math, Ms. Lyons from the chapter-opening vignette examined the most recent group achievement test scores for her class in math and found that Rob was performing two years below grade level. Ms. Lyons then gave

Students' needs can be identified, addressed, and monitored through assessment based on observation, screening, diagnostic testing, program placement and evaluation, curriculum placement, and instructional evaluation. What role do general education teachers play in assessing students' special needs? Michael Newman/PhotoEdit Inc.

Rob some minitests on various math computation skills she had taught to see whether Rob was behind his peers on these skills. Using this information, Ms. Lyons found that a number of students were performing similarly to Rob. She therefore decided not to refer Rob for a more comprehensive evaluation until she first tried making some changes in the classroom with Rob and several other students. Screening assessments are at the heart of prevention-based systems such as RtI where they are referred to as universal screening measures. An explanation of universal screening including how to select and use universal screening measures is presented in the Instructional Edge.

Diagnosis

The major decision related to **diagnosis** concerns eligibility for special education services. Does a student meet established federal guidelines for being classified as having a disability? If so, what are the nature and extent of the student's disability? For example, Paula was a student in Ms. Clark's class. In September, when Paula appeared to be struggling to keep up with the class in reading, Ms. Clark paired her up with a classmate for 15 minutes before reading each day to go over key words and vocabulary. When Paula's reading accuracy and fluency problems persisted even after four weeks of this extra help, Ms. Clark arranged for her to have 30 minutes more practice later in the day with the reading teacher. After a month of this extra help, Paula still showed no improvement. Ms. Clark suspected she had a learning disability and referred her for a case study evaluation. The school psychologist gave Paula a test on cognitive functioning—including a test of memory, attention, and organization—and an individual achievement test. She found that Paula was slow in processing visual information (that is, letters, numbers, and shapes) and that her achievement in reading was significantly lower than that of other students her age. However, her achievement in math was at grade level. Ms. Clark evaluated Paula's classroom reading performance by having her read orally and answer questions from a grade-level trade book that was part of the classroom literature program. Paula's oral reading fluency was well below norms for her grade level, and she was able to answer only 40 percent of the comprehension questions correctly. In the end, Paula was declared eligible to receive services for learning disabilities, because she did not respond favorably to two levels of extra classroom help, she showed problems processing visual information quickly enough, and her achievement was significantly below grade level as measured by both a standardized achievement test and informal classroom reading tests. Working Together highlights effective ways to communicate to parents the results of diagnostic tests, as well as resulting decisions about placement.

Program Placement

The major **program placement** decision involves the setting in which a student's special education services take place (for example, in a general education classroom, resource room, or separate special education classroom). The individualized education program (IEP) team must make this decision carefully. In the past, the tendency was to pull students out of general education classrooms without considering whether they could be supported within the general education program instead. In today's schools, the emphasis is on doing all that can be done within the general education class first. This approach is consistent with guidelines for accessing the general education curriculum outlined in IDEA and RtI, in which students with learning disabilities are identified by monitoring how they respond to evidence-based instruction of varying intensity. Still, students have different needs, and some may require instruction in a specific area at a level of intensity that cannot be delivered in the general education classroom. That is why it is important to make placement decisions based on measures that accurately reflect student performance in class. For example, Carlos was eligible to receive services for learning disabilities in math. His IEP team needed to decide whether his learning needs could be accommodated by

Program placement decisions for students with moderate to severe intellectual disabilities should be based on the supports needed to meet the curricular goals outlined in their IEPs.

INSTRUCTIONAL EDGE

Using Universal Screening in RtI to Identify Students at Risk

What is universal screening?

The problem with identifying children who are experiencing academic difficulties is that by the time they are identified, they are already so far behind that catching up is often a losing proposition. A key feature of RtI is identifying and intervening with students at risk for academic problems early to prevent problems before they become insurmountable. The RtI process of assessing all students to identify those who are having difficulty learning despite an evidence-based Tier 1 program is called universal screening.

What are the qualities of effective universal screening measures?

Effective universal screening measures are accurate and practical, and they should not have negative or unintended consequences for students (for example, be biased) (Hughes & Dexter, 2010; Jenkins, 2009). Universal screening measures must accurately classify students who are at-risk or not at risk for academic failure. This means that only students who need extra support get it, and that students who need support are not overlooked. Overidentifying children who are at-risk (false positives) is costly to schools and can cause unneeded worry. Overlooking students (false negatives) needlessly delays support, creating more serious problems that may be more difficult to remediate later on. Universal screening measures must also be brief and easy to give. Last, effective universal screening measures should do no harm to the student. This means they should avoid leading to inequitable treatment and be linked to effective interventions.

How should a universal screening measure be chosen?

Jenkins (2009) suggests considering these ideas when choosing universal screening measures:

- A screening battery that measures multiple aspects of an academic area is more accurate than a test that measures only one. For example, if you are doing universal screening in reading, you would want to measure phonemic awareness, phonics, fluency, and comprehension. In math you would want to assess both math computation and math problem solving.
- Screening should be conducted more than once per year to detect students who may no longer be at risk or have become at risk.
- There is a research base that shows which universal screening measures are the most accurate. Consult that research base before you select a universal screening measure for your school. Not all universal screening measures are created equal.

How are at-risk students identified?

Currently there is no agreement as to what criteria should be used to identify students who are at-risk in Tier 1 (Hughes & Dexter, 2010). Some programs use a percentile approach whereby students performing below a certain percentile are considered at-risk (Hintze, 2007). For example, all children scoring below the 25th percentile may be considered at-risk.

What measures are commonly used for universal screening?

Most research-based universal screening measures are in the area of reading. Four assessment batteries are most commonly used for universal screening in reading within RtI programs. These include Dynamic Indicators of Basic Skills (DIBELS; http://dibels.uoregon.edu/measures/psf.php), AIMSWEB (http://www.aimsweb.com); Phonological Awareness Literacy Screening (PALS; http://pals.virginia.edu), and Texas Primary Reading Inventory (TPRI; http://www.tpri.org). There are a number of curriculum-based measures (CBM) available for screening in writing and math. Note that many universal screening measures can also be used for progress monitoring, a key part of RtI. For example, AIMSWEB also has universal screening assessments in math including math computation and math concepts and applications.

As you can see, universal screening measures are not as highly developed at the secondary level, largely because of the emphasis on the acquisition of subject matter knowledge rather than basic academic skills. A likely source is student performance on high stakes assessments and/or end-of-grade/class tests.

Internet resources for information about assessment within RtI gathered by Ysseldyke et al. (2010) are shown below.

- Florida Assessment for Instruction in Reading (FAIR)
  http://www.fcrr.org/FAIR_Search_Tool/FAIR_Search_Tool.aspx

- Intervention Central
  http://www.interventioncentral.com

- National Association of State Directors of Special Education
  http://www.nasde.org/Projects/ResponsetoInterventionRtlProject/tabid/411/Default.aspx

- National Research Center on Learning Disabilities
  http://www.nrcld.org/

- Renaissance Learning-Advanced Technology for Data Driven Schools
  http://www.renlearn.com/

- Research Institute on Progress Monitoring
  http://www.progressmonitoring.net/

- RTI Classification Tool and Resource Locator
  http://www.rtictrl.org/resources/

- RTI Action Network
  http://rtinetwork.org/

- System to Enhance Educational Performance (STEEP) and RTI
  http://www.joewitt.org/steep.html

Working TOGETHER

Communicating Effectively with Parents

Mrs. Perez has just attended a multidisciplinary committee meeting for her son Jorge and is distraught. First, being in the same room with all those professionals made Mrs. Perez nervous; she felt like an outsider who was there because she had done something wrong. Second, she was embarrassed that her English wasn't very good, so she was afraid to say anything. She had hoped the meeting would result in Jorge's getting extra help, but that was not what happened at all.

The school psychologist, Mr. Tanner, talked too fast and used a lot of technical language Mrs. Perez didn't understand, such as "performance-based," "verbal IQ," and "age and grade-level expectations." He said Jorge was in the slow-learner range. Mrs. Perez was afraid that he meant her Jorge was stupid. She thought that Jorge was unable to understand tests because his English skills weren't very good, but she was afraid to say so.

When the special education teacher said that Jorge was two to three years below grade level in reading and writing and about one year below level in math, Mrs. Perez wondered whether that meant there was no hope for Jorge. His teacher said that Jorge was having trouble keeping up in class and that last year he had failed to pass the state tests in reading and writing. Mrs. Perez wanted to hear more about what the class was doing and how Jorge was coping with the material, but she was afraid she would offend Jorge's teacher. Mr. Tanner finished by saying that Jorge

was behind in his skills but achieving as expected given his ability. He said that Jorge wasn't eligible for special education services and asked Mrs. Perez if she had any questions.

Mrs. Perez knew that Jorge's English skills were holding him back, but now the committee members were telling her he couldn't get any extra help. Having a million questions but not knowing how to ask them, she nodded her head and left the meeting, afraid that there was no hope for her Jorge in school.

ADDRESSING THE DILEMMA

This interaction illustrates many of the barriers that can exist between parents and teachers. How could you address each of the following issues?

* Few attempts were made to make Mrs. Perez feel comfortable.
* Mrs. Perez has difficulty expressing herself in English.
* The team explained the testing and eligibility process using highly technical language that Mrs. Perez did not understand.
* The standardized tests were hastily explained.
* The team did not clearly ensure that Mrs. Perez agreed with its decisions.
* The team did not address Mrs. Perez's primary concern: Getting help for her son.

adapting the math methods and materials in the general education classroom or whether he should be provided more intensive math instruction in a resource room setting. Carlos's general education teacher gave Carlos and his classmates a series of informal math tests. She found that Carlos was significantly behind his peers on some but not all of the tests; his math problem solving was very deficient compared to that of his classmates, but his math computational skills were fine. The IEP team decided to keep Carlos in his general education class and to support his instruction in problem solving by providing him extra teacher-guided practice whenever a new problem-solving skill was introduced. The team also decided to carefully monitor Carlos's problem-solving skills; if those skills showed little improvement, they would consider other options.

Curriculum Placement

Curriculum placement involves deciding at what level to begin instruction for students. For an elementary school teacher, such a decision may mean choosing which reading or math book a student should use. For example, Ms. Tolhurst has her students read orally and answer questions to find the appropriate trade books for them to read. That is, she determines the level of difficulty at which the books in her classroom reading program are neither too easy nor too hard for them. At the secondary level, curriculum placement decisions are likely to determine which class in a sequence of classes a student should take. For example, Mr. Nowicki, the guidance counselor, was trying to decide whether to place Scott in Algebra 1. He asked the math department to identify basic math skills that all students entering algebra should have. The department constructed a test based on those skills and gave it to Scott as well as other incoming ninth graders.

Of course, information about curriculum placement also provides teachers with a good measure of the extent to which students with disabilities are accessing the general education curriculum, an explicit goal of IDEA. In the examples just mentioned, a student with a disability in Ms. Tolhurst's class who can read only books that are two levels below grade level could be seen as having difficulty accessing the general education reading curriculum. In contrast, a student who enters Mr. Nowicki's algebra class with all of the necessary prerequisite skills is fully accessing the district math curriculum.

Instructional Evaluation

Decisions in **instructional evaluation** involve whether to continue or change instructional procedures that have been initiated with students. These decisions are made by carefully monitoring student progress. For example, Ms. Bridgewater is starting a peer tutoring program to help Cecily, a student with severe intellectual disabilities, read her name and the names of her family members. Each week, Ms. Bridgewater tests Cecily to see how many of the names she has learned. She uses the results of the tests to find out whether the peer-tutoring program is helping Cecily make progress. In another example, Mr. Jackson decides to accompany each of his history lectures with a graphic organizer of the material. He gives weekly quizzes to find out whether the graphic organizer is helping his students better learn the material. Schools implementing RtI use information collected from progress monitoring assessments to assign students to instructional tiers.

Program Evaluation

Program evaluation decisions involve whether a student's special education program should be terminated, continued as is, or modified. One consideration is whether or not the student is accessing the general education curriculum by meeting standards, as evidenced by reaching goals or attaining benchmark levels on assessments. For example, when Addie, a student with a reading disability, attained benchmark levels in reading fluency and comprehension for her grade level, her program was changed. She was integrated into general education for the entire reading block, and her progress was carefully monitored to ensure that her gains were maintained.

Another way to evaluate the success of special education programming is by monitoring the attainment of IEP goals. For example, Amanda is receiving social work services twice per week. Her IEP goal is to decrease the number of times she has a verbal confrontation with Mr. Alvarez, her English teacher. Mr. Alvarez is keeping track of the number of times daily that Amanda refuses to comply with his requests to see whether sessions with the social worker are improving Amanda's behavior.

What Information Sources Are Used in Programming for Students with Special Needs?

A number of information sources are used in programming for students with special needs. The use of multiple assessment sources is consistent with the principle of nondiscriminatory testing, which says that no single measure should be used to establish eligibility for special education services. The measures described in this section include high-stakes achievement tests, standardized achievement tests, psychological tests, alternate assessments, and curriculum-based assessments.

High-Stakes Achievement Tests

A key requirement of IDEA is that students with disabilities have maximum access to the general education curriculum. Unlike in the past, however, access today is defined not as spending a certain amount of time in general education but as making meaningful progress toward meeting general curriculum goals (Nolet & McLaughlin, 2005). In general education today, that means meeting educational standards. Standards, which are set by individual states, comprise what students should be able to know or do as a result of their public education. For the past three decades, general dissatisfaction with public education has dramatically raised learning standards and has led to increased accountability for schools as they teach students to attain those standards.

High-stakes tests are assessments designed to measure whether students have attained learning standards. These tests are a type of assessment referred to as *criterion referenced* because they involve comparing student performance to a specific level of performance, or benchmark, rather than to a norm, or average, as with traditional standardized achievement tests. Most states have created their own high-stakes tests based on an agreed-on set of learning outcomes. For each identified outcome, standards or benchmarks are set that represent an acceptable level of knowledge or competence. Schools are then evaluated on the basis of the percentage of students meeting standards on each of the learning outcomes identified. For example, State A wanted all its fifth graders to be able to comprehend the key elements of short stories, such as character, setting, problem identification, problem resolution, and moral. Reading experts were chosen by the state to create an item that would test student competence in comprehending short stories. The experts chose a short story written at the fifth-grade level and developed a series of multiple-choice questions about the story elements. They then tried out the test on a diverse sample of students and through careful analysis determined that students who could answer at least 90 percent of the story-element questions were competent at identifying story elements. State A then tested all its fifth-grade students on this item to determine the percentage that could identify key elements in short stories.

IDEA requires that most students with disabilities take their states' high-stakes tests. This is how districts can show the degree of access to the general education curriculum attained by students with disabilities. These IDEA requirements were reinforced by the reauthorization of the Elementary and Secondary Education Act of 2002 (ESEA), which requires that all children in each of grades 3 through 8 and at least once in grades 10 through 12 take high-stakes tests to show whether they are meeting state standards or making adequate progress toward them. ESEA requires that at least 95 percent of students with disabilities take high-stakes tests. Both IDEA and ESEA require that the results for students with disabilities be aggregated with the results of the other students and reported publicly. Results for students with disabilities must also be disaggregated and reported separately; students with disabilities who are tested are held to the same standards and levels of adequate yearly progress as their classmates without disabilities.

To ensure that the scores obtained are accurate, students with disabilities are entitled to a range of accommodations while taking high-stakes tests. Common accommodations include changing the setting of the test (for example, allowing students to take tests in special education classrooms), changing the timing of the test (for example, providing extended time or more frequent breaks), changing the response format (for example, allowing students to mark responses in test books rather than on Scantron sheets), and changing the presentation format (for example, using a braille edition of a test or giving directions in sign language) (Roeber, 2002; Thurlow,

RESEARCH NOTE

Solorzano (2008) reviewed the research on the use of high-stakes tests with English language learners. He concluded that high-stakes tests as currently constructed are inappropriate because they fail to take students' cultural and language differences into account. Caution is advised when interpreting them.

www.resources

Common Core Standards in English-language arts and mathematics have been developed for eventual use nation-wide. For more information, go to http://www.corestandards.org.

How do high-stakes tests relate to students meeting educational standards? What are the implications for students with special needs? Cleve Bryant/PhotoEdit Inc.

PROFESSIONAL EDGE

Accommodations for Students with Disabilities on Standardized Tests

Under guidelines from IDEA and NCLB, most students with disabilities are required to take district and state standardized tests, including state high-stakes tests. A list of standard accommodations provided is shown here. Keep in mind that research on effective strategies for determining which students get which accommodations is still being done. Given the range of abilities within all disability groups, it is recommended that teachers avoid using students' labels to make these decisions and instead base them on individual student characteristics.

UNIVERSAL DESIGN

As applied to assessment, universal design is the idea that tests designed with built-in supports minimize the need for accommodations (Lazarus, Thurlow, Lail, & Christensen, 2009). Lazarus et al. (2009) assert that universally designed assessments should have the following qualities:

- accessible, nonbiased items
- simple, clear, and intuitive instructions and procedures
- maximum readability and comprehensibility
- maximum legibility
- precise definition of what is being measured

TYPES OF TESTING ACCOMMODATIONS

Setting

- Provide special lighting.
- Provide adaptive or special furniture.
- Provide special acoustics.
- Administer the test to a small group in a separate location.
- Administer the test individually in a separate location.
- Administer the test in a location with minimal distractions.

Timing

- Allow a flexible schedule.
- Extend the time allotted to complete the test.
- Allow frequent breaks during testing.
- Provide frequent breaks on one subtest but not another.

Scheduling

- Administer the test in several sessions, specifying the duration of each session.
- Administer the test over several days, specifying the duration of each day's session.
- Allow subtests to be taken in a different order.
- Administer the test at a different time of the day.

Presentation

- Provide the test on audiotape.
- Increase spacing between items or reduce number of items per page or line.
- Increase size of answer spaces.
- Provide reading passages with one complete sentence per line.
- Highlight key words or phrases in directions.
- Provide cues (for example, arrows and stop signs) on answer forms.
- Secure papers to work area with tape or magnets.

Responding

- Allow marking of answers in booklet.
- Tape-record responses for later verbatim transcription.
- Allow the use of a scribe.
- Provide copying assistance between drafts.

Other

- Make special test preparations.
- Provide on-task/focusing prompts.
- Make any accommodation that a student needs that does not fit under the existing categories.
- Conduct an alternate assessment.

Source: Testing Students with Disabilities: Practical Strategies for Complying with District and State Requirements (2nd ed.), by M. L. Thurlow, J. L. Elliott, and J. F. Ysseldyke, 2003. Thousand Oaks, CA: Corwin. Reprinted with permission.

---

fyi

Rose (2000) has proposed a system of *universally designed assessments* that, through the use of the latest technology, allow for greater testing accuracy through multiple means of engagement, expression, and representation of information. For more information, go to the Center for Applied Special Technology (CAST) website at http://www.cast.org.

Elliott, & Ysseldyke, 2003). A more complete description of the accommodations available and a process for finding the right accommodations for individual students is provided in the Professional Edge. Up to 3 percent of students with disabilities are entitled to take alternate assessments geared to their individual needs as specified on their IEPs. Alternate assessments are described in more detail later in the chapter.

Why is the issue of high-stakes testing and students with disabilities important for you? The answer is that students with disabilities who are included in your classroom (except for those with significant intellectual disabilities) are expected to meet the same standards as everyone else. Furthermore, in 24 states, students need to pass an exam to receive a high school diploma (Johnson, Stout, & Thurlow, 2009), and at least six states require that students pass a test to be promoted to a certain grade (Thompson & Thurlow, 2003). Therefore, it is critical for you to carefully monitor the progress of your students with disabilities and, if needed, to provide extra supports or resources to ensure that the standards are met. Effective monitoring requires paying close attention to the results of high-stakes tests. More important, it requires you to keep track of student performance on a daily basis using assessments such as the ones described in this chapter.

Standardized Achievement Tests

Another common source of information for making educational decisions is **standardized achievement tests.** These tests are designed to measure academic progress, or what students have retained from the curriculum. Unlike the high-stakes tests just described, standardized achievement tests are *norm referenced*. In a norm-referenced test, the performance of one student is compared to the average performance of other students in the country who are the same age or grade level. Student performance is often summarized using grade equivalents and/or percentile ranks.

Group-Administered Tests   Two major types of standardized achievement tests are group-administered and individually administered diagnostic tests. As the name implies, group-administered standardized achievement tests are completed by large groups of students at one time; this usually means that the general education teacher gives the test to the entire class. These tests assess skills across many areas of the curriculum, none in much depth. For this reason, they are intended to be used solely as screening measures. Nonetheless, caution is advised in using these scores, even if only for screening. As with any test, the general education teacher should be sure that students with disabilities receive appropriate accommodations when taking the test. Otherwise, the resulting score may be a measure more of the disability than of the ability. For example, Alicia has a learning disability in reading and has problems comprehending written directions. When Alicia obtained a low score on a social studies test, it was hard to determine whether her low score was due to a lack of knowledge or her inability to follow the directions.

Another potential problem with group-administered standardized achievement tests is that the norms used to interpret scores are of little use when evaluating students with disabilities; these students are often excluded from the norming group because they have taken the test with accommodations. Also, all students may be affected by the fact that the content of the test might not match what is taught in a particular classroom (Ysseldyke, Burns, Scholin, & Parker, 2010). For example, one teacher stressed problem solving in his science class, whereas the standardized achievement test given in his district stressed the memorization of facts. Therefore, the teacher had to give his own tests to determine whether students were learning the material.

Finally, standardized achievement tests might be culturally biased and historically have led to the overrepresentation of minorities in special education classes (Skiba et al., 2008; deValenzuela et al., 2006). For example, Bill comes from a single-parent home in the city. When he read a story on a standardized achievement test about an affluent two-parent family in the suburbs, he had difficulty predicting the outcome.

Whereas in the past, group-administered standardized achievement tests were used to make administrative and policy decisions on a school district or even national level, it appears that today, high-stakes tests are being used more often for these purposes. Given the time and effort it takes to test an entire school, as well as the value of instructional time to children's learning, many schools have found it more prudent to use only their state's high-stakes accountability test.

Individually Administered Tests   A special education teacher or the school psychologist usually gives **individually administered diagnostic tests** as part of a student's case study evaluation. Although these tests may screen student performance in several curricular areas, they tend to be more diagnostic in nature. For example, an individually administered diagnostic reading test may include test components in

www.resources

For more information on the topic of state and national testing policies, access the website of the National Center on Educational Outcomes (NCEO) at http://education.umn.edu/nceo.

**dimensions of
DIVERSITY**

Poverty often is mentioned as a key factor underlying the overrepresentation of ethnic minorities in special education. Skiba et al. (2005) studied the impact of poverty on representation in special education and found that its contribution was weaker than previously thought, and inconsistent. While poverty in U.S. society needs to be addressed, discriminatory practices within schools also need to be addressed.

the areas of letter identification, word recognition, oral reading, comprehension, and phonetic skills; a diagnostic test in math might include math computation, fractions, geometry, word problems, measurement, and time. Because individually administered diagnostic tests provide information on a range of specific skills, they can be useful as an information source in making educational decisions. For example, Tamara scored two years below grade level on the vocabulary subtest of an individually administered diagnostic test in reading. On the basis of this finding, the teacher of her Tier 2 RtI group added instruction in vocabulary taken from her American History text.

Although individually administered diagnostic tests may be more helpful than group-administered achievement tests, they are still subject to many of the same problems. Again, you should always verify findings from these tests using more informal measures based on the content you teach.

Psychological Tests

Psychological tests are used as part of the process of evaluating students with special needs, particularly to determine whether a student has intellectual or learning disabilities. Reports of the results of these tests are often written by school psychologists and consist of a summary of the findings and the implications for instruction. **Psychological tests** can include intelligence tests and tests related to learning disabilities (Overton, 2009; Salvia, Ysseldyke, & Bolt 2010).

The overall purpose of psychological tests is to measure abilities that affect how efficiently students learn in an instructional situation. These abilities are inferred based on student responses to items that the test author believes represent that particular ability. For example, comprehension, an important learning ability, is often assessed on psychological tests (Salvia et al., 2010). To test comprehension, students may be asked to read and answer questions about a series of directions or other tasks described in printed material. Student scores are then compared to a norm group of other same-age students, with an average score being 100. Other abilities commonly assessed by psychological tests include generalization (the ability to recognize similarities across objects, events, or vocabulary), general or background information, vocabulary, induction (the ability to figure out a rule or principle based on a series of situations), abstract reasoning, and memory (Salvia et al., 2010).

Psychological tests can be helpful if they clarify why students may not be learning in class and lead to effective changes in instruction. For example, the results of Tiffany's test showed that she had difficulty with visual memory. Her biology teacher, Ms. Fasbacher, felt that this was related to her poor performance in labeling parts of the human body on her tests. As a result, Ms. Fasbacher provided Tiffany with extra tutoring prior to each test. Interpreting the results of psychological reports seems less daunting if you follow these five general guidelines:

1. Do not be intimidated by the sometimes generous quantity of technical terms and jargon. You have the right to expect that reports be translated into instructionally relevant language.
2. In the event of discrepancies between psychological reports and your experience, do not automatically discount your experience. The results of psychological tests are most valid when corroborated by classroom experience. Keep in mind that your impressions are the result of many more hours of classroom observation than are psychological evaluations, which are based on fewer samples of student behavior and on samples that represent behavior that takes place outside the classroom.
3. Be sure to check the technical adequacy of the psychological tests included in your report. You may be surprised to find that many of these tests are not acceptable. The recent emphasis in RtI of using students' responses to instruction to identify learning disabilities further reinforces the importance of not relying solely on standardized tests.

---

fyi

Psychological tests may be better measures of expressive language skill, memory, fine motor abilities, and factual knowledge than of potential or reasoning ability (Marston et al., 2003). They also are time consuming to give and only indirectly related to daily classroom instruction.

INSTRUCTIONAL **EDGE**

Strategies for Fair Assessment of Diverse Students

Although today's teachers are much more aware of the possibility of bias in assessing poor students and students from culturally diverse backgrounds (Grossman, 1995), bias and discrimination continue to exist. The following two lists identify areas that can be problematic when assessing diverse students and provide strategies for assessing and interpreting their performance more accurately, respectively.

PROBLEM

1. Students may exhibit test anxiety due to lack of familiarity with the assessment process.
2. Students may lack motivation to perform well on tests because of differing cultural expectations.
3. Students may not respond to traditional motivators.
4. Students' test scores may be depressed because the assessor is unfamiliar or speaks a different language.
5. Students may have different communication styles; for example, they may not feel comfortable asking for help with directions or may respond using fewer words.
6. Students may be unwilling to take risks; for example, they may be reluctant to guess on a test even though it is to their benefit.
7. Students may be accustomed to working at a slower pace.
8. Students may lack exposure to test content.
9. Students may not be proficient in the language used for a test.
10. Students may speak with a dialect that differs from that of the assessor.

RECOMMENDATION

1. Give students practice tests.
2. Qualify test performance with class performance.

3. Individualize reinforcers; use individualistic, competitive, and cooperative goal structures.
4. Allow more time to establish rapport and gain trust.
5. Check for understanding of directions; avoid automatically penalizing students for not saying enough or not giving details.
6. Teach test-taking skills. For example, teach students strategies for when and how to make a best guess on a test.
7. Extend test-taking time to accommodate students' pace.
8. Eliminate unfamiliar content or do not give the test.
9. Assess students using both English and students' native language.
10. Do not count dialectical differences as errors; examine your attitudes about nonstandard dialects for potential bias.

RESEARCH NOTE

Abedi, Hofstetter, and Lord (2004) reviewed the research literature on the effectiveness of testing accommodations for English-language learners in the content areas of math, science, and social studies. The accommodations studied included assessing in the students' native language, modifying the level of English in questions, providing extra time, providing dictionaries and glossaries, and oral administration. In general, the researchers found evidence for the effectiveness of only two accommodations: (1) modifying the language (but not the content) of the test items by reducing low-frequency vocabulary and complex language structures and (2) providing students with definitions or simple paraphrases of potentially unfamiliar or difficult words on the test. Not surprisingly, the authors found that these accommodations helped all students, not just English-language learners. Research shows that curriculum-based assessment also works well with English-language learners, whether the assessment is in their native language or not (Deno, 2003).

---

4. Be sure to check for possible cultural bias. Psychological tests may discriminate against students from culturally diverse or disadvantaged backgrounds. The various ways in which psychological and other tests can be biased, along with suggestions for making them more fair, are presented in the Instructional Edge.
5. Keep in mind that the primary purpose of psychological tests is to establish possible explanations for particular learning, behavioral, or social and emotional problems. Such explanations should be springboards for helping students overcome these problems, not excuses for students' lack of achievement.

Alternate Assessments

As you have learned, IDEA and NCLB require states to include students with disabilities in statewide and districtwide educational assessments. Although most students with disabilities are able to participate when given appropriate accommodations, a small percentage of students are entitled to alternate assessments. The most common group of students taking **alternate assessments** are the 1% of all students with disabilities who typically work on a more individualized curriculum and do not have to meet the

dimensions of DIVERSITY

Psychological tests can be biased against students from diverse backgrounds. Use them only in conjunction with other formal and informal measures.

www.resources

The home page for the National Council on Measurement in Education (NCME), http://www.ncme.org, provides information on the organization and links to other relevant measurement-related websites.

Students with more severe disabilities participate in alternate assessments that stress authentic skills and experiences in real-life environments. What skills do you think are being assessed here? Robin Sachs/PhotoEdit Inc.

 fyi

The NCEO offers these recommendations for developing alternate assessments: (a) define its purpose and identify who is qualified to participate; (b) identify the common core of learning such as what students need to know and be able to do; (c) develop participation guidelines; (d) determine how results are organized and summarized; and (e) integrate results with the general assessment.

fyi

The results of alternate assessments are included when determining whether students in a district are making adequate progress.

same requirements as those students graduating with a standard diploma. In other words, they are required to meet the same broad standards as your other students, but they meet them in different, more basic ways. For example, one of the standards in Ms. Barber's state is that students develop an appreciation for literature. One of the ways that Darrell, a student with a significant intellectual disability, meets that standard is by watching a video of *Oliver Twist* and answering questions using his communication board. School districts may provide this option to up to 1 percent of their students.

While most school districts began using alternate assessments in 2002, the year required for implementation by IDEA, recent research has revealed that guidelines for conducting alternate assessments are still evolving (Towles-Reeves, Kleinert, & Muhomba, 2009). Alternate assessment information can be collected in a number of ways including (1) a portfolio or collection of student work gathered to demonstrate student performance on specific skills and knowledge; (2) an IEP-linked body of evidence or collection of work, similar to a portfolio, demonstrating student performance on standards-based IEP goals and objectives; (3) a performance assessment or direct measures of a student's skill, usually in a one-on-one assessment; (4) a checklist of skills reviewed by persons familiar with the student; and (5) a traditional test requiring student responses, typically with a correct and incorrect forced-choice answer format (Browder, Wakeman, & Flowers, 2006; Towles-Reeves et al., 2009).

The system of alternate assessment used by the state of Kentucky is a good example of a portfolio system (Kleinert & Kearns, 2004). In Kentucky, all students, regardless of disability, are required to meet standards in a range of areas, including using patterns to understand past and present events and to predict future events; using technology effectively; demonstrating knowledge, skills, and values that have lifetime implications for involvement in physical activity; and completing a postsecondary opportunities search (Kearns, Kleinert, Clayton, Burdge, & Williams, 1998). Although the portfolios reflect the same set of outcomes for all students, students with significant intellectual disabilities meet them in different ways. For example, Damon met the standard of completing a search for postsecondary opportunities by compiling a list of his work preferences and specific jobs aligned with his preferences. Sibilie demonstrated her effective use of technology by using an augmentative communication device across a range of school and community settings. Carolyn, a student with multiple disabilities, demonstrated achievement in skills and values related to physical activity by participating in a volleyball game in physical education class. Linus demonstrated his ability to use patterns to understand events by recognizing that on days when his paraprofessional wasn't in school he had less time to get ready for recess.

Here are three questions considered when using alternate assessments with students with severe disabilities:

1. *What are the district's eligibility requirements for alternate assessments?* Keep in mind that only a small number of students have disabilities so severe that they are eligible. The decision to give an alternate assessment should not be based on whether the student is expected to do poorly on the general education assessment.

2. *Is the focus of the assessment on authentic skills and on assessing experiences in community or real-life environments?* For a younger child the community might mean the school, playground, or home; for a high school senior the community might mean the store, bank, or other commercial or public sites.

3. *Is the assessment aligned with state standards?* The skills assessed should have a meaningful relationship to content areas covered by the standards, such as reading and math. For example, one of Clifford's IEP goals in language is to communicate by pointing to pictures on a communication board. Chatrice is learning to give correct coins to the bus driver as a way to meet the math standards. As the general education teacher who is responsible for students' meeting the regular state standards, you may be in the best position to answer this question of standards alignment.

Up to 2 percent of students with disabilities can take alternate assessments based on modified academic achievement standards (U.S. Department of Education, 2007). This alternate assessment option is intended for students whose disabilities have prevented them from achieving grade-level proficiency and who are not likely to reach grade-level achievement within the same timeframe as their classmates without disabilities. Before this provision was added, these students either had to take the grade-level assessment, which often was too difficult, or an alternate assessment intended for students with severe intellectual disabilities, which was too easy.

When the modified academic achievement standards option is used, curricular goals are aligned with grade-level content standards, but the level of achievement expected may be simplified. For example, Josh needs to demonstrate meeting the seventh-grade language arts standard of analyzing how literary elements affect the meaning of text, such as the influence of setting on the conflict and its resolution. Josh does so by reading an easier version of *Swiss Family Robinson* and answering comprehension questions that have lower cognitive demand. It is the responsibility of the IEP team to determine eligibility for this alternate assessment option.

Curriculum-Based Assessments

Because of the limited utility of standardized achievement tests and psychological reports for making day-to-day instructional decisions, you need other tools in order to be a partner in the evaluation process. **Curriculum-based assessment (CBA)** is an effective option that in many instances can be an alternative to standardized tests. CBA has been defined as a method of measuring students' level of achievement in terms of what they are taught in the classroom (for example, Deno, 2003; Hosp, 2008; Tucker, 1985). In CBA, student performance also is measured repeatedly over time, and the results are used to guide instruction (Hosp & Hosp, 2003; Tucker, 1985). CBA has a number of attractive features. When using CBA, you select the skills that are assessed based on what you teach in class, thus ensuring a match between what is taught and what is tested. This match makes CBA measures accurate indicators of student access to the general education curriculum and ideal for use in prereferral or response to intervention (RtI) systems. **Curriculum-based measurement (CBM)** is a particular kind of curriculum-based assessment. CBM is characterized by

www.resources

Learn about the National Assessment of Educational Progress (NAEP), the only ongoing national test of academic progress, at http://www.nagb.org.

fyi

Some states allow students who do not have significant intellectual disabilities but who are reading below grade level to take high-stakes tests at their reading level rather than their grade level. This use of out-of-level testing is not allowed in federal ESEA regulations. The government recommends using alternate assessments with modified standards instead.

a research base establishing its technical adequacy, as well as standardized measurement tasks and scoring procedures that are fluency based (Deno, 2003).

In the chapter-opening vignette, before referring Rob for special education eligibility determination, Ms. Lyons gave him some curriculum-based assessments in math to determine the specific kinds of problems he was having. She then implemented a peer-tutoring program and used these same tests to measure its effectiveness. Mr. Blount used an informal reading assessment based on his U.S. history textbook to see how well his students were able to read the text. Research shows that when teachers use CBA to evaluate student progress and adjust their instruction accordingly, student achievement increases significantly (Deno, 2003; Fuchs, Fuchs, Hamlett, & Stecker, 1991; Shinn, Collins, & Gallagher, 1998).

What Kinds of Curriculum-Based Assessments Can You Create for Your Students?

Two major kinds of CBAs are commonly used: probes of basic academic skills (for example, reading, math, and writing) and probes of content-area knowledge and learning strategies (for example, vocabulary knowledge, prerequisite skills, textbook reading, and note taking). Although probes of basic academic skills relate more directly to elementary school teachers and probes of content-area knowledge and learning strategies to middle and high school teachers, each of these measures is relevant for both groups. For example, high school students need to perform basic skills fluently if they are to have ready access to curriculum content; elementary school students need early training in learning strategies to make the difficult transition to middle and high school instruction easier.

Probes of Basic Academic Skills

Probes are quick and easy measures of student performance in the basic skill areas of reading, math, and written expression. They consist of timed samples of academic behaviors and are designed to assess skill accuracy and fluency. Probes can sample a range of skills in a particular area, as in a mixed probe of fifth-grade math computation

These teachers are using information from assessment probes to make decisions about their students with special needs. How can you use assessment probes to make decisions in your area of teaching? David Young-Wolff/PhotoEdit Inc.

problems in addition, subtraction, multiplication, and division; or they can sample one skill area, such as letter identification or writing lowercase manuscript letters.

Typically, students work on probe sheets for one minute. The teacher then records the rate of correct and incorrect responses as well as any error patterns. Student performance rates have been shown to be useful for making many of the important evaluation decisions described earlier in the chapter: screening, diagnosis, program placement, curriculum placement, instructional evaluation, and program evaluation (Deno, 2003; Hosp, 2008). The Professional Edge describes the importance of considering both student accuracy and student fluency when assessing basic academic skills.

Probes are classified according to how students take in task information (for example, seeing or hearing) and how they respond (for example, writing or speaking). They include four major types: see-say, see-write, hear-write, and think-write. For example, when reading orally from a textbook, students *see* the text and *say* the words. Hence, oral reading is referred to as a see-say probe. Similarly, in a spelling probe, students *hear* the teacher dictate words and *write* the words as they are dictated. This is a hear-write probe. As you develop CBAs, keep in mind the following three suggestions:

1. Identify academic skills that are essential in your particular course or grade. In the elementary grades, include skills in handwriting, spelling, written expression, reading (for example, letter identification, letter sounds, oral reading accuracy, and comprehension), and math (for example, number identification, computation, problem solving, time, and money). In secondary courses these could include key vocabulary, prerequisite skills, and independent learning skills.
2. Select skills representing a *sample* of skills that are taught, not necessarily every skill. Performance on these skills then acts as a checkpoint for identifying students in trouble or measuring student progress. For example, in assessing reading performance, having students read a passage aloud from their reading or literature book and then answer comprehension questions may not represent all the reading skills you have taught (such as words in isolation), but it will include a representative sample of many of these skills.
3. Even though CBA is considered informal assessment, its utility in helping to make instructional decisions depends on the teacher's keeping the difficulty level of the assessment items, as well as the administration and scoring procedures, consistent over time (Deno, 2003; Deno et al., 2009). For example, Ms. Solomon was concerned because her students were using the same words over and over in their writing. After showing them various strategies for increasing their variety of words used, she monitored their progress by taking a writing sample every month and measuring the percentage of different words they used.
4. Remember, curriculum-based assessment has been used successfully by teachers for many years. Therefore, assessments as well as norms or benchmarks may already exist for many of the skills you are teaching.

Probes of Reading Skills The critical reading skills in the elementary years include phonemic awareness, letter sounds, word recognition, vocabulary, and comprehension. Phonemic awareness can be measured using a hear-say probe. Student ability to identify letter names and sounds can be assessed using a see-say probe. Word recognition and comprehension can be assessed using a see-say oral passage reading probe, such as the one in Figure 4.1.

Maze assessments (Shinn, Deno, & Espin, 2000) are curriculum-based measures for assessing reading comprehension that can be given either in groups or using a computer. Maze assessments are graded passages in which every seventh word is deleted; in place of each deleted word are three choices. One of the choices is the correct choice and the other two are distracters. Students read the passage silently and circle the answers they think are correct. Unlike most curriculum-based measures,

PROFESSIONAL **EDGE**

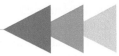

Assessing Student Fluency on Basic Academic Skills

When basic skills or other academic content is assessed informally in the classroom, *student accuracy* is usually stressed. For example, we say that Jill formed 85 percent of her cursive letters correctly, John was 90 percent accurate on his addition facts, or Al identified key pieces of lab equipment with 100 percent accuracy. Although accuracy is important because it tells us whether a student has acquired a skill or section of content, accuracy is not the only useful index of pupil performance. *Student fluency,* or how quickly a student is able to perform a skill or recall academic material, is also relevant. Before you consider the reasons for assessing student fluency provided here, consider this: If your car needed service and you had your choice between two mechanics, both of whom did accurate work and charged $85 an hour but one of whom worked twice as fast as the other, which mechanic would you choose?

THE RATE RATIONALE

1. Students who are proficient in a skill are more likely to remember the skill, even if they do not need to use it very often. If they forget the skill, they need less time to relearn it.
2. Students who are proficient in a basic skill are better able to master more advanced skills. For example, students who can perform addition problems fluently often acquire advanced multiplication skills more easily.
3. Performance of basic skills at an automatic level frees students to perform higher level skills more readily. For example, students who can read fluently with understanding are more likely to be successful in high school classes that require reading lengthy textbook assignments in little time. Students who know their math facts without counting on their fingers can solve word problems more efficiently.
4. Students with special needs are often so labeled because they work more slowly than their peers. Fluency scores allow teachers to compare these students directly with their classmates on this important dimension of speed; they also provide a useful index of student progress, including, for some students, the extent to which supports are needed to access the general education curriculum.

USING THE RESEARCH

If you are interested in learning how your students' oral reading rates compare to national norms, Hasbrouck and Tindal (2006) have compiled national norms based on student oral reading fluency scores from multiple school districts across the country. These norms are shown in the accompanying table. Notice that separate norms

are presented for fall, winter, and spring to account for student growth during the year. So if Simone is reading 80 words correct per minute in February of second grade, she is reading above the 50th percentile for winter of grade 2.

Oral Reading Fluency Norms, Grades 1–8

Grade	Percentile	Fall WCPM	Winter WCPM	Spring WCPM
1	75		47	82
	50		23	53
	25		12	28
2	75	79	100	117
	50	51	72	89
	25	25	42	61
3	75	99	120	137
	50	71	92	107
	25	44	62	78
4	75	119	139	152
	50	94	112	123
	25	68	87	98
5	75	139	156	168
	50	110	127	139
	25	85	99	109
6	75	153	167	177
	50	127	140	150
	25	98	111	122
7	75	156	165	177
	50	128	136	150
	25	102	109	123
8	75	161	173	177
	50	133	146	151
	25	106	115	124

WCPM: Words correct per minute
SD: Standard deviation
Count: Number of student scores

Source: From "Oral reading fluency norms: A valuable assessment tool for reading teachers," by Jan Hasbrouck and Gerald Tindal, *The Reading Teacher, 59*(7), 636–644. Copyright 2006 by the International Reading Association. Reprinted with permission of the International Reading Association (http://www.reading.org) via Copyright Clearance Center.

maze assessments are not timed. The number or percentage of correct responses is scored. Research has shown that maze assessments are an effective, time-saving way of monitoring student progress in reading comprehension (Deno et al., 2009; Shinn et al., 2000).

If you are having your students read trade books, you may need to design your own questions, which can be a difficult task. Carnine, Silbert, Kame'enui, and Tarver (2010) have suggested one practical model for designing comprehension questions,

FIGURE 4.1 See-Say Probe: Oral Passage Reading

Time	1 minute
Materials	*Student*—Stimulus passage *Examiner*—Duplicate copy of stimulus passage, pencil, timer
Directions to Student	"When I say 'Please begin,' read this story out loud to me. Start here [examiner points] and read as quickly and carefully as you can. Try to say each word. Ready? Please begin."
Scoring	As the student reads, place a mark (/) on your copy over any errors (mispronunciations, words skipped, and words given). (If student hesitates for three seconds, give him the word and mark it as an error.) If student inserts words, self-corrects, sounds out, or repeats, do not count as errors. When the student has read for one minute, place a bracket ( ]) on your copy to indicate how far the student read in one minute. (It is usually good practice to let students finish the paragraph or page they are reading rather than stopping them immediately when one minute is over.) Count the total number of words read during the one-minute sample. Tally the total number of errors (words mispronounced, words skipped, and words given) made during the sample. Subtract the total number of errors from the total words covered to get number correct (total words – errors = correct words per minute).

If students complete the passage before the minute is up, compute student rate using this formula:

$$\frac{\text{\#correct words}}{\text{seconds}} \times \frac{60}{1} = \text{correct words per minute}$$

Note	Probe is administered individually. If you use the optional comprehension questions, be sure to have students finish the passage first.

Billy decided to go down by the river and	(9)
demonstrate his fishing ability. He always could deceive	(17)
the fish with his special secret lure. He had his best	(28)
luck in his own place, a wooded shady spot downstream	(38)
that no one knew about. Today he was going to try	(49)
to catch a catfish all the boys called Old Gray. Old Gray	(61)
was a legend in this town, because even though many boys	(72)
had hooked him, he always managed to get away.	(81)
This time Billy knew that if he sat long enough, he could	(93)
catch his dream fish!	(97)

1. Who is the main character in this story?

2. Where does the story take place?

3. What problem is Billy trying to solve?

4. How is Billy going to try to solve the problem?

5. What do you think is going to happen?

Source: From *Curriculum-Based Assessment and Instructional Design,* by E. Lessen, M. Sommers, and W. D. Bursuck, 1987, DeKalb, IL: DeKalb County Special Education Association. Used with permission.

Using Story Grammars

Ms. Padilla's second-grade students have just read the story *The Funny Farola,* by Ann Miranda and Maria Guerrero. The story is about a girl and her family participating in an ethnic festival in their city. The girl, Dora, makes a *farola,* which is a type of lantern people carry while marching in a parade. Dora's family laughs at her farola, because it is in the shape of a frog. However, her unusual farola saves the day when it helps Dora and her parents find Dora's lost brother and sister. Ms. Padilla is assessing Chantille's comprehension of the story using the story grammar retelling format.

Ms. Padilla: Chantille, you have just read *The Funny Farola.* Would you tell me in your own words what the story is about?

Chantille: The story is about a girl named Dora who made this funny frog that she carried in a parade. You see, her brother and sister got lost at the parade 'cause they were having such a good time, but they got found again 'cause they could see Dora's frog.

Ms. Padilla: Chantille, where does this story take place?

Chantille: It took place in a city and the people were having a big festival. That's why they were having the parade.

Ms. Padilla: Chantille, what was the problem with Dora's frog?

Chantille: Well, it was called a *farola,* which is a kind of lantern. Everyone was making them for the parade. Dora's family laughed at her farola 'cause they had never seen a frog farola before.

Ms. Padilla: You said that Dora's sister and brother got lost. What did they do to solve that problem?

Chantille: Well, they saw Dora's frog, so they knew where to find them.

Ms. Padilla: How did you feel at the end of the story?

Chantille: I felt happy.

Ms. Padilla: Why did you feel happy?

Chantille: Well, 'cause Dora's brother and sister found their mom and dad.

Ms. Padilla: Chantille, what lesson do you think this story teaches us?

Chantille: Not to get lost from your mom and dad.

A score sheet that Ms. Padilla completed for Chantille is shown in the accompanying figure. A plus (+) means that Chantille responded accurately to that element without any prompting or questioning; a check mark (✓) means that Chantille mentioned the element after she was questioned or prompted; a minus (−) means that she failed to refer to the element even after questioning or prompts. Look at Chantille's scores. As you can see, she had a good idea of who the main characters were and received a + for this component (Characters). Chantille named two problems in the story: Dora making a farola that her family laughed at, and Dora's brother and sister getting lost. Chantille identified the problem of the lost kids without being prompted, and the problem of the funny farola with prompts; thus, a + and a ✓ were scored for Goal/Problem.

Story Grammar Retelling Checklist

Student Name	Story Elements Evaluated												
	Theme		Setting		Characters		Goal/Problem		Attempts		Resolution		Reactions
Chantille	−		✓		+		+	✓	−		+		+

+ Responded correctly without prompting
✓ Responded correctly after prompting
− Did not identify relevant story component

It was unclear from Chantille's response exactly how the characters tried to solve their problem, so she received a − for Attempts. Chantille did say the problem was solved when Dora's brother and sister saw the frog; she received a + for this element of Resolution. However, she did not say how this resolved the problem of her family laughing at the farola, so she received a −. Chantille's reaction to the story was appropriate, so a + was scored. For Setting, Chantille received a ✓; she identified the setting after Ms. Padilla prompted her. Finally, Chantille received a − for Theme. This response was lacking, even after prompting.

Notice that Ms. Padilla's prompts included explicit references to the various story grammar components. For example, she asked, "You said that Dora's sister and brother got lost. What did they do to solve that problem?" as opposed to asking a more general question, such as "What happened to Dora's sister and brother?" This use of specific language makes the story grammar components more clear, a necessary structure for younger, more naïve learners.

REFLECTION

How could story retellings be incorporated into a classroom literature-based program? How do you think these results will be helpful to Ms. Padilla?

based on story grammar. *Story grammar* is simply the description of the typical elements found frequently in stories. These include theme, setting, character, initiating events, conflict, attempts at resolution, resolution, and reactions. These elements can be used to create comprehension questions that may be more appropriate than traditional main idea and detail questions, because story grammar describes the organization of most stories that elementary school students are likely to read. The Case in Practice shows how a teacher uses story grammar with one of her second-grade students.

At times, you might not wish to ask questions about a story. Specific questions can give students clues to the answers, and they especially help students identify the information you think is important to remember or the way you organize this information. One way to solve this problem is to have students retell stories after they read them. Students themselves then must organize the information they think is important, and you can evaluate the completeness of their recall. Such a situation has two requirements for effective evaluation to occur: a standard set of criteria to evaluate the completeness of the retelling, and the opportunity to evaluate each student's retelling individually.

Probes of Written Expression   Written expression can be assessed using a think-write probe. In this probe, the teacher reads the students a story starter. The students then have one minute to plan a story and three minutes to write it. This probe can be scored in a number of different ways depending on the decisions you will be making. If you are merely interested in screening students for serious writing difficulty, use the number of intelligible words the student is able to write per minute (total words written, or TWW; Powell-Smith & Shinn, 2004). Intelligible words are those that make sense in the story. Norms for this written expression probe are available at this website: http://www.aimsweb.com/measures/written/norms.php. You can modify this measure to make it more appropriate for students in kindergarten and first grade by having them write only two sentences in response to the story starter (Coker & Ritchey, 2010). For students in high school, extending the length of time for writing to 7–10 minutes improves the accuracy and usefulness of the results (Espin, Wallace, Campbell, Lembke, Long, & Ticha, 2008). If you are interested in measuring the overall quality of the writing as well as collecting other diagnostic information, such as grammar usage, spelling, handwriting, punctuation, vocabulary, organization, or ideas, you can score this probe differently or give another probe designed to measure these areas specifically (see Hessler, Conrad, & Alber-Morgan, 2009; Howell & Morehead, 1993; Mercer, Mercer, & Pullen, 2011; and Vaughn & Bos, 2009 for sample informal assessments in these areas).

Probes of Math Skills   Teachers need to measure student math skills in two general areas: computation and concepts. Math computation includes operations in addition, subtraction, multiplication, and division, including math facts in each of these areas. Essential math concepts include money, measurement, word problems, graphs/charts, and geometry. See-write probes for both computation and problem solving have been developed and can be used for making the key special education decisions you have been learning about in this chapter (see Fuchs, Hamlett, & Fuchs, 1998; Fuchs, Hamlett, & Fuchs, 1999; and Howell & Morehead, 1993). Of course, other types of probes might be needed such as think-write probes to measure number-writing skills, and see-say probes for skills such as the identification of numbers, coins, and geometric figures. For those teaching middle and high school math, Foegen (2008) has developed see-write probes to monitor progress in algebra.

Curriculum-Based Assessments in Content Areas

Although content-area teachers can use CBA probes to test student knowledge of subject matter (see Figure 4.2), they may need to take a somewhat different approach to student assessment. Content-area classrooms are characterized by high curricular demands with fewer opportunities for individualization; students are also expected

RESEARCH NOTE

Allinder, Bolling, Oats, and Gagnon (2000) found that students of teachers who regularly asked themselves the following questions when giving curriculum-based measures made more academic progress in math computation: On what skills has the student done well during the last two weeks? What skills should be targeted for the next two weeks? How will I attempt to improve student performance on the targeted skills?

RESEARCH NOTE

Clarke, Baker, Smolkowski, & Chard (2008) developed and tested four curriculum-based measures in math that can be used for universal screening and progress monitoring in RtI: oral counting, number identification, quantity discrimination, and missing number.

FIGURE 4.2 Using Curriculum-Based Assessment (CBA) Probes in Content Areas

Content Area	CBA Examples
Geography	Identify each state's location on a map by writing the correct state abbreviation.
	Match the terrain of an area to corresponding industries and products.
	Compare and contrast regions so that two similarities and two differences are provided.
Science	Given science terms to define, write the correct definitions.
	Identify steps in the scientific process, and describe how to apply each step to a given hypothesis.
	Describe the human body systems so that each system's function and relationship to other systems is stated.

Source: From "Applying Curriculum-Based Assessment in Inclusive Settings," by M. King-Sears, M. Burgess, and T. Lawson, *Teaching Exceptional Children, 32*(1), 1999, pp. 30–38. Copyright 1999 by The Council for Exceptional Children. Reprinted with permission.

to take responsibility for learning much of the material on their own. While IDEA and ESEA clearly state that the curricular expectations for most students with disabilities are the same as for their classmates without disabilities, students who enter a class significantly behind their classmates in either background knowledge or independent learning skills are likely to struggle. Thus, it is important to identify these students early so that they can be better prepared when they enter a content-area class. For example, at the beginning of this chapter, Mr. Blount assessed his U.S. history students' ability to read the class textbook independently because students in his class were expected to read much of the material on their own.

Assessments of Prerequisite Skills   Teachers can find out whether their students possess the knowledge and skills needed to be successful in their classes by using assessments of prerequisite skills. For example, the English department at a high school developed a test of prerequisite skills for ninth-grade English. All students were given this test at the beginning of the year to see what material needed to be reviewed in the first month of school.

The process of developing assessments of prerequisite skills is similar to the process of developing curriculum-based probes described previously in this chapter. This process consists of the following four steps:

1. Identify critical content learning or skills for your class.
2. Identify entry-level content or skills needed. Be certain these are not skills for which a bypass strategy is possible.
3. Develop a measure to assess the identified skills.
4. Administer the measure to your current class. If most of the class is unable to pass the test, you will need to teach and/or review the prerequisite skills or knowledge to the entire class prior to introducing new course material. If only a few students lack the prerequisites, then you will need to arrange for extra tutoring for them. If your school is doing RtI, this extra help could take place in a Tier 2 or Tier 3 instructional group.

Measures of Independent Learning Skills   When students enter high school, they find an environment often not as supportive as the smaller elementary and junior high or middle school environments they left. The student body is often larger and more diverse. Daily routines change and curriculum is more difficult

fyi

King-Sears, Burgess, and Lawson (1999) suggest using the following steps, abbreviated as the mnemonic APPLY, when using CBA in your classroom: Analyze the curriculum, prepare items to meet curriculum objectives, probe frequently, load data using a graph format, and yield to results for making revisions and decisions.

(Sabornie & deBettencourt, 2009). High schools also demand a much higher level of student independence through the application of a range of independent learning skills. These skills, often referred to as *learning strategies,* include note taking, textbook reading, test taking, written expression, and time management. A student's ability to perform these various skills independently can make the difference between passing or failing a class. For example, at the beginning of the chapter, Mr. Blount decided to assess textbook-reading skills because these were important for success in his class. A sample instrument to measure textbook-reading skills, which was originally developed by Voix (1968) and later adapted by Lessen, Sommers, and Bursuck (1987), is shown in Figure 4.3. Notice that the reading tasks for this measure are taken directly from the students' history and science textbooks. Doing this ensures that the results will be relevant for the particular classroom situation. Note also that this textbook-reading assessment can be given to the entire classroom at once, enabling the assessment of many students who have trouble reading their textbooks, not just students with special needs.

When students enter high school, they are likely to face demands for a higher level of independence and responsibility for their own learning. Ken Karp/Prentice Hall School Division

As with the basic and prerequisite skills mentioned previously, probes can be developed to assess independent learning. A key consideration is that the tasks used for assessment should parallel the tasks students are faced with in your classroom: If you are evaluating textbook reading, the reading task should come from the textbook you are using in class; if you are measuring a student's ability to take lecture notes, the task should involve elements similar to a typical lecture delivered in your class.

Once the task has been selected, next decide what kind of measure to use. Three possible choices are direct observation checklists, analysis of student products, and student self-evaluation. With *direct observation checklists,* the teacher develops a list of observable steps necessary to perform a given strategy. Next, the teacher has a student perform a classroom task that requires her to use the strategy and records which behaviors the student performed on the checklist.

Although direct observation of student behavior can provide much more useful information, it is time consuming, particularly when you are a high school teacher who teaches many students each day. For most students, you can use analysis of student products or student self-evaluations. Nonetheless, if you have the luxury of a free moment with an individual student, such as before or after school or during a study hall, the time spent directly observing a student perform a task is very worthwhile.

Analysis of student products involves looking at student notebooks, tests, papers, and other assignments or written activities to find evidence of effective or ineffective strategy performance. In most cases, you can evaluate your whole classroom at once, and you do not have to score the products while you are teaching.

In *student self-evaluations,* students perform a task such as taking a test, are given a checklist of strategy steps, and are then asked to tell which of these steps they used (Mercer, Mercer, & Pullen, 2011; Miller, 1996). Student self-reports are useful for several reasons. They can provide information about strategy behaviors that cannot be directly observed. Student evaluations also stimulate student self-monitoring, a behavior critical for independent learning. Self-report measures can also include interview questions that further clarify strategy usage. For example, one teacher asked, "What was the first thing you did when you received your test?" As with all measures, student self-evaluations need to be corroborated by information from other sources (for example, direct observation checklists and student products). Such corroboration may be particularly important for students with special needs, many of whom have difficulty evaluating their own behavior.

FIGURE 4.3 Evaluating Content-Area Textbook-Reading Skills

Suggestions for specific types of questions are included here. The text in parentheses explains or offers additional information about a particular item.

Using Parts of the Book

1. On what page would you find the chapter called _____? (Tests ability to use table of contents.)

2. Of what value to you are the questions listed at the end of each chapter? (Tests understanding of a specific study aid.)

3. How are the chapters arranged or grouped? (Tests knowledge of text organization.)

4. What part of the book would you use to find the page reference for the topic _____? (Tests knowledge of index.)

5. On what page would you find the answer to each of the following questions? (Tests ability to use index.)

Using Source Materials

1. What library aid tells you the library number of a book so that you are able to find the book on the shelves? (Tests knowledge of functions of cataloging systems.)

2. What is a biography? (Tests knowledge of a type of reference book.)

3. Explain the difference between science fiction and factual science materials. (Tests knowledge of important types of science materials.)

Comprehension

These questions would be based on a three- or four-page selection from the textbook.

Vocabulary

1. Turn to page _____. How does the author define the word _____? (Tests ability to use context clues and the aids the author uses to convey the meaning of a word.)

2. Define _____.

3. What is a _____?

4. *Vocabulary in context:* From the paragraph on page 584 beginning "In Poland, the Soviet Union . . . ," write an appropriate and brief definition of each of the following words: _____, _____, and _____.

Noting Main Ideas

These questions would ask for main points of information, such as the main ideas of longer, important paragraphs of a chapter or the summary of an experiment. (*Examples:* What are atoms composed of? What reason was given for the conservation of human resources? What is the result of the photosynthetic process?)

Noting Details

These questions should ask for specific bits of information, such as an aspect of a process, the application of a law, the principal steps in an experiment, a life cycle, or incidents in the life of a scientist. (*Examples:* Describe the photosynthetic process. What are the different stages in the cycle of precipitation and evaporation? List the major incidents in the life of Marie Curie.)

Drawing Conclusions

Ask questions about the significance or value of a finding, the implication of a description of some species or natural phenomenon, causes and effects, or a comparison of two or more types of organisms. The questions should call for answers that are not stated in the text. (*Examples:* Illustrate the term *balance of life*. What conclusion can you draw from the importance of the photosynthetic process? What is the principal difference between mitosis and meiosis?)

Applying Theoretical Information

These questions would ask for examples of practical uses of scientific law and principles. (*Examples:* Explain the relationship of photosynthesis to the conservation of plant life. Explain the idea that air confined in a small area exerts pressure in all directions in relation to the action of air in a football.)

Following Directions

These questions would ask learners to show the sequence of steps or ideas for solving a problem or performing an experiment or the sequence of a chain of events. (*Examples:* What is the second step of the experiment? What should you do after you have placed the flask over the burner?)

FIGURE 4.3 Evaluating Content-Area Textbook-Reading Skills *(Continued)*

Understanding Formulas and Symbols

These questions test student understanding of how symbols and formulas are used with scientific data. (*Examples:* What does the H refer to in the symbol H_2O? What does 40# mean?)

Maps and Graphs

Use questions that require knowledge of map and graph symbols and how to use them. (*Examples:* Use the graph on page 602 to answer these questions: By 1925, how many millions of people inhabited Earth? How many times over will the world population have increased from 2000 to 2050? Use the map on page 174 to answer these questions: Who ruled Gascony in the 12th century? Who governed the major portion of Flanders after 1550?)

Study Reading

Directions: Read pages 584–586. Take notes. Then, close your book and keep it closed. However, you may use the notes you made to help you answer the following questions. (Have questions on a separate sheet for distribution after notes have been made.) *Note:* Ask detail, main idea, and inference questions.

Sources: Adapted from *Evaluating Reading and Study Skills in the Secondary Classroom: A Guide for Content Teachers*, by R. G. Voix, 1968, Newark, DE: International Reading Association. Copyright 1968 by the International Reading Association. Reprinted with permission.

How Are Curriculum-Based Probes Used to Make Special Education Decisions?

Academic probes can help teachers make many of the assessment decisions discussed previously in this chapter. Several examples are discussed in the following sections.

Peer Comparison in Screening

The key question involved in screening is whether a student is different enough from his peers on important skills in a given academic area (or areas) to indicate that some form of accommodation is necessary. In an RtI school this may mean providing more intensive instruction for a student in a small Tier 2 group. If the difference between a student and his peers continues or worsens despite repeated attempts in the classroom to remediate, placement in a more intensive tier or referral to special education and a more comprehensive assessment may be necessary.

When screening, first select probes in the area(s) of suspected difficulty. Next, give the assessment to the student in question and compare his or her performance to benchmark or norm levels to find out the extent of the achievement gap. Benchmarks or norms are available for probes in most basic skill areas (see WWW Resources on this page). You might also want to assess your entire class to identify other students at risk and obtain valuable feedback about the overall effectiveness of your teaching.

Note the results of an oral reading fluency probe given by a third-grade teacher to his entire class in April, shown in Figure 4.4. Each score represents the number of correct words read orally per minute from a grade-level passage in the classroom reading program. The teacher was particularly interested in the performance of the student who ended up scoring 50 words correct per minute. According to the norms shown on page 114, this student is well below the 25th percentile score for this time of year of 78 words correct per minute, a definite sign of being at risk. Although this student may need extra support from the general education teacher or even a referral for special education eligibility determination, other factors should also be

www.resources

For CBM norms in reading, early literacy, spelling, early numeracy, written expression, and math, go to http://www.aimsweb.com/com/measures. For benchmarks in early literacy skills, go to http://dibels.uoregon.edu/measures.

FIGURE 4.4 Classroom Performance on Academic Skill Probe in Reading

Grade 3, Reading Orally in Context, April 2006

Number of correct words per minute read orally

190	136	103
189	128	99
172	125	97
160	123	86
159	120	84
151	119	80
139	119	50*
136	117	

Median 123
Median/2 61.5
*Denotes score of median/2 or lower

www.resources

The Center for Innovations at the University of Missouri (http://www .cise.missouri.edu/links/research-cbm-links.html) provides teachers with a wealth of resources to help implement research-based practices related to curriculum-based measurement.

considered, including how he performs across other academic skills assessed and whether other students in the class are having similar problems. This low score did prompt the teacher to seek prereferral consultation to get ideas for improving the student's reading performance. The teacher also planned to regularly monitor the student's progress in oral reading fluency to help guide future decision making about his program.

Note that three other students in the class scored 10 or more words below 97, the 50th percentile. According to Hasbrouck and Tindal (2006), this puts them at some risk in reading. The teacher decided to monitor the progress of these students more regularly while also providing them with a peer-tutoring program to give them extra practice in reading fluency. Finally, the teacher learned from this experience that 19 of his 23 students were achieving at acceptable levels on an important indicator of reading ability.

If benchmarks do not exist for the assessment selected, compare the performance of the student in question to half the median of the entire class or a subsample of the class (for example, five average performers). The median, or middlemost score, is used to summarize the scores because it is affected less by extreme scores than is the mean, or average, which could over- or underestimate the performance of the group as a whole. The teacher in Figure 4.4 used a score equal to one-half the median as a cutoff for identifying students who are having trouble with that particular skill (Shinn & Hubbard, 1992). Such a cutoff point typically identifies 6 to 12 percent of a class or grade level that may be experiencing difficulty with a particular skill (Bursuck & Lessen, 1987; Marston, Tindal, & Deno, 1984). As shown, the class scores range from a high of 190 words read correctly per minute to a low of 50 words read correctly per minute. The median, or middlemost, score for the class is 123 words read correctly per minute. A score of 61.5 words read correctly per minute is half the median. Our student in question was the only student scoring below this point. Deno et al. (2002) have shown that using the bottom 20 percent of a class can also be helpful in identifying students who are at risk. Finally, if this teacher were in an RtI school, the students at risk would have been identified earlier as part of schoolwide universal screening. The teacher would have also had the option of placing students into more intensive instructional tiers if needed. The Technology Notes illustrates a way to use software to evaluate the performance of your students.

Computerized Curriculum-Based Measurement

You may be wondering how you are going to assess your students systematically and still have time to prepare and teach your lessons. Researchers have developed a product that may help you (Fuchs, Hamlett, & Fuchs, 1998). They have developed software that makes scoring and interpreting curriculum-based measures in math much easier. In the system of Fuchs et al., students take a weekly probe test that measures required math operations for a given grade level. Students then are taught to enter their own data into a computer program that scores their test and summarizes the results.

The software program summarizes student performance using a display like the one shown in the accompanying figure. The graph shows the student's rate and accuracy on weekly math tests over time. This student (Sheila Hemmer) went from a score of 10 digits correct per minute at the beginning of October to a score of more than 30 digits correct per minute in March. The skills profile chart shows which skills (A1 = first skill in addition; S2 = second skill in subtraction) have been mastered and which may require more instruction.

INDIVIDUAL STUDENT PERFORMANCE

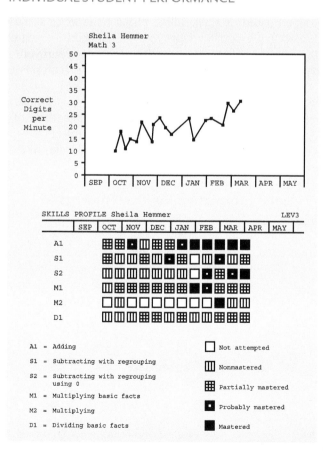

SUMMARY OF CLASS PERFORMANCE

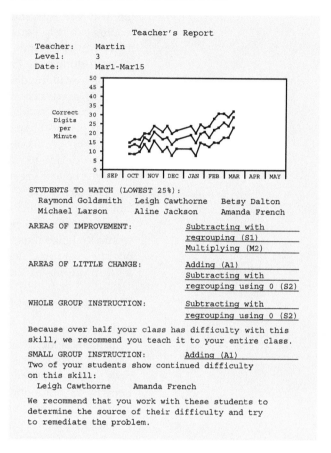

Teachers also receive a display like the one shown above. The graph shows the teacher, Mr. Martin, how his students progressed from October through March. The top line indicates scores at the 75th percentile; the middle line, scores at the 50th percentile; and the bottom line, scores at the 25th percentile. The lists below the graph provide information about which students should be monitored; areas in which the class has improved or not changed; and recommendations for skills that could be covered in whole-group instruction (most of the class needs instruction) or small-group instruction (only one or two students). These data could also be used for screening and progress monitoring in high school since students enrolled in higher-level math courses are often lacking more foundational math skills.

Similar software programs for math concepts and problem solving (Fuchs, Hamlett, & Fuchs, 1999) and reading (Fuchs, Hamlett, & Fuchs, 1997) are also available.

Sources: Figures from "Classwide Curriculum-Based Measurement: Helping General Educators Meet the Challenge of Student Diversity," by Fuchs, Fuchs, Hamlett, Philips, and Bentz, 1994, *Exceptional Children* 60(6), 518–537. Reprinted with permission.

Fluency and Accuracy in Diagnosis

CBA probes also can help teachers diagnose specific skills deficits. For example, a student who performs poorly on a math facts probe may not know the math facts or may simply be unable to write numbers fast enough. You can figure out which situation exists by examining the student's rate, or *fluency,* of think-write number writing. Likewise, keeping track of the number of errors per minute, or *accuracy,* in oral reading can help you detect a particular student's reading problem. Figure 4.5 shows the results of an oral reading probe for two seventh-grade students. The correct rate for both students is 75 words correct per minute. However, Student 1 seems to have a problem with reading fluency. When she reads, she reads accurately; the problem is that 75 words correct per minute is slow for a seventh-grade student. She will need help in fluency building, maybe as part of a Tier 2 RtI group. Student 2, on the other hand, is less accurate in her reading than Student 1; she is making many word identification errors and needs to be assessed further to ascertain whether these errors are a pattern or due to carelessness. If they are part of a pattern, she may require extra support in decoding skills in a resource room or as part of a Tier 3 RtI group.

The fact that CBA probes measure fluency as well as accuracy adds an important diagnostic dimension. For example, if the reading performance of the two students in Figure 4.5 were reported solely as a percentage of accuracy, the results would look like those shown in Figure 4.6. Using percentages alone, Student 1 does not appear to have a problem at all. However, as previously shown, she is reading much more slowly than Student 2.

Skill Mastery and Curriculum Placement

Inclusive education involves the use of a variety of instructional grouping arrangements. Sometimes students are grouped based on their skill levels; at other times a broader range of student skills is desired in a group. Students with special needs benefit from both types of instructional arrangements. You can use CBA probes to group your students by rank ordering and then visually inspecting your students' probe scores. For example, Mr. Glass wanted to form cooperative groups in math. He used scores on a problem-solving task probe, picking one lower performer, two middle performers, and one higher performer for each group. Ms. Robins, in contrast, found that three of her students were having difficulty with capitalization but the rest of the students were not. She formed a small group of those having difficulty to review capitalization rules.The small groups used in RtI are formed based on students' skill levels.

FIGURE 4.5 **Reading Fluency Information for Two Students**

Student 1		Student 2	
Number of words correct per minute	Number of words incorrect per minute	Number of words correct per minute	Number of words incorrect per minute
75	2	75	16

FIGURE 4.6 **Percentage of Accuracy in Passage Reading for Two Students**

Student 1	Student 2
Percentage of accuracy	Percentage of accuracy
96	70

Monitoring Student Progress and Instructional Evaluation

Although education has come a long way in terms of establishing a profession based on evidence-based practices, predicting whether a given practice will work for a given student in a particular situation is still difficult. Thus it is important that you carefully monitor the results of your teaching. This monitoring is particularly relevant for students with special needs who by definition are less likely to respond favorably to commonly used instructional methods.

CBA probes, because they are time efficient, easy to give, and match what is taught in the classroom, are ideal for monitoring student progress in class. For example, Mr. Harris was interested in whether Maria, a student with learning disabilities, was retaining any of the words featured on weekly spelling lists. She had scored 90 and above on her weekly tests, but Mr. Harris was unsure whether she was remembering the words from week to week. He developed a spelling probe using words from previous spelling lists. He gave the probe to his entire class and found that Maria and 10 other students were retaining only 20 percent of the words. As a result, he started a peer-tutoring program to help students review their words. Mr. Harris also set up group competitions and awards for groups scoring the highest on the review probes. Implementing these two activities improved Maria's and the other students' retention significantly.

A final example of a CBA probe is worthy of mention. Mr. Rock's school recently adopted a new algebra text. Mr. Rock wanted to make sure that the new text was meeting the needs of both his higher- and lower-performing students. He gave the class a see-write math probe containing a sample of representative problems taken from the new text and based on the state standards. Mr. Rock found that one of his students scored significantly below the rest of the class on the probe. Mr. Rock decided to provide him with extra math help as part of a Tier 2 after-school program. Mr. Rock also found that two other students got every problem correct, including several that hadn't been covered yet. He decided to place them in a more advanced algebra class.

Teaching approaches, no matter how well they are carried out, can affect students differently. By monitoring the progress of all of his students using CBA probes, Mr. Rock was able to meet their individual needs.

www.resources

For the latest research on student testing, curriculum, and achievement, go to the website of the National Institute on Student Achievement, Curriculum, and Assessment at http://www.ed.gov/offices/OERI/SAI/index.html.

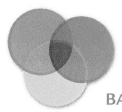

WRAPPING IT UP
BACK TO THE CASES

This section provides opportunities for you to apply the knowledge gained in this chapter to the cases described at the beginning of this chapter. The questions and activities that follow demonstrate how the principles, concepts, and strategies you have learned about in this chapter connect to the everyday activities of general education teachers.

MS. LYONS has determined that Rob's needs should be discussed with the school's instructional assistance team. In addition to presenting information outlining Rob's specific problem areas in mathematics, Ms. Lyons will need to describe what teaching methods, strategies, and/or accommodations she has used to support his learning and how he has responded to them. How might Ms. Lyons document the instructional strategies she has tried with Rob and the results they have provided? Provide a rationale for your choices.

MR. BLOUNT has been proactive in assessing how well his students can use the assigned text in his class and has used the information gathered from those assessments to teach the prerequisite skills needed to learn from the text. However, he is aware that if his students with disabilities have difficulty reading textbooks, they may also have difficulty reading the texts of high-stakes, end-of-grade tests required in his school system. He wants to use appropriate accommodations during these tests. How should Mr. Blount determine which accommodations to use? Further, how might he prepare his students to use these accommodations?

ROBERTO will most likely have difficulty participating in the standardized assessments given in his state. Ms. Benis and Roberto's special education teacher met after school yesterday to discuss what assessment methods they will use to demonstrate Roberto's progress toward meeting state standards. At this meeting, the two teachers reviewed the full range of options available and prepared a list of pros and cons for each option. What would be on your list of options? As you prepare your list, include the pros and cons of each option based on what you know about Roberto.

SUMMARY

- General education teachers can make assessments that contribute to six decision-making areas of special education: screening, diagnosis, program placement, curriculum placement, instructional evaluation, and program evaluation.

- A number of information sources are used in programming for students with special needs including high-stakes tests, group-administered standardized achievement tests, individually administered diagnostic tests, psychological tests, and alternate assessments. All of these assessments are helpful in making instructional decisions for students with special needs, but there is no substitute for observing and measuring how students respond to instruction in class, a key component of RtI.

- A small percentage of students who are typically working on a more individualized curriculum do not have to meet the same requirements as those students graduating with a standard diploma. These students are eligible for alternate assessments whereby they are required to meet the same broad standards as your other students, but they meet them in different, more basic ways.

- Curriculum-based assessment (CBA) measures student achievement in terms of what they are taught in the classroom. There are two major kinds of CBA: probes of basic academic skills and measures of content-area knowledge and strategies.

- CBA is helpful in making a range of special education decisions, particularly those involving day-to-day instruction. CBA norms and peer comparison methods can help screen students in academic difficulty. Probes can also be used to help teachers diagnose specific skill deficits to help form instructional groups and allow teachers to monitor the progress of students in class by measuring student performance over time.

APPLICATIONS IN TEACHING PRACTICE

COLLECTING AND USING ASSESSMENT INFORMATION

Yolanda is a student with a learning disability in your class who has been receiving indirect support or consultation in one area. You are interested in knowing how she is doing relative to the rest of the class. Select the subject area in which Yolanda has been receiving indirect support (reading, math, or written expression). Then select a particular skill in that subject matter that you have been working on in your class (for example, in reading: word identification, passage reading, comprehension, letter or letter–sound identification; in math: any math computation skill, word problems, money, geometry; in written expression: writing mechanics, writing productivity, quality of ideas). Next, describe a curriculum-based assessment strategy you would use to judge how well Yolanda is doing on that skill as compared with her classmates. Respond to the following questions in your description.

QUESTIONS

1. How will you use curriculum-based norms to measure the extent of Yolanda's problem?

2. What additional information will you collect to clarify Yolanda's problem?
3. How will you use probe information to measure the effectiveness of classroom supports for Yolanda?
4. How will you use probe information to help you instruct the rest of the class?

If you are teaching a class for which the ability to read the textbook is an important skill, select a sample textbook from your content area. Then develop a curriculum-based assessment of content-area reading skills using the model shown in Figure 4.3.

QUESTIONS

1. How did you select the skills to be included on your probe?
2. How could you use the information collected to determine the nature and extent of classroom support needed for students with disabilities? For the rest of the class?

PEARSON
myeducationlab

Go to Topic 8: Assessment in the My Education Lab (http://www.myeducationlab.com) for your course, where you can:

- Find learning outcomes for Assessment along with the national standards that connect to these outcomes.
- Complete Assignments and Activities that can help you more deeply understand the chapter content.
- Apply and practice your understanding of the core teaching skills identified in the chapter with the Building Teaching Skills and Dispositions learning units.
- Examine challenging situations and cases presented in the IRIS Center Resources. (optional)
- Access video clips of CCSSO National Teachers of the Year award winners responding to the question, "Why Do I Teach?" in the Teacher Talk section. (optional)
- Check your comprehension on the content covered in the chapter by going to the Study Plan in the Book Resources for your text. Here you will be able to take a chapter quiz, receive feedback on your answers, and then access Review, Practice, and Enrichment activities to enhance your understanding of chapter content. (optional)

Planning Instruction by Analyzing Classroom and Student Needs

From Chapter 5 of *Including Students with Special Needs: A Practical Guide for Classroom Teachers*, 6/e. Marilyn Friend.
William D. Bursuck. Copyright © 2012 by Pearson Education. All rights reserved.

Planning Instruction by Analyzing Classroom and Student Needs

LEARNING Objectives

After you read this chapter, you will be able to

1. Explain what it means to make instructional accommodations and modifications for students with disabilities and other special needs.

2. Describe the steps of the INCLUDE decision-making process for accommodating students with disabilities and other special needs in your classroom.

3. Identify and describe the key elements of a classroom environment.

4. Describe the major components of classroom organization, and explain how they can be adapted for students with disabilities and other special needs.

5. Explain various ways students can be grouped for instruction in an inclusive classroom.

6. Explain how the use of effective classroom materials and instructional methods can benefit students with disabilities and other special needs.

Bob Daemmrich/PhotoEdit Inc.

100

MR. RODRIGUEZ teaches world history at a large urban high school. When he introduces new content to his students, he teaches to the whole class. First, he reviews material that has already been covered, pointing out how that material relates to the new content being presented. Next, he provides any additional background information that he thinks will help students understand the new material better. Before Mr. Rodriguez actually presents new material, he hands out a partially completed outline of the major points he will make. This outline helps students identify the most important information. Every 10 minutes or so, he stops his lecture and allows students to discuss and modify the outline and ask questions. When Mr. Rodriguez completes his lecture, he organizes students into cooperative learning groups of four to answer a series of questions on the lecture. Manuel is a student with a learning disability in Mr. Rodriguez's class. He has a history of difficulty staying on task during lectures and figuring out what information to write down. He also has trouble remembering information from one day to the next. Mr. Rodriguez has noticed that Manuel has a particular interest in soccer and loves to perform for his classmates.

How well do you think Manuel will perform in Mr. Rodriguez's class? What changes in the classroom environment might help Manuel succeed? How might Mr. Rodriguez capitalize on Manuel's interests and strengths?

JOSH has cerebral palsy. He is in the normal range in ability; in fact, he excels in math. However, he has a lot of trouble with muscle movements, has little use of his lower body and legs, and also has problems with fine muscle coordination. As a result, Josh uses a wheelchair, has trouble with his speech (he speaks haltingly and is difficult to understand), and struggles to write letters and numbers correctly. Josh is included in Ms. Stewart's second-grade class.

How can Ms. Stewart set up her classroom to make it easier for Josh to fully participate? What aspects of the classroom environment will Ms. Stewart need to adapt for Josh? How can she use technology to facilitate Josh's inclusion? Why will math be an important subject for Josh in Ms. Stewart's class?

RESEARCH NOTE

The connection between effective instruction and positive student behavior is well established (Scott et al., 2001). Students who are successful have little incentive to disrupt the class or to act in ways that get them excluded from activities.

Disabilities and other special needs arise when characteristics of individual students and various features of students' home and school environments interact. Effective teachers analyze the classroom environment in relation to students' academic and social needs and make accommodations and modifications to ensure students' success in the classroom. For example, Manuel has difficulty staying on task and retaining new information. However, features of Mr. Rodriguez's class make it easier for Manuel to function. The partially completed lecture outlines help Manuel focus his attention on specific information as he tries to listen and stay on task; the pauses help him catch any lecture information he might have missed. The review sessions are intended to help Manuel retain information by giving him a mechanism for rehearsing newly learned material. In another case, Josh has some serious motor problems, but he may be able to function quite independently if Ms. Stewart makes her classroom accessible to a wheelchair and works with special educators to use assistive technology to meet Josh's needs in handwriting and oral communication.

This chapter introduces you to a systematic approach for helping all students with special needs gain access to the general education curriculum, a requirement of the Individuals with Disabilities Education Act (IDEA). Part of that approach is for you to be the best teacher you can be so that fewer of your students require individualized instruction in the first place. Despite your best efforts, however, there will always be students who require a more individualized approach. The **INCLUDE** strategy is provided for these students. Although there are other ways to differentiate instruction for students with disabilities, INCLUDE gives teachers a systematic process for accommodating students based on their individual needs and the classroom demands on, or expectations of the teacher.

The rest of this textbook expands and elaborates on this approach. Later chapters also present a more in-depth look at the relationship between your classroom environment and the diverse needs of learners. An important assumption throughout this text is that the more effective your classroom structure is, the greater the diversity you will be able to accommodate and the fewer individualized classroom changes you will need to make. This idea is incorporated into current RtI models, which focus on problem prevention by establishing a strong base of research-based practices in Tier 1.

How Can the INCLUDE Strategy Help You Make Instructional Accommodations and Modifications for Students with Special Needs?

At a recent conference presentation that included both general education teachers and special education teachers, one of the authors of this text asked the audience how many of those present worked with students with disabilities. A music teacher at the back of the room called out, "Everyone in schools works with students with disabilities!" He is right. As you have learned in the previous chapters, IDEA entitles students with disabilities to "access," "participation," and "progress" in the general education curriculum. These entitlements were reinforced by the Elementary and Secondary Education Act (ESEA; formerly No Child Left Behind), which requires that most students with disabilities meet the same standards as their classmates without disabilities. Therefore, although the professionals who specialize in meeting the needs of students with disabilities are valuable and provide critical instructional and support systems for students, ultimately you and your peers will be the primary teachers for many students with disabilities and other special needs, and you will form partnerships with special educators to meet the needs of others. That makes it critical for you to feel comfortable making accommodations and modifications for students in order for them to have fair access to your curriculum.

The INCLUDE strategy is based on two key assumptions. First, student performance in school is the result of an interaction between the student and the instructional environment (Broderick, Mehta-Parekh, & Reid, 2005; Pisha & Coyne, 2001; Smith, 2004). Consequently, what happens in a classroom can either minimize the impact of students' special needs on their learning or magnify it, making accommodations necessary. In the first chapter-opening example, Mr. Rodriguez engaged in a number of teaching practices that minimized the impact of Manuel's learning disability, such as starting each class with a review of material covered the day before, providing the students with lecture outlines to help them identify important ideas, and engaging his students in regular discussions of the material presented. Nevertheless, if part of Manuel's learning disability is in reading and the classroom text used in Mr. Rodriguez's class is too difficult for Manuel to read independently, Mr. Rodriguez will need to accommodate Manuel's problems in reading. This aspect of the INCLUDE approach is consistent with the idea behind RtI. If all students receive effectively delivered, evidence-based instruction, then fewer will be identified as needing more supports. Further, those eventually identified for special education—the most intensive level of support—will be only those truly in need.

The second key assumption of INCLUDE is that by carefully analyzing students' learning needs and the specific demands of the classroom environment, teachers can reasonably accommodate most students with special needs in their classrooms. You can maximize student success without taking a disproportionate amount of teacher time or diminishing the education of the other students in the class. For example, with the help of the special education teacher, Mr. Rodriguez provided Manuel with a digital text with a built-in speech-to-print component and study guide. Soon Mr. Rodriguez discovered that other students in the class could also benefit from using the digital text and made it available to them. In this way, reasonable accommodations often assist many students in the class.

The INCLUDE strategy contains elements of both universal design and differentiated instruction, two widely recognized approaches to addressing classroom diversity in general and inclusion in particular. The idea of **universal design** originated in the field of architecture, where it was learned that designing buildings for persons with diverse needs from the beginning makes them more accessible and saves money spent on costly retrofits of ramps and automatic doors. As applied to

How does the concept of universal design relate from architecture to teaching? How does this concept simplify the job of a general education teacher? Liz Strenk/SuperStock, Inc.

www.resources

For more information on universal design, go to the Teaching Every Student page of the Center for Applied Special Technology (CAST) website: http://www.cast.org/tes.

classrooms, the idea is that instructional materials, methods, and assessments designed with built-in supports are more likely to be compatible with learners with special needs than those without such supports (Curry, 2003; Hitchcock, Meyer, Rose, & Jackson, 2002; Pisha & Stahl, 2005), and they minimize the need for labor-intensive accommodations later on. For example, print alternatives such as graphics, video, and digital text allow students with reading problems to more readily access subject content. The use of templates with partially filled-in sections and links to more information can help students construct a better essay. Universal design is consistent with RtI's prevention emphasis; when effective practices are in place, many learning problems can be prevented.

The idea behind **differentiated instruction** is that a variety of teaching and learning strategies are necessary to meet the range of needs evident in any given classroom. Students' diverse needs are met by differentiating the content being taught, the process by which it is taught, and the ways students demonstrate what they have learned and their level of knowledge through varied products (Anderson, 2007; Broderick, Mehta-Parekh, & Reid, 2005). Differentiation is achieved by providing materials and tasks at varied levels of difficulty and with varying levels of instructional support, through the use of multiple grouping arrangements, student choice, and varied evaluation strategies (Tomlinson, 2000).

Differentiated instruction is consistent with the approach taken in this text for accommodating students with disabilities and other special needs. In fact, the INCLUDE process of determining student supports based on student needs and classroom demands is an ideal vehicle for implementing differentiated instruction in your classroom. The way differentiated instruction is addressed in INCLUDE also is consistent with the RtI principle that when it comes to providing effective instruction, one size does not fit all.

The INCLUDE strategy for differentiating instruction for students with special needs in the general education classroom follows seven steps:

INCLUDE

Step 1	**I**dentify classroom demands.
Step 2	**N**ote student learning strengths and needs.
Step 3	**C**heck for potential areas of student success.
Step 4	**L**ook for potential problem areas.
Step 5	**U**se information to brainstorm ways to differentiate instruction.
Step 6	**D**ifferentiate instruction.
Step 7	**E**valuate student progress.

These steps are designed to apply to a broad range of student needs and classroom environments. Throughout this text, this icon will denote suggestions for differentiating instruction according to this strategy, with an emphasis on the appropriate step.

INCLUDE

Step 1: Identify Classroom Demands

Because the classroom environment significantly influences what students learn, identifying and analyzing classroom requirements allows teachers to anticipate or explain problems that a given student might experience. Then, by modifying the environment, teachers can solve or reduce the impact of these learning problems. Common classroom demands relate to classroom management, classroom grouping, instructional materials, and instructional methods.

Classroom Management   The ways in which a teacher promotes order and engages students in learning in a classroom are referred to as *classroom management* (Doyle, 1986; Miller & Hall, 2005). Classroom management includes a number of factors:

- *Physical organization,* such as the use of wall and floor space and lighting
- *Classroom routines* for academic and nonacademic activities
- *Classroom climate,* or attitudes toward individual differences

- *Behavior management,* such as classroom rules and monitoring
- *The use of time* for instructional and noninstructional activities

Classroom management strategies can have real benefits for students with disabilities. For example, LaVerna is a student who needs accommodations in physical organization; she uses a wheelchair and requires wide aisles in the classroom and a ramp for the step leading to her classroom. Shawn has behavioral difficulties and thus would benefit from a behavior management system: He might go to his next class prior to the end of each period to eliminate potential opportunities to fight with classmates. He would also benefit from an efficient use of time: Minimizing transition times or the amount of time between activities would eliminate further opportunities for inappropriate interactions with his classmates.

Classroom Grouping   Teachers use a variety of *classroom grouping* arrangements. Sometimes they teach the whole class at once, as when they lecture in a content area such as social studies. At other times teachers may employ small-group or one-to-one instruction. For example, they may teach a small group of students who have similar instructional needs, such as a group of students who all require extra help on multiplication facts or an individual student who needs extra help with an English assignment. Teachers also may group students of differing interests and abilities in an effort to foster cooperative problem solving and/or peer tutoring. Students respond differently to these types of groupings. For example, Mike needs accommodations in classroom grouping in order to succeed; he might do better in a small group in which other students read assignments aloud so that he can participate in responding to them. Using a variety of grouping strategies based on student need is sometimes referred to as *flexible grouping,* an essential part of differentiated instruction (Anderson, 2007).

Instructional Materials   The types of *instructional materials* teachers use can have a major impact on the academic success of students with special needs. Although many teachers choose to develop or collect their own materials, published textbooks are most commonly used. Published textbooks include basic skills texts called *basals,* often used in reading and mathematics, and texts that stress subject-matter content in areas such as history and biology. Other materials commonly used by teachers include concrete representational items such as manipulatives and technological devices, including audiovisual aids, telecommunication systems, and computers. Roberta's use of large-print materials to assist her in seeing her work and Carmen's use of a study guide to help her identify important information in her world history text are both examples of differentiating instruction by making changes in instructional materials.

Instructional Methods   The ways in which teachers present content or skills to students and evaluate whether learning has occurred are the essence of teaching and are crucial for accommodating students with special needs. These are their *instructional methods.* Teachers use a number of different approaches to teach content and skills. Sometimes they teach skills directly, whereas at other times they assume the role of a facilitator and encourage students to learn on their own, providing support only as needed. Instructional methods also involve student practice that occurs either in class, through independent seatwork activities or learning centers, or out of class through homework. Ms. Correli's decision to use a PowerPoint presentation in class and then give Lon a copy of the slides to help his learning is an example of an accommodation in presenting subject matter. Using a paraprofessional to write a student's words is an example of an accommodation in student practice.

Student evaluation, or determining the extent to which students have mastered academic skills or instructional content, is an important aspect of instructional methods. Grades frequently are used to communicate student evaluation. For some students, grading is an appropriate evaluation strategy. But for others, such as Anita, a fifth-grade student who has a moderate intellectual disability and is learning to recognize her name, a narrative report might be a better evaluation tool. When evaluating students with disabilities, teachers must focus on measuring what a student knows rather than the extent of his disability. For example, Alex, who has a severe learning disability in writing, may need to answer test questions orally to convey all he knows; if he gives written answers, only his writing disability may be measured.

INCLUDE

Step 2: Note Student Learning Strengths and Needs

Once instructional demands are specified, the *N* step of INCLUDE calls for noting student strengths and needs. Remember that students with disabilities are a very heterogeneous group; a disability label cannot communicate a student's complete learning profile. For example, some students with intellectual disabilities can learn many life skills and live independently, whereas others will continually need daily assistance. Also keep in mind that students with disabilities are more like their peers without disabilities than different from them. Like their nondisabled peers, they have patterns of learning strengths and weaknesses. Focusing on strengths is essential (Epstein, 2004; Farmer, Farmer, & Brooks, 2010; Shaywitz, 2003). Teachers who see the strengths in students teach positively, helping students to see themselves and others positively, to see learning positively, and to overcome their weaknesses (Tomlinson & Jarvis, 2006). Three areas describe student learning strengths and needs: academics, social-emotional development, and physical development. Problems in any one of these areas may prevent students from meeting classroom requirements, resulting in a need for differentiated instruction. Strengths in any of these areas can help students overcome these problems. For example, a student with good listening skills may be able to compensate for her reading problem by using a digital recording of her civics and government textbook.

Academics   The first part of academics is *basic skills,* including reading, math, and oral and written language. Although these skills might sometimes be bypassed (for example, through the use of a calculator in math), their importance in both elementary and secondary education suggests teachers should consider them carefully. For example, a student with a severe reading problem is likely to have trouble in any subject area that requires reading, including math, social studies, and science and on any assignment with written directions.

Cognitive and learning strategies make up the second part of academics. These strategies involve "learning how to learn" skills, such as memorization, textbook reading, note taking, test taking, and general problem solving. Such skills give students independence that helps them in adult life. Students with problems in these areas experience increasing difficulty as they proceed through the grades. For example, students who have difficulty memorizing basic math facts likely will have trouble learning to multiply fractions, and students who cannot take notes may fall behind in a civics course based on a lecture format.

Survival skills, the third area of academics, are skills practiced by successful students, such as attending school regularly, being organized, completing tasks in and out of school, being independent, taking an interest in school, and displaying positive interpersonal skills (Brown, Kerr, Zigmond, & Harris, 1984; Kerr & Nelson, 2009). Students lacking in these areas usually have difficulty at school. For example, disorganized students are not likely to have work done on time, nor are they likely to deliver parent permission forms for field trips to their parents or return them to school. Survival skills also help some students compensate for their other problems. For example, given two students with identical reading problems, teachers sometimes offer more help to the student who has good attendance and tries hard.

Social-Emotional Development   Students' social-emotional development involves classroom conduct, interpersonal skills, and personal-psychological adjustment. Classroom conduct problems include a number of aggressive and disruptive behaviors, such as hitting, fighting, teasing, hyperactivity, yelling, refusing to comply with requests, crying, and destructiveness. Although most of these behaviors may be exhibited by all children at one time or another, students with special needs may engage in them more frequently and with greater intensity.

Conduct problems seriously interfere with student learning and can lead to problems in interpersonal relations and personal-psychological adjustment. For example, students who are disruptive in class are less likely to learn academic skills and content. Their outbursts also may be resented by their peers and may lead to peer rejection, social isolation, and a poor self-image. Interpersonal skills include but are not limited to initiating and carrying on conversations, coping with conflict, and establishing and maintaining friendships. Although these skills are not ordinarily part of the explicit school curriculum, their overall impact on school adjustment makes them important. For example, students lacking in peer support may have difficulty completing group projects (an example of student practice) or finding someone to help with a difficult assignment (an example of homework).

Personal-psychological adjustment involves the key motivational areas of self-image, frustration tolerance, and proactive learning. For example, students with a poor self-image and low tolerance for frustration may do poorly on tests (an example of student evaluation); students who are inactive learners may have difficulty pursuing an independent science project (an example of student practice).

Physical Development   Physical development includes vision and hearing levels, motor skills, and neurological functioning. Students with vision problems need adapted educational materials. Students with poor fine motor skills may need a computer to do their homework, an accommodation in student practice. Finally, students with attentional deficits may need a wider range of approaches for instruction, including lecture, discussion, small-group work, and independent work.

Step 3: Check for Potential Areas of Student Success

INCLUDE

The next INCLUDE step is *C*, analyzing student strengths in view of the instructional demands identified in Step 1 and checking for activities or tasks students can do successfully. Success enhances student self-image and motivation. Look for strengths in both academic and social-emotional areas. Reading the "Current Levels of Performance" section of the IEP is a good way to begin identifying a student's strengths. For example, Jerry does not read but can draw skillfully. In social studies, his teacher asks him to be the class cartographer, drawing maps for each region of the world as it is studied. Kareem has a moderate intellectual disability and learns very slowly, but he always comes to school on time. His second-grade teacher appoints him attendance monitor. Dwayne has attention deficit–hyperactivity disorder (ADHD), is failing all his classes in school, and is beginning to become difficult to handle at home. His parents and teachers have noticed, however, that he is able to identify personal strengths, has a good sense of humor, and can enjoy a hobby. They support Dwayne's positive interests by enrolling him in the school band.

Step 4: Look for Potential Problem Areas

INCLUDE

In the *L* step of the INCLUDE strategy, student learning needs are reviewed within a particular instructional context, and potential mismatches are identified. For example, Susan has a learning need in the area of expressive writing; she is unable to identify spelling errors in her work. This is an academic learning need. When evaluating students' work, her world cultures teacher, who believes that writing skills should be reinforced in every class, deducts one letter grade from papers that contain one or more spelling errors. Susan also cannot read the history text accurately and fluently enough to understand it. For Susan to succeed in history class, these mismatches need to be addressed. Similarly, Sam has a severe problem that prevents him from speaking fluently. This physical problem creates a learning need. His fourth-grade teacher requires that students present book reports to the class. Again, a potential mismatch exists that could prevent Sam from succeeding. Mismatches such as those experienced by Susan and Sam are resolved by differentiating instruction, the topic of the next two INCLUDE steps.

INCLUDE

Step 5: Use Information to Brainstorm Ways to Differentiate Instruction

Once potential mismatches have been identified, the *U* step of INCLUDE is to use this information to identify possible ways to eliminate or minimize their effects. IDEA stipulates two ways to differentiate for students with disabilities: accommodations and modifications.

Accommodations **Instructional accommodations** typically are defined as supports provided to help students gain full access to class content and instruction, and to demonstrate accurately what they know (Byrnes, 2008; Nolet & McLaughlin, 2005). It is important to remember that with accommodations, school expectations that students meet learning standards remain unchanged. This means that students with disabilities receiving accommodations are expected to learn everything their classmates without disabilities are supposed to learn (Nolet & McLaughlin, 2005). Examples of accommodations include bypassing students' learning needs by allowing them to employ compensatory learning strategies, making an adjustment in classroom teaching materials, using group organization, and teaching students basic or independent learning skills.

Bypass or *compensatory strategies* allow students to gain access to or demonstrate mastery of the school curriculum in alternative ways. For example, Susan, the student with problems in spelling and reading, could benefit from several bypass strategies. For spelling, having a computerized spell checker could help. Alternatively, she could enlist the help of a peer to proofread her work. To help Susan access content in her government text, she could use an electronic reader. She also could be allowed to have her exams read to her so she could demonstrate her knowledge without her reading disability being an obstacle. Bypassing cannot be used in a primary area of instruction, however. For instance, Susan cannot spell check her spelling test, but she can spell check her science homework. Similarly, she cannot have a reading test read to her, but it would be appropriate to have a history test read to her. Also, bypassing a skill does not necessarily mean that the skill should not be remediated. Susan may need both spelling and reading instruction, either as part of her English class or in a more intensive pullout type of setting. Finally, bypass strategies should encourage student independence. For example, Susan might be better off learning to use a spell checker rather than relying on a peer proofreader.

Teachers can also provide accommodations in their *instructional methods, materials, grouping,* and *classroom management* to help students succeed. For example, if Ramos has attention problems, he might be seated near the front of the room, and he might benefit from a special system of rewards and consequences as well as a classroom from which "busy" bulletin board displays are removed. All these are classroom management accommodations. A change in classroom instruction would be to call on Ramos frequently during class discussions and to allow him to earn points toward his grade for appropriate participation. Ramos might pay better attention in a small group—a grouping change—and he might be better able to comprehend his textbooks if the key ideas are highlighted—a materials accommodation. These types of accommodations can be provided as supports in Tiers 1 and 2 in schools implementing RtI.

A third option for accommodating students with special needs is to provide *intensive instruction on basic skills and learning strategies.* Often a special education teacher carries out this instruction in a resource setting. This approach

What classroom demands might this student have difficulty meeting? What bypass strategies or accommodations might help him demonstrate that he has learned his assignment as well as his classmates have?
Shahn Kermani

assumes that basic skills and learning strategies are prerequisites for successful general education experiences. It also assumes that some students require instruction delivered with a greater degree of intensity than can reasonably be provided by a general educator responsible for 20–30 or more students (Bursuck, Smith, Munk, Damer, Mehlig, & Perry, 2004).

Unfortunately, the results of research on whether skills taught in pullout programs transfer to the general education class are mixed (Kavale & Forness, 2000). Some studies show positive results (Freeman & Alkin, 2000; Marston, 1996; Snider, 1997), whereas others show minimal effects (Baker & Zigmond, 1995; Wang, Reynolds, & Walberg, 1988). Studies do suggest that teachers play an important role in determining whether skills taught in a separate setting transfer to their classrooms (Ellis & Lenz, 1996; Sabornie & deBettencourt, 2009). For example, Ms. Henry had Jamie in her English literature class; Jamie was receiving Tier 2 support on taking effective lecture notes. First, Ms. Henry found out what strategy for note taking Jamie was learning. Then she reminded Jamie to perform the strategy before she delivered a lecture and sometimes even during a lecture. Finally, Ms. Henry collected Jamie's notes on a weekly basis to see whether she was performing the strategy correctly, giving specific feedback to her as needed and reporting her progress to the special education teacher.

Of course the general education teacher also can provide this type of instruction. This option is feasible when many students have similar instructional needs and when the teacher can easily monitor skill development. For example, Mr. Higgins, a seventh-grade science teacher, lectures frequently. As a result, students need to be proficient note takers. At the beginning of the school year, Mr. Higgins noticed during a routine check of student notebooks that many students were not taking adequate notes. With assistance from the special education teacher, he taught note taking as part of science. Three students for whom note taking was especially difficult handed in their notes each day so Mr. Higgins could monitor their progress. The Working Together discusses a co-teaching situation in which the general education teacher is developing a strategy to provide accommodations in her classroom with the help of the special educator.

Working TOGETHER

The Reluctant Co-Teacher

Juanita Kirk, a math teacher, initially was excited about co-teaching with Susan Harris, the special educator assigned to the seventh-grade team. Now, though, she is disillusioned. Although Susan was offered paid planning time during the summer, she declined to participate, explaining that she had made her family the focus of her summers and that she would not make professional commitments during that time. Juanita could understand that, but then, at their first meeting in the fall, Susan explained to Juanita that she had always disliked math and had not studied it since she was in high school. She said that she would be most comfortable adjusting to co-teaching by spending the first semester taking notes for students, learning the curriculum, and then helping individual students after instruction had occurred. She stated clearly that she did not have much time for preparing outside class given all her other responsibilities, and she also made it clear that she did not consider it her responsibility to grade student work.

Juanita was surprised. This was not at all what she expected co-teaching to be. She envisioned a partnership in which she and her colleague not only could make instruction more intensive but also could energize math instruction by using various grouping arrangements and brainstorming new ways to reach their students. Now six weeks into the school year, she is beginning to think that co-teaching is more like having an assistant in the classroom—an assistant who is highly paid for not doing very much work. She wonders if this is how co-teaching looks in English, the other seventh-grade course to which Susan is assigned.

ADDRESSING THE DILEMMA

If you were Juanita, how might you address this situation by using ideas in this chapter?

Modifications **Instructional** or curricular **modifications** are made when the content expectations are altered and the performance outcomes expected of students change (Giangreco, 2007; Nolet & McLaughlin, 2005). Typically, students who receive modifications have behavioral and/or intellectual disabilities that are so significant that the curricular expectations in general education are inappropriate. These are usually the same students described in chapter 4 as being eligible for alternate assessments. Instructional modifications are generally of two types: teaching less content and teaching different content (Nolet & McLaughlin, 2005). For example, in order to meet district grade-level science standards, Ms. Lamb's class was learning to label the parts of the human digestive system and state the purpose for each. Manny, a student with a significant intellectual disability included in Ms. Lamb's class, met the same learning standard by pointing to his stomach when asked where food goes when it is eaten. This is an example of teaching less content. In contrast, teaching different content means that the curricular outcomes are different from those of the rest of the class. For example, an instructional goal for Tony, a student with autism, is to remain calm when there is a change in the classroom schedule.

It is important to reserve instructional modifications for students with only the most significant disabilities. Otherwise, instructional modifications reduce a student's opportunity to learn critical knowledge, skills, and concepts in a given subject, leaving gaps in learning that can interfere with meeting school standards and that can be a disadvantage in later school years and beyond. For example, when one class was learning four reasons for the worldwide spread of AIDS, Steven, a student with a learning disability, was required to learn only two reasons, because he had difficulty remembering information. However, when Steven was required to take the state high-stakes science test, he was held responsible for learning the same information about AIDS as everyone else. It would have been more effective for the school to help Steven better remember science content by using a memory-enhancing device rather than reducing the amount of information. In short, reducing or simplifying content inappropriately can lead to watering down the curriculum.

INCLUDE

RESEARCH NOTE

Byrnes (2008) found that written descriptions of accommodations on student IEPs were often ambiguous and led to considerable confusion on the part of teachers as to how to implement them. For suggestions on how to write and interpret IEP descriptions of accommodations, see Byrnes (2010).

Step 6: Differentiate Instruction

After you have brainstormed possible accommodations or modifications, you can implement the *D* step in INCLUDE, which involves selecting strategies to try. A number of guidelines are suggested here to help you decide which strategies to select.

- *Select Age-Appropriate Strategies:* Students' accommodations and modifications should match their age. For example, using a third-grade book as a supplement for an eighth-grade science student who reads at the third-grade level would embarrass the student. In such a situation, a bypass strategy such as a digitally-recorded textbook would be preferable if the student has the necessary background and intellectual skills to listen to the book with understanding. A good rule of thumb is to remember that no students, whether in first or twelfth grade and regardless of their special needs, want to use what they perceive as "baby" books or materials.
- *Select the Easiest Approach First:* Accommodations need to be feasible for the general education teacher. Although making accommodations and modifications often means some additional work for you, it should not require so much time and effort that it interferes with teaching the entire class. For instance, it is easier to circle the 6 out of 12 math problems you want Maria to complete than to create a separate worksheet just for her.
- *Select Accommodations and Modifications You Agree with:* You are more likely to implement an approach successfully if you believe in it (Polloway, Bursuck, Jayanthi, Epstein, & Nelson, 1996), especially in the area of behavior management. For example, in selecting rewards for good behavior, if you are uncomfortable with giving candy, try giving time for desirable activities such as time on the computer.

However, accommodations and modifications should not be considered only in light of teacher beliefs. IDEA is clear that the unique needs of students take precedence over the convenience of schools and professionals. With imagination and some input from special educators, you will undoubtedly find strategies that match your teaching approach while maximizing your students' learning.

- *Determine Whether You Are Dealing with a "Can't" or a "Won't" Problem:* Blankenship and Lilly (1981) describe a "can't" problem as one in which the student, no matter how highly motivated, is unable to do what is expected. A "won't" problem is one in which the student could do what is expected but is not motivated to do so. Each type of problem may require a different accommodation. A student unable to do what is expected might need a bypass strategy; a student unwilling to do the work might need a behavior management strategy. Making this distinction can also save you time. For example, if a student fails a test because she does not feel like working on the day of the test, then a teacher's attempt to provide extra tutorial assistance will likely be wasted effort. "Can't" and "won't" problems are particularly relevant for adolescents, who are often less likely than younger students to work to please their teachers.
- *Give Students Choices:* Adding the element of choice challenges students to make decisions, encourages them to be more responsible for their own learning, and allows them to more readily demonstrate what they know by tapping into their strengths and interests (Anderson, 2007; Carolan & Guinn, 2007).
- *Select Strategies with Demonstrated Effectiveness:* Over the past 30 years, a massive body of professional literature on effective teaching practices has accumulated. Being familiar with this research can help you avoid fads and other unvalidated practices. The strategies suggested throughout this text are based on research and form a starting point for your understanding of validated practices. Such an understanding has always been important, but it is particularly important in view of the recent emphasis placed on evidence-based practices in IDEA and ESEA legislation, as well as in RtI, which requires the use of evidence-based practices in all of its instructional tiers. Ways to select evidence-based practices are described in the Professional Edge.

fyi

To learn more about how to critically read single subject and group experimental research articles see Tankersley et al. (2008) and Cook et al. (2006).

Step 7: Evaluate Student Progress

Although there are many effective teaching practices, it is difficult to predict which will be effective for a given student. As a result, once an accommodation or modification is implemented, the *E* step of INCLUDE is essential: Evaluate strategy effectiveness. You can track effectiveness through grades; observations; analysis of student work; portfolios; performance assessments; and teacher, parent, and student ratings. Monitoring student progress in this way will help you decide whether to continue, change, or discontinue an intervention. In RtI, information obtained through progress monitoring is used to assign students to more intensive instructional tiers, including special education.

INCLUDE

In the next section, the relationship between how you run your classroom and the diverse needs of learners is examined. As you have read, the use of effective practices allows teachers to accommodate more diversity in their classrooms while at the same time reducing the need for making more individualized adaptations. The key features that contribute to a successful classroom are shown in Figure 5.1. These features include classroom management, classroom grouping, instructional materials, and instructional methods.

How Is an Inclusive Classroom Managed?

Classroom management comprises all of the things teachers do to organize students, space, time, and materials to maximize effective teaching and student learning (Wong & Wong, 1998). As described here, classroom management involves physical organization, routines for classroom business, classroom climate, behavior management,

INSTRUCTIONAL **EDGE**

Selecting Evidence-Based Practices for RtI

As you have already learned, evidence-based practices are a key part of RtI. Evidence-based practices are those instructional techniques that have been shown by research to be most likely to improve student outcomes in a meaningful way (Cook, Tankersley, Cook, & Landrum, 2008a). While the primary benefit of using evidence-based practices is boosting student achievement, evidence-based teaching, when implemented with integrity, also can help schools determine when students have learning disabilities and when they fail to learn because of ineffective instruction. That is why using RtI is an accepted alternative for identifying students with learning disabilities in IDEA 2004.

Are evidence-based practices the same as best practices?

Evidence-based practices should not be confused with what are often referred to as best practices. While best practices can be evidence-based, they often include practices that are recommended based on personal experience, opinion, and preference (Cook et al., 2008a). In fact, so many teaching techniques have been referred to as best practices it is not at all clear which ones are based on research and which are not. This situation makes the selection of evidence-based practices for RtI a difficult one.

How do I decide whether a given practice is evidence-based?

Cook et al. (2008a) suggest using two guidelines when deciding whether a given practice is evidence-based, one based on the quality of the research and the other on the quantity. The quality of research means that the research clearly shows that the practice leads to increased student achievement, and that no other explanations are likely. This level of quality, sometimes referred to as experimental control, can be accomplished in two ways: (1) systematically comparing the outcomes of two randomly selected groups, one that uses the practice versus a comparison or control group that does not, or (2) systematically comparing a student's performance when the practice is in place versus when it is not in place (Cook et al., 2008a). The first type of research is called group experimental research and the second type is called single-subject research. Single-subject and group experimental research are not the only valuable kinds of research, but they are the only kinds of research that establish a causal relationship between a teaching practice and student achievement. For example, qualitative research involving interviews, focus groups and/or in-depth observations of individuals or small groups, and quantitative studies that don't involve random assignment or control groups are useful in exploring new techniques that can eventually be put to the causality test using experimental research.

It is not enough, no matter how high the quality of the study, to simply show that an instructional practice worked once. It is also important to show that the technique worked again, with more and/or different students under varied classroom conditions. So the quantity of research, as well as the quality, is important to consider in selecting a practice.

How important is it that I carry out evidence-based practices the same way they are done in the research?

Carrying out the teaching practice the same way it was done in the research is called **treatment fidelity** and it is a critical part of RtI.

When teaching practices are not carried out as designed, students may be unnecessarily placed in more intensive tiers, or even special education. While changes to evidence-based practices can eventually be made, be sure to first give them every chance to work as intended in the research.

If a practice is evidence-based, is it guaranteed to work in my classroom?

Group research, as the term implies, is based on the average performance of groups of students. While a given study may clearly show that the group as a whole performed better, individual students within the group may not have performed as well. Teaching strategies validated by single-subject research may not apply to other students who may differ in some way or may be in classrooms that also differ. There are no guarantees that a teaching strategy will work, even one based on research of high quality and quantity. That is why the progress monitoring component of RtI is so important. When assessments show progress isn't being made, and you are sure that the teaching practice was used as designed, you can make necessary instructional changes before the student falls further behind.

Can I use practices that are not evidence-based?

Some teaching practices may not be evidence-based simply because researchers have not conducted enough studies or have not systematically reviewed the findings from studies that have been done (Cook et al., 2008a). For example, we know a lot more about evidence-based practices in reading than in math and written expression. This means that you can select reading practices with greater certainty that they will work. Whether or not a practice is evidence-based is rarely a yes-no decision; all teaching practices range along a continuum from ineffective to evidence-based, with plenty of gray areas in between. Still, selecting evidence-based practices should not be left to chance; we know enough to improve the chances of a given child considerably, and practices for which we have the most evidence should always be used before selecting practices for which we have less evidence.

Are there sources that can help me select evidence-based practices?

Teachers often don't have time to read and digest research articles, and there are sources that can help. However, be sure to select sources that evaluate research objectively and according to the highest scientific standards. The U.S. Department of Education's What Works Clearinghouse (http://www.whatworks.ed.gov) is a good source of evidence-based practices in many instructional areas. For evidence-based practices in reading, go to the Florida Center for Reading (http://www.FCRR.org) and also consult The Report of The National Reading Panel (http://www.nationalreadingpanel.org). For evidence-based practices in math go to http://ies.ed.gov/ncee/wwc/pdf/practiceguides/rti_math_pg_042109.pdf and the Final Report of the National Math Panel (http://www.ed.gov/about/bdscomm/list/mathpanel/report/final-report.pdf).

FIGURE 5.1 Overview of Classroom Environments

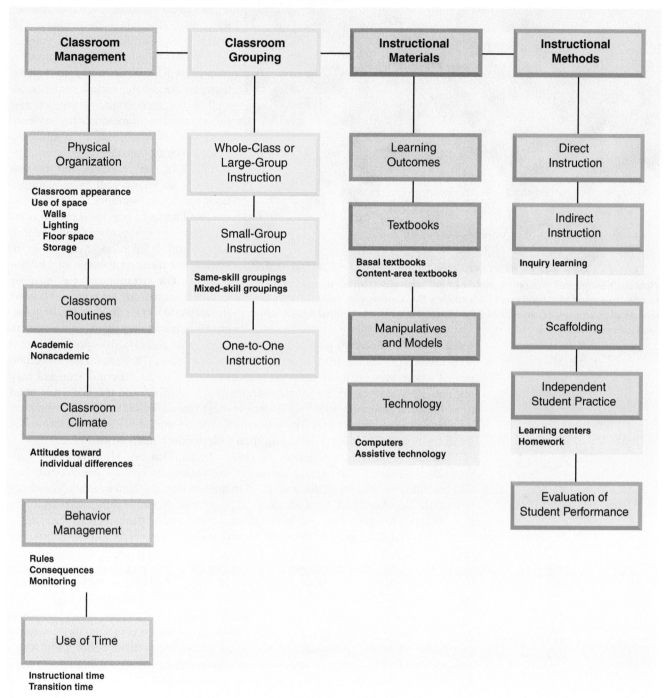

and use of time. The classroom management strategies described in the following sections are part of a larger body of strategies for promoting positive student behavior called *positive behavior supports (PBS)* (Sugai & Horner, 2008). You also may need to use the INCLUDE strategy to make accommodations for students with special needs in all of these areas.

Physical Organization

The way a classroom is physically organized can affect student learning and behavior in a number of areas (Kerr & Nelson, 2009). Carefully arranged classrooms can decrease noise and disruption, improve the level and quality of student interactions, and

This is a teacher-centered grouping arrangement for large-group instruction. What are some advantages and disadvantages of this strategy for students with special needs? What other ways of grouping students should be part of a teacher's instructional repertoire? Michael Newman/PhotoEdit Inc.

increase the percentage of time that students spend on academic tasks (Paine, Radicchi, Rosellini, Deutchman, & Darch, 1983; Sutherland, Lewis-Palmer, Stichter, & Morgan, 2008). The physical organization of a classroom influences learning conditions for all students, as well as the accessibility of instructional presentations and materials for students with sensory and physical disabilities. Physical organization includes the appearance of the classroom and the use of space, including wall areas, lighting, floor space, and storage.

Wall areas can be used for decorating, posting rules, displaying student work, and reinforcing class content, sometimes through the use of bulletin boards. For example, one teacher taught a note-taking strategy and posted the steps on a bulletin board to help her students remember them. In using wall space, keep in mind two possible problems. First, wall displays may divert students with attention problems from concentrating on instruction. These students should be placed where they are least likely to be distracted by displays. Second, students may not notice that important information appears on a display, and teachers may need to direct their attention to it. For example, Ms. Huerta posted a display showing graphic representations of the basic fractions. She reminded her students to look at these fractions while they were doing their independent math work.

Lighting, either from windows or ceiling lights, also can affect students with disabilities. Students with hearing loss might need adequate light to speech-read; they also are likely to have problems with glare in areas where the light source comes from behind the speaker. Students with visual impairments also have difficulty working in areas that are not glare free and well lighted. Occasionally, students with learning or emotional disabilities may be sensitive to and respond negatively to certain types of light. In most cases, problems with lighting can be remedied easily by seating students away from the glare caused by sunshine coming through the classroom windows.

The organization of floor space and the kinds and placement of furniture used also need to be considered. For example, floors that do not have a nonslip surface can make wheelchair and other travel difficult for some students. Furniture that is placed in lanes can block access to the chalkboard or equipment such as computers and make mobility difficult for students in wheelchairs or students with visual impairments. Tables, pencil sharpeners, and chalkboards that are too high may prove inaccessible to students who use wheelchairs. Desks that are too low can interfere with students who have prostheses (artificial limbs). Placement and configuration of special equipment in science labs, computer centers, and vocational areas also can present difficulties in accessibility for students with special needs. For example, the lathe in the woodworking room might be positioned too high for a person in a wheelchair to operate; the space between work areas in the science lab might not be wide enough for a wheelchair to pass. Many of these physical features of classrooms may be beyond your control. If they become a problem, seek assistance from a special education teacher.

The arrangement of your class should be predictable. This means that you should not make major changes without first considering their impact on students with disabilities and then informing these students so they have time to adapt. For example, Mr. Tate decided to move one of the bookshelves in his classroom. He noticed, however, that the new location blocked the passageway from the door to the desk of a student in his class who was blind. Mr. Tate informed the student of the move in advance, and together they worked out an alternative route to the student's desk.

The arrangement of student desks, whether in rows, circles, or small groups, can have considerable impact on students with disabilities and other special needs. For example, traditional row configurations, which provide students with an immediate, unobstructed view of the teacher, have been shown to help students with attention disorders focus better when the teacher is instructing the whole group at one time. However, the placement of desks into clusters of four works better when using mixed-ability, cooperative learning groups to help integrate a student who is socially withdrawn. Another important consideration about floor space concerns student monitoring: Teachers should be able to see all parts of the classroom at all times, whether they are teaching large or small groups or are working at their desks. Designing such visual access means that all specially designated areas in the classroom, such as learning/interest centers, computer stations, small-group instructional areas, and study carrels, need to be positioned so they can be monitored.

An additional area of physical organization is storage. For example, students with visual disabilities may need to store equipment such as audio recorders, large-print books, braille books, and magnifying devices. For students with severe disabilities, space might be needed to store book holders, paper holders, page turners, braces, crutches, and communication boards.

Routines for Classroom Business

Establishing clear routines in both academic and nonacademic areas is important for two reasons. First, routines that are carefully structured (that is, clear to students and used consistently) reduce nonacademic time and increase learning time. Second, you can prevent many discipline problems by having predictable classroom routines.

Most students, especially those with special needs, find stability in knowing that classroom activities will be similar each day. In the absence of this stability, misbehavior often follows. Many examples of misbehavior can be related to breaks in school routines. On the day of a field trip, elementary school students are more likely to hit or push, to delay beginning assignments, and to do poor work. In middle schools and high schools, teachers often dread shortened schedules for assemblies and other school programs because of increased student behavior problems.

You can create daily classroom routines that help students learn. For example, you might expect fourth graders to enter your classroom each morning, begin their morning work, and read quietly if they finish before instruction begins. Having routines for sharing time, setting up science experiments, preparing to go to physical education, moving to the computer lab, and so on helps students meet your expectations. Routines are especially helpful to students who need a strong sense of structure in classroom life. In secondary schools, routines might include having specific lab procedures, starting each class with a five-minute review, or scheduling a particular activity on the same day every week. For example, in a geometry class, students who complete their assignments might choose to begin the day's homework, complete a Math Challenger worksheet from the activity file, or work on research papers or other long-term projects.

Classroom Climate

A number of authors have noted that classroom climate contributes significantly to the number and seriousness of classroom behavior problems (Marzano & Marzano, 2003) as well as student achievement (Hattie, 2009). Classroom climate concerns the overall atmosphere in the classroom—whether it is friendly or unfriendly, pleasant or unpleasant, and so on. Climate is influenced by the attitudes of the teacher and students toward individual differences. For instance, is the classroom characterized by a cooperative or a competitive atmosphere? Is the classroom a safe place for all students to take risks? Are skills for interacting positively with students and adults actively supported in the classroom?

dimensions of
DIVERSITY
Kleinfeld (cited in Gay, 2002), in her 1974/1975 research on Athabascan Inuit and American Indian children, found that the most effective teachers demonstrated personal caring and concern for students while at the same time demanding and facilitating high academic performance. Foster (1995, 1997) and Ladson-Billings (1994) observed similar traits among effective teachers of African-American students.

Teachers who communicate respect and trust to their students are more successful in creating a positive classroom environment in which fewer behavior problems occur (Arends, 2004; Marzano, 2003). For example, Mr. Elliott reprimanded a student who talked out of turn by saying, "I know you have a question about your work, and I'm glad you care enough to ask for help; but I need to have you raise your hand because I can only help people one at a time." Mr. Elliott showed respect for the student and built the student's trust by not putting her down. Yet Mr. Elliott stuck to his rule about not speaking before being called on and explained why it was important. Similarly, Ms. Belson asked Harriet to define the word *diffident*. Harriet gave an incorrect definition, saying it meant "being bored." Ms. Belson said, "Harriet, I can see how you might think the meaning is 'bored' because *diffident* looks a lot like *indifferent*. The word actually means 'lacking in confidence.'"

You can build the overall quality of your communication with your students in many small ways. For example, finding the time each week to speak privately with students lets them know that you care about them as individuals. Asking older students sincere questions about their friends, out-of-school activities, or part-time jobs also conveys your interest in them. Taking the time to write positive comments on papers lets students know that you appreciate their strengths and do not focus only on their special needs. When you encourage each student to achieve his or her own potential without continually comparing students to one another, you are communicating the idea that each class member has a valuable contribution to make. Teachers who fail to take these small steps toward positive communication with students or who publicly embarrass a student or punish a group because of the behavior of a few soon may create a negative classroom climate that thwarts appropriate and effective learning.

A final dimension of teacher–student communication concerns language differences. When students struggle to understand English, their behaviors may at first appear to be challenging. For example, a first grader is asked to complete several directions at one time and has a tantrum as a result of the frustration of not understanding. Similarly, a high school student apparently ignores a teacher's direction to put away project supplies and spend any remaining time beginning the homework assignment. When the teacher addresses this behavior, the student pushes everything off his desk. Is this a behavior problem or an example of misunderstanding and frustration? Teachers working with students who are not proficient English speakers should take care to distinguish problems that result from language differences from misbehavior.

RESEARCH NOTE

Research suggests that the most effective classroom rules are ones that students develop themselves and express with teacher guidance (Bullara, 1993).

dimensions of DIVERSITY

If your classroom includes students who are not native English speakers, you need to make sure that they understand classroom expectations. You may need to explain in concrete terms in a one-to-one situation what you expect, with the possible help of a translator, a student's parents, or both.

Behavior Management

Behavior management refers to teacher activities that directly promote positive student behavior. It includes establishing classroom rules, providing consistent consequences, and monitoring student behavior.

Rules help create a sense of order and expectations for a classroom, and they form a significant first step in setting up a learning environment based on preventive classroom management. Teachers who are effective classroom managers have well-defined rules for their classrooms (Marzano, 2003; Olson, Platt, & Dieker, 2007; Ornstein & Lasley, 2004).

Effective classroom rules share three key characteristics: They are brief and specific, positively worded and clearly understood by students (Alberto & Trautman, 2008; Doyle, 1990), and accommodate students from different cultures (Grossman, 1995).

Be sure to explain rules carefully to your students so that they are understood. Post rules during the first weeks of school, explain and discuss them, and model them for students. Early attention to setting your classroom expectations has a yearlong payoff. By rehearsing and focusing student attention on rules, you make them part of students' understanding of their classroom interactions. If you do not take this time to teach the rules, too often they become merely a bulletin board display, ignored by teachers and students alike.

Also, be sure that your rules accommodate students from different cultures. For example, rules about respecting other students' property may be puzzling for Latino students, for whom sharing one's belongings is a highly valued activity. Similarly, rules related to aggressive behavior may need to be enforced with care for students whose parents expect them to stand up for themselves, especially when someone says something derogatory about a student's family (Grossman, 1995). It is important to note that taking cultural differences into account does not necessarily mean that the rules need to be changed, only that the rules may need to be more carefully explained and enforced.

In addition to having clear expectations, teachers also need to tie their expectations to a set of consistent *consequences*. This means demonstrating that the same consequences apply to everyone and on a consistent basis. For example, Ms. DuBois has a rule that students are to raise their hands before speaking in class. She has also established the consequence that students receive one point for each class period they go without a single talk-out. Points earned figure into each student's grades for the class. Ms. DuBois is careful only to give points to students who meet the criterion of no talk-outs per day, regardless of who is involved or what the circumstances are, because she knows that enforcing rules arbitrarily greatly diminishes their effectiveness. Ms. DuBois also is sure to provide specific verbal praise along with the points to increase students' future chances of behaving appropriately without receiving points. Of course, Ms. DuBois realizes that sometimes rules need to be individualized, as in the case of Justin, a student with Tourette's syndrome, who is allowed one talk-out per class as specified on the behavior intervention plan (BIP) included in his individualized education program (IEP).

Finally, teachers need to *monitor* student classroom behaviors frequently. For example, you should scan the room to check that students are following the rules. To do this, you always need to have a clear view of the entire class, regardless of the activity in which you or the class are engaged. When student behavior is not carefully monitored, students choose not to follow the rules consistently. For example, Charmaine was a student in Ms. Patrick's fifth-grade class who had behavior problems. Ms. Patrick had a rule that students needed to complete all their independent work before they could go to the computer station to play a problem-solving game. Ms. Patrick did not have time to monitor Charmaine's behavior. One day, she saw Charmaine at the computer station and asked her whether she had completed her assignments. Not only had Charmaine not completed her assignments on that day, but she hadn't done any work for the past three days. Thereafter, Ms. Patrick was careful to monitor the work progress of all her students.

Use of Time

The way teachers use time in the classroom is one of the most important aspects of classroom organization. Effectively using instructional time and managing transition time constitute two particularly important tasks.

Using Instructional Time   The amount of time that students are meaningfully and successfully engaged in academic activities in school is referred to as **academic learning time** (Arends, 2004). Research has shown that more academic learning time in a classroom results in increased student learning (Berliner, 1990). Time usage is particularly important for students with special needs, who may need more time to learn than their peers.

Paine et al. (1983) suggest several ways in which teachers can maximize academic learning time. One way is to minimize the time spent on organizational activities such as taking the lunch counts, completing opening activities, getting drinks, sharpening pencils, cleaning out desks, and going to the bathroom. For example, teach students how to perform organizational tasks efficiently and how to observe a firm time schedule when carrying them out. Another way is to select activities that have the greatest teaching potential and that contribute most to students' achieving the core school curriculum. Although learning activities can be fun, they should ultimately be selected for the purpose of teaching students something important. Finally, the research-based

RESEARCH NOTE

Stichter, Stormont, and Lewis (2008) studied the use of time in high and low-poverty schools. They found that teachers in high-poverty schools engaged in more noninstructional talk, had more instructional down time, and had higher numbers of students exiting during instruction. Why do you think this is so?

PROFESSIONAL **EDGE**

Using "Sponges" to Increase Academic Learning Time

You almost always have times during the day when you have a minute or two before a scheduled academic activity or before the class goes to lunch, an assembly, or recess. You can fill that extra time with productive activities by using "sponges." Sponges are activities that fit into brief periods of time and give students practice or review on skills and content you have already covered in class. The following lists of sponges can help you "soak up" that extra classroom time.

EARLY ELEMENTARY SPONGES

1. Tell students to be ready to state one playground rule.
2. Tell students to be ready to list the names of classmates that begin with *J* or *M* and so on.
3. Tell students to be ready to draw something that is drawn only with circles.
4. Tell students to be ready to think of a good health habit.
5. Flash fingers—have students tell how many fingers you hold up.
6. Say numbers, days of the week, and months and have students tell what comes next.
7. Ask what number comes between two numbers: for example, 31 and 33, 45 and 47.
8. Ask students what number comes before or after 46, 52, 13, and so on.
9. Write a word on the board. Have students make a list of words that rhyme with it.
10. Count to 100 by 2s, 5s, 10s, and so on, either orally or in writing.
11. Think of animals that live on a farm, in the jungle, in water, and so forth.
12. Name fruits, vegetables, meats, and the like.
13. List things you can touch, things you can smell, and so on.

DISMISSAL SPONGES

1. "I Spy"—ask students to find something in the room that starts with *M, P,* and so on.
2. Ask students to find something in the room that has the sound of short *a*, long *a*, and so forth.
3. Number rows or tables. Signal the number of the table with fingers, and allow students to leave accordingly.
4. Count in order or by 2s, 5s, and so on.
5. Say the days of the week, the months of the year, and so on.
6. Ask what day it is, what month it is, what date it is, or what year it is. Ask how many months are in a year, how many days are in a week, and so on.

7. Use reward activities:

   "We have had a good day! Who helped it to be a good day for all of us? Betty, you brought flowers to brighten our room. You may leave. John, you remembered to rinse your hands, good for you. You may leave. Ellen showed us that she could be quiet coming into the room today. You may leave, Ellen. Bob remembered his library book all by himself. Dawn walked all the way to the playground—she remembered our safety rules. Lori brought things to share with us. Tom surprised us with a perfect paper—he must have practiced. . . ." Students' good deeds can be grouped together to speed up dismissal. The teacher can finish with, "You're all learning to be very thoughtful. I'm very proud of all of you and you should be very proud of yourselves."
8. Use flashcards. The first correct answer earns dismissal.
9. Review the four basic shapes. Each student names an object in the room in the shape of a triangle, circle, square, or rectangle.

UPPER ELEMENTARY AND MIDDLE SCHOOL SPONGES

1. List the continents.
2. Name as many gems or precious stones as you can.
3. List as many states as you can.
4. Write an abbreviation, a roman numeral, a trademark, a proper name (biological), or a proper name (geographical).
5. Name as many countries and their capitals as you can.
6. List the names of five parts of the body above the neck that are spelled with three letters.
7. List one manufactured item for each letter of the alphabet.
8. List as many nouns in the room as you can.
9. List one proper noun for each letter of the alphabet.
10. Name as many parts of a car as you can.
11. List as many kinds of trees as you can.
12. List as many personal pronouns as you can.
13. Name as many politicians as you can.

How many sponges can you think of for your grade or subject area? Additional ideas for sponges can be found at the Busy Teachers' Web Site K–12: http://www.ceismc.gatech.edu/busyt.

Sources: From "Effective Teaching for Higher Achievement," by D. Sparks and G. M. Sparks, 1984, *Educational Leadership, 49*(7).

---

strategies described in this chapter and throughout this book for managing your classroom, grouping your students, and adapting your methods and materials also help ensure the productive use of your students' time. One specific technique to increase the academic learning time of your students is described in the Professional Edge.

Managing Transition Time Just as important as the amount of time spent in activities is the management of transition time. **Transition time** is the time it takes to change from one activity to another. Transition time occurs when students remain at their seats and change from one subject to another, move from their seats to an activity in another part of the classroom, move from somewhere else in the classroom back to their seats, leave the classroom to go outside or to another part of the school building, or come back into the classroom from outside or from another part of the building (Paine et al., 1983).

Research studies show that teachers sometimes waste academic learning time by not managing transitions carefully (Ornstein & Lasley, 2004). Paine et al. (1983) suggest that you have rules devoted specifically to transitions and that you teach these rules directly to students. As with all rules, those for transitions need to be consistently monitored and reinforced.

The way you organize classroom materials also can affect the management of transitions. For example, you need to have all materials ready for each subject and activity. In addition, materials should be organized so that they are easily accessible. No matter how well organized your transitions are, you still may need to adapt them for some students with disabilities. Students with physical disabilities may need more time to take out or put away their books. Students with physical and visual disabilities may have mobility problems that cause them to take more time with such transitional activities as getting into instructional groups or moving from room to room. Furthermore, you may need an individualized system of rewards or other consequences to guide students with ADHD or behavior disorders through transition times.

dimensions of DIVERSITY

For ideas about designing lesson plans for English-language learners, go to http://coe.sdsu.edu/people/imora/MoraModules/ELDInstruction.htm.

How Can You Group All Your Students for Instruction in Inclusive Classrooms?

Students with special needs benefit from a variety of classroom grouping arrangements, including large- and small-group instruction, one-to-one instruction, and mixed- and same-skill groupings. The flexible use of classroom grouping arrangements is an important part of differentiated instruction (Broderick, Mehta-Parekh, & Reid, 2005). Remember that the particular arrangement you choose depends on your instructional objectives as well as your students' particular needs.

Whole-Class or Large-Group Instruction

Students with special needs benefit from both whole-class (or large-group) and small-group instruction. Tier 1 in RtI is whole-class instruction. One advantage of whole-class instruction is that students spend the entire time with the teacher. In small-group instruction, students spend part of the time with the teacher and also spend time working independently while the teacher works with other small groups. Research shows that the more time students spend with the teacher, the more likely they are to be engaged (Rimm-Kaufman, La Paro, Downer, & Pianta, 2005) and the more they learn (Rosenshine, 1997; Rosenshine & Stevens, 1986). This increase in learning may be because students are more likely to go off task when they are working on their own, particularly when they have learning or behavior problems. Whatever grouping arrangements you use, try to make sure that students spend as much time as possible working with you.

Another advantage of whole-group instruction is that it does not single out students with special needs as being different from their peers. However, you may need to make accommodations within whole-group instruction for students with disabilities. For example, students in Mr. Nichols's fourth-grade class were reading *Charlotte's Web* as a large-group instructional activity. Simone read more slowly than the rest of the class. To help her keep up, Mr. Nichols provided a digital version of the book. He also gave Simone more time to answer comprehension questions about the story in class because it took her longer to look up some of the answers. In another example, before his lectures, a high school science teacher identified technical words he was going to use and then worked before school with a small group of students with vocabulary problems to help them learn the words.

Small-Group Instruction

You may encounter situations in which small-group instruction is more appropriate for students with special needs. You can use same-skill groupings and mixed-skill groupings in setting up your groups.

Same-skill groupings, often referred to as *homogeneous groupings,* are helpful when some but not all students are having trouble mastering a particular skill and need more instruction and practice. For example, Ms. Rodgers was showing her students how to divide fractions that have a common denominator. She gave her class a quiz to see who had learned how to do the problems. She found that all but five students had mastered the skill. The next day, Ms. Rodgers worked with these five students while the rest of the class did an application activity. Small-group instruction is not only for students with disabilities; most students benefit from extra help in a small group at one time or another. In fact, many times students with special needs do not need extra instruction.

Small same-skill groups have also proven effective in basic skill areas when students are performing well below most of the class (Bursuck et al., 2004; Mosteller, Light, & Sachs, 1996). For example, Lori is in Ms. Hubbard's fourth-grade class and is reading at the second-grade level. Lori is learning decoding and vocabulary skills in a small group with other students who read at her level. Because the group is small and homogeneous, Ms. Hubbard is able to proceed in small steps, present many examples, and allow students to master skills before they move on. Lori is making progress and feels good about herself because she is becoming a better reader. Tier 2 and Tier 3 instruction in RtI is usually carried out in small same-skill groups.

Clearly, some students do require instruction that is more individualized and intensive than can be provided in the large group (Bursuck et al., 2004). However, small same-skill groups should be used only when attempts to make accommodations in the large group have been unsuccessful. Same-skill groups tend to become permanent and take on a life of their own. Thus, the ultimate goal of any small group should be its eventual dissolution. Also, on many days students can benefit from instruction with the rest of the class. For example, Lori's group participates in large-group reading when the teacher is reading a story and the class is working on listening comprehension. Another potential problem in using same-skill groupings is the danger that students in a low-achieving group in one area will be placed in low-achieving groups in other areas even though their skill levels do not justify it. For example, just because Lori is in the lowest-level reading group does not automatically mean she needs to be in a low-achieving group in math.

The major advantage of **mixed-skill groupings,** or *heterogeneous groupings,* is that they provide students with special needs a range of positive models for both academic and social behavior. In mixed-skill groupings, students often help each other so such groups can also be a vehicle for providing direct instruction to individual students, something for which classroom teachers often do not have the time. In addition, mixed-skill groups, like large groups, may be less likely to single out students with special needs.

One-to-One Instruction

Providing **one-to-one instruction** for students with special needs can be very effective under some circumstances. In this grouping arrangement, students work with a teacher, a paraprofessional, or a computer on well-sequenced, self-paced materials that are geared to their specific level. For example, Waldo is having trouble with addition and subtraction facts. For 15 minutes each day, he works at the classroom computer station on an individualized drill-and-practice program. Right now he is working on addition facts through 10. When he masters these, the software will automatically provide more difficult problems. Shamika, a student with a moderate intellectual disability, works with a paraprofessional on selecting food items for a balanced lunch while the rest of the class listens to a presentation on the process of performing a nutritional analysis. One-to-one instruction is sometimes an option in the more intensive tiers in RtI.

Although one-to-one instruction may be appropriate in some circumstances, it is not necessarily the grouping arrangement of choice in either general or special education. First, it is inefficient; when it is carried out by the classroom teacher the extensive use of one-to-one instruction will result in less instructional time for everyone. Second, the logistics of one-to-one instruction sometimes require that students complete much independent work while the teacher moves from student to student. This can lead to high levels of off-task behavior, a problem many students with special needs experience (Mercer & Pullen, 2009). Third, the lack of peer models in one-to-one instruction makes it more difficult to motivate students, a problem particularly relevant at the high school level (Ellis & Sabornie, 1990). Sometimes, habitual use of one-to-one instruction can exclude students from critical social interactions. Fourth, there is evidence to suggest that groups as large as three are equally effective (Vaughn et al., 2003). Finally, when a student requires this type of instruction for extended periods of time, further analysis is required of her needs and instructional setting.

The teaching materials you use have a great impact on whether your students meet the standards expected of them (Coyne, Kame'enui, & Carnine, 2007). In evaluating your materials, consider the learning outcomes targeted and the quality with which the materials are designed.

How Can You Evaluate Instructional Materials for Inclusive Classrooms?

Learning Outcomes

Instructional materials are designed to cover a range of *learning outcomes*. These outcomes reflect Bloom's revised taxonomy related to levels of thought. The six levels of thought, from lowest to highest, include remembering, understanding, applying, analyzing, evaluating, and creating (Anderson & Krathwohl, 2001, pp. 67–68):

1. *Remembering* involves retrieving, recognizing, and recalling relevant knowledge from long-term memory. For example, Ms. Lopez's American history class was studying the Revolutionary War. One of her remembering outcomes was for students to recall two major colonial leaders.
2. *Understanding* involves constructing meaning from oral, written, and graphic messages through interpreting, giving examples, classifying, summarizing, inferring, comparing, and explaining. For understanding, Ms. Lopez's students compared the family backgrounds of two colonial leaders.
3. *Applying* involves using information to solve a problem or produce some result. For this level of outcome, Ms. Lopez's students constructed a theory as to why colonial leaders refused to abolish slavery.
4. *Analyzing* is breaking up material into its parts and determining how the parts relate to one another and to an overall structure or purpose through differentiating, organizing, and attributing. For analyzing, Ms. Lopez's students differentiated how the colonists reacted to each British provocation leading up to the start of the Revolutionary War.
5. *Evaluating* involves making judgments based on criteria and standards through checking and critiquing. For this level of thought, students critiqued the colonial leaders as to their qualifications to lead the country as president.
6. *Creating,* the highest level of thought, involves putting together elements to form a coherent whole or reorganizing elements into a new pattern or structure through generating, planning, and producing. For creating, some of Ms. Lopez's students composed a song about the colonial leaders.

Keep in mind several important points when selecting the levels of thought required by your students' learning outcomes. First, in general, select outcomes reflecting a range of levels of thought, even if a range is not represented in the textbooks you are using. Textbooks and teachers tend to stress remembering at the expense of other levels of thought. Second, base your selection of outcomes on your

RESEARCH NOTE

Elbaum et al. (1999) asked third graders what they thought of mixed-skill grouping in reading. All students said that mixed-skill groups were noisy, encouraged disruptions, and made it hard to get help from the teacher. Students with disabilities felt anxious in groups because the groups made their problems more obvious.

PROFESSIONAL **EDGE**

Guidelines for Evaluating Basals and Other Basic Skills Curricula

Before evaluating any material, read the evaluative questions below and place an asterisk next to each that is critical for the type of material you are examining. Answer each question with yes or no. Examine all your responses in a single area, paying special attention to the questions you designated as critical. Rate each area inadequate (1), adequate (2), or excellent (3). If the area is inadequate, designate whether the features can be easily modified (M).

Rating Scale:	Inadequate	Adequate	Excellent	Easily modified
	1	2	3	M

1 2 3 M   **Effectiveness of Material**

Yes   No   Is information provided that indicates successful field testing or class testing of the material?

Yes   No   Has the material been successfully field tested with students similar to the target population?

Yes   No   Are testimonials and publisher claims clearly differentiated from research findings?

1 2 3 M   **Prerequisite Skills**

Yes   No   Are the prerequisite student skills and abilities needed to work with ease in the material specified?

Yes   No   Are the prerequisite student skills and abilities compatible with the objectives of the material?

Yes   No   Are the prerequisite student skills and abilities compatible with the target population?

1 2 3 M   **Content**

Yes   No   Are students provided with specific strategies rather than a series of isolated skills?

Yes   No   Does the selection of subject matter, facts, and skills adequately represent the content area?

Yes   No   Is the content consistent with the stated objectives?

Yes   No   Is the information presented in the material accurate?

Yes   No   Is the information presented in the material current?

Yes   No   Are various points of view—including treatment of cultural diversity, individuals with disabilities, ideologies, social values, gender roles, and socioeconomic status—represented objectively?

Yes   No   Are the content and the topic of the material relevant to the needs of students with disabilities?

1 2 3 M   **Sequence of Instruction**

Yes   No   Is the scope and sequence of the material clearly specified?

Yes   No   Are facts, concepts, and skills ordered logically?

Yes   No   Does the sequence of instruction proceed from simple to complex?

Yes   No   Does the sequence proceed in small, easily attainable steps?

---

students' strengths and needs, not their labels. Teachers tend to choose outcomes requiring lower levels of thought for students with disabilities and other special needs, regardless of their learning profiles. Use the INCLUDE strategy to choose the appropriate level of learning for all of your students.

The nature of the instructional materials you use is another very important consideration in accommodating students with special needs in your classroom. Consider the learning outcomes you desire as you select instructional materials that include textbooks, manipulatives and models, and technology.

Textbooks

Basal textbooks (often called *basals*) are books used for instruction in any subject area that contain all the key components of the curriculum being taught for that subject. The careful evaluation of basals is vital. Well-designed textbooks require fewer accommodations for students with special needs, thereby saving you much time and energy. For example, a math basal that contains plenty of practice activities does not need to be adapted for students who require lots of practice to master a skill. Similarly, a science textbook that highlights critical vocabulary and includes clear context cues to help students figure out the words on their own may make it unnecessary for

Rating Scale:	Inadequate	Adequate	Excellent	Easily modified
	1	2	3	M

1 2 3 M **Behavioral Objectives**

Yes　No　Are objectives or outcomes for the material clearly stated?

Yes　No　Are the objectives or outcomes consistent with the goals for the target population?

Yes　No　Are the objectives or outcomes stated in behavioral terms, including the desired behavior, the conditions for measurement of the behavior, and the desired standard of performance?

1 2 3 M **Initial Assessment and Placement**

Yes　No　Does the material provide a method to determine initial student placement in the curriculum?

Yes　No　Does the initial assessment for placement contain enough items to place the learner accurately?

1 2 3 M **Ongoing Assessment and Evaluation**

Yes　No　Does the material provide evaluation procedures for measuring progress and mastery of objectives?

Yes　No　Are there enough evaluative items to measure learner progress accurately?

Yes　No　Are procedures and/or materials for ongoing record keeping provided?

1 2 3 M **Instructional Input (Teaching Procedures)**

Yes　No　Are instructional procedures for each lesson either clearly specified or self-evident?

Yes　No　Does the instruction provide for active student involvement and responses?

Yes　No　Are the lessons adaptable to small-group and individualized instruction?

Yes　No　Are a variety of cueing and prompting techniques used to gain correct student responses?

Yes　No　When using verbal instruction, does the instruction proceed clearly and logically?

Yes　No　Does the material use teacher modeling and demonstration when appropriate to the skills being taught?

Yes　No　Does the material specify correction and feedback procedures for use during instruction?

1 2 3 M **Practice and Review**

Yes　No　Does the material contain appropriate practice activities that contribute to mastery of the skills and concepts?

Yes　No　Do practice activities relate directly to the desired outcome behaviors?

Yes　No　Does the material provide enough practice for students with learning problems?

Yes　No　Are skills systematically and cumulatively reviewed throughout the curriculum?

Source: From *Instructional Materials for the Mildly Handicapped: Selection, Utilization, and Modification,* by A. Archer, 1977, Eugene: University of Oregon, Northwest Learning Resources System. Used by permission of the author.

teachers to prepare extensive vocabulary study guides. A set of questions to help you evaluate basals and other basic skills materials is included in the Professional Edge.

Carefully evaluating basals helps alert you to any accommodations you may need to make. For example, a spelling basal with little provision for review can be troublesome for students who have problems retaining information; you may want to develop review activities for every three lessons rather than every five, as is done in a given book. Many teachers choose to develop or collect their own materials rather than depend on published basal series. For example, some teachers have their students read trade books instead of traditional reading books; others have their students engage in the actual writing process rather than, or in addition to, answering questions in a book. Still others involve their students in real-life math-problem solving rather than use basal math books. Even if your school does not use basals, the guidelines discussed here for teaching basic skills apply. Of course, the selection of materials is also critical in RtI schools where evidence-based practices are required within all of the instructional tiers. For example, having a research-based reading basal as part of a core curriculum in reading in Tier 1 makes the use of proven practices more likely, provides continuity for children and adults, supplies most necessary teaching tools, and ensures a systematic progression of skills or content, not leaving instruction to chance (Bursuck & Damer, 2011).

RESEARCH NOTE

Harniss, Caros, and Gersten (2007) found that students with special needs learned more when using a text that linked content information into "big ideas," helped students organize information, and provided extensive practice and review.

Content-area textbooks, which are books used for instruction in subject areas such as science and social studies, also need to be evaluated. In secondary schools, students often are expected to read their textbooks to access curriculum content (Sabornie & deBettencourt, 2009; Mercer & Pullen, 2009). Because students are required to read and understand their texts, often without previous instruction, the texts should be written at a level at which students can easily understand them. Armbruster and Anderson (1988) refer to readable textbooks as "considerate." Considerate textbooks are easier for students to use independently and require fewer teacher adaptations. The following guidelines refer to aspects of considerate textbooks involving content, organization, and quality of writing.

Check the Content Covered in the Text to See Whether It Stresses "Big Ideas" Rather Than Facts in Isolation   "Big ideas" are important principles that enable learners to understand the connections among facts and concepts they learn (Coyne et al., 2007). For example, in a text that stressed facts in isolation, students learned that Rosa Parks was an important figure because she led the Montgomery bus boycott in 1955. In a text that stressed big ideas, students learned that the bus boycott, led by Rosa Parks in 1955, was carried out in response to the problem of segregation in the South in the early 1950s and that the boycott was the first in a series of civil rights protests eventually leading to the Civil Rights Act of 1965.

Check to See Whether Support Is Provided for Student Comprehension   Support for student comprehension can be detected in the following three ways:

1. *Check the organization of the headings and subheadings:* Make an outline of the headings and subheadings in a few chapters. How reasonable is the structure revealed? Is it consistent with your knowledge of the subject matter?
2. *Check the consistency of organization in discussions of similar topics:* For example, in a science chapter on vertebrates, information about the different groups of vertebrates should be similarly organized; that is, if the section on amphibians discusses structure, body covering, subgroups, and reproduction, the section on reptiles should discuss the same topics, in the same order.
3. *Look for clear signaling of the structure:* A well-designed text includes information headings and subheadings. The most helpful headings are those that are the most specific about the content in the upcoming section. For example, the heading "Chemical Weathering" is a more helpful content clue than the heading "Another Kind of Weathering." A well-signaled text also includes format clues to organization. Page layouts, paragraphing, marginal notations, graphic aids, and the use of boldface, italics, and/or underlining can all serve to highlight or reinforce the structure. For example, a discussion of the four stages in the life cycle of butterflies could be signaled by using a separate, numbered paragraph for each state (that is, 1. Egg; 2. Larva; 3. Pupa; 4. Adult) and by including a picture for each stage. Finally, look for signal words and phrases that designate particular patterns of organization. For example, the phrases *in contrast* and *on the other hand* signal a compare-and-contrast organization, whereas the words *first, second,* and *third* indicate an enumeration or list pattern.

Check to See That Important Background Knowledge Is Activated   Despite the importance of background knowledge for comprehension (Beck & Mc-Keown, 2002; Marzano, 2004), many textbooks assume unrealistic levels of students' background knowledge (Gersten, Fuchs, Williams, & Baker, 2001). A failure to activate important background knowledge may be especially problematic for students with special needs, who are more likely to lack this information (Hallahan et al., 2005; Lerner & Johns, 2008). A number of textbook features indicate adequate attention to background knowledge. For example, social studies texts often activate background knowledge by providing definitions for important vocabulary content, displaying geographical information on maps, and featuring timelines delineating when key events took place (Coyne et al., 2007). As with all of the dimensions of effective materials we have discussed, using a text that fails to adequately take background knowledge into account means that you will have to provide it.

Check for Quality of Writing   The quality and clarity of writing can also affect student comprehension. Quality of writing can be evaluated in five ways:

1. *Look for explicit or obvious connectives, or conjunctions:* The absence of connectives can be particularly troublesome when the connective is a causal one (for example, *because, since, therefore*), which is frequently the case in content-area textbooks. Therefore, look especially for causal connectives. For example, the sentence *Because the guard cells relax, the openings close* is a better explanation than the sentences *The guard cells relax. The openings close.*

2. *Check for clear references:* Another problem to watch for is confusing pronoun references when more than one noun is used. For example, consider the following: *Both the stem of the plant and the leaf produce chloroform, but in different ways. For one, the sun hits it, and then . . .* Here, the pronouns *one* and *it* could be referring to either the stem or the leaf. Also, look out for vague quantifiers, those that do not modify the noun being quantified (for example, *some, many, few*). For example, the sentence *Some whales have become extinct* is clearer than *Some have become extinct.* In addition, check for definite pronouns without a clear referent (for example, *She saw him,* where the identity of *him* is not specified).

3. *Look for transition statements:* Transitions help the reader move easily from idea to idea. Given that a text covers many topics, make sure that the topic shifts are smooth. For example, in a biology chapter on the respiratory system, the text signals the transition from naming the parts of the respiratory system to describing the actual respiratory process by stating *Next, the role each of these parts of the body plays in the respiratory process will be described.*

4. *Make sure chronological sequences are easy to follow:* In a discussion of a sequence of events, the order of presentation in the text should generally proceed from first to last; any alteration of the order could cause confusion if not clearly signaled.

5. *Make sure graphic aids are clearly related to the text:* Graphic aids should contribute to understanding the material rather than simply provide decoration or fill space, should be easy to read and interpret, and should be clearly titled and labeled and referenced in the text so the reader knows when to look at them.

No matter how well designed conventional basal and content-area texts may be, they are still largely print based and fixed and uniform in format. As a result, conventional materials are likely to present barriers for students with disabilities (Pisha, 2003). For example, students who are blind will need a print alternative, such as braille; students with physical challenges may be unable to turn the pages in a text; students with attention and organizational problems may be unable to identify main ideas; and students with reading disabilities may not be able to read material accurately and quickly enough to comprehend it. Unfortunately, teachers may lack both the time and expertise to adapt these materials.

Modern digital texts can present the same content as conventional printed books but in a format that is more flexible and accessible (Pisha & Stahl, 2005). Digital versions of texts can be easily converted to braille, virtual pages can be turned with the slight press of a switch, and any words in the text can be read aloud.

Manipulatives and Models

Manipulatives and models can help students make connections between the abstractions often presented in school and the real-life products and situations these abstractions represent. *Manipulatives* are concrete objects or representational items, such as blocks and counters (for example, base-10 blocks for math), used as part of instruction. *Models* are also tangible objects; they provide a physical representation of an abstraction (for example, a scale model of the solar system). Strategies to help

dimensions of
DIVERSITY

Duke (2000) studied the use of informational texts in first-grade classrooms. She found few informational texts present, and that only 3.6 minutes of class time per day involved activities with information texts. The use of informational texts was even lower in high-poverty schools. Why is it important to spend time using informational text?

www.resources

Acquiring digital texts can be difficult. Bookshare offers free for all students with disabilities access to thousands of digital books, textbooks, teacher-recommended reading, periodicals, and assistive technology tools. For more information go to http://www.Bookshare.org.

The use of manipulatives and models in this biology class makes learning more concrete. What are ways manipulatives and models can be used to make subject matter content in other areas more concrete? Jupiter Images – Food Pix – Creatas

students make these connections have great potential benefit for students with special needs, who may lack the background knowledge and reasoning skills to understand abstractions (Cass, Cates, Smith, & Jackson, 2003; Smith, 2004). Still, manipulatives and models should be used carefully, because their use with students with special needs has not been heavily researched (Cass et al., 2003; Stein, Kinder, Silbert, & Carnine, 2005). When using these tools, consider the following seven guidelines (Marzola, 1987; Ross & Kurtz, 1993):

1. *Select materials that suit the concept and developmental stage of the students:* When you are first introducing a concept, materials should be easy to comprehend. Generally, the order in which you introduce materials should follow the same order as students' understanding: from the concrete to the representational to the abstract. However, not all students need to start at the same level. For example, in a biology lesson on the heart, many students benefit from viewing a three-dimensional model of a human heart, whereas other students are able to understand how a heart works just by seeing a picture of one.

2. *Use a variety of materials:* Students with disabilities may have trouble transferring their understanding of a concept from one form to another. For example, Curtis's teacher always demonstrated place value using base-10 blocks. When Curtis was given a place-value problem using coffee stirrers, he was unable to do it. Curtis's teacher could have prevented this problem in the first place by demonstrating place value using a range of manipulative materials, such as coffee stirrers, paper clips, and so on.

3. *Use verbal explanations whenever possible to accompany object manipulation:* Models and manipulative demonstrations should be preceded and accompanied by verbal explanations of the concept or skill being demonstrated. Verbal explanations are valuable because students may not be able to identify the important features of the model on their own. For example, Ms. Balou put a model of a two-digit-by-two-digit multiplication problem on the board. She verbally explained to her students all the steps in computing the problem and wrote each step on the whiteboard as it was completed.

4. *Encourage active interaction:* It is not enough just to have the teacher demonstrate with manipulatives or models as students observe. Students need to interact actively with models and manipulatives. Hands-on experience helps them construct their own meaning from the materials.

5. *Elicit student explanations of their manipulations or use of models:* Encourage your students to verbalize what they are doing as they work with models and manipulatives. This is a good way for you to assess whether they really understand the concept or skill. For example, Ms. Conway had her students name the main parts of the human heart using a model. Mr. Abeles had his students explain out loud how they would subtract 43 from 52 using base-10 blocks. Although explanations can help you evaluate how your students process information, students with special needs may not be able to articulate concepts right away because of language problems or a lack of reasoning skills. These students may require frequent demonstrations of how to articulate what they are doing.

---

www.resources

Virtual manipulatives are available online at the following websites: National Library of Virtual Manipulatives (http://nlvm.usu.edu); Math Tools (http://www.mathforum.org/mathtools/); Illuminations (http://illuminations.nctm.org/); Interactivate (http://www.shodor.org/interactivate/activities/); and Arcytech (http://arcytech.org/java/) (Bouck & Flanagan, 2010).

6. *Present clear guidelines for handling manipulatives to prevent management problems:* Although manipulatives can be helpful instructional tools, they also can create management problems, particularly in larger groups when your physical access to students is limited. For example, Ms. Leifheit wanted her students to manipulate blocks to show the sounds in words. Each child received three blocks. When the children heard a word such as *man*, they were to move a block as they said each sound: *m-a-n*. Ms. Leifheit had trouble getting students' attention at the beginning of the lesson because they were busy handling the blocks. She also found that students were not listening to her say the words, again because they were playing with the blocks. Ms. Leifheit decided to break the class into smaller groups so she could more carefully monitor student use of the blocks. She also established a simple rule: When the teacher is talking, students are not to touch their blocks.

7. *Move your students beyond the concrete level when they are ready:* Some students with special needs may have trouble moving from one learning stage to another. One effective way to help students make the transition from the concrete to the abstract is to pair concrete tasks with paper-and-pencil tasks. For example, Ms. Conway had her students label a picture of a human heart (representational stage) after they had observed and discussed a physical model (concrete stage). Mr. Abeles had his second-graders solve subtraction problems using manipulatives and then record their answers on a traditional worksheet without the presence of any pictures (abstract stage).

Technology

Teachers today have available to them a broad array of technologies to enhance the presentation of material to their students. Technologies range from low- to high-tech options. One common use of computers in inclusive classrooms is to provide instruction to students through drill-and-practice programs, tutorials, and simulations. In general, *drill-and-practice programs* are used often with students with special needs. Such programs have been shown to be effective for these students largely because they allow students to learn in small steps, provide systematic feedback, and allow for lots of practice to mastery. Still, not all drill-and-practice programs are created equal (Bursuck & Damer, 2011; Okolo, 2000). Look for programs that

- Directly relate student responding to the instructional objective
- Have animation or graphics that support the skill being practiced
- Provide feedback that helps students locate and correct their mistakes
- Store information about student performance or progress that can be accessed later by the teacher
- Have options for controlling features such as speed of problem presentation, type of feedback, problem difficulty, and amount of practice

Computers also can provide initial, sequenced instruction for students, using tutorials in problem solving, decision making, and risk taking and using simulations. Each of these forms of computer-assisted instruction has potential advantages and disadvantages (Roblyer, Edwards, & Havriluk, 2004). For example, *tutorials* can present instruction to mastery in small, sequential steps, an instructional approach shown to be effective with students with special needs. Tutorials also can provide one-to-one instruction at varying levels of difficulty, something teachers usually do not have time to do. Still, you need to check to be sure that students have the necessary prerequisite skills to benefit from the tutorials. In addition, tutorials may not provide sufficient review for students, and students may not be motivated enough to work through them independently (Roblyer et al., 2004). *Simulations* are of great potential benefit in teaching students to be active learners by confronting real-life situations. However, simulations may be difficult

www.resources

The National Center to Improve Practice in Special Education through Technology, Media and Materials has gathered and synthesized information about technology, disabilities, and instructional practices through a broad range of resources. This site also provides opportunities for teachers to exchange information, build knowledge, and practice through collaborative dialogue: http://www2.edc.org/ncip.

to integrate with academic curriculum, may require much teacher assistance, and can be time consuming (Roblyer et al., 2004).

Assistive technology (AT) is an important part of an inclusive classroom. An assistive-technology device is any piece of equipment that is used to increase, maintain, or improve the functional capabilities of a child with a disability. An assistive-technology service is any service that directly assists a child in the selection, acquisition, or use of an assistive-technology device, according to the Technology-Related Assistance for Individuals with Disabilities Act of 1998. As you have already learned, a range of high- to low-tech AT is available to enable students with disabilities to communicate or to access information by allowing them to bypass their disability. Ways to use INCLUDE to determine the AT needs of students with disabilities are described in the Technology Notes.

···▸ TECHNOLOGY NOTES

Using INCLUDE to Determine Assistive-Technology Needs

According to IDEA, the IEP team must consider whether a child needs assistive-technology (AT) devices and services as part of his or her plan for an appropriate education. This decision is further complicated by the fact that more than 29,000 AT devices exist for individuals with disabilities and aging adults (Baush & Hasselbring, 2004). The INCLUDE strategy can assist greatly in helping the team make this decision. What follows is a series of questions related to AT that teams may want to incorporate into the INCLUDE process. These questions were adapted from ones originally suggested by Beigel (2000); Marino, Marino, and Shaw (2006); and Pedrotty-Bryant, Bryant, and Raskind (1998).

IDENTIFY CLASSROOM DEMANDS

1. How do you present information? For example, teachers who use a lot of classroom discussions place a particular demand on students' speaking abilities; teachers who lecture frequently place a strain on students' writing and organizational skills.

2. What types of grouping arrangements do you use? An emphasis on cooperative learning places a burden on student communication skills.

3. What types of assignments do you make? For example, a project-driven class requires students to find and organize resource materials and then present them to the class in a clear, orderly way.

4. What are the primary ways you assess and evaluate your students? Oral assessments can place a strain on student verbal communication skills; written assessments place demands on written language skills such as handwriting, spelling, and sentence and paragraph construction.

5. How comfortable are you with having a learner who uses AT in the classroom? Your role in this process is very important. Without your support for learning to use AT and then continuing its use, a student may abandon her device.

6. What is the physical structure of your classroom and school? Issues such as whether there are adequate electrical outlets or tables large enough to accommodate a computer and various peripherals need to be considered.

NOTE LEARNER STRENGTHS AND NEEDS AND CHECK FOR POTENTIAL SUCCESS AND PROBLEM AREAS

1. What purposeful motoric movement does the student have? A purposeful movement is one that the learner controls in a conscious, consistent manner (Beigel, 2000, p. 240). Examples of purposeful motoric movement include raising an eyebrow, moving the fingers of one hand in a motion similar to that of typing, and using a pen or pencil to write or draw.

2. How willing is the student to try new activities or tasks? Using AT requires a willingness to change on the part of the student. Your knowledge of the student in this area can help determine the nature of the equipment selected (for example, easy to use or hard to use) as well as the amount of time needed to achieve independent usage.

3. What does the student desire from the use of AT? The personal goals of the learner can greatly influence AT usage. Relevance of the material is an important factor in learning to perform any skill. For example, Tamra had an expressed desire to write poetry and was quite receptive to learning to use a laptop with a large keyboard especially designed for her.

4. What emotional and psychological supports does the student need when learning to use the device? Some students may require considerable emotional and psychological support as they learn to use an AT device. You or other staff working with the student should provide such support when it is needed, as students who become frustrated or disinterested will not likely use the device. It is important to remember that

students cannot be forced to use AT; they can only be encouraged and supported whenever using the device.

5. What level of training do the student and others who interact with the student need? You, the student, and other staff working with the student need to be given the opportunity to see how the various devices work and to see who needs training and in what areas.

6. What impact, if any, do the student's socioeconomic status and cultural background have on the use of AT? Students who live in poverty, as well as their parents, are less likely to have previous experience with technology and may need more extensive training. There is also the question of the impact of culture on the acceptance of AT by students and their families.

BRAINSTORM AND DIFFERENTIATE INSTRUCTION

You need to consider the features of the technical devices as well as the extent to which they help students meet identified IEP goals:

1. How durable is the device? All devices that are used in schools should be able to withstand bumps and jars common in schools.

2. What setup and maintenance issues must be addressed? How easy is the device to update and repair? Do compatibility issues with other technology already in the classroom need to be addressed? Devices that are difficult to maintain, take a long time to repair, are not easily upgraded, or are incompatible with other technology should be avoided because eventually they will be abandoned.

3. How willing is the vendor of the device to provide a trial or loaner period of use for the student? You often need to try several devices in the school environment before a final AT decision can be made.

4. What is the reputation of the company in terms of construction, service, training, and reliability? These questions can be answered by consulting publications that deal with AT (*Team Rehab, TAM Connector*), contacting organizations (Council for Exceptional Children, Center for Applied Special Technology), and asking others who use AT.

5. Does the student have the psychomotor skills needed to use the device in a functional manner? This question should be answered during student assessment. Many devices can be adapted for students with limited motoric control; if a device cannot be adapted, then it is unrealistic to expect that it will be used.

6. Is the device aesthetically acceptable to the student? Some students may prefer a certain color or type of mouse; others may prefer a brightly colored exterior as opposed to the typical colors of blue, black, and beige; still others may want to decorate their equipment (as long as this doesn't interfere with its function). If students' aesthetic needs are not addressed, they may feel the device does not fit into their social milieu and will not likely use it.

7. Does the device meet the student's needs in a way that is easily understood by others? Students should be able to use their devices without causing a distraction. In addition, the device should not be so complex that only the vendor is able to program the device or explain how it can be used.

8. How portable is the device? For AT to be useful, the student or support person must be able to move the device from one class to another—from an elementary classroom to a special class such as art or physical education or between various academic classes in a middle or high school environment.

EVALUATE STUDENT PROGRESS

The ultimate goal of AT is to enable students to more readily meet their IEP goals. Pedrotty-Bryant et al. (1998, p. 55) suggest that teachers ask the following questions when determining whether the assistive technology selected is an appropriate match for the student.

- To what extent does the AT assist the student in compensating for the disability?
- To what degree does the technology promote student independence?
- What is the student's opinion of the technology adaptation?
- What is the family's opinion of the AT?
- Is the AT efficient and easy for the student to use?
- Does the device promote meeting IEP goals and objectives in the least restrictive environment?

How Can You Analyze Instructional Methods in Relation to Student Needs?

Teachers use a number of instructional methods in class, including direct instruction, indirect methods of instruction, scaffolding, independent student practice, and evaluation of student performance. Each of these methods should be analyzed in relation to student needs and then used and/or adapted as needed.

Elements of Direct Instruction

Several decades of research in teaching effectiveness have shown that many students learn skills and subject matter more readily when it is presented systematically and explicitly in what is often referred to as **direct instruction** (Rosenshine & Stevens, 1986; Stronge, 2002). Direct instruction consists of six key elements:

1. *Review and check the previous day's work (and reteach if necessary):* This aspect of direct instruction may include establishing routines for checking homework and reviewing relevant past learning and prerequisite skills. These procedures are important because students with special needs might not retain past learning and/or know how to apply it to new material. For example, on Thursday Ms. Guzik taught her students how to round to the nearest whole number. On Friday she gave her class a word problem to solve that required rounding. Before the students solved the problem, she pointed to a chart in the front of the room that displayed a model of how to round numbers and suggested that they refer to this chart as they solved the problem.

2. *Present new content or skills:* When content or skills are presented, teachers begin the lesson with a short statement of the objectives and a brief overview of what they are going to present and why. Material is presented in small steps, using careful demonstrations that incorporate illustrations and concrete examples to highlight key points. Included within the demonstrations are periodic questions to check for understanding.

3. *Provide guided student practice (and check for understanding):* At first, student practice takes place under the direct guidance of the teacher, who frequently questions all students on material directly related to the new content or skill. You can involve all students in questioning by using unison oral responses or by having students answer questions by holding up answer cards, raising their hands when they think an answer is correct, or holding up a number to show which answer they think is right. For example, when asking a yes-or-no question, tell your students to hold up a 1 when they think the answer is yes and a 2 when they think the answer is no.

   This approach can be used with spelling too. Have your students spell words on an index card and then hold up their answers. Unison responses not only give students more practice but also allow you to monitor student learning more readily. Prompts and additional explanations or demonstrations are provided during guided practice when appropriate. Effective guided practice continues until students meet the lesson objective. For example, Mr. Hayes was teaching his students how to add *es* to words that end in *y*. After modeling two examples at the board, he did several more examples with the students, guiding them as they applied the rule to change the *y* to *i* before they added *es*. Next, Mr. Hayes had students do a word on their own. Students wrote their answers on individual whiteboards and held up the boards when directed by Mr. Hayes. Mr. Hayes noticed that five students did not apply the rule correctly. He called these students up to his desk for additional instruction and had the rest of the students work independently, adding *es* to a list of words on a worksheet.

4. *Provide feedback and correction (and reteach when necessary):* When students answer quickly and confidently, the teacher asks another question or provides a short acknowledgment of correctness (for example, "That's right"). Hesitant but correct responses might be followed by process feedback (for example, "Yes, Yolanda, that's right because . . ."). When students respond incorrectly, the teacher uses corrections to draw out an improved student response. Corrections can include sustaining feedback (that is, simplifying the question, giving clues), explaining or reviewing steps, giving process feedback ("The reason we need to regroup in this subtraction problem is that the top number is smaller than the bottom number"), or reteaching last steps ("Remember, at the end of this experiment you need to tell whether the hypothesis was accepted or rejected. Let me show you what I mean"). Corrections continue until students have met the lesson objective, with praise used in moderation. Specific praise ("I'm impressed by how you drew a picture of that story problem!") is more effective than general praise ("Good job, Leon").

5. *Provide independent student practice:* Students practice independently on tasks directly related to the skills taught until they achieve a high correct rate. Practice activities are actively supervised and students are held accountable for their work.

6. *Review frequently:* Systematic review of previously learned material is provided, including the incorporation of review into homework and tests. Material missed in homework or tests is retaught (Rosenshine & Stevens, 1986).

It is important to note that for older students or for those who have more subject-matter knowledge or skills, these six steps can be modified, such as by presenting more material at one time or spending less time on guided practice. For example, when a second-grade teacher presented a unit on nutrition, she spent a whole week defining and showing examples of complex carbohydrates, fats, sugar, and protein. In an eighth-grade health class, this material was covered in one day, largely because students already had much background information on this topic. Moreover, each of the direct instruction steps is not required for every lesson you teach, although they are particularly helpful to students with learning and behavior problems, who have been shown to benefit greatly from a high level of classroom structure (Hallahan et al., 2005; Mercer & Pullen, 2009; Swanson & Deshler, 2003). The Case in Practice presents an example of a direct instruction lesson. The Instructional Edge describes how direct instruction techniques can be used to enhance Tier 1 instruction in RtI.

RESEARCH NOTE

Students are usually more attentive during fast-paced presentations (Darch & Gersten, 1985). The key to providing a fast-paced presentation is to begin the directions for the next question (or for correction of the current question) immediately after the students respond to the first question. It also helps to limit your own talk.

CASE IN PRACTICE

A Direct Instruction Lesson

This direct instruction lesson is designed to help students use pronouns clearly. Notice that Mr. Francisco first reviews the preskill of what a pronoun is. Then he guides students through the skill of substituting pronouns for nouns.

Mr. Francisco: Remember, yesterday we said that for every noun, there's a more general word called a *pronoun*. So, for the word *boys*, the pronoun is *they*. For the word *car*, the pronoun is *it*. What's the pronoun for the word *James*?

Students: He.

Mr. Francisco: Right. You're going to rewrite sentences so they have no nouns, only pronouns. Here's the first sentence: *Elephants eat grass.* What's the noun in the subject?

Students: Elephants.

Mr. Francisco: What's the pronoun that replaces *elephants*?

Students: They.

Mr. Francisco: What's the noun in the predicate?

Students: Grass.

Mr. Francisco: What's the pronoun that replaces *grass*?

Students: It.

Mr. Francisco: What is the entire sentence with pronouns?

Students: They eat it.

Mr. Francisco: Right. Look at the pronouns written on the board: *he, she, it, they, him, her, them.* You're going to use these words to rewrite sentences so they won't have any nouns, just pronouns. Here's Sentence 1: *George is watching birds.* What noun is the subject?

Students: George.

Mr. Francisco: What's the noun in the predicate?

Students: Birds.

Mr. Francisco: What's the sentence with pronouns in place?

Students: He is watching them.

Mr. Francisco: Good. Look at the next sentence: *Fred and Carlos build houses.* You are going to write it with pronouns in place of the nouns. [Teacher observes students and gives feedback.]

Mr. Francisco: Here's the sentence you should have: *They build them.*

[Teacher repeats with two more examples.]

REFLECTION

What direct instruction steps did Mr. Francisco use here?

Why is direct instruction particularly effective for students with learning and behavior challenges? In what situations would you *not* want to use direct instruction? Why?

Sources: Adapted from *Reasoning and Writing: A Direct Instruction Program,* by S. Engelmann and B. Grossen, 2001, Columbus, OH: SRA/McGraw-Hill.

INSTRUCTIONAL **EDGE**

Enhancing the Effectiveness of Tier 1 Instruction in RtI

You learned earlier in this chapter that the more effective your instruction is in the first place, the fewer the students who will require individualized accommodations. RtI's prevention-based, multitiered system is based on the similar idea that fewer students require instruction in more intensive tiers when evidence-based practices are effectively used in the less-intensive tiers. That is why the quality of instruction in Tier 1, the place where students are first taught, is so important. A successful experience in Tier 1 bodes well for future student success. An unsuccessful experience can lead to the need for "catch-up" in more-intensive tiers, and the process of catching students up is never quick or easy (Francis, Shaywitz, Stuebing, Fletcher & Shaywitz, 1996; Juel, 1988).

You can enhance the effectiveness of Tier 1 instruction by using the following evidence-based teaching techniques validated by Bursuck & Damer (2011). While all students benefit from these enhancements, students who are at risk or who have disabilities derive particular benefit from them.

- Establish a comfortable level of predictability at the beginning of lessons by telling students what they are learning, why they are learning it, and what the behavioral expectations are during the lesson.

- Actively engage students by providing them with many opportunities to respond, frequently through using unison responding.
- Present material to students in concise statements using language they understand.
- Maximize student attention and learning by employing a perky pace throughout every lesson.
- Provide support or scaffolding when students are learning new skills or content by clearly modeling new skills and providing the right amount of guided and independent practice.
- Facilitate retention by adding examples of previously learned material to examples of newly learned material.
- Correct students immediately after an error by modeling the correct answer/skill, guiding students to correct the error, and then asking the same question again so students have another opportunity to answer it.
- Continue instruction until the skill or concept presented is learned to mastery.
- Motivate students by employing a 3:1 ratio of positive to corrective teacher comment.

Indirect Methods of Instruction

Indirect instruction is based on the belief that children are naturally active learners and that given the appropriate instructional environment, they actively construct knowledge and solve problems in developmentally appropriate ways (Knight, 2002). This type of teaching is often referred to as *constructivistic* because of the belief that students are capable of constructing meaning on their own, in most cases without explicit instruction from the teacher (Hallahan et al., 2005; Knight, 2002). Indirect instruction is used by classroom teachers for both basic skills and content areas.

A common indirect method is called **inquiry learning,** or *discovery learning* (Jarolimek, Foster, & Kellough, 2004; Maroney, Finson, Beaver, & Jensen, 2003; National Research Council, 1999). Unlike direct instruction, which is very teacher centered, in the inquiry approach the teacher's role is that of a facilitator who guides learners' inquiry by helping them identify questions and problems (Jarolimek et al., 2004; Knight, 2002). The learners therefore are placed in situations that require considerable initiative and background knowledge in finding things out for themselves. In this way, students are actively involved in their own learning (Jarolimek et al., 2004).

You can see these elements of inquiry learning in a social studies lesson on Inuit or native Alaskan people developed by Lindquist (1995). The goal of the lesson was for students to "realize that there are many different groups of Inuit people, each having unique customs and traditions, but whose culture has been shaped by the Far North" (Lindquist, 1995, p. 54). First, the teacher gave the students five minutes to list everything they knew about the Inuit people. The teacher then had some students share their lists with the class.

Student sharing of their background knowledge was followed by a short film on the Inuit people. After the film, the students were asked to cross out anything on their lists that the film caused them to change their minds about. When the children had revised their lists, the teacher divided the class into pairs; each pair was asked to research a different Inuit tribe. They were to gather information about food, shelter, clothing, and language. Each pair of students recorded information about their particular tribe on a data sheet and reported their information to the class. As each group reported, the teacher synthesized the information on an overhead chart, creating a graphic display for comparing and contrasting similarities and differences among the various tribes.

Scaffolding

Scaffolding is an approach that has been used successfully to support students as they develop problem-solving skills (Larkin, 2001; Olson et al., 2007). Scaffolds are "forms of support provided by the teacher (or another student) to help students bridge the gap between their current abilities and the intended goal" (Rosenshine & Meister, 1992, p. 26).

Before using scaffolding, you need to find out whether students have the necessary background ability to learn a cognitive strategy (Rosenshine & Meister, 1992). For example, a strategy for helping a student read a physics textbook is not useful if the student lacks basic knowledge of mathematics and physical properties. Similarly, teaching a strategy for solving math word problems cannot succeed if the student does not have basic math computation skills. Using scaffolding to teach higher-order cognitive strategies consists of six stages:

1. *Present the new cognitive strategy:* In this stage, the teacher introduces the strategy concretely, using a list of strategy steps. The teacher then models the strategy, including all "thinking" and "doing" steps. For example, Mr. Bridges is teaching his history class how geographic features and natural resources affect the growth and location of cities. First, he introduces the problem-solving strategy to his students: (a) define the problem, (b) propose hypotheses to explain the problem, (c) collect data to evaluate your hypotheses, (d) evaluate the evidence, and (e) make a conclusion. These steps are posted on the chalkboard for easy reference. Mr. Bridges then models the strategy by showing students a map of the state of Illinois and thinking out loud as he applies the steps. For example, he explains how he would sort through many pieces of information in determining which factors led to the development of Chicago (for example, being on Lake Michigan) and which did not (for example, cold climate).

2. *Regulate difficulty during guided practice:* At this stage, students begin practicing the new strategy using simplified materials so they can concentrate on learning

www.resources

Find information on how to scaffold instruction for students at this link: http://iris.peabody.vanderbilt.edu/sca/chalcycle.htm.

With appropriate support, nondirect instruction can be effective for students with special needs. What steps should this teacher take to ensure effective instruction using scaffolding?
Elizabeth Crews/The Image Works

the strategy. First, the strategy is introduced one step at a time. Students are guided carefully through the steps, with the teacher anticipating particularly difficult steps and completing these difficult parts of the task as necessary. Before tackling difficult problems, such as the geography of Chicago, Mr. Bridges has his students use the problem-solving steps to solve simpler problems on topics familiar to them. For example, he has them solve problems such as why the cookies someone made were dry, why a hypothetical student is late for school every day, or why the school lunches taste awful. He also helps students brainstorm ideas for how to collect data, a step that can be difficult. Mr. Bridges does this by compiling an initial list of data collection procedures for each problem. For the problem of why the cookies were dry, Mr. Bridges gives his students a list of possible data collection procedures, such as identifying the ingredients, finding out how long the cookies were baked, and figuring out how old the cookies were.

3. *Provide varying contexts for student practice:* Students practice the strategy on actual classroom tasks under the teacher's direction. The teacher starts out leading the practice, but the students eventually carry out the practice sessions in small cooperative groups. In Mr. Bridges's class, students practice the problem-solving strategy using examples from their history textbooks.

4. *Provide feedback:* The teacher provides corrective feedback to students using evaluative checklists based on models of expert problem solving carefully explained to the students. Students are encouraged to evaluate their performance using these checklists. For example, each time Mr. Bridges's students use the problem-solving strategy, they evaluate their performance by asking themselves questions such as these: Did we clearly state the problem? Did we state a complete list of hypotheses? How thorough were our data collection procedures? Were we able to evaluate all the hypotheses using the information collected? Did we interpret the results accurately? Were our conclusions consistent with our results?

5. *Increase student responsibility:* Next the teacher begins to require students to practice putting all the steps together on their own. Student independence is encouraged by removing elements of the scaffold. For example, prompts and models are diminished, the complexity and difficulty of the materials are increased, and peer support is decreased. The teacher checks for student mastery before going to the last step, independent practice.

6. *Provide independent practice:* Finally, the teacher provides the students with extensive practice and helps them apply what they have learned to new situations. For example, Mr. Bridges shows his students how problem solving can be used in other subjects, such as science.

Independent Student Practice

The major purpose of practice is to help students refine or strengthen their skills in various areas. Consider the following seven guidelines for using practice activities effectively in your classroom:

1. *Students should practice only skills or content they have already learned:* This guideline is particularly important in order for students to be able to perform practice activities independently. Tasks that are too difficult can lead to high levels of off-task behavior.

2. *Practice is more effective when students have a desire to learn what they are practicing:* Whenever possible, point out to students situations in which they can use the skill in other phases of learning. For example, you may explain to your students that if they learn to read more quickly, they will be able to finish their homework in less time.

3. *Practice should be individualized:* Exercises should be organized so that each student can work independently.

4. *Practice should be specific and systematic:* Practice should be directly related to skills and objectives you are working on in class. This guideline is particularly

important for students with special needs, who require more practice to master academic skills.

5. *Students should have much practice on a few skills rather than little practice on many skills:* Focusing on one or two skills at a time is less confusing and gives students more practice on each skill.

6. *Practice should be organized so that students achieve high levels of success:* Correct answers reinforce students and encourage them to do more. Most students need at least 90 percent accuracy when doing practice activities, though higher-achieving students can tolerate a 70 percent rate as long as the teacher is present to assist them (Good & Brophy, 1986).

7. *Practice should be organized so that the students and teacher have immediate feedback:* You need to know how students are progressing so you can decide whether to move to the next skill. Students need to know how they are doing so they can make meaningful corrections to their work (Ornstein & Lasley, 2004).

For students with special needs, consider these additional questions: What are the response demands of the activity? Do students have to answer orally or in writing? How extensive a response is required? Do the students have enough time to finish the activity? Response demands are important because students who are unable to meet them will not be able to do the practice activity independently. For example, Mr. Edwards is having his class practice weekly vocabulary words by orally stating their definitions. Ross stutters and is unable to answer out loud. Mr. Edwards allows Ross to submit a written list of definitions. Ms. Osborne is having her students complete short-answer questions in their chemistry books. Clarice has a physical disability and is unable to write her answers independently. She uses an adapted classroom computer to prepare her answers. Mr. Nusbaum has asked his students to write a paragraph summarizing the reasons for the stock market crash of 1929. Maurice cannot write a coherent paragraph but can answer orally into an audio recorder. Amanda writes very slowly, so Mr. Nusbaum gives her more time to complete the activity.

Learning Centers   One common way of providing practice for students is through *learning centers,* classroom areas where students work alone or in groups as they engage in a variety of activities, often without the assistance of the classroom teacher (Opitz, 2007). Learning centers are called by a variety of names, including "interest centers, learning stations, activity areas, free choice areas, booths, and enrichment centers" (Patillo & Vaughn, 1992, p. 12). Well-designed learning centers can provide students with disabilities opportunities to be more actively engaged in learning, practice new skills, increase proficiency in skills acquired, and apply knowledge and skills to novel situations (King-Sears, 2007, p. 138). Learning centers can provide teachers with ways to provide differentiated instruction.

The key to effective use of learning centers is to design activities that are meaningful and can be accomplished independently. To do that, you must have a clear idea of what you want your students to learn ("Where are we going?"), how your students can practice information taught ("Who needs to practice what?"), and what your students' learning levels are ("What kinds of activities allow students to meaningfully practice and/or apply information learned?") (King-Sears, 2007, p. 138). Use the INCLUDE strategy to make accommodations for individual students as necessary. You can also employ a special type of teacher-led learning center by using the station-teaching option for co-teaching.

Homework   Another common form of practice used by teachers is *homework.* Research shows that homework has a positive effect on student achievement, when it is properly assigned and monitored (Cooper, 1989). Effects are greatest at upper grade levels and for lower-level tasks (Hattie, 2009).

Homework is often a challenge for students with special needs. For example, most teachers expect homework to be completed independently, and students must have the sensory, academic, and organizational skills to do so. A student with a severe reading disability might be unable to read a chapter in a geometry book and answer the questions without some form of accommodation such as a peer reader or recorded text. Similarly, a student with fine motor difficulties might be unable to answer the questions unless allowed to do so orally or with an adapted word processor. In addition, you may need to provide this same student more time or to assign fewer questions. Therefore, it is important that you carefully examine your own particular homework requirements and modify them to ensure full participation by all your students.

Evaluation of Student Performance

The major purpose of student evaluation is to determine the extent to which students have mastered academic skills or instructional content. Chapter 4 discussed formal and informal assessments that can be used to evaluate student progress. Student evaluations are also communicated through grades, which are determined in a number of ways, including classroom tests and assignments. Because student evaluation is so important, you need to consider how classroom tests and assignments may interact with student learning needs. Most critical is that the method of evaluation measures skill or content mastery, not a student's disability. For example, Carson, a student who has ADHD, should be given tests in small segments to ensure that the tests measure his knowledge, not his attention span. Similarly, Riesa, a student with a severe learning disability in writing, needs to take an oral essay test in physics if the test is to be a valid measure of her knowledge of physics rather than her writing disability. The type of report-card grade used, as well as the system used to arrive at that grade, might also need to be modified for some students. For example, Hal was discouraged about always getting a C in English, no matter how hard he tried. His teacher decided to supplement his grade with an A for effort to encourage Hal to keep trying. Mr. Henning encouraged his students to come to class on time by giving them credit for punctuality.

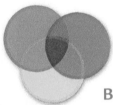

WRAPPING IT UP
BACK TO THE CASES

This section provides opportunities for you to apply the knowledge gained in this chapter to the cases described at the beginning of this chapter. The questions and activities that follow demonstrate how the principles and concepts you have learned about in this chapter connect to the everyday activities of all teachers.

MR. RODRIGUEZ has provided a digital copy of the text and a daily review of previously presented content, outlines of lectures, and small-group discussions to support Manuel's learning of content. Step 7 of the INCLUDE strategy asks teachers to evaluate student progress. Using information in this chapter and Chapter 4, suggest two assessment methods that Mr. Rodriguez might use to monitor Manuel's progress. Explain why you selected these two methods.

JOSH may face peers who have difficulty adjusting to his speech. As a result, they may shy away from interactions with him. Based on information provided in this chapter, describe two ways Ms. Stewart can use classroom management, grouping, instructional materials, or specific teaching methods to support Josh's interactions with peers. Explain why you think these methods would be helpful for Josh.

SUMMARY

- Instructional accommodations are support provided to help students gain full access to class content and instruction, and to demonstrate accurately what they know. Instructional or curricular modifications are made when the content expectations are altered and the performance outcomes expected of students change.

- The INCLUDE strategy is a decision-making process to help teachers make accommodations and modifications for stu-

dents with special needs. The steps in INCLUDE are identify classroom demands; note student learning strengths and needs; check for potential areas of student success; look for potential problem areas; use information to brainstorm ways to differentiate instruction; differentiate instruction; and evaluate student progress.

- An important part of the INCLUDE strategy is analyzing classroom demands. Demands covering four major areas should be analyzed: classroom management, classroom grouping, instructional materials, and instructional methods.

- Classroom organization includes physical organization, classroom routines, classroom climate, behavior management (including classroom rules, consequences, and monitoring), and use of time.

- Key aspects of classroom grouping involve the use of whole-class and small instructional groups, same-skill and mixed-skill groups, and one-to-one instruction.

- Instructional materials that need to be evaluated are basal textbooks, content-area textbooks, manipulatives and models, and instructional and assistive technology.

- Instructional methods should be analyzed in terms of student needs. Common methods to consider are direct and indirect instruction, independent student practice, and student evaluation. Sometimes students with disabilities or other special needs require extra support in order to be successful. These supports are called scaffolds.

APPLICATIONS IN TEACHING PRACTICE

PLANNING ACCOMMODATIONS IN THE INSTRUCTIONAL ENVIRONMENT

Consider the following two scenarios:

- Verna is a student with a learning disability in Ms. Chang's fourth-grade class. Ms. Chang uses whole-group instruction in math. This method is sometimes hard for Verna, who is behind her peers in math. Verna is slow to remember math facts, has trouble keeping numbers straight in columns, and sometimes forgets a step or two when she is computing a problem that requires several steps.

- Mr. Howard teaches U.S. history. About half of his fourth-hour class struggle in reading; four students receive special education services for learning disabilities. Mr. Howard has been assigned a special education teacher, Ms. Riley, to co-teach the class with him. Mr. Howard and Ms. Riley think the class can benefit from learning the following textbook-reading strategy (Bartelt, Marchio, & Reynolds, 1994):

  R *Review* headings and subheadings.
  E *Examine* boldface words.
  A *Ask* "What do I expect to learn?"
  D *Do* it: Read!
  S *Summarize* in your own words.

QUESTIONS

1. Identify the demands in Ms. Chang's class that are likely to be challenging for Verna.
2. How can Ms. Chang use the remaining steps in the INCLUDE strategy to help Verna succeed in the large group?
3. How can Ms. Chang use direct instruction to teach students to round numbers to the nearest 10? Design such a lesson.
4. How can Mr. Howard and Ms. Riley use the approaches for co-teaching you learned about in Chapter 3 to teach the reading strategy and still cover the history content required by the state?
5. How can they use scaffolding to teach the READS strategy?
6. Find a drill-and-practice computer program for elementary or high school students and evaluate it. Does it meet the criteria discussed in this chapter?

PEARSON myeducationlab

Go to Topic 10: Instructional Practices and Learning Strategies in the MyEducationLab (http://www.myeducationlab.com) for your course, where you can:

- Find learning outcomes for Instructional Practices and Learning Strategies along with the national standards that connect to these outcomes.
- Complete Assignments and Activities that can help you more deeply understand the chapter content.
- Apply and practice your understanding of the core teaching skills identified in the chapter with the Building Teaching Skills and Dispositions learning units.
- Examine challenging situations and cases presented in the IRIS Center Resources. (optional)
- Access video clips of CCSSO National Teachers of the Year award winners responding to the question, "Why Do I Teach?" in the Teacher Talk section. (optional)
- Check your comprehension on the content covered in the chapter by going to the Study Plan in the Book Resources for your text. Here you will be able to take a chapter quiz, receive feedback on your answers, and then access Review, Practice, and Enrichment activities to enhance your understanding of chapter content. (optional)

Strategies for Independent Learning

Strategies for Independent Learning

After you read this chapter, you will be able to

1. State ways that teachers can encourage student self-awareness, self-advocacy, and self-determination.
2. Explain how teachers can create their own learning strategies.
3. Describe the steps involved in teaching learning strategies. Analyze each step, discussing why it is important for building independent strategy usage.
4. List and describe research-based learning strategies in the areas of reading and reading comprehension, listening and note taking, written expression, math problem solving, and time and resource management. Discuss how they can be applied to the students you will be teaching.
5. Describe ways that teachers can help students perform learning strategies independently after they have learned how to do them.

Getty Images Inc. – Image Source Royalty Free

GERALD is a student with learning disabilities in Mr. McCrae's ninth-grade English class. Gerald has had problems in the area of written expression throughout his school years, consistently failing to meet standards on the state high-stakes assessment. It is not that he does not have good ideas. When Gerald talks about what he is going to write, it sounds great. However, when he tries to get his ideas on paper, he becomes very frustrated. Writing is difficult for Gerald. One problem is that his papers lack organization. They rarely have a good introduction and conclusion, and the body is usually out of sequence. Gerald also makes a lot of mechanical errors; his papers are full of misspellings, and he frequently leaves out punctuation marks and capital letters. When asked by Mr. McCrae why he does not proofread his papers, Gerald responded that he does.

What can Mr. McCrae do to help Gerald learn to organize his papers better? How can he help Gerald proofread his papers better for mechanical errors?

TRACI is a student in Ms. Cord's fourth-grade class. Last year, Traci didn't meet standards on the state high-stakes assessment in math, but her scores were not low enough to make her eligible for special education services. Traci has trouble solving word problems in math because she does not have a systematic way of working on them. When she starts a problem, she looks for the numbers right away rather than first reading the problem carefully. For example, one day she saw the numbers 23 and 46 in a problem and automatically added them to get a sum of 69. The problem called for subtraction, but Traci did not know that, because she had not read the problem.

What can Ms. Cord do to help Traci solve math word problems more successfully? How can Ms. Cord help Traci become a more successful independent problem solver?

RON is a twelfth-grade student with a moderate intellectual disability who has problems with organization. He is often late for school, because, according to his parents, he rarely plans ahead and is always getting his materials ready for school at the last minute. Ron is usually late for class as well. He says that he cannot keep track of what he needs to bring to each class, so he is constantly going back to his locker, which makes him late. His locker is a complete mess. In the afternoons, Ron has a part-time job helping to clean copying and fax machines as part of a work-study program. His supervisor has expressed concern that Ron has been late for work several times and frequently misses his bus, causing his co-workers to have to drive him home.

What can Ron's teachers do to help him become better organized?

Gerald, Traci, and Ron share a common problem: They are unable to meet independently the academic and organizational demands of school. Being able to work and solve problems independently has become increasingly important as more and more students are expected to meet state and federal standards and as the demands of the twenty-first-century job market have become increasingly complex. Gerald needs to be able to organize his papers better, not just in English but in all areas, because teachers often judge quality on the basis of organization, neatness, and the number of spelling or punctuation errors. Traci needs to solve problems more systematically, not just in math but in other classes and outside school as well. Ron needs a strategy for managing his time: Being punctual and having the necessary supplies or materials are essential for success on his alternate assessments as well as eventually in the world of work. The fact is, as students move through the grades and on to careers or postsecondary education, more and more independence is expected and necessary for success.

Students need to perform independently in five key areas: gaining information, storing and retrieving information, expressing information, self-advocating, and managing time (Ellis & Lenz, 1996). Gaining information involves skills in listening to directions during lessons and on the job and in reading and interpreting textbooks, source books, and other media. Storing information consists of strategies for taking notes and preparing for tests or other evaluations. Students also need to retrieve information when needed. For example, they need to remember how to carry out a task such as cleaning and clearing a table or how to follow safety procedures during science lab. Expressing information includes the tasks of taking tests and writing papers. It also involves employment tasks such as developing a printed menu for a fast-food restaurant. Self-advocacy skills build student self-determination, helping students set realistic school or life goals and develop and carry out a plan to meet those goals. Finally, students need to have the time management skills to organize their time and efforts toward meeting their goals.

Although all these skills become more important as students progress through school, independence should be stressed at all levels of instruction. Unfortunately, many students, including those who are at risk or have other special needs, lack basic independent learning skills. Traditionally, when students needed learning-strategy instruction, they were referred to special education classes, remedial reading or math programs, or special study-skills courses. But in inclusive classrooms, learning strategies can be taught to students with disabilities or other special needs in several ways. Moreover, learning strategies often can be covered in class so that all students can benefit. For example, when Mr. Cooper discovered that many of his students in U.S. history were having trouble taking notes, he presented a note-taking strategy to his whole class. Similarly, Ms. Carpenter taught her biology class a strategy for taking multiple-choice tests because her students were scoring low as a group on these kinds of questions.

When students have more intensive skill needs, more individualized strategy instruction might take place outside the classroom, sometimes in a Tier 2 RtI group. For example, some students with special needs may need to have a strategy broken down into small steps, view multiple demonstrations of a strategy, and practice the strategy many times before they learn it. If the collaborative support of other education professionals is lacking, this level of instruction may be difficult to deliver within the time and curricular constraints of the general education classroom. Ron, from the chapter-opening case, has just such extraordinary needs. He needs a strategy designed specifically for his organizational problems; a plan for getting to his afternoon job on time would not be relevant for the rest of his classmates. In cases such as these—in which a special educator teaches a strategy to individual students—your job is to encourage and monitor student use of the strategy in your class and to provide students with feedback on their performance. However, in most cases, you can teach many of these skills in your class while still covering the required academic content. In fact, teaching learning strategies to students allows you to cover more material because your students become able to learn on their own.

You should do all you can to encourage the use of independent learning strategies and teach them to your students. This chapter focuses on ways you can build student independence in learning by encouraging student self-awareness and self-advocacy skills, developing and teaching independent learning strategies directly in class, and teaching students to use specific strategies on their own.

How Can You Encourage Student Self-Awareness, Self-Advocacy, and Self-Determination?

As students move through elementary, middle, and high school and on to postsecondary education or the world of work, the level of independence expected by those around them increases. Teachers expect students to come to class on time, master content through reading and lectures, keep track of assignments, organize study and homework time, set realistic career goals, and participate in curricular and extracurricular activities to meet these career goals. Students also must recognize when they have a problem and know where to go for help. Clearly, students need to look out for themselves, to become self-advocates. **Self-advocacy** is an important part of self-determination, or the ability to make decisions and direct behavior so that the desired goals are achieved (Holverstott, 2005). While the goal of becoming self-determined is important for all students, it is particularly important for students with special needs, who are at risk for learned helplessness and low self-esteem.

Adjusting to changing expectations can be difficult for all students, but especially for those with disabilities. Many students with special needs are not aware of their strengths and weaknesses (Brinckerhoff, 1994; Scanlon & Mellard, 2002) and lack self-advocacy skills (Durlak, Rose, & Bursuck, 1994; Janiga & Costenbader, 2002). Self-advocacy skills can be taught to students of all ages and disabilities (Test, Fowler, Brewer, & Wood, 2005).

In effective student self-advocacy training, students learn their strengths and weaknesses, the potential impact of these strengths and weaknesses on their performance, the support they need to succeed, and the skills required to communicate their needs positively and assertively. Generally speaking, special educators have much of the responsibility for teaching self-advocacy directly. However, general education teachers are in a good position to teach all students about the opportunities and expectations of the adult world related to self-awareness and self-advocacy. For example, in applying the steps in INCLUDE, when Ms. Gay observed that Meredith was getting Fs on her independent work in class, Ms. Gay surmised that Meredith's problem was at least in part due to her being afraid to ask for help. Ms. Gay decided to spend five minutes with the whole class to talk about knowing when and how to ask for help. She felt this discussion would help Meredith and other students in the class be more assertive when they encountered difficulty in their work. In another situation, Cecil, a student with a vision impairment who was in Mr. Jordan's algebra class, sat in the front row but was still unable to see the problems on the board because Mr. Jordan wrote the numbers too small. However, Cecil did not feel comfortable asking Mr. Jordan to write larger. With his special education teacher, Cecil practiced asking Mr. Jordan for help. Cecil then asked Mr. Jordan directly, who responded that it would be no problem to write bigger. Mr. Jordan also gave Cecil some additional pointers on how to describe his disability and how to ask his teachers for accommodations. The Working Together stresses the importance of teachers working together as a team when helping students acquire self-advocacy skills.

INCLUDE

RESEARCH NOTE

Neale and Test (2010) successfully taught third- and fourth-grade students with high-incidence disabilities to express their learning preferences in an IEP meeting using a learning strategy called "I Can Use Effort."

Working TOGETHER

Fostering Team Communication and Self-Advocacy

Avery was a student in Mr. Katz's biology class. During the third week of school, Avery approached Mr. Katz after class. Avery said he had a learning disability and that his special education teacher said he had a legal right to receive more time to take his classroom tests. Mr. Katz was concerned. He felt that it wasn't fair to let Avery have extra time when he couldn't do that for the rest of the class. Mr. Katz also knew that the state test in science would be given soon and that getting more time to take classroom tests was not a good way to prepare Avery for them. In Mr. Katz's eyes, if Avery failed to meet standards in science, he, Avery's teacher, would be accountable. Furthermore, Mr. Katz was furious that no one had told him about this issue. He knew Avery had learning disabilities and that he might need extra help, but no one had said anything about changing how he took tests. Mr. Katz remembered that he had been unable to attend Avery's individualized education program (IEP) meeting due to a scheduling conflict, but shouldn't someone have told him about something as important as this?

Why is it important for students with disabilities to be able to advocate for themselves?

Why do you think a problem has occurred in this case?

What steps should Mr. Katz take to get the IEP team working together to support Avery?

www.resources

The following websites can be valuable resources for students as they develop self-advocacy skills:
Wrightslaw: http://www.wrightslaw.com
Disability Rights Education and Defense Fund (DREDF): http://edhd.bgsu.edu/isod

INCLUDE

How Can You Effectively Teach Independent Learning Strategies in Class?

In addition to teaching students to advocate for their own educational needs, another way you can help your students become more independent is to teach them strategies for learning how to learn (Lenz, 2006). These methods are collectively referred to as learning strategies. **Learning strategies** are techniques, principles, and rules that enable a student to learn to solve problems and complete tasks independently (Lenz, Ellis, & Scanlon, 1996; Schumaker, Deshler, & Denton, 1984). Learning strategies, which are similar to study skills, not only emphasize the steps needed to perform a strategy (for example, steps to follow in reading a textbook) but also stress why and when to use that strategy as well as how to monitor its usage. For example, when Ms. Blankenship taught her students a strategy for reading their textbook, she pointed out that the strategy would save them time yet improve their test scores. She also taught them to judge how well they were using the strategy by filling out a simple checklist as they read. The Case in Practice shows how the INCLUDE strategy can be used to select the appropriate learning strategies for your students.

An important component of teaching learning strategies effectively is that they be well-designed. As you recall from the discussions of effective materials, the better your materials are designed, the greater the chance that they will work for your students with disabilities or other special needs without requiring you to make major accommodations. Some effective guidelines for designing learning strategies are presented in the Professional Edge.

For students to use learning strategies independently, they must first learn to perform them accurately and fluently. Research shows that most students benefit when the teacher directly explains how learning strategies can help them complete academic tasks (Lenz, 2006). However, students vary in the amount of structure they need to acquire learning strategies (Lenz, 2006). Some students can construct successful strategies on their own from repeatedly completing tasks in their classes (Pressley & Hilden, 2006). Other students may need simple prompts and models to develop strategies. This level of structure usually can be delivered by the general education teacher in a large-group setting. Still other students may require more intensive instruction, often in a small group, that includes explicit describing and

CASE IN PRACTICE

Using INCLUDE to Guide Instruction in Learning Strategies

Mr. Devereau taught social studies at Martin Luther King Jr. Middle School. He had a reputation for expecting a lot from his students; throughout the year, he expected them to be able to learn an increasing amount of subject matter independently.

Prior to the first day of school, Mr. Devereau was informed that his first-period class included eight students with learning disabilities and two with behavior disorders. He was also told that a special education teacher, Ms. Finch, was assigned to the class as a co-teacher. Mr. Devereau had never before had this many students with disabilities in one class; he also had never worked with a co-teacher. Still, he was hopeful that Ms. Finch would be able to help him, so he set up an appointment to meet with her.

Ms. Finch: What demands do students have to meet to be successful in your class?

Mr. Devereau: I expect students to begin to learn on their own. That is what is expected when they get to high school. I assign most of the reading of the text to be done outside of class, and I require students to take notes from class lectures and DVDs that I show. With my lectures, I use mainly PowerPoint slides. I distribute copies of the slides to students before class.

Ms. Finch: How does your grading system work?

Mr. Devereau: Grades are based on student performance on two multiple-choice tests and a five-page report on a famous person in pre–Civil War America.

Ms. Finch: Based on how your class is structured, my concern is that the students' IEPs show that they all are likely to have problems finding main ideas in both the textbook and the class lectures. But I know of some learning strategies that would help them be more successful in these areas.

Mr. Devereau: That sounds good. It's likely that other students in the class would benefit from these strategies as well.

Mr. Devereau and Ms. Finch decided to each take a strategy. Mr. Devereau would teach the note-taking strategy while he was lecturing in class. Ms. Finch would assist by modeling note taking at the board and/or monitoring student note-taking performance and providing corrective feedback as necessary. Ms. Finch was to teach the students two textbook-reading strategies: one for scanning a text and another for summarizing the big ideas in the text. She was to work on these strategies daily during the last 15 minutes of class until the students were able to perform them independently. While Ms. Finch and Mr. Devereau thought that the students with special needs also would have trouble with the multiple-choice tests and the five-page report, they decided that covering these strategies at the same time would be too much. However, they agreed to show the students how the strategies they were learning for note taking and textbook reading could also help them with their tests and research paper.

REFLECTION

How did Mr. Devereau and Ms. Finch use INCLUDE to help their students? Was it appropriate for them to teach the strategies to the entire class? Why? Which specific strategies described in this chapter might be appropriate for Mr. Devereau and Ms. Finch to use?

---

modeling of a specific strategy as well as extensive practice and feedback about how to apply the strategy to their course demands (Swanson, 2001). This more intensive instruction can be delivered in Tier 2 or 3 of an RtI system, depending on the degree of student need. The following steps for teaching learning strategies are research-based (Deshler et al., 1996):

1. Assess current strategy use.
2. Clarify expectations.
3. Demonstrate strategy use.
4. Encourage students to memorize strategy steps.
5. Provide guided and independent practice.
6. Administer posttests.

These steps incorporate many of the effective teaching practices and would also qualify as evidence-based practices for RtI. Use the INCLUDE strategy to help you determine the level of structure you need to provide to students as you deliver each step. Guidelines for differentiating instruction in Tier 3 in RtI are provided in the Instructional Edge.

INCLUDE

PROFESSIONAL EDGE

Developing Your Own Learning Strategies

You can use the guidelines here either to create your own learning strategies or to evaluate ones that are commercially produced. By following these suggestions, you can develop learning strategies tailored for the students in your class.

1. Identify skill areas that are problematic for most of your students, such as taking multiple-choice tests or writing lecture notes.

2. For each skill area, specify student outcomes, such as scoring at least 10 percent higher on multiple-choice tests or writing down key main ideas and details from a lecture.

3. List a set of specific steps students need to follow to reach the identified outcomes. You may want to ask other students who have good test-taking and note-taking skills what they do. Presented here is a sample reading comprehension strategy called *RAP* (Ellis & Lenz, 1987):

   R *Read* a paragraph.

   A *Ask* yourself what were the main idea and two details.

   P *Put* the main idea and details in your own words.

4. Your strategy should contain no more than eight steps. Having more steps makes the strategy difficult to remember.

5. Your steps should be brief; each should begin with a verb that directly relates to the strategy.

6. To help students remember the steps, encase the strategy in a mnemonic device (for example, the acronym RAP for the reading strategy just presented).

7. The strategy should cue students to perform behaviors for thinking (remembering), for doing (reading), and for self-evaluation (surveying or checking their work).

8. A textbook-reading strategy developed by teachers (Bartelt, Marchio, & Reynolds, 1994) that meets the guidelines for developing an effective learning strategy follows:

   R *Review* headings and subheadings.

   E *Examine* boldface words.

   A *Ask,* "What do I expect to learn?"

   D *Do* it—Read!

   S *Summarize* in your own words.

Source: Adapted from "Generalization and Adaptation of Learning Strategies to Natural Environments: Part 2. Research into Practice," by E. Ellis, K. Lenz, and E. Sabornie, 1987, *Remedial and Special Education, 8*(2), pp. 6–23. Copyright © 1987 by Hammill Institute on Disability. Reprinted with permission.

Assess Current Strategy Use

INCLUDE

Students often are receptive to instruction when they can clearly see what problems they are having and how the strategy you are teaching can help them overcome these problems. Therefore, learning-strategy instruction begins with an assessment of how well your students can currently perform a skill, a part of the N and C steps of INCLUDE. Specific learning strategies can be assessed using direct observation checklists, analyses of student products, and student self-evaluations.

You also need to assess whether your students have the preskills necessary to perform the strategy. For example, students who can discriminate between main ideas and details in a lecture are ideal candidates for learning a note-taking strategy; students who can read all the words on a test and understand the class content will benefit most from a test-taking strategy. In contrast, students who cannot identify most of the words in their texts are not logical candidates for learning a textbook-reading strategy; students whose assignments are too difficult for them will not benefit from a strategy to help them organize their independent practice activities.

As you have learned, students with special needs often lack critical preskills. Before you decide to teach a particular strategy, you should identify its preskills and assess them separately. If most students lack the preskills, they can be taught as part of your everyday instruction. If only a few have problems with preskills, these students need to receive additional instruction in class, with a peer or adult tutor, through co-taught lessons, or in a learning center, Tier 2, Tier 3, or special education setting.

Clarify Expectations

Learning strategies have the potential of empowering your students because they enable them to learn and succeed in and out of school on their own, without undue help from others. When you introduce learning strategies to students, you need to

INSTRUCTIONAL **EDGE**

Providing Differentiated Instruction in Tier 3 in RtI

You have learned that in RtI, professionals accommodate individual differences using instruction of varying intensities called tiers, and that students who fail to make adequate progress in the least intensive tier, Tier 1, receive extra practice on targeted foundational skills in Tier 2. A smaller number of students continue to struggle, despite well-delivered evidence-based Tier 2 instruction. These students need even more intensive instruction in Tier 3.

What is Tier 3 instruction?

In Tier 3, students receive highly intensive instruction matched to their individual needs (Reschley, 2007). Tier 3 can be special education, but not always. Tier 3 instruction is more concentrated than Tiers 1 and 2, focusing on a small set of foundational skills, usually in math, reading, writing, and behavior, that may or may not be at grade level (Lemons, 2007). Intensity in Tier 3 is addressed through (a) more frequent sessions, often of longer duration, (b) smaller groups, and (c) highly systematic and explicit instruction characterized by control of task difficulty, careful sequencing of tasks, frequent teacher modeling, guided practice and feedback, a mastery learning orientation (whereby students don't move to the next skill, lesson, or activity until the previous one is learned), and motivators to help students regulate their attention and behavior and work hard (Gersten et al., 2009a; Gersten et al., 2009b). Prepackaged and/or commercially produced programs can be used for Tier 3 as long as they are highly systematic, explicit, and evidence based (Bursuck & Damer, 2011). One example of such a program is the University of Kansas Strategic Instruction Model (SIM) learning strategy materials (http://www.ku-crl.org/sim/).

Who is eligible for Tier 3 instruction?

Students enter Tier 3 when the results of their progress monitoring show a clear lack of progress towards meeting specified benchmarks. If special education is involved, then a comprehensive evaluation to determine special education needs and eligibility is required. Tier 3 typically includes approximately 2–6% of students (Lyon, 2009). In a class of 25 students this would amount to 1 or 2 students, though this figure may be higher in some high-poverty schools (Bursuck et al., 2004).

Where, when, and for how long does Tier 3 instruction take place?

Tier 3 instruction usually takes place outside the general education classroom. In middle or high school, Tier 3 can occur during time scheduled for elective classes or study halls (Mellard & Prewett,

2010). On average, students participating in Tier 3 receive interventions daily, totaling from 45–120 extra minutes of instruction per week in addition to time spent in their core general education program (Gersten et al., 2009a). In many instances Tier 3 time in high school is longer because in areas such as reading there is no core general education program. Length is dependent on multiple issues including problem severity, subject, intervention method, and scheduling. Sometimes Tier 3 instruction is delivered in the form of a "double dose," whereby student daily time in instruction is doubled. With regard to group size, one-to-one instruction appears to be most effective (Gersten et al., 2009a), although groups as large as 3 are used in situations of limited resources and middle and high schools.

Who teaches Tier 3 groups?

Tier 3 groups are most commonly taught by special education teachers, even when Tier 3 is not special education, although Tier 3 groups can be taught by general educators, speech and language pathologists, and Title 1 teachers. Tier 3 interventions involving behavior are likely to involve the school psychologist.

How long do students remain in Tier 3 groups?

Because the skill deficits of students receiving Tier 3 services are very significant, Tier 3 groups are longer term than Tier 2 groups, extending for as long as one or two years (Reschley, 2007). While in Tier 3, students' progress is monitored continually; the results are used to change instruction as needed as well as determine eventual readiness to exit Tier 3 and reenter Tiers 1 and 2.

What is the role of the general education teacher in teaching Tier 3 students?

Even though general education teachers do not usually teach Tier 3 groups, they teach Tier 3 students at other times during the day. By applying the INCLUDE strategy, teachers can readily find out how well their Tier 3 students are meeting their classroom demands. This "window on reality" is an important part of progress monitoring for the RtI team as they continually evaluate the extent to which the gap between Tier 3 students and their peers is narrowing. Of course, information gathered using INCLUDE also can help teachers successfully accommodate Tier 3 students in their classrooms. Keep in mind that when RtI is implemented, all teachers are responsible for all students, regardless of tier. Also, the fact that students require intensive instruction in one area does not mean they cannot be successful in other areas of the general education curriculum.

point out their potential benefits clearly and specifically. Carefully explained expected outcomes can be motivating, particularly as students get older and teacher encouragement alone may no longer be enough to keep them interested.

The first step in getting and keeping students motivated to learn is to provide a strong rationale for why learning the strategy is important. This rationale should be directly tied to current student performance as well as to the demands of your class, two essential pieces of information derived from the INCLUDE process. For example, when introducing a new note-taking strategy, Mr. Washington pointed out that

INCLUDE

Demonstrating the use of a learning strategy involves explaining both the thinking and the doing parts of a process, showing examples and nonexamples of effective strategy use, and checking learners' understanding. How do these steps help students with special needs acquire learning strategies? Shuttershock

the class was able to identify on average only half of the main ideas presented on a note-taking pretest. He also told his class that half of the material on his tests would come from information presented during his lectures. Finally, Mr. Washington explained that taking good notes can help students outside school as well; in many job situations, employers give directions that need to be written down.

The next step in clarifying expectations is to explain specifically what students should be able to accomplish when they have learned the skill. For example, Ms. Thompson told her class that after learning a textbook-reading strategy, they would be able to do their homework faster. Also, give students an idea of how long it will take them to learn the strategy. You could make a chart showing the instructional activities to be covered each day and the approximate number of days it will take to learn the strategy. The advantage of presenting the information on a chart is that steps can be checked off as completed. The act of checking off completed activities can be very motivating for students, and it is also a way of demonstrating self-monitoring, an effective independent learning skill discussed later in this chapter.

Demonstrate Strategy Use

In demonstrating strategies, keep in mind three important points. First, remember that the process one goes through in performing a task or solving a problem should be carefully explained. For example, demonstrate both thinking and doing behaviors. Talking aloud to yourself while performing the skill is particularly important for many students with disabilities, who often do not develop spontaneously organized thinking patterns.

Second, present both positive and negative examples of appropriate strategy use, carefully explaining why they are positive or negative. This explanation can help students tell the difference between doing a strategy the right way and doing it incorrectly, a distinction that can be difficult for students with special needs to make without direct instruction. For example, Mr. Washington demonstrated effective and ineffective notetaking strategies using a Smartboard ©. As students listened to a short videotaped lecture, he took notes systematically, writing down key ideas and details. Next, using the same lecture, he demonstrated ineffective note taking by trying to write down every word.

Third, after you demonstrate, ask frequent questions to monitor student understanding and determine whether more demonstration is needed. Keep in mind that for many students, including those with disabilities, one demonstration may not be enough.

Encourage Students to Memorize Strategy Steps

The purpose of having students memorize the steps in the strategy is to make it easier for them to recall the strategy when they need to use it. To help students learn the steps, you can post them prominently in your classroom at first so that you and your students can refer to them throughout the class or day. Students also may need to be drilled on saying the strategy steps. To practice, students could pair off and quiz each other, or you could ask students the strategy steps before and after class. For example, each day during the last several minutes of class, Ms. Henry quizzed four of her social studies students on the steps of a strategy for paraphrasing text. This type of help also can be given in a Tier 2 RtI group.

Even though memorizing a strategy can help students recall it, you may not want to spend too much time on this step, particularly for some of your students with learning disabilities, who may have memory problems. For these students, you might include the steps to all the strategies they are learning in a special section of their assignment notebooks. For strategies used most often, cue cards listing strategy steps can be taped to the inside cover of textbooks or notebooks.

Provide Guided and Independent Practice

Because students must learn how to perform strategies accurately and fluently before they can attempt them independently, they need considerable practice. Five ways of providing practice on learning strategies are suggested. One way is to have students use controlled materials when they are first learning a strategy. **Controlled materials** generally are materials at the student's reading level, of high interest, and relatively free of complex vocabulary and concepts. Because controlled materials remove many content demands on the learner, they allow students to focus all their energy on learning the strategy. Controlled materials also foster initial success, which is important for motivation. For example, Mr. Bernard was teaching his students a strategy for taking essay tests in current events. At first, he had his students practice this strategy on simply worded, one-part essay questions about material familiar to the students, such as people and events in the areas of rock music, movies, television, and sports. As students became better at using the strategy, Mr. Bernard gradually introduced more complex questions on less familiar topics, such as the AIDS epidemic in Africa and the drug war in Mexico. Finally, he used sample test questions.

A second way to provide students with practice is first to guide them and then to allow them to perform independently. *Guided practice* means giving students verbal cues when they are first attempting a skill. For example, before and while her students were practicing a strategy, Ms. Waters asked them questions such as, "What will you do first?" "Why did you do that?" "What should you do after you are done with the strategy steps?" "Which key words are you going to look for in the questions?" "How will you know which are the main ideas?" and "Was the sentence I just read a main idea? Why?" Once most students seem able to answer your reminder questions, you can gradually stop asking them so that students are eventually performing independently. Some students may need little guided practice or none at all and can be allowed to work independently right away.

A third practice technique is to give feedback that is specific and encourages students to evaluate themselves (Lenz, 2006; Lenz et al., 1996). For example, Dominique has just performed the steps of a proofreading strategy in front of the class. Her teacher says, "Good job, Dominique! I knew you could do it." Denise performed the same strategy in front of her class and her teacher asked, "How do you think you did? What do you need to focus on most the next time?" The feedback Dominique received does not clearly tell her what she did right, nor does it encourage self-evaluation. The feedback given to Denise encourages self-evaluation, a critical part of independent learning. Of course, if Denise cannot evaluate her own performance at first, the key parts of good performance have to be pointed out to her and practice on self-evaluation provided.

A fourth aspect of practicing learning strategies is to praise students only when they have produced work that is praiseworthy. Praise that is not tied to student performance or is exaggerated, often for the purpose of enhancing student self-image, may only reinforce the student's sense of inadequacy. For example, because of a history of failure in learning situations, students with special needs often see little relationship between their efforts and classroom success. When you give nonspecific praise to these students, it is easier for them to attribute your praise to something other than competence, such as sympathy ("I'm so bad at this, she has to pretend I did well").

Fifth, encourage students to reinforce themselves and to take responsibility for both their successes and their failures. For example, after doing well on a note-taking strategy, Alicia was encouraged by her teacher to say, "I did a good job. This time I paid attention and wrote down all the main ideas. I need to do the same the next time." Alicia's teacher was showing her how to attribute her success to factors under her control. This approach can help her become a more active, independent learner.

Administer Posttests

When it appears from your practice sessions that most students have acquired the strategy, give them the pretest again, this time as a posttest, to test their mastery. If, according to your posttest, students have not acquired the strategy, identify where the breakdown occurred and then provide additional instruction and/or practice. If more than 20 percent of the students need extra practice or instruction, they can receive additional help in a large or small group. If your school is using RtI, the extra help could be provided in a Tier 2 group. If fewer than 20 percent of the students require more assistance, they can be provided with more individualized practice by the teacher before or after school, by a special education teacher or other support staff, or in a Tier 3 group.

What Are Some Examples of Successful Learning Strategies?

There is a growing number of research-based learning strategies that work for students who are at risk or who have special needs. These strategies cover many areas, including reading and reading comprehension, listening and note taking, written expression, math-problem solving, and time and resource management. An array of strategies that incorporate many of these effective practices are summarized in the following sections. Many of these strategies can be used with students at all levels—elementary, middle, and high school.

Word-Identification and Reading Fluency Strategies

Students cannot always depend on the teacher to help them figure out difficult words. They also need to read fluently enough so that they can understand what they are reading and finish assignments in a timely manner. The next two strategies are designed to help students help themselves in the important areas of word identification and reading fluency.

Identifying Words in Textbook Reading Middle and high school students are likely to encounter technical words in their content-area textbooks that have multiple syllables, making them difficult for some students to identify. One strategy designed to help students with special needs identify difficult words in their textbook reading (Archer, Gleason, & Vachon, 2003, p. 95) helps students break apart words and then put them back together. First, teach your students to break words apart on paper by having them do the following:

1. Circle the word parts at the beginning of the word (prefixes).
2. Circle the word parts at the end of the word (suffixes).
3. Underline the letters representing vowel sounds in the rest of the word.
4. Say the parts of the word.
5. Say the parts fast.
6. Make it a real word.

Here is an example of this strategy:

Once your students can perform all of these steps by writing them, they are gradually encouraged to perform the steps in their heads, as follows (Archer et al., 2003, p. 95):

1. Look for word parts at the beginning and end of the word, and vowel sounds in the rest of the word.
2. Say the parts of the word.
3. Say the parts fast.
4. Make it a real word.

To be successful with this strategy, students need to be able to perform two critical preskills. They need to know sounds the vowels make, and they need to be able to pronounce prefixes and suffixes. Students lacking these preskills need to be taught them prior to strategy instruction. With RtI, preskill training can take place in Tier 2. For words that have parts difficult to decode, encourage students to say the parts they know and then use the strategy described next for using the context to figure out the word. Of course, it is fair to get help from a classmate or the teacher if all of these strategies have been tried and students are still unable to figure out the word.

WARF To be successful in understanding content-area textbooks, students need to read quickly enough so that they can think about word meaning rather than squander their energy on word identification. Students also may have to adjust their rate of reading, depending on their purpose for reading (Mercer & Pullen, 2009). Minskoff and Allsopp (2003) suggest a strategy to help students who can read accurately at least at the third-grade level but need to increase and/or adjust their reading speed. It is called *WARF:*

W *Widen* your eye span.
A *Avoid* skip-backs.
R *Read* silently.
F *Flex* your reading rate.

Students first are taught to widen their eye span and not read word by word. They are taught to group words, not reading the articles (for example, *the* or *a*) or auxiliary words (for example, *is* or *are*), so they can focus on words that give meaning. As part of this **W** step, they also are taught to try to group words meaningfully (for example, for the words *a sunny day*, focus on *sunny* and *day*). In the **A** step, avoiding skip-backs, students are taught to keep reading if they do not understand something, using context clues to gain understanding. They are told to go back only if this is unsuccessful. In the **R** step, students are taught to read silently, avoiding reading aloud in a whisper by pressing their lips together. In the final step, **F,** students learn to change their reading rate depending on the difficulty and/or familiarity of the material. For example, when students are looking for information, they need to know to read quickly as they search for key words on the page. When students read important information they must understand or memorize, they need to be aware to read more slowly. Conversely, if students are reading information they know well, they can adjust their rate and read faster.

Vocabulary Strategies

In addition to being able to identify technical vocabulary, students also must know what words mean if they are to understand what they read. Strategies for using direct instruction to teach new vocabulary were covered in Chapter 9. Realistically, however, teachers have the time to teach only about two vocabulary words per day (Armbruster, Lehr, & Osborn, 2001).

A strategy that your students can use to help them figure out the meaning of words independently is shown in Figures 10.1 and 10.2. To perform this strategy, students must first learn the meaning of common morphemes.

FIGURE 10.1 **Word-Part Clues**

1. Look for the *root word,* which is a single word that cannot be broken into smaller words or word parts. See if you know what the root word means.
2. Look for a *prefix,* which is a word part added to the beginning of a word that changes its meaning. See if you know what the prefix means.
3. Look for a *suffix,* which is a word part added to the end of a word that changes its meaning. See if you know what the suffix means.
4. Put the meaning of the *root word* and any prefix or suffix together and see if you can build the meaning of the word.

Source: "Vocabulary Tricks: Effects of Instruction in Morphology and Context on Fifth-Grade Students' Ability to Derive and Infer Word Meanings," by J. Baumann, E. Edwards, E. Boland, S. Olejnik, & E. Kame'enui, 2003, *American Educational Research Journal, 40*(2), pp. 447–494.

FIGURE 10.2 **Vocabulary Clues**

When you come to a word and you don't know what it means, use these clues:

1. *Context clues:* Read the sentences around the word to see if there are clues to its meaning.
2. *Word-part clues:* See if you can break the word into a root word, prefix, or suffix to help figure out its meaning.
3. *Context clues:* Read the sentences around the word again to see if you have figured out its meaning.

Source: "Vocabulary Tricks: Effects of Instruction in Morphology and Context on Fifth-Grade Students' Ability to Derive and Infer Word Meanings," by J. Baumann, E. Edwards, E. Boland, S. Olejnik, & E. Kame'enui, 2003, *American Educational Research Journal, 40*(2), pp. 447–494.

Reading Comprehension Strategies

Reading comprehension strategies are intended to help students meet the independent reading demands of content-area classes, particularly in the middle and upper grades. Although reading primarily involves textbooks, students must be able to read and understand a variety of source books as well. The following are examples of proven reading comprehension strategies for students of all grade levels.

SCROL   One example of a reading comprehension strategy is *SCROL* (Grant, 1993). The SCROL strategy enables students to take notes while they are reading, an important study strategy, and to use text headings to aid their comprehension and help them find and remember important information. The SCROL strategy has five steps:

S   *Survey* the headings. In the assigned text selection, read each heading and subheading. For each heading and subheading, try to answer the following questions: What do I already know about this topic? What information might the writer present?

C   *Connect.* Ask yourself, How do the headings relate to one another? Write down key words from the headings that might provide connections between them.

R   *Read* the text. As you read, look for words and phrases that express important information about the headings. Mark the text to point out important ideas and details. Stop to make sure that you understand the major ideas and supporting details. If you do not understand, reread.

RESEARCH NOTE

Reading strategies are more effective when combined with instruction in written expression. Teachers taught both *TWA* (**T**hink before reading; think **W**hile reading; think **A**fter reading) and *PLANS* (**P**ick goals; **L**ist ways to meet goals; **A**nd make **N**otes and **S**equence notes). The combined use of TWA and PLANS led to student gains in reading comprehension and writing (Mason et al., 2006).

O   *Outline.* Using indentations to reflect structure, outline the major ideas and supporting details in the heading segment. Write the heading and then try to outline each heading segment without looking back at the text.

L   *Look* back. Now look back at the text and check the accuracy of the major ideas and details you wrote. Correct any inaccurate information in your outline. If you marked the text as you read, use this information to help you verify the accuracy of your outline.

Advise students to follow steps 3–5 (**R–L**) every time they encounter a section with headings in the text they are reading. Taking notes using SCROL improves student comprehension while also providing students with a product that can help them study more effectively for tests.

Students often struggle with the R step of SCROL that involves marking the important ideas and details. Mariage, Englert, and Okolo (2009) developed the *Highlight It!* and *Mark It!* strategies to help students identify and then elaborate on main ideas and details. Cue cards used to guide students through the *Highlight-It!* and *Mark-It!* steps are shown in Figures 10.3 and 10.4 *Highlight It!* focuses on the meaning in the text, while in *Mark-It!* students elaborate on the meaning by questioning the author's ideas and themselves, making personal connections, predicting

FIGURE 10.4

FIGURE 10.3

Highlight It!

1.   Read section.

2.   Pause and Think.

3.   Highlight.

4.   Re-read Highlighting.

5.   Self-Check:
      Does it make sense?
      Do I have the main idea(s)?
      Do I have several key details?

6.   Pair/Share/Compare
      "I highlighted . . ."
      "I highlighted this because . . ."
      (Justify and Explain Thinking)

7.   Discussion: How is our highlighting similar and different?

8.   Community Share: Report Out

Source: From "Teaching Organizational Skills to Promote Academic Achievement in Behaviorally Challenged Students," by D. H. Anderson, V. H. Munk, K. R. Young, L. Conley, and P. Caldarella, 2008, *Teaching Exceptional Children, 40*(4), 6–13.

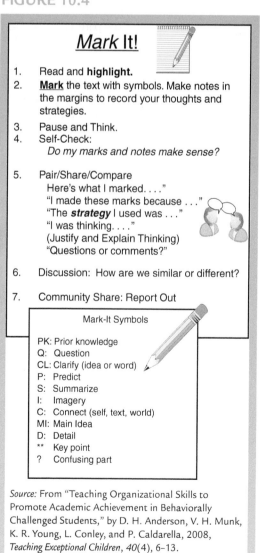

Mark It!

1.   Read and **highlight.**
2.   **Mark** the text with symbols. Make notes in the margins to record your thoughts and strategies.
3.   Pause and Think.
4.   Self-Check:
      Do my marks and notes make sense?

5.   Pair/Share/Compare
      Here's what I marked. . . ."
      "I made these marks because . . ."
      "The **strategy** I used was . . ."
      "I was thinking. . . ."
      (Justify and Explain Thinking)
      "Questions or comments?"

6.   Discussion: How are we similar or different?

7.   Community Share: Report Out

Mark-It Symbols

PK: Prior knowledge
Q: Question
CL: Clarify (idea or word)
P: Predict
S: Summarize
I: Imagery
C: Connect (self, text, world)
MI: Main Idea
D: Detail
**   Key point
?   Confusing part

Source: From "Teaching Organizational Skills to Promote Academic Achievement in Behaviorally Challenged Students," by D. H. Anderson, V. H. Munk, K. R. Young, L. Conley, and P. Caldarella, 2008, *Teaching Exceptional Children, 40*(4), 6–13.

ideas, using imagery, and clarifying text. To teach both strategies, first model the strategies. Then perform the strategies with your students, focusing on a section of text. Last, have your students collaborate with partners on performing the strategies and share the results with the class.

PARS *PARS* is a simplified textbook-reading strategy that is good for younger students and students without much experience using textbook-reading strategies (Cheek & Cheek, 1983). The four steps of PARS follow:

P *Preview* the material by scanning the chapter and surveying the introductory statement, headings, graphic aids, and chapter summary to identify main ideas.

A *Ask* questions that relate to the main ideas discovered when surveying the chapter.

R *Read* the chapter to answer the questions developed.

S *Summarize* the main ideas in the chapter.

Remember that just telling students the steps of a learning strategy is not enough. Letting students watch you perform the strategy and then carefully guiding students as they learn to perform it are essential if students are to learn to use PARS to gain access to the content of their textbooks more independently.

CAPS You have learned that students who can comprehend stories are able to identify key parts of stories called story grammars. *CAPS* is a self-questioning strategy that guides students as they look for these important story elements (Leinhardt & Zigmond, 1988). The strategy is composed of the following steps:

C Who are the *characters?*

A What is the *aim* of the story?

P What *problem* happens?

S How is the problem *solved?*

CAPS is particularly effective for students in elementary school, where key reading demands involve understanding stories.

SLiCK A common accommodation for students with reading disabilities is the bypass strategy of providing them with an oral text. However, some students still struggle to understand a text, even when they no longer have to read it. *SLiCK* (Boyle et al., 2002) is a strategy designed to help students comprehend digitally recorded textbooks. It involves the following steps:

S *Set* it up.

L *Look* ahead through the chapter.

C *Comprehend.*

K *Keep* it together.

In the **S** step, the student sets it up by opening the textbook to the start of the assigned section; readying a worksheet containing the SLiCK strategy steps at the top, with spaces to record key information such as headings, subheadings, and key vocabulary words. In the **L** step, the student looks ahead through the chapter using the recorded book, player, and print textbook. The student notes keywords, headings, and subheadings and records them on the worksheet. In the comprehend, or **C**, step, the student reads along with the recording, pausing to record important details under the headings and subheadings previously identified. The student is encouraged to think of big ideas by writing minisummaries as he or she reads. In the final step, **K,** the student combines all of the minisummaries to get the big picture about what the section of text means. Boyle et al., (2002) report that students acquire the **S** and **L** steps quickly, while the **C** and **K** steps require considerable teacher modeling and practice before they are learned.

RUDPC You have learned that successful comprehension requires an understanding of how information in stories and expository text is organized and that students with learning disabilities and attention deficit–hyperactivity disorder (ADHD) often have trouble identifying organizational patterns. While we typically think of organizational patterns as applying to written text, information presented on computer screens has an organizational scheme as well (Minskoff & Allsopp, 2003). Assignments in school routinely require students to access information on the Internet. Research shows that students need to learn how to navigate the different parts of a website to acquire efficiently the information sought (Kuiper, Volman, & Terwel, 2005). Often this involves ignoring the many distractions that can appear on the computer screen.

Minskoff and Allsopp (2003) developed the *RUDPC* strategy for helping students derive important information from a webpage. The steps are as follows:

R *Read* the title and headings.
U *Use* the cursor to skim the page.
D *Decide* whether you need the page.
P *Print* the page.
C *Copy* the bibliographic information.

When reading a website, students need to make quick decisions about whether a given section of a webpage provides information they are looking for. Reading everything on the screen is inefficient. Students with special needs may need explicit instruction on the **D** step in order to learn to make these judgments. Minskoff and Allsopp (2003) also suggest that for some students, printing pages prevents them from being distracted by graphics or frustrated by small fonts.

POSSE Another reading comprehension strategy is *POSSE* (Englert, 2009; Englert & Mariage, 1991). This strategy includes many reading practices that have been shown to aid reading comprehension, such as graphic organizers, text structures, stimulation of student background knowledge, and self-monitoring. The steps in this strategy are as follows:

P *Predict* ideas.
O *Organize* the ideas.
S *Search* for the structure.
S *Summarize* the main ideas.
E *Evaluate* your understanding.

When students are predicting, they can be given a sentence starter such as *I predict that . . .* For this step, students are taught to use signals from a variety of sources, including title, headings in bold, pictures, keywords, and so on. Brainstorming is very important in this step. A technique used for teaching the POSSE strategy steps is a process called reciprocal teaching. **Reciprocal teaching** is a way to teach students to comprehend reading material by providing them with teacher and peer models of thinking behavior and then allowing them to practice these thinking behaviors with their peers (Palincsar & Brown, 1988). At first, the teacher leads the dialogue, demonstrating how the strategies can be used during reading. As instruction goes on, the teacher gives the students more and more responsibility for maintaining the dialogue. Eventually, students are largely responsible

These students are engaged in a structured dialogue about the test they are reading, a peer-mediated comprehension strategy called reciprocal teaching. What strategies must students be taught before they can practice reciprocal teaching? © Kathy deWitt/Alamy

for the dialogue, though the teacher still provides help as necessary. The most important part of the technique is the teacher's releasing control and turning the dialogue over to the students (Englert & Mariage, 1991).

A sample dialogue for reciprocal teaching is presented in the Case in Practice. After reading it, think of the reasons reciprocal teaching is such a powerful technique for teaching reading comprehension to students who are at risk or who have other special needs. In what other areas could reciprocal teaching be used? The Technology Notes feature describes an electronic textbook geared to students' individual reading levels that teaches students the same reading comprehension strategies stressed in POSSE, and more.

RESEARCH NOTE

Kim et al. (2006) improved the reading comprehension skills of middle school students with disabilities using reciprocal teaching adapted for use with a computer.

Listening and Note-Taking Strategies

Students in all grades need to be able to understand information presented orally by their teachers. In elementary school, students are required to follow many oral directions and listen when the teacher is reading aloud or presenting information. In middle school, junior high, and high school, where lecturing is a common way for teachers to present subject-area content, students are required to discern and record key information in lectures so they can study it later. As you have already learned, students with special needs may have problems understanding information presented orally. These problems can make access to the general education curriculum more difficult for them.

CASE IN PRACTICE

Teaching Script for Demonstrating POSSE

The students in this class have just read a section of text that focuses on Loch Ness. They are now applying the search, summarize, and evaluate steps of POSSE.

Teacher: What is the main topic the text is talking about?

Peg: The Loch Ness monster.

Teacher: What was this section about? What was the main idea?

Peg: Oh, the lake. I have two questions: "What is a lake?" and "What lives in it?"

Teacher: Do you mean this particular lake or any lake?

Peg: This lake. Joe?

Joe: It's foggy, it's deep, and it's long and narrow.

Peg: Don?

Don: The land beside the lake, you don't know if it is real soft and you could fall through it.

Teacher: So it could be soft and swampy.

Ann: I think the Loch Ness monster lives there.

Teacher: Is Ann answering your question, Peg?

Peg: No.

Teacher: What was your question?

Peg: I had two: "What is a lake?" and "What lives in the lake?"

Joe: But the book never answered that. I have a question about the main idea. Aren't we supposed to do a question about the main idea?

Teacher: Just about what we read.

Joe: Yes, but Peg asked us, "What lives in the lake?" but it doesn't really mention that in the book.

Teacher: That's true. The major idea has to do with Loch Ness and what it looks like. A minor idea that we really inferred rather than directly read in the article was that the Loch Ness monster lives in the lake.

Peg: Are there any clarifications?

Students: [No response.]

Teacher: I have a clarification. You had trouble reading some of these words and I wondered if you know what some of them mean. What does *ancestors* mean?

[The teacher continues discussing vocabulary.]

Sources: From "Making Students Partners in the Comprehension Process: Organizing the Reading 'POSSE,'" by C. S. Englert and T. V. Mariage, 1991, *Learning Disability Quarterly, 14,* pp. 133–134. Used by permission of Council for Learning Disabilities.

Thinking Reader: The Textbook of the Future

FIGURE 10.5 **Sample Daily Lesson Plan Format**

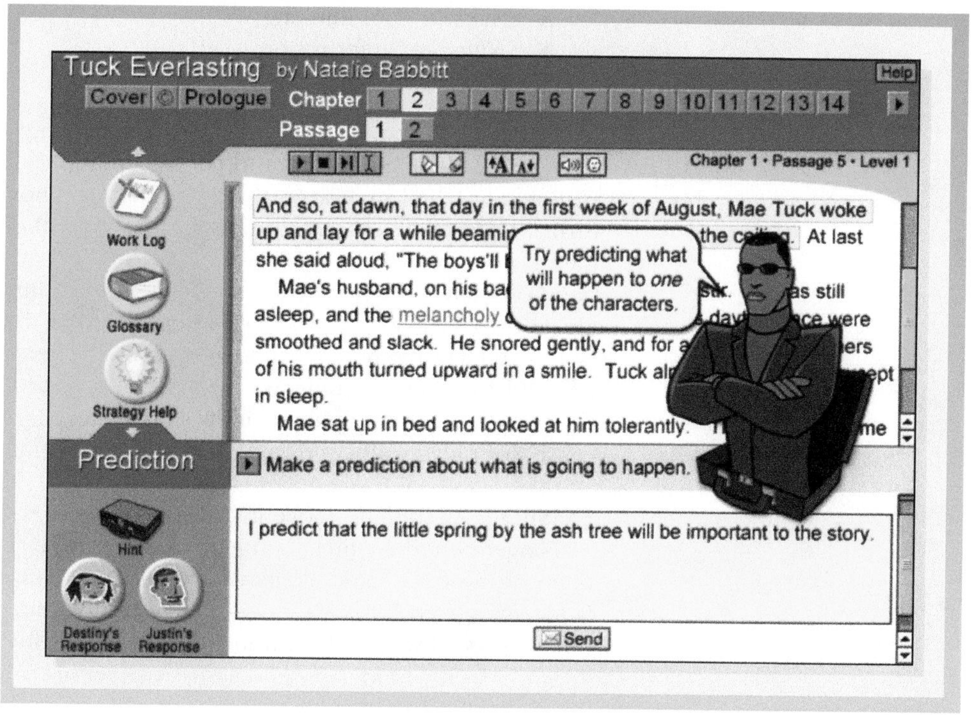

Textbooks are the most common method of delivering subject-area information to students of all grades but particularly to those who are in middle school or high school. Yet many students with and without special needs experience problems comprehending their textbooks. Whereas some of these problems are due to reading slowly and/or inaccurately, students also lack strategies for locating and retaining important information in their texts. Unfortunately, standard textbooks provide teachers and students with little support in teaching and learning important comprehension strategies. Enter the Thinking Reader.

The Thinking Reader incorporates a variety of supports into electronic text in order to teach research-based reading comprehension strategies such as summarizing, questioning, clarifying, predicting, and visualizing. The supports can be customized to accommodate individual student reading abilities by systematically reducing the level of structure as students become more proficient in the reading comprehension strategies. The goal is for students to select independently the strategy that best fits their comprehension needs.

The specific supports in the program include a human voice feature that reads the text while highlighting it and natural intonation to support the finding of main ideas and the development of fluency. Comprehension is supported through a series of strategy prompts that guide students as they practice the comprehension strategies. For example, at the end of each passage, students might be asked to predict what will happen in the story, clarify something that they find confusing, summarize the passage, or visualize what is happening. Students respond to the prompts in three formats: open-ended, fill-in-the-blank, and oral. There are also supports for vocabulary development, including a contextual glossary with Spanish translations for English-language learners.

Perhaps the most helpful aspect of the Thinking Reader is the availability of supports to help students think about the passage. The program employs an *agent* who provides hints for each strategy (for example, "Try predicting what will happen to one of the characters") or think-alouds (for example, "I remembered that both Winnie's grandmother and the stranger are very interested in music. She is excited to hear the music again, and he seems to find it meaningful that she has heard it before. So I predict that the music will be important in some way"). A sample screen display is shown in Figure 10.5.

Note: The Thinking Reader was developed by Dr. David Rose and Dr. Bridget Dalton at the Center for Applied Special Technology (CAST). The program is based on research cited in this text, including a report of the National Reading Panel (2000), principles of universal design (Dalton & Pisha, 2001), and reciprocal teaching (Palincsar & Brown, 1988). The Thinking Reader has been used successfully to teach comprehension strategies to students with learning disabilities (Dalton & Pisha, 2001).

◆◇◆

The listening and note-taking strategies described in the next section were designed to help all students learn more successfully from their teachers' presentations.

SLANT   Students who are engaged in class are more likely to be successful (Larkin & Ellis, 1998). The *SLANT* strategy is designed to increase student involvement in class lectures or discussions. Greater student involvement increases the likelihood that students will listen more carefully and take better notes. *SLANT* includes the following steps:

S *Sit* up.
L *Lean* forward.
A *Activate* your thinking.
N *Name* key information.
T *Track* the talker.

In the **S** step, Sit up, remind students that slouching or putting their heads down in class makes their bodies want to fall asleep and causes them to miss a lot of information. For **L**, tell students that leaning forward shows they are interested in the information, even when they are not, and that often they can train their minds to follow their bodies. **A**ctivating your thinking involves having your students ask themselves question such as, "What is this about?" or "What is important to remember?" This step also involves asking the teacher a question when they don't understand (Vaughn & Bos, 2008). For the **N** step, students answer teacher questions, share their ideas, and respond to others' comments (Ellis, 1991). For the final step **T**, Track the talker, encourage students to keep their eyes on the teacher or whomever else is talking because this prevents them from daydreaming or being distracted by other things.

TASSELL   As students move into the upper grades, they are required to take notes for longer periods of time. Longer lectures require sustained attention, a skill that is often problematic for students with disabilities (Smith, 2004). The *TASSELL* strategy is recommended for students who have trouble maintaining their level of attention (Minskoff & Allsopp, 2003). It includes the following steps:

T *Try* not to doodle.
A *Arrive* at class prepared.
S *Sit* near the front.
S *Sit* away from friends.
E *End* daydreaming.
L *Look* at the teacher.

For the **E** step, encourage students to monitor their attention. When they find they are daydreaming, they should immediately change their position, sit forward, and make eye contact with the teacher. Then they should write down whatever the teacher is saying, regardless of its importance (Minskoff & Allsopp, 2003). For the **L** step, encourage students to keep their eyes on the teacher when they are not taking notes or looking at the chalkboard, overhead, PowerPoint presentation, or computer screen (Minskoff & Allsopp, 2003).

CALL UP   *CALL UP* is a research-based strategy for taking lecture notes. It has the following steps (Czarnecki, Rosko, & Fine, 1998):

C *Copy* from the board or PowerPoint.
A *Add* details.
L *Listen* and write the question.
L *Listen* and write the answer.
U *Utilize* the text.
P *Put* in your own words.

When copying from the board, a transparency, or a PowerPoint slide, students listen and look for cue words and phrases that identify main ideas, copy them down in the margin, and underline them. Students also listen for details, writing them 1 inch from the margin with a dash (——) in front of each detail. Students listen for teacher or student questions that they think can inform their understanding and write them, indented, under the appropriate main ideas. Students also record answers under the main ideas. The last two steps can be carried out at home or in study hall. Students first read about the main ideas in their textbooks and then paraphrase the information under each main idea in a space previously left blank. Students record relevant text pages in the margins so they can refer to the text at a later time if needed. Try posting the CALL UP steps prominently in your classroom. As you lecture, model the various steps while explicitly telling your students which steps you are performing and why. For example, Mr. Sauter was lecturing his class on the topic of the respiratory system. He wrote *respiratory system* on the board and directed his students to write down this main idea of the lecture. He then told them to add the details of the parts of the respiratory system (for example, *nose, lungs, mouth,* and *windpipe*) to their notes. Mr. Sauter posed important questions as he lectured such as "What is the purpose of the bronchial tubes?" He directed students to copy down these questions as he raised them. Finally, Mr. Sauter asked students to answer all questions raised for homework.

Of course, to learn this or any other note-taking strategy, students need the preskill of being able to tell the difference between main ideas and details. Some students choose key words that represent main ideas, but others attempt to write down everything and should be taught directly how to differentiate main ideas and details. For example, Mr. Abeles discovered that many students in his world history class were unable to identify the main ideas in his lectures. First, he explained the difference between main ideas and details: A *main idea* is what a whole section or passage is about; a *detail* is what just one part of a section or passage is about. For several weeks he stopped after presenting a section of material and put three pieces of information on the board—one main idea and two details. He asked the students which was the main idea and why. When his students were doing well at these tasks, Mr. Abeles had them write their own main ideas for a section of a lecture, which were shared with the class, and then he provided corrective feedback as necessary.

Writing Strategies

Another area that requires student independence is writing and proofreading papers. Several research-based strategies are useful to help students in this area.

POWER   One strategy that helps students organize all the steps in the writing process is called *POWER* (Englert et al., 1988). The process involves the use of self-questioning, graphic organizers, and peer editing using the following steps:

P   *Planning*
O   *Organizing*
W   *Writing*
E   *Editing*
R   *Revising*

The POWER strategy teaches students four different organizational structures for writing papers: stories, comparison/contrast, explanations, and problem/solution (Englert et al., 1988). When writing stories, students use key story elements—Who? When? Where? What happened? How did it end?—to organize their papers. A comparison/contrast structure includes information on what subjects are being compared (for example, atoms and molecules), on what characteristic of those subjects is being compared (size), and on how the subjects are alike and/or different in relation to that characteristic (atoms are the smallest particles; molecules are composed of two or more atoms). Explanations involve telling how to do something, such as explaining the steps in changing a tire. In a problem/solution structure, a problem is identified (for example, it took too long to travel from the East to the West in the early 1800s in the United States), the cause of the problem is explained (the only way to go from the East to the West was by stagecoach), and the solution is stated (the transcontinental railroad was built).

For the *planning* stage, students focus on the audience for the paper, the purpose, and the background knowledge that is necessary to write the paper. In the *organizing* step, students decide which organizational pattern fits their paper (for example, story, comparison/contrast) and then complete a pattern guide to help them organize their ideas. A **pattern guide** is a graphic organizer designed to help students organize their papers. A sample pattern guide for a comparison/contrast paper is shown in Figure 10.6. Notice that the words not in boxes—*Both same, In contrast to, Similarly,* and *However*—are key words frequently used when making comparisons. These words help students make the transition to writing sentences. For example, in Figure 10.6, two kinds of pizza are being compared and contrasted. The student might write, "The crusts of deep dish and regular pizza are the same in that they both are made of white flour. This is in contrast to their thickness; deep dish pizza crust is much thicker."

In the *writing* stage, the teacher demonstrates and thinks aloud to show students how to take the information gathered in the planning and organizing steps and produce a first draft. For example, you can compose an essay comparing two kinds of pizza using an overhead projector, thinking out loud as you write. You can involve students by asking questions such as, "What would a good topic sentence be? Is this a good example? How do you think I should end this? Why?" You could also have students write the paper along with you.

The *editing* step teaches students to critique their own writing and to identify areas in which they need clarification or assistance, an important self-evaluation skill. Editing is a two-step process involving student self-evaluation and peer editing. For self-evaluation, students reread and evaluate their drafts, starring sections of the

www.resources

Your students can research their papers more independently by accessing Kids Web (http://www .npac.syr.edu/), a digital library specifically designed for children.

FIGURE 10.6 Pattern Guide for Comparison/Contrast Paper

Compare/Contrast

What is being compared and contrasted?
Deep dish pizza and regular pizza

On what characteristics?
Crust

Both same | Alike? White flour | Different? Deep dish is thicker | In contrast to

On what characteristics?

Similarly | Alike? | Different? | However

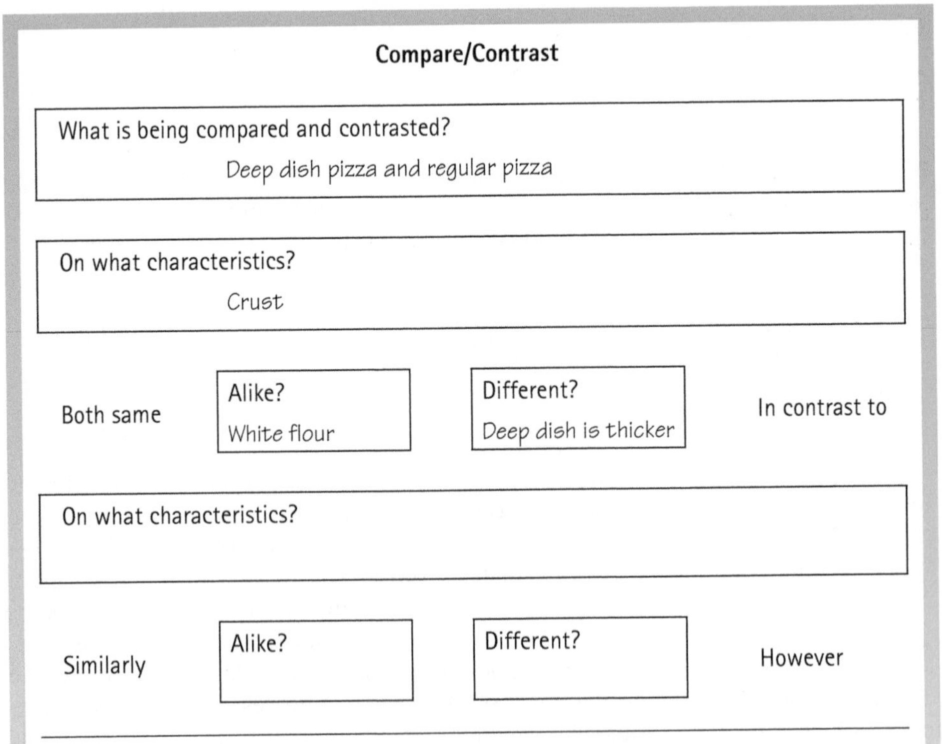

Source: From "A Case for Writing Intervention: Strategies for Writing Informational Text," by C. S. Englert, T. E. Raphael, L. M. Anderson, H. M. Anthony, K. L. Fear, and S. L. Gregg, 1988, *Learning Disability Quarterly, 3*(2), p. 108. Reprinted with permission.

paper they like best and putting question marks in the margins beside passages they think may be unclear. Finally, students think of two questions to ask their peer editors. For example, Jorge asked his peer editor whether he had used capital letters and punctuation correctly. He was also concerned about whether his paper was long enough and asked for suggestions on how to add information.

For **peer editing,** several steps are followed. First, the writer reads the paper to a peer editor while the editor listens. The peer editor then summarizes the paper. Next, the editor evaluates the paper, sharing with the writer an analysis of salient features of the writing that might guide a revision or lead to improvement. For example, the peer editor might suggest that the writer add key words or reorganize the paper for clarity. Then the peer editor and the writer brainstorm ways to improve the paper.

A research-based strategy called *TAG* also can help students with the peer-editing process (Carlson & Henning, 1993; MacArthur & Stoddard, 1990). The TAG strategy involves three simple steps:

T *Tell* what you like.
A *Ask* questions.
G *Give* suggestions.

As with all strategies, students need to be provided with models and guided practice for doing these steps prior to doing them independently. In the *revising* step, students decide on changes to be made using their self-evaluation marks and peer feedback. Englert et al. (1988) suggest that the teacher model how to insert or change the order of information, providing a rationale for any changes. All modifications are made directly on the first draft. Last, the teacher and student have a conference, and changes in writing mechanics are suggested. Following this conference, a final draft is composed on clean sheets of paper.

COPS When students have to proofread their papers independently, they might use a strategy called *COPS* (Alley, 1988). In the COPS strategy, students question themselves as follows:

C Have I *capitalized* the first word and proper nouns?
O How is the *overall appearance* of my paper? Have I made any handwriting, margin, or messy errors?
P Have I used end *punctuation,* commas, and semicolons carefully?
S Do words look like they are *spelled* right? Can I sound them out or use the dictionary?

Although COPS has been shown to be effective, students need preskills to perform this strategy adequately. Before teaching COPS, consider the following questions: Can the students recognize misspelled words? Do the students know rules for using capital letters and punctuation? Can they apply these rules? Can the students use a dictionary? If the answer to any of these questions is no, teach these skills directly before teaching students the COPS strategy.

W-W-W What=2 How=2 This strategy was developed and researched by Harris, Graham, and Mason (2003) to help elementary-age students write stories:

W *Who* is the main character?
W *When* does the story take place?
W *Where* does the story take place?
W *What* does the main character do or want to do? What do other characters do?
W *What* happens then? What happens with other characters?
H *How* does the story end?
H *How* does the main character feel? How do the other characters feel?

dimensions of
DIVERSITY
Cohen and Riel (1989) studied the effects of writing for authentic audiences of peers from different cultures using the Internet. They found that essays written for distant peers were more explicit and detailed than essays written to be graded by their teachers.

INCLUDE

Students with weak writing skills and other language difficulties will require more support with the vocabulary and concepts. Their instruction can be differentiated by giving them more practice or by using a graphic organizer and picture cues, such as the one in Figure 10.7.

Report Writing   Report writing is something many students prefer to avoid, largely because they lack a systematic way of writing successfully. Graham, Harris, and MacArthur (2006) report success teaching students a six-step report-writing strategy originally developed by MacArthur et al. (1996). The steps in the strategy are as follow:

1. Choose a topic.
2. Brainstorm all you know and would like to know about the topic.
3. Organize your ideas by main points and details on a web-type graphic organizer, where main ideas and subordinate ideas are linked together through the use of lines and arrows.
4. Read to find new information and verify the accuracy of information already generated. (Add, delete, and modify items on the Web as necessary.)

FIGURE 10.7 Practice Cue Cards for W-W-W What=2 HOW=2

Source: Adapted from "Self-Regulated Strategy Development in the Classroom: Part of a Balanced Approach to Writing Instruction for Students with Disabilities," by K. R. Harris, S. Graham, and L. H. Mason, *Focus on Exceptional Children, 35*(7), 1–17.

5. Write your report using the information you organized on the Web, but continue planning as you write.
6. Check to be sure you used everything you wanted from the Web (p. 291).

In Graham et al. (2006), the report-writing strategy was co-taught by general and special educators using many of the suggestions for teaching a learning strategy described earlier in the chapter. First, they clarified expectations by carefully describing the qualities of a good report and showing the students actual examples of well-written reports. Next the teachers encouraged students to memorize the strategy, and then the special education teacher demonstrated how to use the strategy while holding a running dialogue with herself. For example, to show the students how to keep themselves focused, she asked herself, "What do I need to do?" To show the students how to keep themselves on task, the teacher said to herself, "Keep going." To demonstrate how to self-monitor, the teacher said, "Does this part make sense?" To show students how to cope with frustration, she said, "I can do this."

For guided practice, the teachers differentiated instruction. The special education teacher co-wrote reports with some of the students with special needs in a small group, while the general education teacher worked with the remainder of the class in a large group, providing reduced support. Once students were writing independently, the teachers required them to reflect on what they were doing in a daily journal. Students were also reminded to continue to manage the writing process by talking to themselves. In all, it took the students six weeks to master the report-writing strategy—time that the teachers felt was well spent, given the improvement in student reports that resulted.

Learning Spelling Words   A study strategy can help students learn unknown spelling words (Graham & Freeman, 1986). Students are required to carry out the following five steps:

1. Say the word.
2. Write and say the word.
3. Check the word.
4. Trace and say the word.
5. Write the word from memory and check your spelling.

If students misspell the word in step 5, they need to repeat all five steps.

Strategies for Using Technology to Improve Student Writing

Revising Essays   This strategy uses a word processor for revising essays (Graham & Harris, 1987). Students instruct themselves using the following six steps:

1. Read your essay.
2. Find the sentence that tells you what you believe—is it clear?
3. Add two reasons why you believe it.
4. SCAN each sentence:

   S   Does it make *sense?*
   C   Is it *connected* to your belief?
   A   Can you *add* more?
   N   *Note* errors.

5. Make changes on the computer.
6. Reread your essay and make final changes.

Using Spell Checkers Effectively   Spell checkers can help students identify misspelled words and correct them. However, one problem with spell checkers is that the correctly spelled version of a word that the student is attempting to write

fyi

You can see a writing strategy co-taught in a videotape published by the Association of Supervision and Curriculum Development (Alexandria, Virginia) titled *Teaching Students with Learning Disabilities: Using Learning Strategies* (2002).

www.resources

The Write Site (http://www .writesite.org) allows students to take on the roles of journalists and editors to research, write, and publish their own newspaper. The site provides unit outlines, handouts, exercises, downloadable teaching materials, information about how to write, and more.

is not always presented as an alternative. This happens when the combination of letters that the student has typed does not approximate closely enough the intended word for the software to offer the needed choices. Because the correct word does not appear on the first attempt, students often click on "Go to Next Word" or "Skip Word" without making a change. The result can be a paper with many misspelled words.

Ashton (1999) describes the *CHECK* strategy, a sequence of steps designed to help students use any spell checker more effectively. The sequence of steps in the strategy is as follows:

C **Check** *the beginning sounds.* Most spell checkers search for similar words beginning with the same letter as the word typed. Therefore, the correctly spelled version of the word is more likely to appear when at least the first letter is correct. For this step, students check the beginning sound of the word and ask themselves what other letter could make that beginning sound. For example, if the student is attempting to spell the word *elephant* but has begun the word with *ul*, teach him or her to ask what other letter(s) make that beginning sound.

H **Hunt for** *the correct consonants.* If trying a new beginning sound does not help, have students change other consonants in the word. Ashton (1999, p. 26) tells of a boy who was writing about Egypt and wanted to use the word *pyramid*. His first spelling attempt was *perament,* but the only suggested word was *per*. The boy continued to sound out the word and changed the spelling to *peramed*. This still did not produce the word he was looking for, so he changed his spelling again to *peramid*. *Pyramid* then appeared in the suggested word list, and the student recognized it as being the correct spelling.

E **Examine** *the vowels.* Selecting the correct vowel when spelling is especially difficult because vowels make so many sounds. Spell checkers can help students figure out which sound to use for a particular vowel or vowel combination. For example, a student spelled the place where she ate lunch as *cafitirea*. After substituting other possible vowels in the word, she came close enough to the actual spelling to elicit the word *cafeteria* on the suggested list.

C **Changes** *in word lists give hints.* Sometimes students can use words in the suggested word list to find the correct spelling. For example, a student trying to spell the word *favorite* first tried *fovoriute*. When this spelling did not produce the correct alternative, she changed her original spelling to *foariute,* then *fovaritue,* then *favaritue*. After the last try, the word *favor* was given as a suggested spelling. Using that word, she typed *favorite,* which brought *favorite* to the list—the correct spelling, which she recognized.

K **Keep repeating** *steps 1 through 4.* The most important aspect of using this strategy effectively is to give it repeated chances, students trying as many different letter combinations as they can. However, at some point students may want to use another source, such as a dictionary, personalized word list (a continually updated list of words students have looked up before), classmate, teacher, or parent.

Strategies for Problem Solving in Math

Increasingly, teachers are focusing on problem solving as a major component of the math curriculum. This concentration is consistent with the math standards developed by the National Council of Teachers of Mathematics (2000) as well as the recommendations of the more recent report of the National Mathematics Advisory Panel (2008), which stress the importance of teaching problem solving. However, research indicates that if students with special needs are to become good problem solvers, they must be taught how to problem solve directly. A common (but by no means

RESEARCH NOTE

DeLaPaz (1999) reviewed the research on dictation and speech-recognition systems and concluded that these systems can allow students with disabilities to bypass handwriting, spelling, and punctuation problems, freeing them to focus on planning and generating content.

RESEARCH NOTE

Hetzroni and Shrieber (2004) found a clear difference in quality between handwritten and computer-produced writing. Using paper and pencil, students wrote papers that had more spelling mistakes and lower overall quality of organization and structure.

PROFESSIONAL **EDGE**

The Key Word Strategy for Solving Math Word Problems: Is There a Better Way?

The key word strategy is an example of an ineffective strategy that many students with special needs use or are taught to use in solving math word problems (Kelly & Carnine, 1996). In this approach, students associate key words such as *more, in all, gave away,* and *left over* with certain mathematical operations. The key word strategy is attractive to teachers and students because sometimes it works. For example, the word *more* is commonly associated with subtraction, as in the following problem:

Jose has 15 cents. Carmen has 10 cents. How much *more* money does Jose have?

Unfortunately, many times the word *more* appears in word problems that call for addition, as in the following problem:

Charmaine had 15 cents. Her mother gave her 10 *more* cents. How many cents does she have now?

Kelly and Carnine (1996) suggest teaching students with special needs a more effective strategy for solving math word problems using problem maps and math fact families. Their strategy for teaching single-operation addition and subtraction problems follows:

For any addition/subtraction situation, there are two "small" numbers and a "big" number (the sum).

An addition/subtraction number family is mapped this way:

$$\xrightarrow{7\quad 9} 16$$

The preceding family represents the following addition/subtraction facts:

$$7 + 9 = 16 \qquad 16 - 9 = 7$$
$$9 + 7 = 16 \qquad 16 - 7 = 9$$

A missing *big* number implies addition:

$$\xrightarrow{8\quad 22} \square \qquad 8 + 22 = \square$$

A missing *small* number implies subtraction:

$$\xrightarrow{\square\quad 22} 30 \qquad 30 - 22 = \square$$

or

$$\xrightarrow{8\quad \square} 30 \qquad 30 - 8 = \square$$

These maps can then be applied to a variety of addition and subtraction word problems. Kelly and Carnine (1996, p. 6) give the following example involving comparison problems:

In comparison problems, the difference between two values being compared may be information given in a problem (for example, Marco sold 57 fewer subscriptions than Lui) or the unknown in a problem (for example, How much heavier was Mary?). Because of the words *sold fewer* in the following problem, many students with LD will subtract.

Marco sold 57 fewer magazine subscriptions than Lui. Marco sold 112 subscriptions. How many subscriptions did Lui sell?

Students can use number families to avoid this confusion. The first step is to represent the problem using a number family; students must determine whether each of the two numbers given in the problem is a small number or the big number. The students are shown a simple way to do this:

They find the sentence that tells about the comparison and read it without the difference number. For example, students are taught to read the first sentence without the 57: "Marco sold fewer subscriptions than Lui." Because Marco sold fewer subscriptions, Marco is represented by a small number. By default, Lui is the big number. The students write M for Marco and L for Lui:

$$\xrightarrow{M} L$$

The word problem also gives a number for the difference between Marco and Lui. That number always has to be a small number. Marco sold 57 fewer, so 57 is the other small number:

$$\xrightarrow{57\quad M} L$$

Next, the students read the rest of the problem. The problem asks about Lui and gives a number for Marco, so the students draw a box around L and replace the M with 112:

$$\xrightarrow{57\quad \overset{112}{\cancel{M}}} \boxed{L}$$

Because the problem gives both small numbers, the students write an addition problem.

$$\begin{array}{r} 57 \\ +112 \\ \hline \end{array}$$

The answer tells how many magazine subscriptions Lui sold.

Stein, Kinder, Silbert, and Carnine (2005) and Seethaler, Powell, and Fuchs (2010) offer similar word problem strategies as applied to multiplication, division, and multistep word problems.

Source: Excerpt from "The 'Key Word' Strategy for Solving Math Story Problems," by B. Kelly and D. Carnine, 1996, reprinted by permission of Council for Learning Disabilities.

See Seethaler, Powell, and Fuchs (2010) to learn about PIRATES, a research-based strategy for solving word problems.

the only) way to introduce problem solving to students in a classroom context is through word problems. An effective technique for teaching word problems for students with special needs is presented in the Professional Edge on the previous page.

STAR The *STAR* strategy has been used successfully to teach older students with disabilities to solve math problems, including algebra (Gagnon & Maccini, 2001, p. 10). It consists of the following steps:

S *Search* the word problem, reading the problem carefully and writing down knowns or facts.

T *Translate* the word problem into an equation in picture form by choosing a variable, identifying the operation, and representing the problem through manipulatives or picture form.

A *Answer* the problem.

R *Review* the solution by rereading the problem and checking the reasonableness of the answer.

Examples of how STAR can be used to solve division problems with integers are shown in Figure 10.8.

FIGURE 10.8 Using the STAR Strategy to Solve Division Problems with Integers

Sample problem: Suppose the temperature changed by an average of −2°F per hour. The total temperature change was −16°F. How many hours did it take for the temperature to change?

Phase of Instruction   **Star Strategy**

1. Concrete Application

Students use blocks to represent the problem. General guidelines: inverse operation of multiplication.

Algebra tiles: ▣ = 1 unit

Prompts students to:

Search problem (read carefully, ask questions, write down facts); translate the problem using blocks; answer the problem using the tiles; and review the solution (reread the problem, check reasonableness and calculations).

1) Students begin with no tiles on the workmat.

2)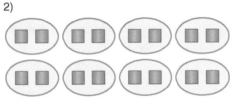

3)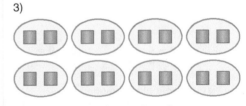

a. Count the number of sets of −2 needed to obtain −16.

b. Students add 8 sets.

c. Students count the number of sets needed (8).

2. Semiconcrete Application

Students draw pictures of the representations.

Prompts students to:

Search problem (read carefully, ask questions, write down facts); translate (represent) the problem via drawings and write down the equation; answer the problem using drawings and write the answer; and review the solution (reread the problem, check reasonableness and calculations).

3. Abstract Application

Students first write numerical representations:

$-16 \div 2 = x$, apply the rule for dividing integers to obtain $x = +8$, and reread and check the answer.

Prompts students to:

Search problem (read carefully, ask questions, write down facts); translate the problem into an equation; answer the problem (apply the rule for division integers); and review the solution (reread the problem, check reasonableness and calculations).

Source: "Preparing Students with Disabilities for Algebra," by J. C. Gagnon and P. Maccini, 2001, *Teaching Exceptional Children, 34*(1), 8–15. Copyright 2001 by the Council for Exceptional Children Reprinted with permission.

Note how the teacher moves students beyond the concrete application phase and into semiconcrete and abstract phases. For example, she starts with blocks (concrete) and moves to pictures (semiconcrete) and then to numerals (abstract). Moving students beyond concrete representations is important for students with special needs, because if they are to become independent learners, they must be able to work at an abstract level. While these students benefit from working with manipulatives and other concrete representations, teachers must make sure to move them to more abstract levels as soon as they are able.

LAMPS The *LAMPS* strategy (Reetz & Rasmussen, 1988) can be used as an aid to help remember the steps in regrouping or carrying in addition:

L *Line up* the numbers according to their decimal points.
A *Add* the right column of numbers and ask . . .
M *"More* than 9?" If so, continue to the next step.
P *Put* the 1s below the column.
S *Send* the 10s to the top of the next column.

SLOBS To help with borrowing in subtraction, teach students to follow the steps in the *SLOBS* strategy (Reetz & Rasmussen, 1988):

S *Smaller:* Follow steps.
L *Larger:* Leap to subtract.
O *Cross off* the number in the next column.
B *Borrow* by taking one 10 and adding to the next column.
S *Subtract.*

For the problem

$$\begin{array}{r} 72 \\ -46 \\ \hline \end{array}$$

students look at the top number on the right to see whether it is smaller or larger than the bottom right number. If it is smaller, the students follow the rest of the steps. They cross off the number in the next column to the left to borrow one unit from that column (reducing that number by one) and add it to the other column. In the problem shown, they borrow 10 from the left column and then subtract. If the number is larger, students proceed directly to the subtract step. They repeat the steps if more digits are to be subtracted.

FOIL The *FOIL* strategy (Crawford, 1980) helps prevent algebra students from missing one of the four products needed to calculate multiplication of a binomial by another binomial. Students follow these four steps:

F Multiply *first* terms.
O Multiply *outermost* terms.
I Multiply *innermost* terms.
L Multiply *last* terms.

For example, the FOIL strategy can be applied to the following problem:

$$(x + 4)(x + 3)$$
$$\text{A} \quad \text{B} \quad \text{C} \quad \text{D}$$

In the **F** step, the student multiplies the first two factors in each binomial, $x \times x = x^2$, or using the letters, *AC.* Next, in the **O** step, the student multiplies the first factor in the first binomial and the second factor in the second binomial, $x \times 3 = 3x$, or *AD.* Then, in the **I** step, the student multiplies the second factor of the first binomial and the first factor of the second binomial, $4 \times x = 4x$, or *BC.* Finally, in the **L** step, the second factors of both binomials are multiplied: $4 \times 3 = 12$, or *BD.* This strategy applies only to the special case of multiplying two binomials.

RESEARCH NOTE

Fuchs et al. (2008) identified seven evidence-based principles of effective instruction for students with math disabilities: instructional explicitness, instructional design to minimize the learning challenge, strong conceptual basis, drill and practice, cumulative review, motivators to help students regulate their attention and behavior to work hard, and ongoing progress monitoring.

Strategies for Managing Time and Resources

A lack of organization is a common characteristic of students with disabilities (Lerner & Johns, 2009; Silver, 2006), as is true for Ron, one of the students introduced at the beginning of the chapter. Organizing study materials involves having the appropriate school supplies, making sure these supplies are brought to class when they are needed, and having an organized notebook to ensure easy access to information. First, you can make sure that students obtain the appropriate school supplies by requiring that they tell their parents what materials they need daily, because you will not be able to call each of their parents individually each day to remind them. In many cases, teachers tell their students what to bring and assume that the students will do the rest on their own. However, this method may not be structured enough for some students who, like Ron, are likely to forget what you said.

Second, you can encourage students to write the information down rather than try to remember it. Having the information on the board or projected helps ensure that their lists are accurate. You may also want to duplicate the list and distribute it to students who cannot easily write it themselves.

Finally, encourage your students to ask themselves the following or similar questions, which can help them remember school supplies as well as assignments throughout the school year:

- What is due tomorrow in school?
- What do I need to do to get it done tonight?
- What materials or other things do I need to get the job done?
- Whom can I ask for help in doing this?

These questions can at first be posted on the board to help students remember them and to prompt their use. You can help motivate students to bring needed materials by providing positive recognition for those who do bring their supplies to school. For example, Mr. Gutierrez gave school pencils to students who had all their supplies in school. Ms. Habner put the names of her students on a "responsible students" list, from which she chose people for classroom jobs.

You may need to make accommodations for students with special needs. For example, students with complex physical disabilities may need a classmate or parent

Strategies for managing time and organizing materials help provide the structured routines that many students need to succeed in school. What are the three steps in teaching students how to use weekly assignment calendars? Michael Newman/PhotoEdit Inc.

to carry their supplies into school. Students who live in poverty might be unable to afford supplies other than materials the school or teacher provides.

Besides having to organize their materials, students also need to organize their time, particularly as they get older and the demands made on their time increase. More schools are teaching students to use schedule books to help them arrange their time (Bryan, Burstein, & Bryan, 2001; Jenson, Sheridan, Olympia, & Andrews, 1994; Patton, 1994). Anderson, Munk, Young, Conley, & Caldarella (2008) developed an organizational skills form for this purpose. A sample form is shown in Figure 10.9. Students are taught to use one form for each of their classes using these steps.

- Students organize their notebooks by inserting divider tabs and blank notebook paper for each class.
- Students are introduced to the activity forms for each class and given a rationale for their use such as: "These will help you get your work done on time and get better grades."

www.resources

TimeLiner is a software program designed to help students organize information for research projects using a timeline. For more information, go to http://www.teachtsp.com.

FIGURE 10.9 Organizational Skills Form

Student Name _____ Subject _____ Week _____ Term _____

Day/ Date	On time or Absent (Step 3)	*Prepared (Step 3)	**Tests and/or Assignments (Steps 4 and 5)	*** ✓ = "Completed" and Turned in (Step 6)	% Correct (Teacher) (Step 7)	Components Complete (Step 8)
MON	OT A	Binder Pencil Pouch Form Labels Paper Correct sections	---------------			
Tue	OT A	Binder Pencil Pouch Form Labels Paper Correct sections	---------------			

*Prepared

1. Binder
2. Pencil daily in class
3. Form for the week
4. Divider labels for each subject
5. Paper, 5 sheets behind each label
6. Papers in correct sections
7. Pencil pouch

**Tests and Assignments

W = worksheet, assignments listed
T = test, tests listed
V = video
L = lecture
N/A = nothing due

***Turned In

Check mark (✓) = assignment handed to teacher
Estimated grade for this term _____
I could improve my grade by:

- Students begin to use the form by self-recording in column 2 whether they have the necessary materials for class by turning the terms in column 3 into self-questions such as, "Do I have a pencil?" or "Are the papers for this class in the right section of my binder?"
- Students record their assignments for the day; if there are no written assignments, using a code, they record what was covered in class that day such as a "V" for video, "L" for lecture, etc.
- Students check whether the assignment was completed and turned in, thus providing themselves with self-reinforcement for finishing the assignment. The teacher can initial students' boxes when work is turned in to provide additional accountability.
- Students record their scores on the assignment, thus providing themselves with written records of their grades so there are no surprises at the end of the grading period.
- Students record the number of items completed. This helps the teacher monitor students' use of the form, and the students self-monitor their performance.

How Can Students Learn to Use Strategies Independently?

Some students may have trouble using a learning strategy independently, even after they have learned how to do it. Their problem could be that they do not know when to use a strategy or how to keep track of how well they are using it, and how to change their behavior, if necessary.

Three strategies that can help students perform tasks more independently are self-instruction, self-monitoring, and self-questioning. Like all learning strategies, these "self" strategies may need to be carefully taught using the teaching practices described in this chapter.

Self-Instruction

In **self-instruction,** learners are taught to use language to guide their performance. In essence, students are taught to talk themselves through a task. The idea is that if they can talk themselves through a task, they will not need help from anyone else. Self-instruction has been successfully used to teach students with disabilities strategies for math, test taking, reading comprehension, and writing (Uberti, Mastropieri, & Scruggs, 2004).

The first step to teach students self-instruction techniques is to explain that self-instruction involves giving oneself directions on how to do a task. For example, self-instruction can be used to help get seatwork done or to remember to use a strategy for a multiple-choice test. Next, ask students to identify a situation that requires the use of a specific skill, such as getting their seatwork done in reading or taking a 10-minute science quiz on Friday. Demonstrate how to write down the steps needed to perform that task. For example, to get independent classwork done, the student first decides how much effort to put into this task. Next, he or she decides what is supposed to be done. Finally, the student decides what the first step in completing the task should be, what the next step should be, and so forth, until the assignment is done. When students are finished, they praise themselves for a job well done. Ask students to rehearse the steps through self-talk or peer review, going over all the steps involved in completing a written classwork task from beginning to end.

After you have demonstrated how to apply self-instruction, have the students practice in a role-play situation, and give them feedback. In the independent classwork task, for example, you could project a sample reading task and demonstrate the steps by thinking out loud. The students could then practice in pairs and give

FIGURE 10.10 Sample Reading Strategies Notebook

Alonzo's Reading Strategies Notebook
Table of Contents

	Page
Identifying hard words	
Using word parts	3
Reading fluency	
WARF	4
Reading comprehension	
SCROL	5
Highlight It!	6
Mark It!	7

Source: Adapted from "Supporting Self-Regulated Learning with Exceptional Children," by J. J. Wery and J. L. Niefield. *Teaching Exceptional Children, 42*(4), 70–78.

each other feedback, with you monitoring and also giving feedback. Even after all of this careful instruction, students still can forget the purpose of certain strategies, forget to use the strategies, or not understand when and where to use the strategies. Wery and Niefield (2010) developed the form shown in Figure 10.10 to guide students as they try to independently use learning strategies they have been taught to perform in class.

Self-Monitoring

In **self-monitoring,** students watch and check themselves to make sure they have performed targeted behaviors. Self-monitoring has been shown to be effective in making positive changes in the academic and social behavior of students with disabilities (Daly & Ranalli, 2003). It is a critical aspect of independent learning, which often requires students to check their performance to see whether it is effective and make a change when a particular strategy is not working (Hallahan et al., 2005; Reid, 1996). Self-monitoring also can be a strong motivator for students by providing them concrete evidence of their progress.

In teaching self-monitoring to your students, first explain to them that it is a way they can check their own behavior to make sure they are doing the right thing. Ask the students to identify a learning strategy they need to use in class. For example, students may select a strategy such as the COPS proofreading strategy described earlier in the chapter.

The next step is to select a practical and expedient way for students to measure the behavior. One possibility is to have them use a checklist of strategy steps and then record the percentage of steps completed. For example, Yashika recorded the steps of the SCROL strategy he completed when reading a section in his science text.

Teach students to use the measurement system through demonstration, practice, and feedback, and continue to encourage and reinforce the use of self-monitoring in your class. Self-monitoring can be applied to any learning strategy.

Self-Questioning

Self-questioning is a form of self-instruction in which students guide their performance by asking themselves questions. The idea behind self-questioning is that if students can guide their own behavior by asking themselves questions, then they will not always need a teacher or other adult present to perform.

 fyi

Brimijoin et al. (2003) report a teacher using a car windshield metaphor to teach students to monitor their understanding. The teacher asked, "How many [of you] are clear as glass about how greatest common factor works? How many have bugs on your windshields? How many have windshields covered with mud?" (p. 70).

RESEARCH NOTE

Wehmeyer et al. (2003) studied the use of self-monitoring with students with developmental and intellectual disabilities. They found that the use of "self" strategies improved the students' class participation and decreased their rate of problem behaviors.

FIGURE 10.11 **Using Self-Instruction, Self-Monitoring, and Self-Questioning in a Math-Problem-Solving Strategy**

Math-Problem Solving

Read (for understanding)

Say:	Read the problem. If I don't understand it, read it again.
Ask:	Have I read and understood the problem?
Check:	For understanding as I solve the problem.

Paraphrase (in your own words)

Say:	Underline the important information.
	Put the problem in my own words.
Ask:	Have I underlined the important information?
	What is the question? What am I looking for?
Check:	That the information goes with the question.

Visualize (a picture or a diagram)

Say:	Make a drawing or a diagram.
Ask:	Does the picture fit the problem?
Check:	The picture against the problem information.

Hypothesize (a plan to solve the problem)

Say:	Decide how many steps and operations are needed.
	Write the operations symbols $(+, -, \times, \div)$
Ask:	If I do . . . , what will I get?
	If I do . . . , then what do I need to do next?
	How many steps are needed?
Check:	That the plan makes sense.

Estimate (predict the answer)

Say:	Round the numbers, do the problem in my head, and write the estimate.
Ask:	Did I round up and down?
	Did I write the estimate?
Check:	That I use the important information.

Compute (do the arithmetic)

Say:	Do the operations in the right order.
Ask:	How does my answer compare with my estimate?
	Does my answer make sense?
	Are the decimals or money signs in the right places?
Check:	That all the operations are done in the right order.

Check (make sure everything is right)

Say:	Check the computation.
Ask:	Have I checked every step?
	Have I checked the computation?
	Is my answer right?
Check:	That everything is right. If not, go back.
	Then ask for help if I need it.

Source: From "Solve It! Strategy Instruction to Improve Mathematical Problem Solving," by M. Montague, C. Warger, and T. H. Morgan, 2000, *Learning Disabilities: Research and Practice, 15*(2), pp. 110–116. Reprinted by permission of Blackwell Publishing.

In teaching students self-questioning, have them first identify the duties or tasks that are required in class. For example, students can identify steps needed to proofread a written paper, such as checking the correct use of capital letters, punctuation, spelling, and appearance. Have students write these tasks in question form, asking, for example, "Have I capitalized all words correctly? Have I used the right punctuation marks in the right places? Have I spelled all the words correctly? Is my paper neat?"

As in self-monitoring, the next step is to select a practical and expedient way for students to measure the behavior, such as recording behaviors as they occur using a checklist. Students might practice self-questioning in pairs for feedback. Other practical measures include keeping task questions on index cards and putting them in a convenient place. For example, students might put the proofreading questions on an index card and tape it to the inside cover of their notebooks. Recall that in the classroom organization form just described, students were taught to use self-questioning to prompt themselves about whether they had the necessary materials for class.

Montague, Warger, and Morgan (2000) taught students with disabilities to solve math word problems using a strategy that included elements of self-instruction, self-monitoring, and self-questioning. The strategy is shown in Figure 10.11.

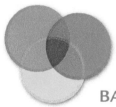

WRAPPING IT UP

BACK TO THE CASES

This section provides opportunities for you to apply the knowledge gained in this chapter to the cases described at the beginning of this chapter. The questions and activities that follow demonstrate how these principles, along with other concepts that you have learned about in this chapter, connect to the everyday activities of all teachers.

GERALD has problems in written expression including organization and mechanical errors. Mr. McCrae has determined that organization is most important, because the mechanical errors can be corrected after Gerald has produced an organized written product. Mr. McCrae has selected the POWER strategy to teach Gerald. You are interested in applying this strategy in your teaching, so you work with Mr. McCrae to develop a script for teaching it. (See the Case in Practice "Teaching Script for Demonstrating POSSE" for a sample script.) In the planning portion of POWER, you may want to consider an editing strategy such as COPS and a graphic organizer. After you have written your script, compare scripts with a peer partner from your class.

TRACI, as you may recall, struggled with solving word problems. After helping her with a strategy for solving such problems, Ms. Cord reflects on Traci's skills in other academic areas. Traci often cannot answer comprehension questions regarding main ideas and details in short passages of text or storybooks. Ms. McCord wonders whether Traci's difficulties in reading might be similar to the ones she experienced in word problems. What do you think? Explain your thinking. Suppose that she does discover that the difficulties are similar. What strategies would you teach Traci that would be useful for reading word problems? Provide a reason for each of your choices.

RON often came unprepared to class. However, after several weeks of his teachers working with him, he now is coming to class with all of the books and materials he needs. In fact, he completed his homework assignments every day this week. He is proud that he has been remembering to check his schedule book and the checklist in his locker. However, he still experiences difficulty getting to school and work on time, and on four days last week, he missed the bus that takes him home. After deciding that the next step is to teach Ron to use self-instruction and self-monitoring strategies for the home and work situations, you have learned about a website (http://coe.jmu.edu/Learningtoolbox/index .html) where you can find a strategy that will help Ron manage time when he is away from the school environment. Once you are at this website, enter as a teacher and select the "Strategy List" from the column on the left. Select two strategies that you think will work for Ron and share your choices with two peers. After all of you have shared your strategies and the reasons for your choices, select two you would present to Ron so that he can choose the one he wants to use.

SUMMARY

- General education teachers can help all their students, including students with disabilities and other special needs, become independent learners. One way teachers can build student independence is to encourage student self-awareness, self-advocacy, and self-determination.

- Another way to help your students become more independent is to design and teach effective learning strategies in class. Methods of teaching learning strategies to students include assessing current strategy use, clarifying expectations, demonstrating strategy use, encouraging students to memorize strategy steps,

providing guided and independent practice, and administering posttests.

- Many successful strategies that can help students become independent learners are available in the areas of reading and reading comprehension, listening and note taking, writing, problem solving in math, and managing time and resources.

- Three strategies that can help students learn to use learning strategies independently are self-instruction, self-monitoring, and self-questioning.

APPLICATIONS IN TEACHING PRACTICE

DESIGNING STRATEGIES FOR INDEPENDENCE

Latasha is a student who has a moderate hearing loss. Although her hearing aid helps, she still has to depend on speech reading to communicate. She also speaks slowly and has trouble saying high-frequency sounds such as *sh* and *t*. Latasha has a poor self-image and is reluctant to interact with her peers and teachers. Design a self-advocacy program for Latasha.

QUESTIONS

1. What skills would you teach Latasha to use for self-advocacy?
2. How would you get Latasha to use these skills in your class and in other in-school and out-of-school situations?

Cal is a student with organizational problems; he is chronically late for class and rarely finishes his homework. Design an organizational strategy for Cal using the guidelines for developing strategies covered in this chapter.

QUESTIONS

1. How would you teach the organizational strategy you have designed using the guidelines covered in this chapter for effectively teaching a learning strategy?
2. How would you teach Cal to apply the strategy independently using self-instruction? Self-monitoring? Self-questioning?

QUESTIONS

1. Is there anything you would change about the strategy? How would you teach the strategy using the six steps described in this chapter?
2. How would you help students apply the strategy independently using the three "self" strategies discussed in this chapter?

PEARSON
myeducationlab

Go to Topics 10: Instructional Practices and Learning Strategies, 11: Reading Instruction, and 12: Content Area Teaching in the MyEducationLab (www.myeducationlab.com) for your course, where you can:

- Find learning outcomes for Instructional Practices and Learning Strategies, Reading Instruction, and Content Area Teaching along with the national standards that connect to these outcomes.
- Complete Assignments and Activities that can help you more deeply understand the chapter content.
- Apply and practice your understanding of the core teaching skills identified in the chapter with the Building Teaching Skills and Dispositions learning units.
- Examine challenging situations and cases presented in the IRIS Center Resources. (optional)
- Access video clips of CCSSO National Teachers of the Year award winners responding to the question, "Why Do I Teach?" in the Teacher Talk section. (optional)
- Check your comprehension on the content covered in the chapter by going to the Study Plan in the Book Resources for your text. Here you will be able to take a chapter quiz, receive feedback on your answers, and then access Review, Practice, and Enrichment activities to enhance your understanding of chapter content. (optional)

Differentiating Instruction

Differentiating Instruction

LEARNING Objectives

After you read this chapter, you will be able to

1. Describe ways you can differentiate instruction for students by teaching preskills; sequencing instructional examples; and providing additional instruction, practice, and review.

2. Describe accommodations you can make when activating background knowledge, organizing content, and teaching terms and concepts.

3. Make lessons accessible for students with special needs by improving the clarity of your written and oral communication.

4. Describe strategies for involving parents in teaching their children.

5. Adapt independent practice activities for students.

6. Describe how you can make modifications in your classroom materials and activities for students with moderate to severe intellectual disabilities.

Katelyn Metzger/Merrill

MS. DIAZ was teaching her fourth-grade class how to write percentages for fractions using this example from her math book:

Write a percent for $\frac{7}{8}$.

$\frac{7}{8}$ means $7 \div 8$.

$$0.87\frac{4}{8} = 0.87\frac{1}{2} = 87\frac{1}{2}\%$$

$$8\overline{)7.00}$$
$$\underline{64}$$
$$60$$
$$\underline{56}$$
$$4$$

Divide until the answer is in hundredths. Give the remainder as a fraction.

$\frac{7}{8} = 87\frac{1}{2}\%$, or 87.5%

To show her students how to do this problem, Ms. Diaz wrote the example on the board, pointing out that the fraction 7/8 means 7 divided by 8. She then explained that they would have to divide until the answer was in hundredths and would have to give the remainder as a fraction. Following this instruction, Ms. Diaz assigned the students ten similar problems to do independently. Abdul, who is a student in this class, has a learning disability. Abdul has experienced some difficulties with math skills since he entered the second grade. He has difficulty learning new skills unless he is given many opportunities for instruction and practice. Abdul answered none of the ten problems correctly. He missed converting the fraction to a percentage because he forgot that it means 7 divided by 8; Abdul divided 8 by 7 instead.

How could this lesson have been taught to Abdul to prevent this misunderstanding? How can Ms. Diaz differentiate instruction for him if he continues to struggle with problems of this type?

CECILY is a student with a hearing loss who is in Ms. Boyd's U.S. history class. Cecily has failed every test so far, because the tests are based mainly on the textbook, which she has difficulty reading. Cecily can read most of the words in the text but is unable to pick out the main ideas. Cecily also has trouble figuring out the meanings of key vocabulary words in context, even though they are highlighted in the text, and she does not know how to use the glossary. Last week, Cecily was assigned a chapter to read for homework. She spent almost two hours trying to comprehend 15 pages of text, and when she was done, she cried in frustration because she could not remember anything she had read. Until recently, Cecily has enjoyed a small group of friends who teach her popular phrases while she teaches them sign language for their favorite topics—clothes, movies, and boys. However, her friends are doing much better in class than Cecily and she's embarrassed.

What can Ms. Boyd do to help Cecily read and remember key ideas in her textbook? What can she do to help Cecily understand new vocabulary words?

ALBERT has attention deficit–hyperactivity disorder (ADHD) and is included in Ms. Olivieri's second grade class. Ms. Olivieri uses learning centers as a way of giving her students extra practice on skills she has already taught in class. Sometimes she has her students read text and answer questions independently. For example, yesterday students reread a story covered in reading class and completed a graphic organizer requiring them to identify key story parts such as setting, main characters, problem, and problem resolution. Other days she has students work together playing learning games like vocabulary dominoes, or timing each other reciting math facts, word parts, or science vocabulary. Albert struggles with the independent activities. He complains that the work is too hard for him, and he has particular difficulty with assignments that have multistep directions and more than one part. As a result, he often wanders away from the centers, either getting help from other students in class or bothering them. Ms. Olivieri feels she is already spending too much time helping Albert.

What can Ms. Olivieri do to make centers a more successful experience for Albert and give herself more time to work with other students?

fyi

This chapter presents instructional accommodations and modifications for steps 5 and 6 of the INCLUDE strategy:

Step 5   Use information from steps 1–4 to brainstorm ways to differentiate instruction.

Step 6   Differentiate instruction.

INCLUDE

INCLUDE

As you have already learned, the curriculum methods and materials teachers use have a strong influence on how readily students learn in the classroom. In fact, the better the materials and the teaching, the fewer the individual accommodations required for students with special needs. However, for a variety of reasons, you may not have control over the materials used in your school. Furthermore, despite your best teaching efforts, some students will still need individual accommodations or modifications to gain access to important skills and content. For example, in the cases just described, merely showing Abdul how to do one problem is not enough. He needs guidance through a number of examples before he is ready to do problems independently. In addition, you can help Cecily focus on important information in her textbook by giving her a study guide that has questions pertaining to the most important content in each chapter. You can also have Cecily identify vocabulary she does not know and ask a classmate to help her with the meanings before she reads. For Albert, you can make sure all directions are clearly written using words he can identify; you can also give directions for center activities orally, guide students through several practice examples before they are required to work independently, and break his assignments into several shorter activities. Of course, you also want to be sure that Albert has the academic skills necessary to complete center assignments independently.

The purpose of this chapter is to provide you with strategies for differentiating instruction by making accommodations and modifications in curriculum materials, teacher instruction, and student practice activities that are reasonable to carry out and increase the likelihood of success for students with disabilities. Remember, most students with disabilities included in your classroom are expected to meet the same curricular goals as their classmates without disabilities. Therefore, most of the strategies for differentiating instruction covered in this chapter fall into the category of accommodations, which are supports that allow students to more readily access the general education curriculum. In addition, with RtI being used in many schools, differentiated instruction is often carried out using more intensive instructional tiers. For example, Cecily might be given extra instruction in vocabulary in a small Tier 2 group.

It is also important to note that the instructional accommodations described in this chapter can sometimes be carried out with your entire class. At other times, they might be presented with individual students or as a part of small groups. The way you choose to accommodate your students with special needs depends on classroom demands, the characteristics of individual students, and the overall level of functioning of your class. For example, in the case of Abdul, if he has many other classmates who are struggling to write percentages for fractions and if he can attend to a task in a large group, then Ms. Diaz can accommodate him by building more guided practice into her large-group instruction. If only Abdul and a few of his classmates are having trouble learning percents or if Abdul has trouble paying attention in a large group, then Ms. Diaz might better accommodate Abdul by instructing him either one-to-one or in a small group. You can use the INCLUDE strategy to help you make decisions about the best way to make accommodations for your students with special needs.

Instructional modifications are used for students who have more significant disabilities and who have alternative curricula specified on their individualized education programs (IEPs). Strategies for making appropriate instructional modifications are covered at the end of this chapter.

How Can You Make Accommodations for Students with Special Needs in Basic Skills Instruction?

Basic skills instruction means primarily instruction in the academic skills of reading, writing, and math. However, you may also apply effective principles for differentiating basic skills instruction to content areas such as science. Four aspects of basic skills instruction for which you may need to make accommodations for students with disabilities are preskills; the selection and sequencing of examples; the rate of introduction of new skills; and direct instruction, practice, and review.

Teaching Preskills

Darrell is in Ms. Rayburn's second-grade class. In language arts, he is experiencing a problem common to many students with special needs. On Tuesday, Darrell was at his desk reading a book on his favorite topic: magic. However, when Ms. Rayburn asked Darrell specific questions about the book, he was unable to answer them. It turned out that Darrell was unable to identify most of the words in the book and was just pretending to read. Another student, Tamika, is in Mr. Thomas's Algebra 1 class. She is having difficulty solving basic equations with one unknown because she has yet to master basic math computational skills.

Preskills are basic skills necessary for performing more complex skills. Prior to teaching a skill, you should assess students on the relevant preskills and, if necessary, teach these skills. Darrell was unable to comprehend the book about magic because he lacked the word identification skills needed to read the words. He may need instruction in word attack skills; he may also need to be encouraged to read trade books at his reading level. Tamika needs additional instruction and practice on her computational skills if she is going to be successful in Algebra 1. Because textbooks do not generally list preskills, you need to ask yourself continually what preskills are required, and you should be vigilant for students who lack them. Looking at the instructional demands in this way is a key part of applying the INCLUDE strategy. Determining the potential impact of student preskills on instruction may mean informally assessing such skills using curriculum-based assessments.

If you are teaching a skill and find that most of your students lack the necessary preskills, teach these preskills directly before teaching the more complex skill. If only one or two students lack preskills, you can accommodate them with extra practice and instruction through a peer or parent volunteer or with the help of a special service provider or paraprofessional. For example, Ms. Cooper was preparing a lesson on how to find the area of a rectangle. Before beginning the lesson, she gave her students a multiplication probe and found that almost half the class was still having problems with their multiplication facts. Ms. Cooper set up a peer tutoring program in which students who knew their facts were paired with students who did not; the pairs practiced facts for 10 minutes each day for a week. Students who preferred to work alone practiced their math facts using a drill-and-practice computer-based program. Ms. Cooper still introduced finding the area of rectangles as scheduled, but she allowed students to use calculators, a bypass strategy, until they had mastered their facts.

Selecting and Sequencing Examples

The way you select and sequence instructional examples also can affect how easily your students learn. For example, Alex's practice activities for a week in Mr. Huang's third-grade math class are shown in Figure 9.1. Mr. Huang has been covering two-digit subtraction with regrouping. On Monday through Thursday, Alex was given five of these problems and got them all right. On Friday, he was asked to do a mixture of problems, some requiring regrouping and some not. Alex got only three of the problems correct because he was unable to discriminate between subtraction problems that required regrouping and those that did not. He was unable to differentiate these two types of problems in part because his daily practice pages had included only one problem type. Carefully preparing the **example selection** you use for instruction and student practice can help students learn to differentiate among problem types.

You can help students make key discriminations between current and previous problem types by using examples that at first require the application of only one particular skill (Carnine, Silbert, Kame'enui, & Tarver, 2010). When students can

INCLUDE

FIGURE 9.1 Alex's Math Work

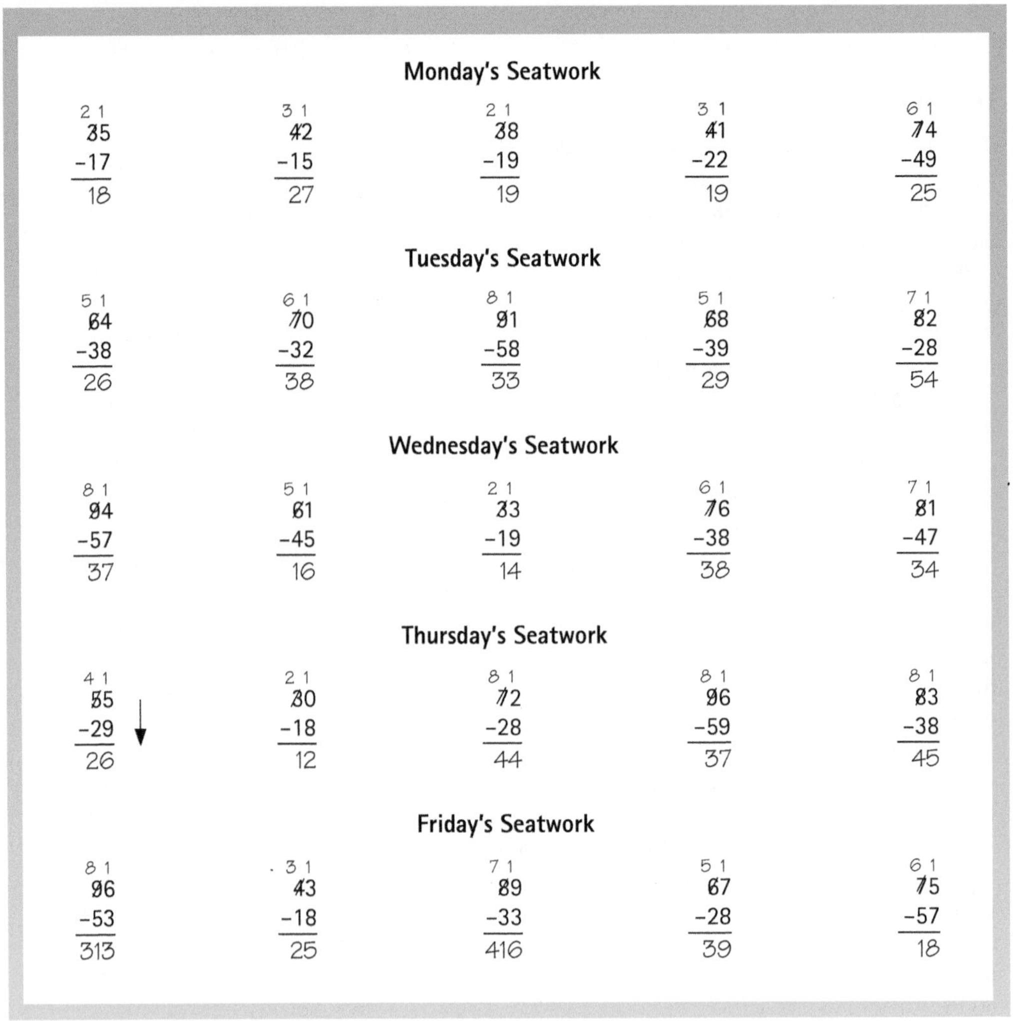

Monday's Seatwork

$^{2\ 1}$ 35	$^{3\ 1}$ 42	$^{2\ 1}$ 38	$^{3\ 1}$ 41	$^{6\ 1}$ 74
−17	−15	−19	−22	−49
18	27	19	19	25

Tuesday's Seatwork

$^{5\ 1}$ 64	$^{6\ 1}$ 70	$^{8\ 1}$ 91	$^{5\ 1}$ 68	$^{7\ 1}$ 82
−38	−32	−58	−39	−28
26	38	33	29	54

Wednesday's Seatwork

$^{8\ 1}$ 94	$^{5\ 1}$ 61	$^{2\ 1}$ 33	$^{6\ 1}$ 76	$^{7\ 1}$ 81
−57	−45	−19	−38	−47
37	16	14	38	34

Thursday's Seatwork

$^{4\ 1}$ 55	$^{2\ 1}$ 30	$^{8\ 1}$ 72	$^{8\ 1}$ 96	$^{8\ 1}$ 83
−29	−18	−28	−59	−38
26	12	44	37	45

Friday's Seatwork

$^{8\ 1}$ 96	$^{3\ 1}$ 43	$^{7\ 1}$ 89	$^{5\ 1}$ 67	$^{6\ 1}$ 75
−53	−18	−33	−28	−57
313	25	416	39	18

perform these problems without error, add examples of skills previously taught to help students discriminate between the different problem types. Doing this also provides students with needed review. An easy accommodation for Alex would have been to add several problems that did not require regrouping to each daily teaching and practice session once he had demonstrated that he could compute the regrouping problems accurately when they were presented alone.

Ms. Owens ran into a different example-related problem when teaching her students word problems in math. In her examples, when a word problem included the word *more,* getting the correct answer always involved subtracting, as in the following problem:

> Alicia had 22 pennies. Juanita had 13. How many more pennies does Alicia have than Juanita?

However, on her test, Ms. Owens included the following problem:

> Mark read 3 books in March. He read 4 more books in April. How many books did Mark read?

Several students with special needs in Ms. Owens's class subtracted 3 from 4 because they thought the presence of the word *more* signaled subtraction. Ms. Owens needed to include problems of this latter type in her teaching to prevent such misconceptions.

Consider this example: When Mr. Yoshida taught his students how to add *ed* to a word ending in *y*, he demonstrated on the board as follows:

carry + ed = carried hurry + ed = hurried

Next, Mr. Yoshida had his students add *ed* to five words ending in *y*. Finally, he assigned students ten practice problems in their English books that looked like this:

Write the past tense of *marry*.

A number of students were unable to answer the questions in the book, even though they knew how to add *ed* to words ending in *y*, because the practice examples in the book required students to know the meaning of "past tense" and how to form the past tense by adding *ed*. The book's practice activity was very different from the instructional examples Mr. Yoshida used, which only required students to add *ed* to words ending in *y*.

Both Ms. Owens's and Mr. Yoshida's examples demonstrate an important aspect of selecting instructional examples: The range of your instructional examples should match the range of the problem types used when you assess student learning. Ms. Owens could have prevented problems in her class by expanding her range of examples to include word problems that contained the word *more* but were not solved by subtracting. Mr. Yoshida could have better prepared his students for the practice activities in the English book by using examples that referred directly to forming the past tense by adding *ed*. Note that some students with special needs still may struggle even when appropriate instructional examples are used. These students may require an individual accommodation that could be as simple as a reminder that the word *more* can have more than one meaning or that the past tense is formed by adding *ed* to a verb. Or the accommodation could be as involved as providing additional instruction using concrete representations of the different meanings of *more* or verbs ending in *ed*.

The following shows a different example selection problem. Tawana's class was learning several high-frequency sight words that appeared in their classroom reading program. On Wednesday, Tawana learned the word *man*, but on Thursday, after the word *men* was presented, she was unable to read *man* correctly. Tawana's word identification problem illustrates another example selection problem, namely, **example sequencing**. The visual and auditory similarities of *man* and *men* make learning these words difficult for many students who are at risk and students with learning disabilities, who may have trouble differentiating words that look and/or sound the same. One way to prevent this problem is to separate the introduction of *man* and *men* by introducing other dissimilar high-frequency words, such as *dog, house,* and *cat*. Students with special needs also may need differentiated instruction such as more practice learning the words, color coding the vowels *a* and *e,* and spelling the two words using letter blocks.

This same sequencing idea can be applied to teaching letter sounds. For example, when deciding on the order in which to teach the sounds, consider separating letters that look and sound the same, such as *b* and *d, m* and *n,* and *p* and *b*. The careful sequencing of instruction can also be applied to teaching higher-level content. For example, when Mr. Roosevelt, a chemistry teacher, taught the chemical elements, he separated those symbols that look and/or sound similar, such as bromine (Br) and rubidium (Rb), and silicon (Si) and strontium (Sr). Knowledge of how sequencing can affect learning can help you recognize the need to differentiate instruction. For example, Ms. Mann, unlike Mr. Roosevelt, was unable to change the order in which she taught the chemical elements without drastically modifying her chemistry text. When she noticed that bromine and rubidium were taught closely together, she allowed more time for students to practice in their study groups before introducing another element.

fyi

Student errors and misconceptions also stem from the over- or under-generalization of concepts. Careful selection and sequencing of a range of examples can help prevent these kinds of errors.

Deciding the Rate of Introduction of New Skills

Students sometimes have difficulty learning skills that are introduced at too fast a rate. For example, Mr. Henry was teaching his ninth-grade English students how to proofread rough drafts of their writing for errors in using capital letters and punctuation marks. He reviewed the rules for using capital letters, periods, commas, question marks, and exclamation points. Next, he had students take out their most recent writing samples from their portfolios to look for capitalization and punctuation errors. Carmine found that he had left out capital letters at the beginning of two sentences, but he did not find any of the punctuation errors he had made. A number of other students in the class had the same problem. The dilemma was that Mr. Henry had taught his students to proofread their papers for capital letters and punctuation marks simultaneously. A better pace might have been first to work on proofreading for capitalization errors and then to add one punctuation mark at a time (first periods, then commas, followed by question marks, and then exclamation points).

In another example of the **rate of skill introduction,** Ms. Stevens was working on reading comprehension with her students. She introduced three new comprehension strategies at once: detecting the sequence, determining cause and effect, and making predictions. However, when applying the INCLUDE strategy using results from her universal screening measure, she recognized that Carlos, a student with a mild intellectual disability, learned best when he was taught one strategy at a time. Ms. Stevens accommodated Carlos by forming a Tier 2 group with three other students who, like Carlos, would benefit from learning these comprehension strategies one by one before being asked to carry them out simultaneously. Mr. Wallace, the special education co-teacher, taught the group, starting with instruction on detecting the sequence. You can learn more about working with special education teachers in the Working Together.

These examples demonstrate an important principle about introducing new skills to students with special needs: New skills should be introduced in small steps and at a rate slow enough to ensure mastery before teaching more new skills. Further, you may want to prioritize skills and even postpone some, as Ms. Stevens did. Many commercially produced materials introduce skills at a rate that is too fast for students with disabilities. As just illustrated, a common accommodation is to slow down the rate of skill introduction and provide more practice. Other students in the class, including those with no formally identified special needs, often benefit from

Listening is the weakest skill for English-language learners. Khisty (2002) suggests: (1) displaying words as they are spoken or pointing to words in prepared text as they are delivered; (2) contextualizing instruction through models, real objects, drawings, and other visual aids; and (3) having students act out problems or concepts.

INCLUDE

www.resources
The ProQuest K–12 website, at http://www.proquestk12.com, provides lesson plans that include modifications for students with special needs.

Working TOGETHER

Asking for Help

Ms. Gabriel is starting her first year as a high school history teacher. She just found out that she will have four students with learning disabilities included in her fifth-period U.S. history class. The special education teacher, Mr. Colbert, left the students' IEPs in her mailbox with a brief note asking her to look them over to see what kinds of accommodations she is required to make in her teaching. The IEPs state that she is supposed to modify their homework assignments and adapt the textbook.

Ms. Gabriel is confused. In the first place, she is unsure exactly what an *accommodation* is. Second, she doesn't know what the IEP means by *modifying* homework and *adapting* the text. She's particularly worried about homework because she knows students won't like it if they know that other students are doing less

homework. Ms. Gabriel feels that Mr. Colbert should have met with her to explain more clearly what she needed to do. Still, she is new to the school and is afraid to admit she doesn't know what to do. Mr. Colbert is also the wrestling coach, and Ms. Gabriel doesn't feel very comfortable communicating with him.

- How could Ms. Gabriel request a meeting with Mr. Colbert while at the same time setting a positive tone for working together?
- What communication strategies can Ms. Gabriel employ at the meeting to both get the information she needs and establish a good working relationship with Mr. Colbert in the future?

such accommodations as well. If a student happens to be the only one having a problem, you can seek additional support from special needs staff, paraprofessionals, peers, and/or parent volunteers.

Given the current atmosphere of accountability in U.S. schools, it is often hard for teachers to slow down the rate at which they introduce new information for fear they will be unable to cover all the material that will appear on high-stakes tests. Although covering content efficiently is an important consideration, learning is usually best served when teachers carefully construct a foundation of skills and concepts based on student performance rather than on the school calendar.

Slowing down the rate of skills introduced is an accommodation in the way curriculum is presented, but it is not the same thing as reducing the amount of curriculum to be learned. You need to be careful not to reduce the expectations for your students with special needs who are expected to meet the goals of the general education curriculum. Otherwise, they will have difficulty meeting state standards. However, for your students with moderate to severe intellectual disabilities, it may be appropriate to make an instructional modification by decreasing the amount of curriculum. For example, Ms. Evers modified Robin's curriculum by shortening her spelling lists from 15 to 3 words and selecting only high-frequency words as specified on her IEP.

Providing Direct Instruction and Opportunities for Practice and Review

Students who are at risk or have disabilities may require more direct instruction and review if they are to acquire basic academic skills. Consider the following example. Youn is in Ms. Howard's spelling class. On Monday, Ms. Howard gave students a pretest on the 15 new words for the week. On Tuesday, the students were required to use each word in a sentence. On Wednesday, the teacher scrambled up the letters in all the words and had the students put them in the correct order. On Thursday, students answered 15 fill-in-the-blank questions, each of which required one of the new spelling words. On Friday, Youn failed her spelling test even though she had successfully completed all the spelling activities for that week. Youn performed poorly because the daily spelling activities did not provide her with enough direct instruction and practice on the spelling words. Although activities such as using spelling words in sentences are valuable in the right context, they do not provide practice on the primary objective of this particular lesson, which is spelling all 15 words correctly from dictation. One way to differentiate Youn's instruction would be to have a peer tutor give her a daily dictation test on all 15 words; have Youn write each missed word three times, saying each letter in the word as she writes; and then retest her on all 15 words again.

This example demonstrates another problem that students with special needs have when learning basic skills: retention. Melissa had mastered addition facts with sums to 10 as measured by a probe test in October, but when she was given the same test in January, she got only half of the facts correct. Similarly, Thomas, in his civics class, could define the equal protection clause of the Constitution in November, but he could not remember what it was when asked to define it in February. A common way to differentiate instruction for such students is to schedule more review for them. This review should be more frequent following your initial presentation of the material and then can become less frequent as learning is established. For example, instead of waiting until January to review addition facts, Melissa's teacher could first provide review weekly, then every other week, and then every month. Thomas's civics teacher could periodically review key concepts and information that Thomas may need to apply later, either through homework, a learning center activity, an instructional game or contest, or an activity in a co-taught class. If Thomas and Melissa were the only ones in their classes in need of review, their teachers could accommodate them individually by giving them extra help before school while the rest of the class was working independently, or as part of a Tier 2 small group in RtI. You can learn more about Tier 2 groups in RtI in the Instructional Edge.

RESEARCH NOTE

Research shows that many students with learning disabilities need direct instruction in letter sounds in order to eventually learn to identify words systematically (Ehri, 2004).

INSTRUCTIONAL **EDGE**

Providing Differentiated Instruction Using Tier 2 in RtI

While Tier 1 in RtI is evidence-based, it is also the least intensive tier, mainly employing large-group instruction with fewer supports for student learning. Some students need more intensive instruction in Tier 2, the subject of this feature. As you read about Tier 2, remember that much of the research on RtI has been done in the area of elementary school reading, so caution is advised when applying these recommendations to other subject matter areas and grade levels (Gersten et al., 2009).

WHAT IS TIER 2 INSTRUCTION?

Tier 2 consists of instruction provided in Tier 1, plus additional small group sessions that provide extra practice of targeted skills and content covered in Tier 1. As in Tier 1, all instruction in Tier 2 is evidence-based. In some schools, instruction in Tier 2 is carefully scripted using the same research-based intervention for all children having similar problems in a given area. This is called the standard protocol model. Other RtI schools use a more individualized approach whereby interventions are chosen based on graphed individual student data. Greater intensity is achieved in Tier 2 through more systematic and focused instruction, smaller instructional groups, and more frequent progress monitoring.

WHO IS ELIGIBLE FOR TIER 2 INSTRUCTION?

Students enter Tier 2 when their performance on universal screening measures dips below benchmark scores, a set percentile, or below standard on a high stakes or end-of-grade test. While the number of students eligible for Tier 2 varies, it is estimated as being around 15%. In a class of 25 students, this would amount to 3–4 students.

WHERE, WHEN, AND FOR HOW LONG DOES TIER 2 INSTRUCTION TAKE PLACE?

Tier 2 instruction usually takes place in small, same-skill groupings of 3–4 students. These groups meet 3–5 times per week, for 20 to 40 minutes in elementary school, up to 60 minutes per session in high school (Bursuck & Damer, 2011). Tier 2 groups can take place either inside or outside the general education classroom, with some middle school groups taking place in literacy labs and even within after-school programs (Johnson & Smith, 2008).

WHO TEACHES TIER 2 GROUPS?

Tier 2 instruction can be carried out by a variety of staff including general education teachers, Title 1 teachers, special education teachers, and paraprofessionals, all carefully prepared to ensure instructional quality.

HOW LONG DO STUDENTS REMAIN IN TIER 2 GROUPS?

The amount of time students spend in Tier 2 varies, but in many systems time in Tier 2 is of a limited duration, ranging from 8–12 weeks. During that time student progress is regularly monitored. Students who progress to grade level exit Tier 2, although they continue to be monitored to ensure their performance is maintained. Students who fail to show progress despite receiving well-delivered Tier 2 instruction usually move to more intensive instruction in Tier 3, although students can remain in Tier 2 longer if they show significant improvement despite still performing below benchmark levels.

WHAT IS THE ROLE OF THE GENERAL EDUCATION TEACHER IN TIER 2?

The role of the general education teacher in Tier 2 varies. Perhaps your most important role is to teach Tier 1 so well that fewer students require Tier 2 instruction. Beyond that, general education teachers play an important role in progress monitoring by regularly measuring student performance and using the results to help the RtI team decide who exits Tier 2 and who remains. Last, while general education teachers can teach Tier 2 groups themselves, it can be difficult to do so with quality and consistency while still discharging your many other instructional responsibilities.

A related concern is that teaching approaches that are indirect and provide little practice may be appropriate for some students but may need to be supplemented for others. For example, Felix and Bill were learning to read in Ms. Farrell's class. Neither boy had learned the *ch* sound (as in *chin*). On Monday, Felix came across the word *chair* in a trade book he was reading. His teacher pronounced the word and said, "That sound at the beginning of *chair* is the same sound you hear at the beginning of *cherry*." The next day, Felix came to the word *chip* in his book, and he figured it out; he remembered what Ms. Farrell had told him the day before and was able to make the connection between the beginning sound in the orally presented word *cherry*, and the *ch* in *chair*, and then *chip*. For Felix, one example in his book and a brief teacher explanation were enough for learning to occur. On Monday, Bill also came across a *ch* word, and he too was told what the word was and that it began with the same sound as the word *cherry*. Unlike Felix, however, when Bill came across another *ch* word the next day, he could not remember the sound of these letters. Having the teacher tell him another word that *ch* began with was too

TABLE 9.1 Direct Instruction of *ch* Sound

Teacher	Student
I. Teach directly the ch sound in isolation. Teacher writes on the board: *ch, or, ee, ch, th, sh, ch,* and *ing.*	
1. Teacher models by saying the sound of the new letter combination and tests by having the students pronounce it. Teacher points to *ch.* "These letters usually say *ch.* What sound?"	"*ch*"
2. Teacher alternates between the new combination and other combinations. Teacher points to a letter combination, pauses 2 seconds, and asks, "What sound?"	Say the combination sound
3. Teacher calls on several individual students to identify one or more letter combinations.	
II. Teach directly the ch sound in words. Teacher writes on the board: *chin, chair, chip, boot, beam, chomp, stain, chum, moon,* and *chat.*	
1. a. Students identify the sound of the letter combination in *chin,* then read the word. Teacher points under the combination letters and asks, "What sound?"	"*ch*"
b. Teacher points to left of word. "What word?"	"*chin*"
c. Teacher repeats step 1(a–b) with remaining words.	
2. a. Students reread the list without first identifying the sound of the letter combination. Teacher points to *chin,* pauses 2 seconds, and asks, "What word?"	"*chin*"
b. Teacher repeats step 2(a) with remaining words.	
3. Teacher calls on individual students to read one or more words.	

Source: Adapted from *Direct Instruction Reading* (5th ed.), by D. Carnine, J. Silbert, E. J. Kame'enui, and S. G. Tarver, 2010, Upper Saddle River, NJ: Merrill/Pearson Education. Copyright © 2010. Reprinted with the permission of Pearson Education, Inc., Upper Saddle River, NJ.

indirect; he needed the teacher to say, "The sound of *ch* is /ch/. What's the sound of *ch?*" In addition, one practice example was not enough. Bill required more direct instruction and practice than did Felix, such as that provided in the activity shown in Table 9.1.

This discussion of Felix and Bill raises an important issue: General education teachers need to know more than one approach to meet the needs of individual students, an idea at the heart of differentiated instruction as well as of RtI. Felix can learn sounds with minimal instruction while reading books; Bill cannot. Bill's teacher may need to accommodate Bill and other students in the class by providing them with some direct instruction on letter–sound correspondence. This direct instruction can involve having students both say and write their sounds.

Another example reinforces the idea that some of your students may need more direct instruction and practice. Mr. Diaz was teaching his English students how to write a persuasive essay, including how to develop a thesis, add supporting details, reject counterarguments, and end with a conclusion. He described the steps in writing a persuasive essay while showing students an example of a well-written persuasive essay. He then asked the students to write a one-page persuasive essay for homework. Brenda handed in her essay the next day; although her paper showed some potential, her thesis lacked clarity, her details were sketchy, and she forgot to reject possible counterarguments. Brenda needed more instruction and guided practice on how to write a persuasive essay than Mr. Diaz had provided. Mr. Diaz could have applied the INCLUDE strategy, anticipated Brenda's problems, and provided guided practice by writing essays with the class until even lower performers such as Brenda seemed comfortable performing the task. He also could have had the students write a persuasive essay independently in class so that he could monitor their performance and accommodate individual students using corrective feedback and more instruction, if necessary.

dimensions of DIVERSITY

In Native American cultures, children learn skills by first observing them and then doing them. Native American students benefit from direct teaching that first stresses modeling or demonstrations. You can enhance demonstrations for your Native American students by showing them the final product before the demonstration (Sparks, 2000).

INCLUDE

CASE IN PRACTICE

Applying INCLUDE to a Basic Skills Lesson

Ms. Dettman loves to look on the Internet for what she calls "teacher-tested" lesson plans. She found a lesson yesterday on the topic of math word problems (Bowen, n.d.), an area in which her students often struggle and in which she is always looking for something different to do. The teacher who used this technique claimed that it had had a positive impact on her class's performance last year on the state's high-stakes test in math. Ms. Dettman decided to try it.

In this lesson, the teacher posts a daily word problem on tagboard. The skill targeted (for example, division, fractions) varies from day to day. The problem is read aloud first thing in the morning and students have until lunchtime to solve it. The students keep a special file folder containing an answer sheet for the week's problems. Students are required to show their work. After lunch, three or four students go to the board to solve the problem. They talk aloud about how they solved the problem. Each child has an incentive chart posted in class. Every day, two students collect and score papers and points are awarded for correct answers. Students receive a prize when they reach a certain number of points, and then a new chart is posted.

Ms. Dettman has a group of four students in class who have trouble in math; three of these students have learning disabilities in both reading and math. Because the curricular goals for these students are the same as those for everyone else in the class, instructional modifications are not required. Ms. Dettman reviewed the demands of this activity to see whether any accommodations were needed. She identified the following seven demands:

1. Read the problem.
2. Identify the operation needed to solve the problem (for example, add, subtract).
3. Write a number sentence.
4. Convert the number sentence to a computation problem.
5. Solve the computation problem.
6. Label the answer.
7. Check work.

Next, Ms. Dettman thought about areas where she might need to make accommodations. She considered the students' preskills. Three of the students have reading problems, but the fact that the story problems would be read out loud eliminated the need for an accommodation such as a bypass strategy. However, Ms. Dettman thought the students would have trouble translating the story problems into a sentence; they all have reading comprehension problems and had previously struggled to pick the correct operation when they solved word problems in class. The four students also don't know their math facts, and their computational accuracy is inconsistent, even though they understand the concepts behind the four basic operations. Computation could be a definite problem as well. None of the students struggles with handwriting, so the writing demands of solving the word problem would not be problematic. In addition, one student is artistically inclined, a strength that Ms. Dettman planned to build on.

Ms. Dettman was concerned about the fact that different types of story problems were selected for the activity each day in the lesson plan. She thought that this variety might confuse the four students who seem to work best when new problem types are added gradually as others are learned. Ms. Dettman was also concerned that student modeling of problem solving at the board by thinking out loud was a great idea, but she felt the students with problems in math might not benefit from it without more careful structuring.

Ms. Dettman decided to make the following accommodations for the four students. Although she would continue to work with them on improving the accuracy of their math computation skills, for this activity she would allow them to bypass their current difficulties in this area by letting them use calculators.

Ms. Dettman also decided to provide the students with a visual diagram to guide them through the problem-solving steps, along with small-group guided practice to ensure they used the strategy appropriately. Part of that small-group guided practice would include teacher and student think-alouds to make the problem-solving steps more conspicuous for the students. Also, when students came to the board to solve problems out loud in the large group, bonus points would be awarded to those students paying careful attention, particularly to the think-aloud part. Ms. Dettman would use only story problems that the students were capable of solving independently. That way, they would get needed independent practice as well as a realistic opportunity to earn points and cash them in for a prize at the end of the week.

Finally, Ms. Dettman would appoint the student with artistic talent to be the class artist. She would come to the board and draw a picture representing the problem.

REFLECTION

Why do you think Ms. Dettman made instructional *accommodations* for the four struggling students rather than instructional *modifications*? How did Ms. Dettman use the INCLUDE strategy to come up with instructional accommodations for those students? How effective and feasible are these accommodations? What would you do differently if you were the teacher?

Finally, it is important to remember that practice is most effective when it *follows* direct instruction; practice is never an adequate substitute for direct instruction. For example, Mr. Hanesworth designed a board game in which students get to move ahead if they can answer a division fact problem. The problem is that five students in his class still do not understand the concept of division. For them, the board game practice activity is likely to result in failure. Mr. Hanesworth can accommodate these learners in a small group by providing additional instruction on division for them while allowing the rest of the class to play the board game independently. Of course, later on, Mr. Hanesworth can reward the hard work of the small group by allowing them to practice a skill they know using a game-like format.

Clearly, you may need to differentiate instruction to enable students with special needs to acquire basic skills. An example of how to differentiate basic skills instruction using INCLUDE is presented in the Case in Practice. In addition, the Technology Notes introduces ways to use technology to assist students with special needs with their writing. Students also may need accommodations when subject-area content is presented, the primary teaching focus as students move into the upper grades.

How Can You Make Accommodations for Students with Special Needs When Teaching Subject-Area Content?

The instruction of academic content includes areas such as social studies and science. This instruction often involves the use of textbooks and lecture–discussion formats, but it also can include other activities, such as videos, films, hands-on activities, and cooperative learning. Although content-area instruction generally is associated with instruction in secondary schools, the information presented here is relevant for elementary teachers as well. Social studies and science have always been taught at the elementary level, and now there are even high-stakes science tests that may be administered as early as third grade. In this section, you learn how you can differentiate instruction to help students with special needs learn subject-area content. Strategies for making accommodations are stressed for activating background knowledge, organizing content, and teaching terms and concepts. As with basic skills, you can provide accommodations for students with disabilities by changing how you teach the entire class or by making individualized accommodations either one to one or in small groups.

Activating Background Knowledge

The amount of background knowledge students have can greatly influence whether they can read subject matter with understanding. To illustrate, read this list of words:

are	making	between
only	consists	often
continuously	vary	corresponding
one	curve	points
draws	relation	variation
set	graph	table
if	values	isolated
variables	known	

INCLUDE

dimensions of
DIVERSITY

Relating content to students' background knowledge makes material more relevant. It also motivates students to draw on their own background knowledge when they encounter new information, helping them assume responsibility for learning (Gersten, Baker, & Marks, 1998).

Using Web-Based Programs to Improve Student Writing Performance

Students with disabilities face many challenges with writing (Graham, 2006). Tele-Web (Technology-Enhanced Learning Environments on the Web) is an Internet-based software program that can help students with disabilities overcome these problems. Tele-Web helps students write expository text that is well organized; contains an introduction, body paragraphs, and a conclusion; and meets the knowledge demands of the reader (Englert, Zhao, Dunsmore, Collings, & Wolberg, 2007). Tele-Web uses two devices to support student writing. First, mapping tools are used to help students generate ideas and details for their papers. Students are taught to move their ideas, or supporting details, to their respective boxed categories using a click-and-drag feature that is also part of Tele-Web.

The second device is a template known as the *supported report.* First, a printed reminder of the teacher's oral instructions appears at the top of the screen. To help students stage their ideas, *Title* and *Introduction to Paper* boxes appear. Next, a *Topic Sentence Box* prompts students to generate a topic sentence for their first paragraph. Immediately following the topic sentence box is a *Supporting Details Box* used to cue students to choose details that support their topic sentence. Each time students click to add a paragraph, new topic sentence and paragraph boxes appear. Finally, a *Concluding Sentence Box* is provided near the bottom of the computer screen prompting students to conclude their papers.

In addition to these features, Tele-Web uses a pop-up window to prompt students to evaluate their writing through a series of self-questions. Example questions include: Did I tell what the pet looks like? Did I use a topic sentence? Did I use concluding sentences? The questions disappear when students return to composing their papers, fostering independence by providing only temporary support.

Tele-Web has three additional features that allow students to access online support: (1) a spell checker that matches words in the paper against an online dictionary; (2) a text-to-speech function that allows the computer to read back student text; and (3) an online submission feature through which teachers provide feedback and students revise and publish their papers.

Englert et al. (2007) tested Tele-Web against a paper-and-pencil approach to teaching writing that offered similar supports but without the use of computers. The papers of students with disabilities who used Tele-Web had a greater range of information about their writing topics and were better organized, showing a clear relationship among the introduction, body, and conclusion.

Shown below is a list of other Internet sources for software that can help students with writing assignments (Gillette, 2006):

SOFTWARE PROGRAMS THAT CAN READ DIGITIZED TEXT

- Write OutLoud (Don Johnston Incorporated)
  http://www.donjohnston.com

- Read OutLoud (Don Johnston Incorporated)
  http://www.donjohnston.com

- Kurzweil 3000 (Kurzweil Educational Systems)
  http://www.kurzweiledu.com

- Read & Write Gold
  http://www.texthelp.com

SOFTWARE PROGRAMS THAT ASSIST STUDENTS WITH PLANNING COMPOSITIONS

- Draft Builder (Don Johnston Incorporated)
  http://www.donjohnston.com

- Inspiration (Inspiration)
  http://www.inspiration.com/store/main/index.cfm

TALKING WORD PROCESSORS

- IntelliTalk III (IntelliTools) Intellitools
  http://www.intellitools.com

- Word 2010 (Microsoft)
  http://www.microsoft.com/office/word/produinfo/default.mspx

VOICE RECOGNITION SOFTWARE

- Scansoft Dragon Naturally Speaking
  http://www.nuance.com/naturallyspeaking/standard

- Word 2010 (Microsoft)
  http://www.microsoft.com/office/word/prodinfo/default.mspx

WORD PREDICTION SOFTWARE

- Co:Writer (Don Johnston Incorporated)
  http://www.donjohnston.com

- Read & Write Gold
  http://www.texthelp.com

How might speech-synthesis and word-prediction programs help this student with her journal entries? What other types of assistive technology might help her with her writing?
Will Faller

◦-◦-●

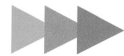

INSTRUCTIONAL **EDGE**

Strategies for Teaching Science to English-Language Learners

ELLs struggle in science, yet information about teaching science to ELLs can be hard to find (Watson, 2004). While ELLs share the characteristic of having limited English proficiency, it is important to realize that they are a diverse group. ELLs come to your science classroom with different levels of background knowledge, literacy in their native language, family involvement in their education, intellectual ability, and motivation to do well in school, to name a few areas. All of these factors, in addition to English proficiency, should be considered when differentiating ELLs' science instruction using these strategies (Short & Echevarria, 2004/2005; Watson, 2004):

- For students in your class who speak little or no English, label parts of your classroom and lab equipment with both English names and names from the students' native language. Using Spanish, for example, the labels would be *science book/ciencialibro*. Besides helping to initiate communication with your ELLs, labeling in English and another language also demonstrates to English-speaking students the difficulties students face when learning a new language. Requiring all of your students to learn both names effectively reinforces this idea.

- Place less emphasis on the traditional approach of having students read the textbook prior to engaging in a laboratory activity. Instead, start with the laboratory experience. The concreteness of laboratory experiences makes the text more comprehensible.

- Whenever possible, show objects, draw pictures, or act out the meanings of key terms. For example, when teaching the concept of *scientific classification*, one teacher demonstrated the concept by having students take off their left shoes and put them in a pile in the front of the room. The students classified the shoes in different ways, such as shoes that lace, slip on, and buckle.

- Repeat instructions, actions, and demonstrations as needed, speaking slowly and using simple sentence structure whenever possible.

- Demonstrate procedures and provide clarifying diagrams and illustrations before students begin lab work. For example, before students begin a lab exercise, provide them with a written procedural guide, go over key terms by placing them on the board, demonstrate the procedures, and actively monitor students' performance by circulating among them as they are completing the lab.

- Assign lab partners to ELLs. The lab partners should be strong in science and work well with other students. Placing two ELLs together in a group along with one English speaker is also effective, particularly if one of the ELLs is more advanced than the other in English skills. Encouraging ELLs to express their thoughts to a partner before reporting to the whole class promotes language learning and the confidence to speak out in class.

- If appropriate, enlist the support of parents in building students' background knowledge about topics before they are introduced in class. Background knowledge provided in students' native language allows them to better follow what is discussed, even if they don't know every word.

- Schedule time for review at the end of each lesson, pointing out key concepts and vocabulary while making connections to lesson objectives and state standards. This is essential, because ELLs may concentrate so intently on processing language during instruction that they are unable to identify the most important information expressed.

- Give feedback to your students on their language use in class. For example, model for your students how scientists talk about their experimental findings. Have students try to use the language of scientists when orally presenting their lab reports, and give them feedback on their performance.

Were you able to read all of them? Do you know the meanings of all these words? Now read the following passage:

> If the known relation between the variables consists of a table of corresponding values, the graph consists only of the corresponding set of isolated points. If the variables are known to vary continuously, one often draws a curve to show the variation. (From Michaelson, 1945, as cited in Lavoie, 1991)

Chances are, unless you are a math major, if you were asked to summarize what you just read, you would be unable to do so despite the fact that you probably answered yes when asked whether you could read and understand all the words individually. You may lack the background knowledge necessary to understand this very technical paragraph. The knowledge students bring to a content-area lesson is often as important for understanding as the quality of the textbook or instructional presentation (Marzano, 2004; Pressley, 2000). For students to understand content material, they need to relate it to information they already know.

Unfortunately, teachers often fail to consider background information. Students with disabilities and students who are at risk may have two problems related to background knowledge: They may simply lack the necessary knowledge, or they may know the information but be unable to recall it or relate it to the new information being presented.

Using the Prep Strategy   One teaching strategy for determining how much knowledge students already have about a topic so that you can decide how much background information to present in class prior to a reading assignment is called the **PReP (PreReading Plan) strategy** (Langer, 1984). The PReP strategy has three major steps:

1. *Preview the text or lesson, and choose two to three important concepts.* For example, for a science lesson, Mr. Amin chose the concept of photosynthesis and the keywords *cycle* and *oxygen*.
2. *Conduct a brainstorming session with students.* This process involves three phases. In Phase 1, students tell you what comes to mind when they hear the concept. This gives you a first glance at how much they already know about the topic. Student responses in Phase 1 can be written or oral. The advantage of written responses is that you can assess the background knowledge of your entire class at once. The disadvantage of written responses is that for students who struggle to write, it is difficult to gauge whether an unacceptable response is due to a lack of knowledge about the topic or simply the result of a writing problem. This is a good time to differentiate your instruction using INCLUDE. If students have a writing problem, modify your approach by questioning them orally. In Phase 2, students tell you what made them think of their responses in Phase 1. This information can help you judge the depth of, and/or basis for their responses, and it also provides a springboard for students to refine their responses in Phase 3. In Mr. Amin's class, he discovered in Phases 1 and 2 that two of the students mistakenly thought that photosynthesis had to do with photography because of the presence of *photo* in the word. This error provided an opportunity to build on students' knowledge. Mr. Amin explained that *photo* means light and that in photography, a camera takes in light to make pictures. He then said that plants take in light too, and when the light combines with chemicals in the plant, carbohydrates and oxygen are made. This process is called *photosynthesis.* In this way, Mr. Amin used what the students already knew to teach them a concept they did not know. In Phase 3, students can add to their responses based on the discussion in Phase 2.
3. *Evaluate student responses to determine the depth of their prior knowledge of the topic.* During this step, you can decide whether students are ready to read the text and/or listen to a lecture on photosynthesis or whether they first need more information. Determining the needs of your students with respect to the demands of your instruction is an important part of INCLUDE. In Mr. Amin's class, two students continued to have trouble understanding that photosynthesis was something plants did with light to make carbohydrates and oxygen. They needed more information before they were ready to read the chapter. Mr. Amin accommodated these students by showing them a video illustration of photosynthesis in the morning before school began. The video includes concrete examples that weren't necessary to use with the rest of the class.

INCLUDE

Preparing Anticipation Guides   Anticipation guides can help you activate student knowledge about a particular topic and construct bridges to new information by encouraging students to make predictions (Readence, Moore, & Rickelman, 2000; Vacca & Vacca, 2007). **Anticipation guides** consist of a series of statements, some of which may not be true, related to the material that students are about to read (Roe, Smith, & Burns, 2005). Before teaching, students read these statements that either challenge or support ideas they may already have about the subject. This process catches their interest and gives them a reason for listening and reading. Providing questions or statements prior to reading also aids comprehension for all students, including those with disabilities.

For example, Ms. Henry constructed an anticipation guide prior to teaching a unit on the nervous system. Her anticipation guide included the following statements:

- A person cannot function without the nervous system.
- The nervous system helps us study and learn about new things.
- There are gaps between the nerve cells in our bodies.
- Nerve cells do different jobs in the body.
- The central nervous system is only one part of the nervous system.
- Our brains do not control our reflexes.
- Persons cannot hold their breath until they die.
- Some people can swim without thinking about it.

When using the anticipation guide, Ms. Henry needed to differentiate her instruction for several of her students with reading problems. After distributing the guide, she met with these students in a small group and read each item out loud, clarifying terms such as *central nervous system, reflexes,* and *nerve cells.* Ms. Henry also accommodated students with reading problems by highlighting important ideas from the selection, dividing the text into smaller sections, having these students complete the anticipation guide with peer buddies, and giving students a chance to read the text at home before discussing it in school (Kozen, Murray, & Windell, 2006).

Providing Planning Think Sheets Activating background information and building bridges to current knowledge are also of concern to teachers when asking students to write. Some researchers recommend **planning think sheets** to help writers focus on background information as well as on the audience and purpose of a paper (Englert et al., 1988). For audience, students are asked to consider who will read the paper. For purpose, students clarify why they are writing the paper (for example, to tell a story, to convey information, or to persuade someone). Finally, students activate background knowledge and organize that knowledge by asking themselves questions such as "What do I know about the topic?" and "How can I group or label my facts?" (Englert et al., 1988; Vaughn & Bos, 2009). A planning think sheet for a paper assignment might contain write-on lines for students to answer the following questions (Raphael, Kirschner, & Englert, 1986):

- What is my topic?
- Why do I want to write on this topic?
- What are two things I already know that will make it easy to write this paper?
- Who will read my paper?
- Why will the reader be interested in this topic?

Students may need more teacher modeling and guided practice before being able to complete think sheets independently. You can deliver these accommodations using a small teacher-led group. You can further differentiate instruction and motivate students by providing a range of paper topics that students can choose from. Students also can be permitted to respond orally to the questions.

Organizing Content

Research shows that many students, including students with special needs, have difficulty understanding important ideas and their interrelationships in content areas (Baker, Kame'enui, Simmons, & Simonsen, 2007). These students can benefit from the use of supports or scaffolds that help them identify and understand important information. One form of support is to organize the curriculum according to big ideas rather than facts in isolation. Another form of support is to make these big ideas more evident to students through the use of advance organizers, cue words for organizational patterns, study guides, and graphic organizers.

www.resources

For the latest research on using background knowledge to improve student comprehension go to: http://www.cast.org/publications/ncacbackknowledge.html.

www.resources

The TESOL (Teachers of English to Speakers of Other Languages) website, at http://www.tesol.org, provides news and links regarding the fastest-growing sector of school-age children: those who come from non-English-speaking backgrounds.

Using Advance Organizers   **Advance organizers** include information presented verbally and/or visually that makes content more understandable by putting it within a more general framework. They are particularly effective for students with special needs who may have limited background knowledge and reading and listening comprehension skills (Swanson & Deshler, 2003). Examples of advance organizers include the following (Lenz, 1983):

- identifying major topics and activities
- presenting an outline of content
- providing background information
- stating concepts and ideas to be learned in the lesson
- motivating students to learn by showing the relevance of the activity
- stating the objectives or outcomes of the lesson

While a well-constructed advance organizer presented to the entire class will meet the needs of most students, those with disabilities or other special needs may benefit from a more individualized approach. For example, Mr. Serano motivated Zak by tying an advance organizer for a lesson about weather to Zak's interest in aviation. Ms. Williams explained to Rinaldo that his lesson objective was to identify and write numbers from 10 to 100. The rest of the class was learning to add two-digit numbers. Ms. Hardy used an individualized advance organizer to communicate to Carlos, who struggles with writing, that he could demonstrate what he learned in the unit on explorers by designing a map showing the countries the major explorers came from. The rest of the class wrote two-page papers about the countries involved in exploration, including the major explorers from each country.

Employing Cue Words for Organizational Patterns   Big ideas are often the central focus of an **organizational pattern** of information. The most common patterns of information include the descriptive list including the sequence of events in time, comparison/contrast, cause/effect, and problem/solution (Baxendell, 2003; Ellis, 1996). Each of these patterns of information can be made more conspicuous for students through the use of cue words. For example, cue words for a list, description, or sequence might include *first, second,* and *third;* cue words for comparison/contrast would be *similar, different, on the one hand,* and *on the other hand;* cue words for cause/effect might be *causes, effects, because,* and *so that;* and cue words for problem/solution would be *problem, solution,* and *resolve.* Cue words are important for students with disabilities, many of whom have difficulty telling the difference between important and unimportant information (Hallahan et al., 2005; Kame'enui et al., 2007).

Text that does not contain clear cue words requires students to make a number of inferences, which may be difficult for students. Rewriting the book is obviously not a reasonable way to differentiate instruction. Instead, you can accommodate students by helping to make the key concepts more explicit using teaching strategies described in this text, such as study guides and graphic organizers. Or, you can use alternative means of presenting the same information, such as videos or books that are more clearly written.

Constructing Study Guides   The general term **study guide** refers to outlines, abstracts, or questions that emphasize important information in texts (Conderman & Bresnahan, 2010; Mercer, Mercer, & Pullen, 2011). Study guides are helpful in improving comprehension for students with special needs in content-area classrooms (Lovitt, Rudsit, Jenkins, Pious, & Benedetti, 1985). For example, at the beginning of this chapter, Cecily was having trouble picking out key ideas in her U.S. history text, a common problem for students at all educational levels. She might benefit from a study guide that cues students to important information by asking them questions about it. Procedures for constructing study guides are shown in the Professional Edge two pages ahead. A sample study guide for a section of a social studies text on Truman's Fair Deal is shown in Figure 9.2.

FIGURE 9.2 Sample Study Guide for Truman's Fair Deal Vocabulary

---

Consumables are products that _____.

Some positive examples of consumables are _____, _____, and _____.
A negative example of a consumable is _____.

Big Ideas

The **problem** was that after World War II, price controls were lifted and the cost of _____,
_____, and other consumer goods went _____.

The **solution** was for workers to _____.

The **effect** was that _____ and _____.

Study guides can be used with the entire class or as an accommodation for individuals or small groups of students. Horton (1987) suggests the following ways to differentiate instruction using study guides:

1. Allow 2 or 3 inches of margin space in the study guide in which students can take notes. Draw a vertical line to indicate the margin clearly. For example, in the study guide in Figure 9.2, the answer to the first vocabulary question is "*Consumables* are products that cannot be used over again." You may want to have students write this vocabulary word along with its complete definition in the margin. Some students find a new word easier to understand if you first use the overhead or PowerPoint to discuss the definition along with a series of positive and negative examples. Specific strategies for presenting new vocabulary are presented later in the chapter.
2. Print page numbers next to the sentences in the study guide to show where to find missing words in the textbook.
3. Print the missing words at the bottom of the page to serve as cues.
4. Leave out several words for more advanced students and fewer for students with special needs. For example, in Figure 9.2, the *effect* part of the big idea could be simplified as "The *effect* of strikes such as the railroad strike was that the stability of the American economy was threatened and ____."
5. Model how to use the study guides by completing a sample study guide in front of the class while thinking out loud (Conderman & Bresnahan, 2010).
6. Arrange for reciprocal peer-teaching situations; pair students and have them take turns being the teacher and the student.
7. Use the study guide for homework assignments. Assign students a passage in the text and give them accompanying study guides (either with or without the pages marked for easy reference). Have them complete the guides and study the material for homework.
8. Ask students to keep and organize their study guides from a number of passages and to study them as they review for unit or end-of-semester tests.
9. Place reading passages, study guides, and tests on a computer. Design the study guide using a hypertext format with highlighted questions or key words containing a link to the website that will help answer the question (Conderman & Bresnahan, 2010). Be sure to take into account your students' capabilities using computers, using INCLUDE to make accommodations as needed. Use print-to-speech software for students who have difficulty with word reading.
10. Whenever possible, write the study guide at a reading level that fits most of your students. Students with reading and writing problems may need to have the study guide read to them or respond to the questions orally.
11. To discourage students from only learning material on the study guide, supplement the study guide with other instructional methods and construct test questions that are not taken word-for-word from the study guide (Conderman & Bresnahan, 2010).

www.resources

The Education Development Center's webpage for the National Center to Improve Practice in Special Education through Technology, Media, and Materials, at http://www2.edc.org/ncip, provides many ideas on how to implement research-based teaching practices with students with special needs.

PROFESSIONAL **EDGE**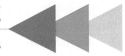

How to Develop Study Guides

Study guides help improve the comprehension of all students, especially those with special needs who are included in content-area classrooms. Follow these steps to develop a study guide from a content-area textbook:

1. Go through the entire book and mark the chapters you want to cover for the term and those you do not.
2. Indicate the sequence in which you will assign the chapters; that is, note the one that comes first, second, and so forth.
3. Read the material in the first chapter carefully. Mark the important vocabulary, facts, and concepts that you expect students to learn. Cross out any material you do not intend to cover.
4. Divide the chapter into logical sections of 1,000- to 1,500-word passages. (The length will depend, of course, on how detailed the material is and how much of it you deem important.)
5. Write brief sentences that explain the main ideas or emphasize the vocabulary, facts, or concepts in the passage. Write 15 sentences per passage.
6. Place these sentences in order so the material in one leads to the next and so forth.
7. To create questions, either leave out a few words in each sentence or change each sentence into a question. For example, the following statement was identified as important in a chapter on natural disasters:

> A 2 percent sales tax was passed to pay for relief efforts after the massive floods of 2005.

This statement could be turned into a question by leaving out several words:

> _____ was passed to pay for relief efforts after the massive floods of 2005.

You could also change the statement into a question:

> How did the people pay for the relief efforts after the massive floods of 2005?

8. Project the sentences and/or questions using large type.
9. Prepare sheets for the students, using regular type.
10. Prepare an answer sheet for the teacher.
11. Develop a multiple-choice test to cover the material in the study guide. The test should have 10–15 items, with four possible choices for each question.

Source: From "How to Develop Study Guides," by Thomas C. Lovitt and Steven V. Horton, from *Reading and Writing Quarterly,* January 1987, Volume 3, Issue 4, pp. 333–343.

INCLUDE

12. Use INCLUDE to decide whether to put related but more basic information in the guide. For students with more significant challenges, make an instructional modification by changing the content load so it remains related to the topic at hand but is more basic. For example, Ms. Hall required that Al, a student with a mild intellectual disability in her fourth-grade class, identify fruits and vegetables that were high in fiber, while the rest of the class responded to questions about the biochemical processes involved when the body digests fiber. When the students were tested on the content covered in the guide, Al was held responsible for answering his more basic questions, which covered content that had been previously specified on his IEP.

Study guides are not a substitute for direct instruction. The amount of direct instruction necessary varies with the difficulty of the material. In general, students need more help completing study guides for texts that assume high levels of student background knowledge and in which key information needs to be inferred as opposed to being explicitly presented. The INCLUDE strategy can help you determine whether more direct instruction is needed and whether it needs to be delivered as part of large- or small-group instruction, or a Tier 1 or Tier 2 group.

Creating Graphic Organizers   Another way teachers can help students organize content is to use **graphic organizers.** This strategy gives students a visual format to organize their thoughts while looking for main ideas (Baxendell, 2003). Archer and Gleason (2010) suggest the following five guidelines for constructing graphic organizers:

1. Determine the critical content (for example, vocabulary, concepts, ideas, generalizations, events, details, facts) that you wish to teach your students. Helping students focus on the most critical information is important for several reasons. First, students with disabilities may have trouble identifying the most important information in an oral lesson or textbook chapter. In most cases this

FIGURE 9.3 Comparison/Contrast Concept Map

Attribute	Native Americans	Settlers
Land	Shared Lived close to it without changing it Respected it	Owned Cleared it Used it

Summary

Native Americans and settlers had different ideas about land. Native Americans shared the land whereas the settlers owned individual pieces of it. Native Americans lived close to the land; they respected it and did not change it. Settlers used the land for their own gain.

will be content stressed in your state's standards. Second, it is easier for students to remember several main ideas than to remember many isolated details. Third, putting too much information on a graphic organizer can make it so visually complex that students may have trouble interpreting it.

2. Organize concepts into a **concept map,** a type of graphic organizer or visual representation that reflects the structure of the content, such as stories, hierarchies (top-down and bottom-up), feature analysis, diagrams, compare/contrast, and timelines. Because the purpose of a graphic organizer is to clarify interrelationships among ideas and information, you should keep it as simple as possible. Figure 9.3 shows a completed comparison/contrast concept map.

3. Design a completed concept map. Completing the map before you teach with it will ensure that the information is clear and accurate and can be presented to your students in a timely manner.

4. Create a partially completed concept map to be completed by students during instruction. Having students fill out the map as you present your lesson is an excellent way to keep them on task. Also, many students with disabilities benefit from a multisensory approach; seeing the information on the graphic, hearing it from the teacher, and writing it on the map helps them better retain the information presented.

5. Create a blank concept map for students to use as a postreading or review exercise. This structure for review is easy for students to use.

Once you have constructed graphic organizers, you can use them as follows (Archer & Gleason, 2010):

1. Distribute partially completed concept maps to your students.

2. Project the map on a screen using PowerPoint or an overhead projector, displaying only those portions you wish students to attend to. Limiting the amount of information you present at one time will help students with attention problems who have trouble focusing on more than one piece of information at a time.

3. Introduce the information on the concept map proceeding in a logical order; stress the relationships among the vocabulary, concepts, events, details, facts, and so on.

4. At natural junctures, review the concepts you have introduced. You can do this by projecting the blank map and asking students questions about the content. This review is essential for students who have difficulty learning large amounts of information at one time.

5. At the end of the lesson, review the critical content again using the blank concept map. You can also have students complete the blank maps for homework. These maps will help students organize their studying and also help you find out what they have learned.

In most cases, using graphic organizers will be helpful for your entire class. Students with attention or listening problems may benefit from the additional accommodations of having a completed graphic explained to them prior to instruction for

www.resources

These two sites provide collections of many ready-to-use graphic organizers: http://www.teachervision.fen.com/graphic-organizers/printable/6293.html and http://www.graphic.org.

use as an advance organizer and then completing a blank organizer after instruction with the teacher or a peer for extra practice and review. Students with gaps in background knowledge may benefit from additional work with graphic organizers that summarize background information. This can be provided as part of small-group or one-to-one instruction. For example, to prepare some of his students with special needs to complete the graphic organizer shown in Figure 9.3, Mr. Jackson read sections of two stories: one about the settlers in Ohio in the 1700s and another about the Delaware tribe, who also lived in Ohio at the time. He also differentiated instruction by providing additional ways for students to demonstrate their knowledge of this and other differences between settlers and Native Americans by having students write short stories or produce their own picture books.

Teaching Terms and Concepts

Content-area instruction is often characterized by a large number of new and/or technical vocabulary words and concepts. Students who have special needs or who are at risk are likely to have difficulty with the vocabulary and concept demands of many content-area texts and presentations. For example, consider the following passage from a general science text:

> Thousands of years ago, Scandinavia was covered by a thick ice sheet. The mass of the ice forced the crust deeper into the denser mantle. Then the ice melted. The mantle has been slowly pushing the land upward since then. This motion will continue until a state of balance between the crust and mantle is reached again. This state of balance is called *isostasy* (ie-sosstuh-see). (Ramsey, Gabriel, McGuirk, Phillips, & Watenpaugh, 1983)

Although the term *isostasy* is italicized for emphasis, other technical terms and concepts, such as *crust* and *mass,* also may pose a problem for students and require special attention. These words may be particularly difficult because students are likely to be familiar with their nonscientific meanings, which are quite different from their technical meanings (for example, *mass* as in church; *crust* as in bread). You need to check student understanding and teach vocabulary directly, if necessary, using one of the strategies covered in this section.

This teacher is modeling positive and negative examples to clarify the meaning of a new concept. How can using both examples and nonexamples help make the meaning of new terms and concepts clear? Paul Conklin/PhotoEdit Inc.

Using Definitions   Carnine et al. (2010) propose an approach to teaching terms and concepts using definitions that employ positive and negative examples following three steps:

1. State your definitions clearly and simply. Your definitions should only contain words that students already know.

   Consider the following definition of consumables, a word from the study guide in Figure 9.2:

   consumables: a resource whose availability is permanently changed by its usage.

   This definition uses a number of words that younger or even at-risk middle or high school students might not know. Instead, consider the following more learner-friendly definition:

   consumables: products used by persons and businesses that must be replaced regularly because they wear out or are used up.

2. Ask students a series of questions to find out whether they can discriminate positive examples from negative examples. For examples, if you were teaching *consumables* using a definition, you might say the following:

   Consumables are products used by persons and businesses that must be replaced regularly because they wear out or are used up. What are consumables? ("Consumables are products used by persons and businesses that must be replaced regularly because they wear out or are used up.")

   Last month we had to replace three of our light bulbs. Are light bulbs consumables? ("Yes, light bulbs are consumables.") How do you know? ("They are products that wear out and need to be replaced.")

   In Ellen's neighborhood most people have lived in the same house for more than 20 years. Are houses consumables? ("No, houses aren't consumables") How do you know? ("Houses don't need to be replaced regularly because they don't wear out.")

   Sarah was out of skin cream and hand lotion and had to go to the store to get some more. Are Sarah's skin cream and hand lotion consumables? ("Yes, Sarah's skin cream and hand lotion are consumables.") Why do you say that? ("Because she used them up and they had to be replaced.")

   Randy went to the gas station to fill his tank and change his oil. Are gas and oil consumables? ("Yes, gas and oil are consumables.") How do you know? ("Because they can be used up and have to be refilled.")

   The class went to the park for a picnic and went swimming in the river. Is the river a consumable? ("No, the river is not a consumable.") Why do you say that? ("Because it is not a product and can't be replaced.")

   What are consumables? ("Consumables are products used by persons and businesses that must be replaced regularly because they wear out or are used up.")

3. Ask a series of open-ended questions to discover whether students can discriminate the new word from words they learned previously. For example, after teaching consumables, ask, "What are consumables?" Also ask for the definitions of words previously introduced: "What are durable goods? natural resources?"

Note that having students repeat the definition after it is first presented helps keep it in working memory and makes it easier for them to answer the questions that follow. Also, requiring students to answer in complete sentences using the new word rather than answer with only a yes or no forces them to use the word. The more times students use a new word, the greater the likelihood they will learn it. Responding in complete sentences reinforces important expressive language skills that are often problematic for students with special needs. If students have been taught a word using a definition or synonym, follow your question with "How do you know?" Their reasons for answering yes or no will reveal whether they are correctly using the definition or just guessing.

FIGURE 9.4 **Concept Diagram**

Concept Name:	Nonviolent resistance	
Definition:	Protesting in a peaceful way	

Always	Sometimes	Never
Peaceful	Done in a group	Violent
	Done individually	

	Positive Examples	Negative Examples
	Picketing	Shouting match
	Boycott	Physical attack
	Sit-in	Revolutionary war
	Hunger strike	Riot

fyi

Stahl and Shiel estimate that teachers can realistically teach 300 words per year, which translates to about 8–10 per week (as cited in Armbruster, Lehr, & Osborn, 2001). Since there will never be enough time to teach all of the words students are unlikely to know, words taught need to be selected carefully.

English-language learners and other learners with special needs cannot rely solely on linguistic information to learn and retain vocabulary. For these students, accommodations can include bringing in real objects and visuals, such as photographs; matching your actions with your words by conducting demonstrations; allowing students to hear and see vocabulary by using films, DVDs, and books on tape; and having students engage in hands-on activities by performing pantomime and drawing pictures (Hill & Flynn, 2006). Students can also be motivated by personalizing the questions in your vocabulary instruction. For example, when Ms. Hendrix taught her students the meaning of *vehicle,* she included in her presentation photos of the family cars of her hard-to-motivate students. She further engaged Rohan by giving him the job of holding up the photos in front of the class during the presentation.

Making Concept Diagrams   Constructing **concept diagrams** is a method that combines graphic organizers with the methods just described using definitions and positive and negative examples (Bulgren, Schumaker, & Deshler, 1988). A sample concept diagram for the concept of nonviolent resistance is shown in Figure 9.4. First, the teacher selects a keyword from a story or lecture. Next, she constructs a diagram that features the definition of the word; the characteristics that are always present, sometimes present, and never present; and positive and negative examples that can be used to model the word. Finally, the teacher presents the concept diagram to students as follows (Carnine et al., 2010):

1. Present the word and its definition.
2. Discuss which characteristics are always, sometimes, and never present.
3. Discuss one of the positive examples and one of the negative examples in relation to the characteristics.
4. Check other positive and negative examples to discover whether they match the characteristics.

How Can You Improve Clarity in Written and Oral Communication?

In effective instruction, ideas are clearly tied together, which enables students to understand them more easily. The need for instructional clarity applies to both your written communication and oral communication. Written communication, in many school situations, involves the use of textbooks and other printed materials, such as handouts, homework, and written tests. Oral communication can include instructional behaviors such as giving directions, asking questions, and delivering lectures.

When a textbook is not written clearly or a lecture is not presented clearly, students have to make critical connections between ideas on their own, a skill that many students who are at risk may not have. Students may not be able to recognize that they do not understand the material, or they may not be aware of strategies to try when instruction is difficult to understand. For example, when reading a text, they may not know how to use keywords and headings or how to look at the end-of-chapter questions to get main ideas. During oral presentations, students may not feel comfortable asking questions to clarify the information presented because often they are not sure what to ask and are afraid of looking stupid. Finally, students may lack the background knowledge necessary to construct meaning on their own. If you communicate clearly and use materials that do so as well, students with special needs can be more successful and the need for differentiated instruction will be reduced.

Clarity in Written Communication

The importance of clearly written communication is illustrated by these two textbook passages about western migration in the United States:

> Many of the farmers who moved in from New England were independent farmers. Land cost about a dollar an acre. Most men could afford to set up their own farms. Livestock farming was quite common on the frontier. Hogs could be fed in the forests. The cost of raising hogs was low. (Senesh, 1973, as cited in Armbruster, 1984)

> Most of the farmers who moved in from New England were independent farmers. Being an independent farmer means that the farmer can afford to own his own farm. Around 1815, most men could afford their own farms because lands were cheap—it cost only about a dollar an acre. Many of these independent farms were livestock farms. For example, many frontier farmers raised hogs. Hog farming was common because hogs were inexpensive to keep. The cost of raising hogs was low because the farmer did not have to buy special feed for the hogs. The hogs did not need special feed because they could eat plants that grew in the surrounding forests. (Armbruster, 1984)

The second passage is much easier to understand; it requires fewer inferences by the reader and fewer accommodations by the teacher. It also defines *independent farmer* for the reader. If students were reading the first passage, you might have to provide this definition—which you could do orally or in a study guide. The reason farmers turned to raising livestock can be inferred from the first paragraph, but it is stated directly in the second. For students reading the first paragraph, teachers may need to pose questions prior to reading to establish an understanding of this relationship: for example, "Why did the farmers turn to raising livestock?" Vocabulary not explained clearly in context may need to be covered more directly in large or small groups using strategies for teaching vocabulary covered in this and the next chapters.

Another aspect of written language that can make comprehension more difficult is the use of pronouns. A general rule of thumb is that the closer a pronoun is to its referent, the easier it is to translate. Consider the following section of text:

> Now life began to change. The Eskimo hunters could see that these tools were useful. So they became traders, too. They trapped more furs than their families needed. Then they brought the furs to the trading posts. There they could trade the furs for supplies they had never had before. Because the new tools helped Eskimo hunters get along better, they became part of the Eskimo environment. (Brandwein & Bauer, 1980)

Many readers may have trouble figuring out whom *they* refers to in this passage. Although the placement of most pronouns is not this problematic, understanding pronouns can be difficult for students with special needs. However, students can be taught to make sense of pronouns (Carnine et al., 2010). Before students read, identify unclear pronouns. Have students underline the pronouns in a passage. Then show them how to find the pronouns' referents by asking questions. Consider the following example:

Passage

Curtis and Dorva skipped school. They were grounded for a week. He was sorry. She got mad.

www.resources

The CAST (Center for Applied Special Technology) website, at http://www.cast.org, has many helpful suggestions for the universal design of learning materials and teaching practices. This site provides a link to the National Center on Accessing the General Curriculum webpage, which offers research, solutions, and resources for universal design.

Student Questioning

Teacher: "Curtis and Dorva skipped school." Who skipped school?
Students: Curtis and Dorva.
Teacher: "They were grounded for a week." Was Curtis grounded?
Students: Yes.
Teacher: Was Dorva grounded?
Students: Yes.
Teacher: "He was sorry." Was Curtis sorry?
Students: Yes.
Teacher: Was Dorva sorry?
Students: No.
Teacher: "She got mad." Did Dorva get mad?
Students: Yes.

Depending on the level of sophistication of your class, this instruction could be done with the entire class or performed as differentiated instruction for individual students who struggle to understand sentences containing pronouns. The accommodation could also be made as part of a Tier 2 group.

Clarity in Oral Communication

Just as the quality of textbook writing affects student learning, so too does the quality of teachers' oral language. Three particularly important areas of oral language are giving directions, asking questions, and presenting subject matter (such as in a lecture).

Giving Directions   Giving oral directions is the most common way that teachers tell their students what they want them to do. When directions are not clear and have to be repeated, valuable instructional time is wasted. Consider this set of directions given by a middle school teacher at the beginning of a social studies lesson:

Unclear Instruction

All right, everyone, let's settle down and get quiet. I want you all to get ready for social studies. Shh. . . . Let's get ready. Alice and Tim, I want you to put those work-sheets away. We need our books and notebooks. (Evertson et al., 1983, p. 143)

How clear is the teacher about what she wants her students to do? Now read this alternative set of directions:

Clearer Instruction

All right, everyone, I want all of you in your seats facing me for social studies. [Teacher pauses.] Now, I want you to get out three things: your social studies book, your spiral notebook, and a pencil. Put everything else away so that you have just those three things—the social studies book, the spiral notebook, and the pencil—out on your desk. [As students get out their materials, the teacher writes "Social Studies, page 55, Chapter 7 on Italy" on the chalkboard. She waits until students have their supplies ready and are listening before she begins talking.] (Evertson et al., 1983, p. 143)

In the first example, the teacher does not get the students' attention before giving them directions. She is also unclear in communicating what she wants her students to do. For example, the words *settle down* and *get ready* are not defined for the students. In the second example, the teacher first gets her students' attention and then very specifically states all the things they need to do.

Lavoie (1989) has suggested four guidelines for giving directions that are helpful either for your entire class or as accommodations for individual students with special needs:

1. State commands specifically, using concrete terms. In the Clearer Instruction example, the teacher was very specific about what the students needed to do to get

ready for social studies. They had to get out three things: their books, notebooks, and pencils. The first teacher told them only to "get ready."

2. Give "bite-size" directions; avoid a long series of directions. The second teacher first had her students sit down and face her; then she had them take out their materials; finally, she had them turn to the chapter they were going to read that day.

3. Whenever possible, accompany explanations with a demonstration. For example, Mr. Gaswami asked his students to take out their science books, turn to the beginning of the chapter, identify five keywords, and define them using the glossary. Mr. Gaswami showed his students what he wanted them to do by opening his book to the chapter, pointing out that the keywords were italicized, and then defining several keywords to demonstrate how to find and paraphrase the meanings using the glossary in the back of the book. He also displayed pictorial images of these directions on the board to help students read and remember all the steps.

4. Use cuing words such as "Look up here" and "Listen, please" before giving directions. Gestures such as a raised hand are also effective in getting students' attention.

Asking Questions   Asking students questions is a vital part of instructional clarity. The way you question your students is important for several reasons. Questioning is a quick way of assessing what your students have learned. In addition, questioning through the use of follow-up probes can help you analyze your students' errors.

Wilen, Ishler, Hutchinson, and Kindsvatter (1999) suggest the following guidelines for using questions in your classroom:

1. *Phrase questions clearly to ensure that students know how to respond.* For example, a vague question such as "Why were bank failures and the stock market crash of 1929 important?" forces students to guess rather than to consider carefully a direct response to the question. Better wording would be "What were the two primary causes of the Great Depression?"

2. *Provide a balance between higher- and lower-level questions.* The important point to keep in mind is that both kinds of questions are important. Lower-level, or convergent, questions help you find out whether students have the basic understanding necessary for higher-level thought. Further, critical and creative thinking can be developed by using convergent and evaluative questions. Although incorporating more higher-level skills into the curriculum is positive, it is important to realize that lower-level knowledge is still important, particularly for students with special needs, who may not readily acquire lower-level knowledge. Failing to help these students acquire this understanding can prevent them from ever developing higher-level understanding. Also, lower-level questions can give students an opportunity to succeed in class. Finally, research suggests that lower-level questions may be most appropriate in teaching basic skills to students who are at risk (Berliner, 1984; Emmer, Evertson, Sanford, Clements, & Worsham, 1983).

3. *Adapt questions to the language and skill level of the class, including individual students in the class.* Your questions should accommodate a range of needs, from lower-performing students to gifted students. For example, a question for a lower-performing student might be, "From what you have just read, how does the demand for a product affect its supply?" For students with more skills, the question might become, "Going beyond the article a little, how does price affect supply and demand and at what point is market equilibrium reached?"

4. *Vary the wait time depending on the nature of the question asked.* If the question covers review material or material of little difficulty, the wait time—or time you allow your students to think about the answer—is brief. However, if a question covers material that is new and/or difficult for your students, give them more time to think before responding. In general, teachers tend to give their students too little think time (Cotton, 1989). Extending thinking time to just 3 seconds

Another use of cueing is to let a student know that he or she can expect to be called on to respond orally when you present a particular signal that only the student knows. This way the student can attend to a lesson with less anxiety about speaking in class.

between the end of a question and the start of an answer benefits students in a number of ways:

- Students give longer, more accurate answers.
- The number of times students don't respond decreases.
- Many more students volunteer answers.
- More students with special needs volunteer answers.
- More capable students are less likely to dominate class discussions. (Bursuck & Damer, 2011, pp. 283–284)

5. *Involve all students in classroom questioning by calling on nonvolunteers as well as volunteers.* Calling on all students also allows you to monitor student learning efficiently. In addition, calling on nonvolunteers (who frequently are students with disabilities or other special needs) demonstrates that you hold them accountable for listening and leads to higher levels of on-task behavior. However, as mentioned before, you should match questions with student ability to maximize the likelihood of student success. Finally, for lower-level questions, consider using choral responding, or having all students respond at once together. Unison responding allows more student opportunities for practice and recitation and can lead to higher levels of correct responses and on-task behavior (Carnine, 1981).

6. *Scaffold incorrect answers and "no responses."* Often students with disabilities will not attempt to answer questions because they are worried about making errors in front of their classmates or are unsure of their speech. Even when you increase your thinking time, some of these students will not volunteer answers and, when you call on them, will say, *"I don't know,"* or silently shrug their shoulders. Increase your support for these students using this four-step "cue-clueing procedure" suggested by Bursuck and Damer (2011). For example, Ms. Baroody asked the class, *"What is one detail in this section that led me to decide the main idea as 'Mae was fascinated by science?'"* She scaffolded her instruction for Lovelle, a student whose hand wasn't raised, as follows:

1. First Ms. Baroody provided a cue, *"Lovelle, what are some of the things that Mae was doing in this section that showed she was fascinated with learning science?"*
2. Next, Ms. Baroody gave Lovelle a 3-second thinking pause to formulate an answer. He still didn't respond so she moved to step 3.
3. Ms. Baroody increased her support and provided a cue so obvious she was certain it would lead Lovelle to the right answer. *"Lovelle, look at sentence 4 and read it."* (Lovelle read: "Mae spent many hours at the library reading books about science and space.") Then Ms. Baroody asked, *"So where did she go to learn more about science?"* (Lovelle answered, "The library.")
4. Ms. Baroody then reinforced and expanded Lovelle's answer to bolster his confidence: *"Yes, that's absolutely right, Lovelle. The information in the book describing how Mae went to the library and spent all that time reading about science and space was a clue that she must really like science."* (Bursuck & Damer, 2011, p. 284).

Use the INCLUDE strategy to ensure that the questions you ask in class match the instructional levels of your students. For example, as part of a curriculum modification stated on her IEP, Melissa was learning to identify numbers from 100 to 999; the rest of the class was learning long division. During a class presentation on how to solve three-digit division problems, Mr. Henry called on Melissa to identify the hundreds-place number that was being divided. Sam, another student in the class, was expected to learn the same long division problems as everyone else, but he was clearly having trouble doing so, as judged by his homework and in-class performance. Mr. Henry questioned him in a different way by asking him to explain the first step in solving the problem after it had already been solved at the board.

Presenting Subject Matter Communicating clearly to your students when you are presenting subject-area content orally, such as in a lecture, also is important. The following section of a lecture was delivered during a geography lesson on Italy:

INCLUDE

Teacher 1

Italy is in southern Europe, down by France and the Mediterranean Sea. It's a peninsula in the Mediterranean. There are a lot of beautiful islands in the Mediterranean off of Italy and Greece as well. Sardinia and Sicily are islands that are part of Italy. Corsica, Capri, and some other islands like Crete and Cyprus are in the same part of the world, but they don't belong to, although they may be close to, Italy. You could turn to the map of Europe that's in your text to see where Italy is. (Evertson et al., 1983, pp. 143–144)

The language used by this teacher lacks clarity. For example, he presents information about a number of islands but is unclear in explaining how these islands relate to the main topic, which seems to be the location of Italy. The teacher is also vague when he says, "[The islands] don't belong to, although they may be close to, Italy." In addition, the teacher uses the word *peninsula* but does not define it. Finally, this explanation needs the visual display of a map to bring clarity to it, but the teacher refers to a map only at the end of the explanation, almost as an afterthought. Then, rather than require students to refer to it, he leaves them with the impression that its use is voluntary. The only students who will know where Italy is after this lecture are those who already knew before the lecture. Many students with special needs will likely be left behind. An example of another lecture on the same topic is much clearer:

Teacher 2

Now, I want all eyes on me. [The teacher then gestures to the world map next to her. The continent of Europe is highlighted.] The continent we have been studying the past month is highlighted here on this map of the world. What continent is it? [The teacher calls on a nonvolunteer who is also a struggling student to identify the continent. The teacher then shows a map of Europe with the countries they have already studied highlighted: France, Switzerland, and Austria.] What are the names of these countries that we have already studied? [The teacher has the class respond in unison and then shows the map of Europe with Italy highlighted.] This is the new country we are studying today. It is called *Italy*. [The teacher writes the word *Italy* on the board as she says it.] What is this country called? [The teacher has the class respond in unison.] Italy is a large peninsula shaped like a boot that extends into the Mediterranean Sea. [The teacher writes *peninsula* on the board, sounding out the syllables as she writes.] What's the word everyone? [Because students have studied the word once before, the teacher calls on a nonvolunteer to define it.] Corrine, what is a *peninsula*?

While this teacher's presentation is much clearer, she may still need to differentiate instruction for her students. For example, Juan, a student with attention problems, may respond better to a video than to a teacher lecture. Carmen, who has a learning disability, has trouble organizing information presented orally and may benefit from using a graphic organizer of the key geographical features of Italy. Damon, a struggling student who has difficulty retaining information, may be assisted by completing a blank copy of the graphic organizer as part of a student study team. Of course other students in the class may benefit from these accommodations as well.

How Can You Involve Parents in Teaching Their Children?

Teachers are always looking for ways to find extra help for students who take more time to learn new content or skills. That is why we often hear teachers say, "If only his parents would work with him more at home." Although we know parents can promote learning by showing affection for their children, by displaying interest in their children's schoolwork, and by expecting academic success, the effectiveness of parents tutoring their children at home is less clear. The results of research on the effectiveness of parent teaching are mixed; some experts say it is effective whereas others question it (Erion, 2006; Mercer & Pullen, 2009). When determining whether to involve parents in tutoring their children, Mercer and Pullen (2009) suggest taking the following factors into account:

1. Are there reasons for deciding against tutoring (for example, mother–father disagreement over the necessity of tutoring, health problems, financial problems, marital problems, or a large family with extensive demands on parental time)?
2. Do parents have the resources of a professional (for example, a teacher) to answer their questions about the tutoring? The success of home tutoring may depend on cooperative efforts.
3. Can the sessions be arranged at a time when there is no interruption from siblings, callers, or other demands? Children need sustained attention in order to learn.
4. Will the child become overwhelmed with academic instruction and resent the home sessions or feel overly pressured?
5. Do the parents become frustrated, tense, disappointed, or impatient during the tutorial sessions? These parents may spend their time better with the child in activities that are mutually enjoyable.
6. Do the tutorial sessions create tensions among family members? For instance, do the siblings view the sessions as preferential treatment?
7. Does the parent resent tutoring the child or feel guilty every time a session is shortened or missed? Are the sessions usually enjoyable and rewarding?

Of course, if you decide to have parents tutor their child, the same strategies for teaching skills and content to students with special needs covered earlier in this chapter still apply. For example, only skills or content at a student's level should be presented, and the progression of skills or content should be gradual and based on student mastery. In addition, parents should be carefully trained to present new information or skills clearly and enthusiastically and to provide appropriate corrections and encouragement as needed. Parents should also limit the length of the tutoring sessions to 15 minutes for children up to grade 6 and 30 minutes for older students and should begin and end each session with an activity that the child enjoys and is successful at (Cummings & Maddux, 1985, as cited in Mercer & Pullen, 2009). Also, care must be taken to select the most appropriate time to tutor and to select a place that does not restrict the activities of other family members and is not too distracting. Finally, tutoring should be held at the same time and place to establish a clear routine (Mercer & Pullen, 2009, p. 125).

What Accommodations Can You Make for Students to Help Them Succeed in Independent Practice?

The main purpose of practice activities is to provide students with opportunities to refine skills or solidify content that they have already learned and to allow you to monitor their performance. To achieve these purposes, students should be able to complete independently practice activities such as seatwork, practice that is included as part of learning centers, and homework assignments.

Even under ideal circumstances and with the best intentions, it is difficult to design practice activities that meet the needs of all students in your class. Problems arise because of individual characteristics, and individual accommodations need to be made using INCLUDE. For example, students with severe reading problems may have difficulty reading directions that are clear to everyone else. Students with attention problems may have trouble answering questions that have multiple steps. Students with physical disabilities may be unable to perform the writing requirements of their

INCLUDE

assignments. In the case of students with severe intellectual disabilities, practice activities may need to be modified totally so they are consistent with the students' skill levels and the goals and objectives on their IEPs.

Differentiating Seatwork Assignments

Affleck, Lowenbraun, and Archer (1980) have suggested five accommodations you can make to directions to ensure that students with special needs know what to do before working independently. Use INCLUDE to figure out whether these accommodations need to be done with your entire class or with only one or a small group of students:

1. Verbally present the tasks. This strategy can be applied to the whole class, particularly when many students are having problems with the directions. You can accommodate the needs of individual students by pairing a worksheet with a digital recording that explains the directions.
2. Add practice examples that you can do with the whole class or a small group of students who are having particular difficulty.
3. Write alternative sets of directions. You can project these, or you can distribute individual copies to students.
4. Highlight the important words in the directions.
5. Have students help each other when the directions are difficult.

Differentiating Learning Center Activities

Another way to provide extra practice for students is in classroom learning centers. Examples of how to differentiate activities in learning centers are shown in Figure 9.5.

INCLUDE

fyi

Before starting independent practice, complete sample items for the students. Talk through each step, modeling your thought process and decision making. Use questioning to check that students understand directions.

FIGURE 9.5 Examples of Differentiated Learning Center Activities

OUTCOME:
Students read or listen to information and then write or type responses to questions about the information.

MATERIALS:
Books, audio books, computer software for typing, worksheets with varied levels of questions about the information.

DIFFERENTIATION:
- Some students complete fill-in-the-blank responses.
- Some students respond to a prompt and write an essay response.
- Some students complete an outline as they are listening.

Source: Adapted from "Designing and Delivering Learning Center Instruction," by M. E. King-Sears, 2007, *Intervention in School and Clinic, 42*(3), pp. 137–147.

Differentiating Homework Assignments

As they do with in-class practice activities, students with special needs may have difficulty completing traditional homework assignments. A major reason for student failure to complete homework assignments independently, successfully, and without undue stress is that the assignments are too difficult to begin with. Before you give your students an assignment, ask yourself the following questions:

1. What skill (for example, reading, written expression, or math) demands does the assignment make on the students? Are the students capable of meeting these skill demands?
2. What background knowledge (for example, vocabulary or concepts) does the assignment demand of the students? Are the students capable of meeting the demand for background knowledge?
3. Is the purpose of the assignment clear to students?
4. If the assignment involves skill practice, does it include a lot of practice on a few skills rather than a little practice on a lot of skills?
5. Are clear, written directions provided for how to complete the assignment?
6. Is enough time allotted to complete the assignment?

Even if you answered yes to all these questions, students with special needs may require additional accommodations. For example, students with reading problems may need extra assistance with homework directions. Students with physical disabilities may need assignments shortened, or they may need to respond orally rather than in writing. Remember to use the INCLUDE strategy to make accommodations that fit your assignments and the individual characteristics of your students with special needs. Finally, the success of homework also depends on the involvement of parents. Parent involvement is particularly important for students with disabilities because they are more likely to struggle with homework (Bursuck et al., 1999). Parents play two key roles: overseeing the homework process while their children are at home and communicating with the school regularly about homework. Parents can oversee the homework process by having daily discussions about homework with their children, creating an environment at home that is conducive to getting homework done, supervising homework activities periodically during the time set for homework, and providing support and encouragement for homework completion (Bursuck et al., 1999).

INCLUDE

Despite the importance of homework, home–school communication about it sometimes is a problem (Harniss, Epstein, Bursuck, Nelson, & Jayanthi, 2001; Munk et al., 2001). Parents of students with special needs may want much more communication with teachers about homework and feel that teachers should make more of an effort to initiate such communication (Munk et al., 2001). Likewise, teachers may feel that parents do not initiate communication about homework often enough, take homework seriously enough, and follow through with commitments they make about helping their children with homework (Epstein et al., 1997).

Contacts with parents about homework can be increased by conducting parent–teacher meetings in the evening for working parents and by taking advantage of e-mail, a great potential time-saver (Harniss et al., 2001). Another strategy for increasing communication is to establish a homework hotline that can be accessed by phone or a website that provides certain types of homework assistance. You can also involve parents in the homework process at the beginning of the school year and on an ongoing basis thereafter using checklists, newsletters, informed notes, phone calls, and parent discussion groups (Margolis, 2005). For example, at the open house at the beginning of the school year, Ms. Ordonez gives parents information about course assignments for the semester, homework support available in the classroom, and policies on missed homework and extra-credit assignments. She then sends

All students can benefit from homework and other independent practice activities. What are some strategies you can use to make homework and other assignments more effective for students with special needs? © Jim West/Alamy

home school progress updates every four weeks; the progress reports include a section on homework completion.

Teachers also can ask parents whether they want to have homework information sent home daily, to sign that they reviewed their children's homework, and to note their children's efforts and describe their difficulties. By signing assignments and indicating their children's effort or difficulty in completing them, parents communicate to their children that they and the teacher are working together and care about homework being completed (Margolis, 2005). It is also important to understand that homework may be a lower priority for families when compared to other home issues. For example, Mr. Gentry knew that Dominique's family had recently been evicted from their apartment and were living in their car. Until Dominique's family was able to find another place to live, Mr. Gentry arranged for him to complete his homework before or after school. Ultimately, the most effective way of warming parents to the homework process is to only send home work that students can complete successfully and independently.

How Can You Make Instructional Modifications for Students with Moderate to Severe Intellectual Disabilities?

Students with moderate to severe intellectual disabilities often cannot perform some or all of the steps in tasks carried out every day by students without disabilities. In the past, this inability to perform tasks in the same way as other students was interpreted to mean that these students could not benefit from these activities. Today, the emphasis is on making modifications for students with moderate to severe disabilities so that they can meet the same curricular standards but in a more functional way, as guided by their IEPs (Lowell-York, Doyle, & Kronberg, 1995; Nolet & McLaughlin, 2005).

One way to modify materials and activities for students with moderate to severe disabilities is to conduct an **environmental inventory.** The purpose of an environmental inventory is to find out what modifications are needed to increase the participation of these students in the classroom as well as in community environments (Vandercook, York, & Forest, 1989) and to help them meet functional curricular objectives specified on their IEPs. The environmental inventory process involves asking yourself four questions:

1. What does a person who does not have a disability do in this environment?
2. What does a person who has a disability do in this environment? What is the discrepancy?
3. What types of supports and/or modifications can be put in place to increase the participation level or independence of the student with special needs?
4. What functional outcomes can the student meet as a result of this participation?

An example of how this process is used in a classroom environment is shown in Figure 9.6. This example involves Roberto, a student with moderate to severe intellectual disabilities. Roberto is in Ms. Benis's sixth-grade social studies class. The class is working in small groups on depicting the steps in the recycling process for paper, metal, and plastic. Each group is studying a different recycled material. Roberto lacks the motor and cognitive skills necessary to participate like everyone else.

Ms. Benis decides to modify instruction for Roberto. She assigns him to the group that his friend Seth is in. She also decides to use different materials with Roberto. Ms. Benis has a paraprofessional help Roberto find pictures of recycled products; Seth helps Roberto paste these pictures onto the group's diagram. Mr. Howard, Roberto's special education teacher, helps Roberto identify recycled products in grocery stores and restaurants. Roberto's parents help him sort the recycling at home. All of these activities help Roberto meet his IEP goal of participating in community recycling efforts. Examples of making instructional modifications using INCLUDE are described in the Case in Practice.

RESEARCH NOTE

Nelson et al. (1998) asked middle school students their preferences for homework accommodations. Most preferred were completing assignments entirely at school, working on assignments in small groups, starting homework in class with the teacher, and allowing extra-credit assignments. Least preferred accommodations were individualizing assignments and assignment notebooks.

www.resources

Do you want to post your own homework assignments on the Internet without a website of your own? Go to Ed Gate's SchoolNotes webpage, at http://www.schoolnotes.com.

FIGURE 9.6 Environmental Inventory Process

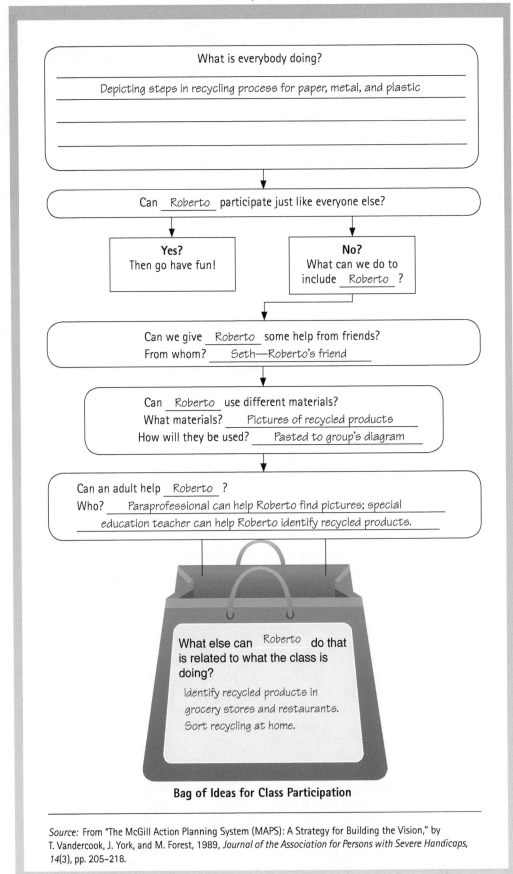

What is everybody doing?

Depicting steps in recycling process for paper, metal, and plastic

Can Roberto participate just like everyone else?

Yes?
Then go have fun!

No?
What can we do to
include Roberto ?

Can we give Roberto some help from friends?
From whom? Seth—Roberto's friend

Can Roberto use different materials?
What materials? Pictures of recycled products
How will they be used? Pasted to group's diagram

Can an adult help Roberto ?
Who? Paraprofessional can help Roberto find pictures; special
education teacher can help Roberto identify recycled products.

What else can Roberto do that
is related to what the class is
doing?

Identify recycled products in
grocery stores and restaurants.
Sort recycling at home.

Bag of Ideas for Class Participation

Source: From "The McGill Action Planning System (MAPS): A Strategy for Building the Vision," by
T. Vandercook, J. York, and M. Forest, 1989, *Journal of the Association for Persons with Severe Handicaps,*
14(3), pp. 205–218.

CASE IN PRACTICE

Making Instructional Modifications in a Middle School Consumer and Food Science Class

Mr. Gagliano teaches a middle school consumer and food science class. He recently taught a unit on cooking and nutrition, including how to shop for food. The targeted state standards for the unit were as follows:

1. Students demonstrate the knowledge and skills needed to remain physically healthy.
2. Students evaluate consumer products and services and make effective consumer decisions.

One part of the unit covered vegetarianism. The goal was for the students to plan, shop for, and cook a vegetarian meal. After defining *vegetarianism* and providing a brief history of vegetarianism in the United States, Mr. Gagliano planned to show a video on the Food and Drug Administration (FDA) nutritional guidelines, including how to decipher nutritional information on a food product label. Mr. Gagliano then planned to break the class into four groups and assign each group the task of designing a vegetarian meal meeting FDA nutritional guidelines.

Ramone is a student with moderate intellectual disabilities who is included in Mr. Gagliano's class. Ramone can do basic math at about the second-grade level and reads below the first-grade level. Although his oral language skills are adequate to carry on a conversation, his ability to interact with others in a small group is limited. Ramone's IEP objectives include the following:

1. Prepare three basic meals independently.
2. Use a calculator to budget money while shopping.
3. Make purchases with the "next-dollar" strategy (for example, paying $6.00 and "one more dollar for cents" for an item that costs $6.62).
4. Increase functional sight-word vocabulary to 200 words.
5. Work appropriately in small groups for up to 50 minutes.

Mr. Gagliano and Ms. Henning, Ramone's special education teacher, met to decide how Ramone's instruction during this unit could be modified. They agreed that the curricular demands for the rest of the class were not appropriate for Ramone, and they planned the following instructional modifications based on Ramone's IEP:

1. Ramone will record the possible choices for the menu (for example, main dishes, dessert, drink). He will actively participate in the making of the final choices. A classmate will help him with spelling as needed.
2. Ramone will record the choices for the grocery list. He will also be assigned the job of checking the kitchen to make sure that items on the list are not already there.
3. Ramone will practice reading the words from the grocery list with the help of his group.
4. Ramone will assist with the shopping, using his calculator to budget the group's money, making purchases using the "next-dollar" strategy, and reading his grocery words to find his items. Ramone will be assisted by his group as needed.
5. Ramone will assist the group in cooking the meal.

Following the activity, Ramone, with assistance from Mr. Gagliano and Ms. Henning, evaluated his performance using checklists based on his related IEP objectives. The evaluations were placed in Ramone's alternate assessment portfolio.

REFLECTION

Do you think it was appropriate for the teachers to plan instructional modifications for Ramone rather than instructional accommodations? How were the expectations for Ramone different from those for his classmates? How were they similar? Should students such as Ramone get credit for meeting state standards when their instruction is modified? How useful is the INCLUDE strategy in planning instructional modifications for students with moderate to severe disabilities?

Source: Adapted from "Creating and Using Meaningful Alternate Assessments," by H. Kleinert, P. Green, M. Hurte, J. Clayton, and C. Oetinger, 2002, *Teaching Exceptional Children, 34*(4), pp. 40–47. Copyright 2002 by the Council for Exceptional Children. Reprinted with permission.

WRAPPING IT UP

BACK TO THE CASES

This section provides opportunities for you to apply the knowledge gained in this chapter to the cases described at the beginning of this chapter. The questions and activities that follow demonstrate how these standards and principles, along with other concepts that you have learned about in this chapter, connect to the everyday activities of all teachers.

MS. DIAZ notes that lately Abdul has been showing signs of losing the motivation to try new math skills. She has increased the number of examples and practice opportunities each time she introduces a new skill and provides oral and written directions for all seatwork activities. Another teacher has suggested that she use an advance organizer whenever she introduces a new skill. Develop an advance organizer for the lesson in the case study for teaching conversion of fractions into percentages. After you have completed that task, explain why using advance organizers might help increase Abdul's motivation to learn new skills, especially math skills.

CECILY, as you may remember, struggles with reading comprehension. At the end of this case, we ask how Ms. Boyd might help her read and remember content in her history text. Later in the chapter, we suggest that a study guide might be a useful tool for Cecily. Developing effective study guides that move beyond the *remembering* level of Bloom's taxonomy (see the Learning Outcomes section in Chapter 5) is a skill that requires practice. Construct a study guide that would effectively support and extend Cecily's learning as she listens to the history text, using the following instructions.

Ask one to three classmates to form a work group. Select a portion of a chapter from this text and individually develop a study guide for that portion (see the Professional Edge "How to Develop Study Guides"). Once everyone in the group has completed a study guide, compare your guides using these questions:

- Do you and your peers agree on the important or key topics? Do you agree on the important vocabulary words to be included? Note and discuss differences.
- Do the study guides match the objectives listed at the beginning of the chapter?
- Are your questions written to help Cecily understand the material at the higher levels of Bloom's taxonomy (applying, analyzing, evaluating, and creating)? Are they also written to help her with knowledge and comprehension of specific facts?
- Collaborate with your peers to incorporate everyone's ideas into a single study guide that will meet Cecily's needs.

ALBERT, as you may remember, struggles to independently complete practice activities in learning centers. Ms. Olivieri has taken several steps to help him. First, before including an independent practice activity in a center, she makes sure all of her students, including Albert, are able to perform accurately the skill involved. She makes sure she reviews previously learned skills that apply to the skills being practiced too. Ms. Olivieri also offers numerous examples of work that she expects students to complete while working in the centers. Finally, she provides clear, step-by-step directions in both oral and written formats. She has noted that Albert's ability to do correct work has improved. However, he still has difficulty completing the same quantity of work that his peers are able to complete. Once he has completed some portion of the work, he is out of his seat to sharpen a pencil, throw away scrap paper, or chat with a friend. Since Ms. Olivieri has experienced some success with Albert, she is encouraged to continue working to help him become independent in completing his work in centers. What might she try next? Explain why you selected these strategies or interventions.

SUMMARY

- Teachers may need to differentiate basic skill instruction in the areas of preskills; selecting and sequencing examples; the rate of introduction of new skills; and the amount of direct instruction, practice, and review.

- In teaching subject-area content to students with special needs, teachers may need to differentiate instruction when activating background knowledge, organizing content, and teaching terms and concepts.

- Teachers can improve clarity in written communication by selecting printed materials that clearly tie ideas together, have clear pronoun referents, and require fewer student inferences.

Teachers can improve oral communication by giving clear directions, asking questions appropriately, and presenting subject matter using direct, unambiguous language.

- Teachers may need to differentiate independent practice activities such as seatwork, those found in learning centers, and homework.

- Students with moderate to severe intellectual disabilities often cannot perform some or all of the steps in everyday tasks. These students require instructional modifications based on an alternative curriculum set forth on their IEPs. Teachers can use an environmental inventory as well as the INCLUDE strategy to modify classroom activities for these students.

APPLICATIONS IN TEACHING PRACTICE

DEVELOPING A REPERTOIRE OF INSTRUCTIONAL ACCOMMODATIONS

You want to teach a group of at-risk students to spell the following contractions: *can't, aren't, couldn't, shouldn't, wouldn't, don't, won't,* and *isn't.*

QUESTIONS

1. What preskills should you be concerned with, how can you assess them, and what can you do with students who do not know them?
2. How can you sequence instruction? Why did you choose this particular sequence?
3. How can you provide direct instruction, practice, and review for your students?
4. At what rate should you introduce the contractions?
5. How can you evaluate whether your students have learned the contractions?

Develop a graphic organizer for a major concept in Chapter 1 of this text.

QUESTIONS

1. How did you select the concept? Is it a big idea?
2. How would you use the graphic organizer to teach students who are at risk or other students with special needs?

Design a lesson to teach the concept of *differentiated instruction* using a definition.

QUESTIONS

1. Is your definition stated clearly, simply, and concisely?
2. What positive and negative examples did you use?
3. How can you find out whether your students know the meaning of the concept?
4. How can you find out whether your students can differentiate this concept from other concepts presented in the text?
5. How would you teach the concept using a concept diagram format?

You are teaching a lesson on the respiratory system. First you describe the respiratory process (for example, diaphragm contracts; air rushes into nose and/or mouth; air travels down trachea; air enters lungs through bronchial tubes; and so forth) using a chart showing the key parts of the respiratory system (for example, nose, throat and trachea, bronchial tubes, lungs). Next you plan to have students work in small, heterogeneous groups on labeling a model of the respiratory system and describing all the key steps in the respiratory process.

QUESTIONS

1. Based on this lesson, complete an environmental inventory for a student with a moderate to severe intellectual disability.
2. Using INCLUDE, what other modifications might you make for this student?

myeducationlab

Go to Topics 10: Instructional Practices and Learning Strategies, 11: Reading Instruction, and 12: Content Area Teaching in the MyEducationLab (www.myeducationlab.com) for your course, where you can:

- Find learning outcomes for Instructional Practices and Learning Strategies, Reading Instruction, and Content Area Teaching along with the national standards that connect to these outcomes.
- Complete Assignments and Activities that can help you more deeply understand the chapter content.
- Apply and practice your understanding of the core teaching skills identified in the chapter with the Building Teaching Skills and Dispositions learning units.
- Examine challenging situations and cases presented in the IRIS Center Resources. (optional)
- Access video clips of CCSSO National Teachers of the Year award winners responding to the question, "Why Do I Teach?" in the Teacher Talk section. (optional)
- Check your comprehension on the content covered in the chapter by going to the Study Plan in the Book Resources for your text. Here you will be able to take a chapter quiz, receive feedback on your answers, and then access Review, Practice, and Enrichment activities to enhance your understanding of chapter content. (optional)

Index

Page references followed by "f" indicate illustrated figures or photographs; followed by "t" indicates a table.